DICTIONARY OF HISTORICAL TERMS

SECOND EDITION

CHRIS COOK

GRAMERCY BOOKS
New York

Preface and Acknowledgements

This book has attempted to bring together, in a single volume, as many as possible of the historical terms that are frequently encountered by both undergraduates and research students. These terms may be technical definitions (particularly from the medieval period), foreign words that have become part of the historical vocabulary (such as Ausgleich or Risorgimento), or recent terms and phrases that have not yet made their way into conventional historical works of reference. The book has attempted to cover these terms on a worldwide basis. Inevitably, no medium-size reference book can be entirely comprehensive, but it is hoped that this volume will make an important addition to the reference shelves of students and teachers of history. Many colleagues have helped with advice and practical assistance in preparing this book. I would like to thank Ted Cater and Pat Mercer for their help and, most of all, Richard Clayton for many hours of research. Nigel Griffin was able to make very valuable corrections for the revised reprint of this book.

For the preparation of the second edition of the Dictionary, I am grateful to John Stevenson for his many suggestions and to Dr. Harry Harmer for his very great practical assistance. At my publisher, I must thank Margot Levy and Penelope Allport for their encouragement and help. My thanks are also due to Nigel Quinney and Ruth Carim.

CHRIS COOK

Copyright © The Macmillan Press Ltd., 1983, 1989. All rights reserved under International and Pan-American Copyright Conventions.

No part of this book may be reproduced or transmitted in any form or by any means, electronic or mechanical, including photocopying, recording, or by any information storage and retrieval system, without permission in writing from the publisher.

This 1998 edition is published by Gramercy Books®, a division of Random House Value Publishing, Inc., 201 East 50th Street, New York, NY 10022, by arrangement with Peter Bedrick Books, 156 Fifth Avenue, New York, NY 10010. This 1998 edition is a reprint of the 1991 Peter Bedrick Books edition, published by agreement with The Macmillan Press Ltd., London and Basingstoke.

Gramercy Books® and design are registered trademarks of Random House Value Publishing, Inc.

Random House
New York • Toronto • London • Sydney • Auckland
http://www.randomhouse.com/

Printed in the United States of America

Library of Congress Cataloging-in-Publication Data
Cook, Chris, 1945-
    Dictionary of historical terms / Chris Cook. — 2nd ed.
      p.   cm.
    This edition originally published in the U.S. in 1990 by Peter Bedrick Books.
    Includes bibliographical references and index.
    ISBN 0-517-18871-6
    1. History—Dictionaries. I. Title.
D9.C67 1998
903—DC21

97-30835
CIP

8 7 6 5 4 3 2 1

A

AAA. Agricultural Adjustment Agency, set up by the NEW DEAL to administer farming subsidies. *See also* ALPHABET AGENCIES.

Abbasid. Moslem dynasty which ruled in the Middle East 750–1258. It came to power in the revolution led by Abu Muslim, a member of the Hashimiyya (an extremist religious sect) which was under Abbasid control. The Umayyad Caliphate – already weakened by Shi'ah opposition; unrest among the Mawali (new converts to Islam) who were denied equal status with the Arab warrior class; and by tribal Arab feuds – collapsed in the face of the revolution. The basis of the Abbasid dynasty was really laid by the Caliph al-Mansur who ruled 754–55. The Caliphate falls into three phases: *c*750–850, an age of trade, great wealth and the assimilation of the philosophic and scientific knowledge of the ancient world through translations into Arabic of Greek and Syriac works; *c*850–1050, a time of political disintegration and the rise of independent dynasties; *c*1050–1258, an age of invasions by Seljuk Turks, Crusaders and finally by Mongols who overran Persia in 1255 and ended the dynasty. However, a line of nominal Abbasid Caliphs continued to rule Egypt until 1517. *See* CALIPH.

ABC countries. Term common in the 1950s for the grouping of Argentina, Brazil and Chile.

abdication crisis. English constitutional crisis which commenced on 16 November 1936 when King Edward VIII told the Prime Minister, Stanley Baldwin (1867–1947) that he wished to marry an American divorcee, Mrs Wallis Simpson. Baldwin, his cabinet, the leaders of the Labour and Liberal parties, the heads of overseas dominions and most of the House of Commons were of the opinion that the marriage was unsuitable, given Edward's titular position as 'Supreme Governor' of the Church of England. A private Act might have been passed arranging for a morganatic marriage, in which the king's wife would not become queen, but such a measure was considered unsatisfactory. The British press maintained a voluntary silence on the issue until 3 December. On 10 December, the king decided to abdicate; two days later he left for voluntary exile in France. His successor George VI made him Duke of Windsor, and on 3 June 1937 he married Mrs Simpson at Château de Cande.

Abecedarians. ANABAPTIST sect founded in 16th-century Germany by Stork, a disciple of Luther. Its members held all human knowledge to be

1

valueless and declined to learn even the alphabet.

Abhorrers. Alternative name given to the TORY party in the 17th century during the reign of Charles II, derived from the use of the word 'abhor' in addresses to the king protesting against the petitions in favour of summoning parliament in 1679.

Abolitionists. Party opposed to slavery founded in the northern states of the USA in the late 18th century. In 1774 an Abolitionist Congress was held and in April 1776 legislation against slavery was attempted in the US Congress. Abolitionist sentiment, previously only loosely co-ordinated, was given a focal point in 1833 when William Lloyd Garrison founded the American Anti-Slavery Society. Originating in Boston, by 1840 the movement had some 200,000 members nationwide. However, in 1839 the national organization had split into a radical wing, led by Garrison, which denounced the US constitution as proslavery, and a more conservative wing. In 1840 a splinter group, the American and Foreign Anti-Slavery Society, founded the Liberal Party to represent directly the abolitionist cause in national politics. Greatest activity took place at state and local levels, ensuring that the anti-slavery cause remained an important element in US politics: it was promoted by the FREESOILERS and the Republican Party. The victory of the north in the Civil War (1861–65) led to the emancipation of slaves and the American Anti-Slavery Society formally dissolved itself in 1870.

absolutism (deriv. Lat. *legibus absolutus*, absolved from the laws). System of unlimited government in which the governed possess no representation, right to vote or part in the administration and in which there are no legal or constitutional restraints on the ruler.

Abwehr (Germ., defence). Espionage, counter-espionage, and sabotage service of the German High Command in World War II.

ACAS. Arbitration and Conciliation Advisory Service, established in Britain in 1975. The Employment Protection Bill introduced by the Labour government in that year and based on a TUC 20-point plan gave to ACAS duties that were previously carried out by the Department of Employment. ACAS was placed on a statutory footing and empowered to intervene in industrial disputes concerning recognition of trade unions. Further responsibilities included the issue of a code of practice on the disclosure of information to unions by employers. The Conservative opposition agreed to perpetuate ACAS. It has since intervened in a number of serious industrial disputes, not always with success. Critics allege that in its desire to arrange agreements between unions and employers it fudges the issues which have caused the disputes, thereby avoiding permanent settlements and storing up trouble for the future. Employers have argued that ACAS tends to lend support too readily to union demands.

acceptance speech. Speech by which a candidate for the US presidency accepts nomination at the party convention, usually outlining his programme for office.

Acordada (Span.). Special tribunal established in 1710 to deal with the rapid growth of banditry in colonial Mexico. It had the power to pass severe sentences with no appeal until the last decade of the 18th century when the viceroy and a committee began to review its sentences before execution.

ACP states. States which in the 1950s were Atom Controlling Powers, that is, which had the ability to promote nuclear fission and thereby generate atomic energy either for peaceful use or to manufacture nuclear weapons. The USA developed its atom bomb in the MANHATTAN PROJECT; and the USSR exploded one in 1949, Britain in 1952, France in 1960 and China in 1964.

Action Directe. French anarchist group formed in 1979 by libertarians, Maoists, Trotskyists and left-wing fascists, connected with international terrorist movements and responsible for a number of assassinations and bombings in the 1980s.

Action Française. Right-wing political movement founded in France in 1899 by the journalist and poet Charles Maurras (1868–1952), which was royalist, nationalistic and anti-semitic and which criticized the Third French Republic for decadence. Although a freethinker, Maurras approved of Roman Catholicism, believing that its traditions were a counterforce to democratic republicanism. In 1908 he and Leon Daudet (1867–1942), a pamphleteer and essayist, began joint editorship of the movement's newspaper,*Action Française.* The Vatican became estranged from the movement after 1926 and it drew increasingly close to fascism. Between 1940 and 1944 it gave strong support to the VICHY government and was accordingly suppressed after France was liberated; Maurras was sentenced to life imprisonment for collaboration with the Germans.

activists. Members of a political group prepared to take action as opposed to those whose membership is passive, involving only, for example, payment of membership fees. In the 1960s and early 1970s the term was applied widely to those members of left-wing and youth 'movements' who attended demonstrations and rallies, usually against US involvement in Vietnam, or more generally against various aspects of Western capitalism.

In the 1980s the term has been used in the UK mainly to describe members of constituency Labour parties who have sought to reform the party's procedures and inject a more socialist element into its policies.

acuerdo (Span.). Agreement or resolution.

Addled Parliament. Parliament summoned to grant supplies to James I which sat from 5 April to 7 June 1614. It refused the King the revenues he desired unless he was prepared to abandon IMPOSITIONS and reinstate the clergy deprived of office in 1604. The Parliament passed no acts, hence the name 'addled'.

adelantado (Span., one who goes before). An officer of the kings of Castile from the early middle ages, who acted as a Crown-appointed governor of frontier territories.Ferdinand III (1217–52) gave such officers judicial and administrative powers which they retained until the 16th century. From the mid-16th to the late 18th centuries, the term refers to the officials charged with advancing the frontiers of the Spanish empire during Spain's civil and judicial authority

Adi Granth. The sacred book of the SIKHS.

adjutators (*also* agitators). Delegates

elected by each regiment or troop of the NEW MODEL ARMY in 1647 to act with the officers in bringing the army's demands and grievances before parliament.

Adler-Tag (Germ., Eagle Day). Name given by the LUFTWAFFE to 13 August 1940, the date on which they began the destruction of the Royal Air Force Fighter Command in the air and on the ground prior to invasion of Britain. The Germans flew 1,500 sorties, but poor intelligence led to wastage of bombs on the wrong airfields. However, Germany claimed to have destroyed 98 planes and 8 major bases. Eagle Day might be regarded as marking the beginning of the period known as the BATTLE OF BRITAIN but its exact duration is subject to dispute. Futhermore, 15 August, the day of maximum German effort on which 1,800 sorties were flown, is perhaps more deserving of the name.

Adullamites. A small section of the Liberal Party, led by Robert Lowe (later Lord Sherbrooke), which opposed Gladstone's 1866 Reform Bill. The term was coined by John Bright, who likened the Liberal dissidents to those who took refuge with David in the Cave of Adullam (I Samuel 22:1).

Adventurers. English financiers who in 1642 contributed £1 million towards the cost of the forces used to suppress the Irish rebellion. They subsequently received 2.5 million acres of land confiscated from the rebels and were confirmed in their possession by the 1652 and 1662 Acts of Settlement.

Advocatus Dei (Lat., God's advocate). *See* ADVOCATUS DIABOLI.

Advocatus Diaboli (Lat., Devil's advocate). A functionary of the Roman Catholic Church appointed to state the objections to a proposed canonization. The argument in favour of canonization of the deceased is put by the Advocatus Dei.

advowson. In Britain, right of presentation to a clerical benefice by either clerical or lay patrons. Dating from the 8th century, it became subject to many abuses after the 1164 Constitutions of Clarendon when it was recognized as a right of property. It still exists today as a property right tenable by non-Catholics.

aetheling (OE). In Anglo-Saxon England, a prince of the royal blood. The last was Edgar (d. 1125), great-nephew of Edward the Confessor (1003–66), whose claim to the throne was ignored on Edward's death when Harold Godwineson was crowned. Following the Norman conquest of 1066 various revolts were raised in championship of Edgar's claims and for a time he had to flee the country. He was reconciled to the Norman, William I (1028–87), in 1074.

affidavit (Lat. *affidare*, declare on oath). Statement in writing, made under oath, sworn before a person having the authority to administer it.

afrancesados. Supporters in Spain and the Spanish colonies of Napoleon Bonaparte (1769–1821). The term is used of all those responsible for the penetration of French ideas into Spain.

African National Congress. *See* ANC.

Agency for International Development. (AID). Agency created by the US government in November 1961 for the co-ordination and administration of US economic aid. It superseded the INTERNATIONAL CO-OPERATION ADMINISTRATION and the DEVELOPMENT LOAN FUND.

agent provocateur (Fr.). A person placed in the ranks of the enemy during social, political or industrial conflicts, to damage or compromise the enemy, provoking actions that might not otherwise have taken place. Agents provocateurs have been employed to provoke armed clashes between police and strikers or to induce strikers to act illegally. They have also been used by government agencies against revolutionary groups and in international politics to create disorder or 'incidents' as an excuse for war or intervention in others' affairs.

Age of Affluence. From a book on the post-World War II boom by the American economist J.K. Galbraith entitled *The Age of Affluence*. In Britain, the period from 1951 to 1964, of low unemployment, a 50% rise in real living standards, and the increased spread of consumer goods – largely as a result of hire purchase (consumer credit) rather than any shift in the proportion of national income going to wage-earners.

aggression. An attack, often difficult to identify clearly: aggressors often claim to be motivated by self-defence or to be defending law and order. At the Convention for the Definition of Aggression on 3 July 1933 between the USSR, Estonia, Latvia, Afghanistan, Persia, Turkey, Poland and Rumania, it was held that an act of aggression occurred whenever (1) war was declared against another state; (2) the armed forces of one state invaded the territory of another without a declaration of war; (3) the armed forces of one state attacked the territory, naval vessels or aircraft of another without a declaration of war; (4) a naval BLOCKADE was instituted by one state on the coastline or ports of another; or (5) a state gave aid to armed bands formed on its territory to attack another state. This definition closely followed that suggested by the Committee on Security Questions of the Disarmament Conference in May 1933. The UN Charter makes no attempt to define the term.

agiotistas (Span., profiteers or usurers). A term particularly applied to businessmen in 19th-century Mexico who lent money to the government for short terms at high rates of interest, in return for mortgages on government property or on customs duties. When the mortgages became payable the agiotistas collected huge profits; as a result, government revenues were reduced and revolution often followed. Since they stood to benefit from government deficits the agiotistas often helped to foment disorder.

agitators. *See* ADJUTATORS.

agitprop. Agitation Propaganda, a theatrical device employed by the left-wing in Europe and the USA during the 1950s; in the 1960s it developed into what is now termed 'street theatre'. Its purpose was to convey a political message, or political education, by seeking to interest and entertain.

Agraviados (Span., men with a grievance). Title adopted by Catalan insurgents in 1825.

agrogorad (Russ., agro-town). Soviet agricultural institution first proposed by Khruschev in 1949. The idea, to build blocks of apartments in which farm workers would live like city dwellers and to provide them with private plots of land grouped together in a large common area, was dropped after criticism in *Pravda* and at the XIXth Party Congress. However, Khruschev revived it in 1958 after becoming Chairman of the Council of Ministers. The plan was put into effect between 1959 and 1965, notably in the Ukraine, but under a different name.

Agudas Yisrael, Aguda. The 'Association of Israel', an ultra-religious right-wing political party.

ahimsā (Sansk., non-injury). Term used particularly with reference to the policy pursued by Mahatma Gandhi in India between 1920 and 1945.

aids. Taxes levied by English kings on their feudatories from the 9th century onwards. They fell into two classes: feudal aids and gracious aids. MAGNA CARTA provided that feudal aids could be levied only with the consent of the Great Council, other than in exceptional circumstances, i.e. the ransom of the king, the knighting of his eldest son and the marriage of his eldest daughter. Gracious aids (scarcely voluntary despite the name) were levied for other special purposes such as war or payment of the lord's debts. When the king imposed gracious aids they fell heavily on the towns of the ancient demesne; however, the tax was preferred to TALLAGE since it was, by implication, voluntary and therefore free of the stigma of VIL-LEIN. Aids declined from the 13th century onwards as new forms of taxation developed.

ailing giants. Declining industries in the 1920s and 30s – coal, textiles, shipbuilding, iron and steel – which had formed the basis of Britain's 19th-century supremacy. Weakened by outdated techniques and management, falling demand and foreign competition, they accounted for the bulk of long-term unemployment.

Alascans. Foreign Protestant refugees in England in the reign of Edward VI (1547–53) named after Laski, the superintendent of foreign church communities.

Albigensians (*also* Albigenses). The medieval heretic Cathars of southern France. The name is derived from the Albi region of Provence, where many Cathars were located under the protection of Raymond, Count of Toulouse. The sect appeared in the 11th century. Its beliefs largely reflected and were ultimately derived from those of Manichaeism. Like Manichaeism, the Albigensian heresy challenged orthodox Catholicism on two levels. Firstly, it held that matter was evil, the demesne of Satan, and that the spiritual alone was godly. God was locked in perpetual combat with the forces of evil which dominated the material world. Only by the rejection of the material world (e.g., the denial of sensual desires) was salvation to be reached. This belief constituted a direct denial of the orthodox doctrine of the nature of Christ, who became incarnate (i.e. material) and yet remained God. Moreover, the heresy implied that God was not the creator and master of all things both spiritual and material, and suggested that the path to salvation lay not in the sacraments of the Church but in the strict pursuit of an ascetic life.

Secondly, the sect had its own organization separate from that of the Church. Those following a rigidly ascetic life were known as the 'perfect', while those living under less severe discipline were 'believers'. The 'perfect' were held to have direct access to heaven when they died.

This concept of a hierarchical elite was a direct affront to orthodox teaching.

The sect was condemned for heresy by Pope Innocent III (1198–1216), who inaugurated the Albigensian Crusade, the first crusade against Christians. Originally led by Simon de Montfort, the crusade lasted from 1208–1229; at the siege of Béziers in 1209, 15,000 Albigensians are said to have been massacred. An inquisition against the Albigensians was established at Toulouse; its culmination was the capture of the fortress at Montségur in 1244.

alcabala (Span.). A sales tax on all commodities, imposed in Spain in 1341, which survived until as recently as 1845. Although the alcabala was the single most important source of Crown revenue, it severely hampered trade. Attempts to impose it in the Netherlands in 1569 were so bitterly opposed that it had to be postponed for two years and when it was introduced, it resulted in cessation of trade. In Spain's colonies an alcabala of 2–6% was imposed on all commercial transactions (except those between Indians) between 1575 and 1591.

alcalde (Span. deriv. Arab. *al-qādi*, judge). Spanish system of judiciary established between 1492 and 1550, by which time it had taken the definitive form it kept up to the late 18th century. Its officers wielded judicial, political and administrative authority, and were also chairmen of the town councils. The system was exported to the South American colonies, but the officers gradually lost their political powers, which were abolished completely in 1870.

alderman (deriv. OE *ealdorman*). In England, a civic dignitary, co-opted onto a local council, and next in rank to the mayor. The office, an old one with a varied history, was abolished in 1972. A list of aldermen exists dating from 1290; by a statute of 1394 aldermen could be chosen for life; a statute of 1741 made them JUSTICES OF THE PEACE. Their position was regularized by the 1835 Municipal Corporations Act and confirmed by the 1888 Local Government (County Councils) Act. Aldermen, appointed to local councils to provide stability and continuity, were elected by the councillors from amongst themselves or from people otherwise qualified to serve. They comprised one third of the council except in the county and boroughs of London, where they comprised one sixth. Their term of office was six years, one half standing for election every three years.

alhondiga. In Spanish colonial South America (16th–19th centuries), public granaries in main towns, from which the government attempted to ensure a steady supply of reasonably priced bread for the population.

aliya (Heb., going up). Among the Jews, the call to read in the synagogue a passage from the Torah (the first five books of the Bible), a considerable social honour. The passage read on the Sabbath morning is subdivided so that at least seven people are called. Cohens (descendants of Aaron, the first priest) and Levites (of the priestly tribe of Levi) have a prior right to be called. Among the Jews of the DIASPORA, the ability to read Hebrew had become so rare by the 14th century that it was necessary to have a trained reader for the passage, while the one called merely presided and recited blessings. At one time it was common to sell the honour of the aliya but this practice has now disappeared. In the 20th century, the term is also applied to the 'going up' of the Jews in the Diaspora to Israel.

Al-jama'ah (Arab., group, assembly). Orthodox majority of the Islamic community who follow what they claim to be the true 'way' (*sunnah*) as opposed to heretical or sectarian groups.

allegiance. In the middle ages, the bond of a vassal to his lord and of a subject to the Crown. It was secured by LIEGE HOMAGE. In modern times, allegiance is achieved by bonds of national sentiment, by precise legal definitions of nationality and the duties of the citizen and, in the case of officers of the state, by oath.

allodial land. A land system which developed among the Franks in the 9th century on the disintegration of the CAROLINGIAN monarchy. Land was held in absolute proprietorship rather than as a fief, the possession of which depended on a feudal lord. Allodial lands were not subject to any burden save the call to national defence; on the death of the proprietor they passed equally to all children or, failing issue, to the next of kin. The system operated up to the 13th century in France and in parts of Germany, notably Saxony; and in England up to the Norman Conquest in 1066. It disappeared as monarchies reasserted their authority.

alphabet agencies. Informal name for the many economic and social agencies established in the USA under the NEW DEAL including, for example, the Agricultural Adjustment Administration (AAA), the National Recovery Administration (NRA), the Reconstruction Finance Corporation (RFC), the Federal Housing Agency (FHA), and the Tennessee Valley Authority (TVA). Such agencies were generally referred to by their initials only.

alternative vote. Voting system in which the voter states both first and second preference. If a candidate gains an absolute majority of first preference votes, the second preference is ignored. But if no candidate achieves this, any voting paper naming him as a second preference is added to his first preference papers and if the new total of votes gives him a majority, he is then elected. There are variations on the system and the number of preferences a voter may be asked to state can be extended.

Althing (ON, assembly of all the people). In Iceland, the national assembly, in contrast to the THING, the local assembly found in Norway. Until its annexation by Norway in 1263, Iceland was an independent republic; its Althing has existed continuously since 930 AD. Its 52 members elect one-third of their number to form an upper chamber, the remaining two-thirds sitting in a lower house. The president, elected by popular vote every four years, is the focus of executive power.

Alumbrados (Span., enlightened). Groups of mystics which emerged in Spain c1510 and attacked by the INQUISITION. They were the spiritual forefathers of the better known ILLUMINATI of Germany.

Amalricians (*also* Amalricini). 12th-century pantheist sect, the somewhat confused followers of Amaury of Bène, condemned by the pope for heresy in 1210.

amercement (Afr., at the mercy of). In Anglo-Saxon or Norman England, system of penalties for those convicted for offences against the king's peace. FORFEITURE might be imposed, although under the Normans money fines were usual for lesser offences. The system was widespread by the 13th century but was then gradually replaced by statutory penalties.

Amethyst incident. Incident on 20 April 1949 when HMS *Amethyst*, a British naval frigate engaged on carrying supplies to the British community in Nanking, was fired upon by communist guns sailing up the Yangtze-Kiang. Some 17 men were killed and a further 30 wounded. The ship was trapped off an island in the river for 14 weeks, attempts by other vessels to rescue her being unsuccessful. On the night of 30–31 July, Lieut.-Commander J.S.Kerans succeeded in getting 140 miles downriver to the sea: by sailing at over 22 knots the ship managed to avoid the guns of five forts on the way to the coast. The reason for the detention of the *Amethyst* remains unclear, but it was presumably an attempt to assert Chinese sovereignty over an international river on the part of the revolutionary authorities.

Ami des hommes (Fr., friend of men). Sobriquet of the Marquis de Mirabeau (1715–89).

Ami du Peuple (Fr., friend of the people). Sobriquet of the French revolutionary leader Jean Paul Marat (1743–93); also the title of the journal he edited.

amnesty (deriv. Gk. *amnesia*, forgetting or oblivion). Action of a state in pardoning offenders, either by commuting or revoking sentences or by promising not to press charges. It is a useful tool in effecting political reconciliation between former enemies: in the USA, for example, the most extensive use of amnesty came after the civil war (1861–65), when it was widely granted to residents, soldiers and politicians of the rebel CONFEDERACY. Its most recent widescale application was in 1977

when Pres. Carter granted it to US citizens who had evaded conscription for the Vietnam War (1965–73), though it was not extended to military deserters.

Amnesty International. Privately-sponsored international organisation, founded in 1961 by a British barrister, Peter Benenson, whose main purpose is to campaign for the release of political prisoners who have neither committed nor advocated acts of violence. It also seeks to help the families of such prisoners and to improve international standards of the treatment of prisoners and other detainees. The organisation has done much to highlight cases of torture, murder and unjust detention. It has 50,000 members in 57 countries and is financed entirely by private subscription; the headquarters are in London. It has no political or religious affiliations and in 1972 received the Nobel Peace Prize.

Anabaptists (re-baptisers). Fanatical religious sect which arose in Westphalia in the early 16th century. It advocated political and social radicalism, including polygamy. In 1535, under the leadership of Boccold (also known as John of Leyden), they seized the city of Munster, but were overpowered and their leaders executed. In England the term was used abusively in the 17th century to describe BAPTISTS.

anarchism (deriv. Gk. *anarchia*, nonrule). Doctrine advocating the abolition of all organised authority, since, in the words of Josiah Warren, 'every man should be his own government, his own law, his own church'. The first systematic exposition of anarchism was in William Godwin's *Enquiry Concerning Political Justice* (1793) which claimed that since men, when given free choice, are rational, sociable and co-operative, they will form voluntary groups and live in social harmony without state control or the institution of property. Such a situation would be achieved not by revolution but by rational discussion. Pierre Joseph Proudhon (1809–65), a French economist, elevated anarchism to the status of a mass movement in *Qu'est-ce que la propriété?* (What is property?), published in 1840. In it he concluded that property is theft and that 'governments are the scourge of God'. He urged the establishment of non-profit-making co-operative credit banks to provide interest-free capital. He disapproved of violence and of organized groups, including trade unions. These ideas were combined with a revolutionary philosophy by communistic anarchists, notably the Russians Michael Bakunin (1814–76) and Peter Kropotkin (1842–1921), who favoured 'direct action' by the workers to topple the state by all possible means, including assassination. In 1868 anarchists joined the FIRST INTERNATIONAL, which was later split following conflicts between Marxists and the followers of Bakunin. Anarchists were later responsible for the assassination of Tsar Alexander II, King Humbert of Italy, Empress Elizabeth of Austria, President Mackinley of America and President Carnot of France.

Anarchism differs from COMMUNISM in its opposition to the state and its refusal to form political parties. Not all anarchists advocate violence. Philosophical anarchists such as the American Henry Thoreau (1817–62) were primarily individualists believing in a return to nature, non-payment of taxes and passive resistance to state control. Leo Tolstoy (1828–1916) professed a Christian anarchism, believing the state to be inconsistent with Christianity and holding that refusal to pay taxes, render military service or recognize the courts would topple the established order. Such ideas influenced Gandhi. In Spain the anarchists actually participated in government (1936–7) but the conflict between anarchists and communists within the Spanish Republican ranks during the Civil War, together with the mounting prestige of Soviet communism between 1941 and 1948 led to a decline in the international influence of anarchism. But in the 1960s anarchist sentiment revived in the student movement's revulsion at capitalism, coinciding with disillusionment at Soviet foreign policy. In recent anarchist movements such as the BAADER-MEINHOF group and the Italian RED BRIGADES, terrorism is prevalent. *See also* MARXISM, SYNDICALISM.

ANC. African National Congress, party formed in 1912 at Bloemfontein to protect the interests of black people in South Africa. It developed from the Native Education Association formed in 1882 in Cape Colony. In 1926 it decided to work for a democratic and racially integrated South Africa. It pursued non-violent tactics and many young Africans left it because of its lack of militancy. The South African government made it illegal in 1961. In the same year the ANC's leader, Nelson Mandela, was tried for treason and acquitted. He was however, subsequently convicted of sabotage (1964) and sentenced to life imprisonment. Despite Mandela's continuing detention he remains the most potent symbol of the anti-apartheid movement and the ANC is still widely recognized – even by many white South Africans – as the most formidable champion of black rights.

ancien régime (Fr., old government, old order). The governmental and social structure which prevailed in Europe prior to the French Revolution of 1789. Its main characteristics are taken to have been an absolute or despotic monarchy, based on the DIVINE RIGHT OF KINGS and the rigid division of society into three orders – the aristocracy, the Church, and the THIRD ESTATE.

Angevins (deriv. Fr. Anjou). The Plantagenet kings of England from Henry II (1154) to Richard II (d. 1400). The name comes from Geoffrey, Count of Anjou, the father of Henry II.

Anglo-Catholic. That strand in the Church of England which stresses the church's Catholic heritage, rejects the term 'Protestant' and espouses much of Roman Catholic ritual and dogma.

Angry Brigade. British anarchist group responsible for bombings and gun attacks on government buildings, commercial premises, embassies and cabinet ministers' homes between 1968 and 1971. Eight alleged members were tried in 1972, four were acquitted and four imprisoned.

annate (deriv. Lat. *annus*, year). A fee or tax paid to the Pope in respect of ecclesiastical preferment, consisting originally of the whole of the first year's income from the office. Annates, introduced into England in the 13th century,were annexed to the Crown under Henry VIII and transferred in 1704 to a perpetual fund for the benefit of the poorer clergy (known as Queen Anne's Bounty). On 1 April 1948 Queen Anne's Bounty was abolished and the Ecclesiastical Commissioners administering it were embodied in the Church Commissioners for England.

annexation. Process whereby a state assumes possession of territory unilaterally and without the consent of the former owner. Unlike a protectorate, military occupation or UN trusteeship, full sovereign rights are conferred but the population of the annexed territory become subjects of the new possessor state. Annexations may be made by force, by treaty or by other means. Examples are Germany's annexation of the Sudetenland in 1938 and Israel's annexation of Jordanian areas of Jerusalem in 1967.

Anschluss (Germ., union). The union of Germany and Austria proclaimed on 13 March 1938. Pressure for the union of the two war allies, building up since the collapse of the Habsburg monarchy in 1918, increased when Adolf Hitler, an ardent advocate of union, became German Chancellor in 1933. By threats of military action, Hitler secured the resignation of the Austrian Chancellor Schushnigg and installed in his place the pro-Nazi Seyss-Inquart who, in concert with Hitler, invited Germany to occupy Austria on the pretext of restoring internal law and order.

anti-clericalism. Opposition to organized religion, particularly the power and privileges of the Roman Catholic Church. Anti-clericalism, though not a coherent political doctrine, has a long history. In England it is traceable to the 14th century when Wyclif insisted that all men had a right of access to the scriptures. In Tudor times, anti-clericalism arose from a variety of motives ranging from greed and a desire to plunder the monasteries to a genuine dislike of priestly powers and abuses. Modern anti-clericalism was prevalent in revolutionary France and remained characteristic of French radicalism during the 19th century. Anti-clericalism has broken out sporadically in Spain (notably in 1873, 1909–13 and 1931–36) and in Latin America. In Germany it was confined to the KULTURKAMPF and the later Nazi persecution of individual Church leaders. In Italy there has been a long history of anti-clericalism stemming from opposition to the territorial claims of the Pope and, more recently, over the Catholic Church's attitude to divorce and contraception. In some communist states, anti-clericalism has arisen from the government's identification of the clergy with former fascist regimes and as part of an ideological battle for the loyalty of the masses.

Anti-Comintern pact. Agreement between NAZI Germany and Japan proclaiming their joint hostility to international communism, signed by the two countries on 25 November 1936 and by Italy the following year. It was the work of the German foreign minister, Ribbentrop (1893–1946), whose aim was to reflect Nazi ideology in his conduct of foreign affairs. The pact also gave German recognition to the Japanese-backed 'puppet' régime that ruled Manchuria, occupied by Japan since 1931.

Anti-Corn Law League. English association dedicated to securing the repeal of the CORN LAWS, founded in Manchester in 1839 by 'representatives from all the great sections of our manufacturing and commercial population'. Its leaders were Richard Cobden (1804–65), a textile manufacturer, and John Bright (1811–89), a cotton-mill owner, both believers in free trade. The League was predominantly middle-class in composition but attracted working-class support when enthusiasm for CHARTISM waned. It made the use of mass meetings and popular oratory an accept-

able part of English political life. It was also quick to adopt the 'penny post', introduced in 1840, as a means of disseminating propaganda. A public subscription of £50,000 opened by the League in November 1842 reached the full amount within three months. The following year a subscription of £100,000 was opened and filled by mid-1845. The League's magazine had a circulation of 20,000 and thousands attended meetings. Such evidence of the League's popularity finally helped persuade the Conservative Prime Minister Peel to renege on past pledges and to repeal the corn laws in June 1846, opening an era of free trade. The League, its aims achieved, then disbanded.

Anti-Parnellites. Irish Nationalist MPs, led by Justin McCarthy, who refused to support Parnell's leadership after the 1890 O'Shea divorce case. The expression was also occasionally used between 1885 and 1890 to describe those who opposed Irish HOME RULE. *See also* PARNELLITES.

Anti-Pope. Applied to Popes Clement VII and Benedict XIII who resided at Avignon during the GREAT SCHISM and were elected in opposition to the canonically chosen Pope.

anti-semitism. Term first applied in the mid-19th century to denote animosity towards the Jews. Throughout the middle ages the Jews faced hostility on religious grounds and because, unlike Catholics, they were allowed to practise usury. Modern anti-semitism differs in being largely politically and economically motivated, doctrinaire, and based on a pseudo-scientific rationale devised by, for example, Gobineau (1816–82), Houston Stewart Chamberlain (1855–1927) and Nazi 'philosophers'. In the 1870s a group of German writers, using the linguistic distinctions 'Semitic' and 'Aryan' as racial terms, began speaking of the Jews as a distinct and inferior race. Anti-semitic political parties were active in both Germany and Austria-Hungary in the 1880s while POGROMS began in Russia in 1882. In France the 1894 Dreyfus case revealed a large core of anti-semitic feeling. Between 1905 and 1909 anti-Jewish violence on a large scale again broke out in Tsarist Russia, particularly in Lithuania and Poland. In the late 19th and early 20th centuries thousands of Jews from eastern Europe fled to Britain and the USA. From 1920 to 1933 Hitler expounded theories of Aryan racial supremacy and blamed the Jews for Germany's misfortunes. The Nuremberg Laws of 1935 codified Nazi theories of race, denied Jews German citizenship and forbade them to marry Aryans; in 1938 Jewish property was confiscated. During World War II over five million Jews were murdered in CONCENTRATION CAMPS. Since 1945 anti-semitism has usually been a reaction to ZIONISM and the state of Israel. In the USSR anti-semitism re-emerged in 1953 and there was serious violence against Jewish communities in 1958–9. In 1962–3 Jews were executed for 'economic crimes' and until recently many Jews seeking to emigrate to Israel have been imprisoned.

ANZAC (acronym). The Australian and New Zealand Army Corps which achieved fame for its part in the Gallipoli campaign of 1915.

Anziani (Ital.). The Council of Ancients established in Florence in the mid-13th century. Consisting of fourteen leading citizens, it controlled all matters relating to government.

ANZUS Pact (acronym). Tripartite security treaty concluded on 1 September 1951 in San Francisco between Australia, New Zealand and the United States, providing for mutual collaboration should any of the three be subject to an armed attack in the Pacific area. The pact marked a new independence from British control in the foreign affairs of Australia and New Zealand. New Zealand was later to withdraw from the ANZUS Pact.

apartheid (S. Afr., apartness). Policy of 'separate development' pursued by the South African government. Based on beliefs in the *baaskap* (white supremacy) and in racial purity, it involves total racial discrimination between blacks and whites in South Africa. Some degree of racial segregation has existed in South Africa since the mid-17th century and was continued under the United Party, led by Smuts and Hertzog from 1934. Since the National Party came to power in 1948, oppressive measures against the non-white population have steadily increased under the premierships of Malan, Strijdom, Verwoerd and Vorster. Since 1953 strikes by African workers have been prohibited, schools have been segregated and mixed marriages made illegal. In 1956 the Cape Coloured voters were partially disenfranchised.

Official policy is to create separate self-governing black states in which Africans may be guided to self-government and, it is claimed, independence. The Bantu Self-Government Act of 1959 provided for seven such BANTUSTANS which would give Africans, who constitute 70 per cent of the population, 14 per cent of the total land; the first was created by the 1963 Transkei Constitution Act. Total apartheid cannot be feasible, however, since Africans, by a system of labour and travel permits which often breaks up families, provide a source of low-paid labour for white-owned industries, particularly the mines. In March 1960 an anti-apartheid demonstration at Sharpeville led to the deaths of 67 Africans; in March 1961 apartheid was condemned by a conference of Commonwealth prime ministers.

In June 1976, 176 people were killed in riots in Soweto; in September 1977 the moderate black leader Steve Biko was killed while in police detention. The second Bantustan of Bophutatswana received 'independence' in 1977, followed by Venda in 1979. During 1977 the Roman Catholic Church allowed all races into its schools and a conference of bishops issued a 21-point plan for improving the position of blacks. A number of American firms stated that they would end segregation in their South African branches while EEC governments laid down guidelines requiring their firms to give equal treatment to blacks. The national government of Natal produced plans for a new constitution giving more rights to Indians and coloureds, but not to blacks who were to be dealt with by the bantustan policy. However, in 1980 conservatives in South Africa benefited at the expense of reformers in a government reshuffle. In 1982 a group of ultra-conservatives under Treurnicht left the governing National Party; they have since gained increasing support, notably in the 1988 local elections in the Transvaal.

Apocrypha (Gk., hidden). Books included in the Septuagint (Greek) and Vulgate (Latin) versions of the Old Testament, but excluded from the sacred canon by Protestants at the REFORMATION. The reason given for exclusion was that the books were not originally written in Hebrew and were not regarded as genuine by the Jews. The books of the Apocrypha are: 1 and 2 Esdras, Tobit, Judith, additions to Esther, Wisdom of Solomon, Ecclesiasticus, Baruch, Song of the Three Children, Susannah, Bel & the Dragon, Prayer of Manasseh, and 1 and 2 Maccabees.

The Apocrypha is generally regarded as an appendage to the Old Testament, but it has some direct relevance to Christian works. 2 Esdras contains visions of the Apocalypse which echo the New Testament's Revelations; the liturgical poetry of the Song of the Three Children is used in Christian worship as the *Benedicite* while Ecclesiasticus includes a later Christian synopsis of the teachings of Jesus, son of Sirach. The Roman Catholic Church has cited various parts of the Apocrypha as proof of the value of prayers for the dead and of good works such as alms-giving, an authority denied by Protestants.

Apostles. An élitist society founded in the 18th century centred on King's College, Cambridge. Its members were primarily intellectuals and politicians and the revelation that they included communist spies Kim Philby, Guy Burgess, Donald Maclean and Anthony Blunt, allegedly recruited by Soviet agents in the 1930s, gave the society some notoriety. *See* MI5.

Apostolic Brethren (*also* Apostolics). An order founded by Gerard Segarelli in Parma in 1260, holding heretical doctrines on perfection and poverty in exaggerated imitation of the FRANCISCANS. They were responsible for a rebellion under the leadership of Dolcino di Novara, who was burnt in 1307.

appanages (Fr. deriv. Lat., to provide with means of subsistence). In France, the provision made from the 13th to the 16th centuries for the younger sons of kings, consisting of feudal lands owned by the Crown. In 1790 they were reduced to pensions and rents and later abolished. In 1810 they were re-established as pensions, then finally abolished in 1832. The name was also given to the Imperial estates in pre-revolutionary Russia.

apparatchik (pl., *apparatchki*). Full-time paid officials working in the Soviet Communist Party *apparat* (party machine), particularly in the Central Party Secretariat and its various sections.

apparentement (Fr., an electoral alliance between political parties). A term used particularly of an arrangement introduced for the 1951 elections. By the system of proportional representation operative in multi-member constituencies under the Fourth Republic, parties forming an *apparentement* counted as a single party. This allowed the parties in alliance to claim more seats, for if the *apparentement* won an absolute majority in a constituency it took all the seats. The system, designed to strengthen the moderate centre parties at the expense of the far left and the GAULLISTS, did not, however, result in stable government as was anticipated.

appeasement. Foreign policy based on the conciliation of the grievances of rival states, usually involving some form of concession as an attempt to avoid conflict or war. The term is most often applied to the pre-World War II policy of Britain and France of attempting to satisfy the demands of Hitler with regard to Germany's grievances over the Versailles settlement. The policy, based on

agreements with Germany and Italy, is particularly associated with Neville Chamberlain's premiership (1937–40). As a result of appeasement Germany was able to occupy the Rhineland, the Sudetenland areas of Czechoslovakia and to achieve ANSCHLUSS with Austria. The policy is held to have ended when Hitler broke the 1938 Munich agreement and occupied the rest of Czechoslovakia in March 1939.

Appellant, Lords. *See* LORDS APPELLANT.

approvers. In medieval England, self-confessed criminals who as common informers and in the hope of pardon undertook appeals of felony and the consequent trial by battle. During the 13th century they had to win five trials to obtain a pardon and in return were maintained and equipped by the Crown. If an appeal failed, or a battle was lost, they were hanged. Approvers were always regarded with distaste and the custom disappeared during the 15th century.

Arab League. Loose association of Arab states formed in March 1945 at Bludan, Syria, following a preparatory conference in September 1944 at Alexandria, Egypt. Founder-members were Egypt, Iraq, Lebanon, Saudi Arabia, Syria, Jordan and the Yemen. Other states which later joined the League are Libya in 1951; Sudan in 1956; Tunisia and Morocco in 1958; Kuwait in 1961; Algeria in 1962; South Yemen in 1968; Bahrain, Qatar, Oman and the TRUCIAL STATES in 1971.

The council of the League meets in Cairo where a delegate of each member-state, plus a spokesman for the Palestinians, attends. Its purpose is to increase economic and technical co-operation between the Arab states, to promote Arab culture and to end inter-Arab conflicts. For many years its primary concern was to secure the expulsion of the French from Arab territory, but since 1967 its main activity has been co-ordinating opposition to Israel. The rise of the PLO has led to a decline in its influence though it continues to function as a force for economic unity.

aristocracy of labour. The skilled section of the 19th- and early 20th-century British working class in the staple industries, economically and consciously culturally distinct from the mass of workers, which provided the core and the leadership of the trade union movement. A Marxist view that its influence held the Labour movement back from revolutionary politics is widely disputed.

Armagnacs. The party of the Orleans princes, followers of the Comte d'Armagnac. In 1407 John of Burgundy arranged the murder of Louis, Duke of Orleans; in 1410 open warfare broke out between the BURGUNDIANS and the Armagnacs. The Armagnacs drew their power from the south and south-east of France, were strong among the great nobles and favoured an anti-English war policy. In 1418 their opponents seized control of Paris by treachery and the Armagnac leaders were imprisoned. The Paris mob, always hostile to the Armagnac cause, broke into the prisons and murdered them. Some 3,500 are said to have perished, including the Comte d'Armagnac. Many of those engaged on the Armagnac side later enlisted in the forces of Frederick III of Germany in the war with the Swiss (1446) which became known as the Armagnac War. *See also* CABOCHIENS.

Armatoli. Greek mercenaries in the employ of the sultans of Turkey from the 15th to the early 19th centuries.

arme blanche (Fr., white force). A term for cavalry much in vogue before World War I. For those who used it, the term usually signified devotion to a concept of warfare as a glorious, fast-moving affair in which victory was won by rapid and imaginative deployments of cavalry. The conditions on the WESTERN FRONT rendered cavalry virtually obsolete, however, and tanks began to play a crucial role analogous to that of cavalry in pre-mechanized times.

Armenian Massacres. Massacres of Armenians, a Monophysite Christian people living within the OTTOMAN empire, by Moslem Turks between 1894 and 1895. They led to outrage in Britain and ended Britain's attempts to preserve the integrity of the empire (*see* EASTERN QUESTION). In 1914–15 the Turks exterminated a large part of the Armenian population and deported the remainder of it from Armenia in 1915.

Arminians. The followers of Jacob Arminius (1560–1609), a Leyden professor who in the early 17th century dissented from the strict Calvinism of Dutch Protestantism. They rejected the doctrine of PREDESTINATION, emphasizing instead the teachings of the early Church on free will. In 1618 the Synod of Dort issued a decree banishing the Arminian preachers; the Great Pensioner, Barneveldt, their chief lay supporter, was executed. In mid-17th century England, Archbishop Laud was accused by his opponents of Arminianism – i.e. of favouring the doctrine of free will above that of predestination, but the latter remained part of Anglican orthodoxy. For the enemies of James I and

Charles I, the appellation 'Arminian' served as a term of abuse for the Court and those divines who implemented its religious policies. Parliament, mainly Puritan and Calvinist, used it as a pejorative label for any holder of views that it disliked and suspected.

armistice. Truce or ceasefire.

Armistice Day. 11th November 1918, when the ARMISTICE ending hostilities on the WESTERN FRONT took effect. The same date every year now commemorates the fallen in all wars since 1914.

arms race. Continuous competition between the USSR and the Western powers, particularly the USA, to establish technical and numerical supremacy in arms production.

Army Bureau of Current Affairs (ABCA). Established in June 1941, it organized compulsory weekly platoon discussions on topics of contemporary interest, notably post-war reconstruction. Uncontroversial in practice, the Bureau aroused fears among senior military and political figures, including Churchill, who attempted to have it wound up. Credited, probably wrongly, with influencing troops to vote Labour in large numbers at the 1945 British General Election.

Arnoldists. Members of a 12th-century north Italian movement which attempted to impose a form of apostolic poverty upon the Church. They were followers of Arnold of Brescia (c1100–1155) who held DONATIST and anti-clerical views. After condemnation at the Synod of Verona in 1184, the influence of the heresy waned, although it remained one of a number of manifestations of discontent with the state of the established Church.

Arrabiati. Party of the Medici at the time of the Florentine Republic, established in 1493.

Array, Commissions of. A system in medieval England whereby all free men and, from the 13th century, the unfree also, were obliged to serve in their country's defence. Commissioners were appointed to 'array' able-bodied men between 15 and 60 years of age in each shire and select the best of them for the king's service. The weapons which they were obliged to keep ready were prescribed by successive ASSIZES. Commissions of Array continued into the 17th century; they were issued by Charles I in 1642 to raise his forces for the Civil War.

arrière fief (AFr.). Feudal term denoting the land held by the vassal of a vassal.

arrondissement (Fr.). In France, a subdivision of the larger political and administrative unit, the *département*.

artel (Russ., workers). In pre-revolutionary Russia, an association of workmen living and working together and sharing the profits of each job. Artels varied in character; some were temporary but others developed the characteristics of a guild. The artel of bank porters, for instance, was responsible to the employers for the actions of its members.

Aryan (deriv. Sansk., lord). Originally, a philological term referring to a group of inter-related Indian languages. The idea that a particular race existed which spoke these languages was put forward by the German-born scholar Friedrich Max

Müller (1823–1900), who suggested a warlike North Indian people known as 'aryas', referred to in Sanskrit documents dating from 3,000 BC, spoke the first or primeval Indo-European language and that a whole range of modern languages from English to Hindustani originated from it. Müller also suggested that they were the Urvolk or primeval race, but later wrote several works retracting those theories.

But the myth of an Aryan Urvolk who spread over India and Persia from North India and across the steppes into Europe was developed by nationalists and romanticists in Europe and the USA. They were portrayed as a master-race with qualities of beauty, intelligence, courage, profundity and a talent for political organization and, as such, the founders of civilization. All Europeans and some Asian peoples were said to be descended from them. There is no scientific evidence whatsoever to support the myth, since languages may easily migrate without a related physical migration of peoples, but it was widely adopted by racists and became closely associated with ANTI-SEMITISM. It was the basic tenet of NAZI philosophy.

Aryanization. Nazi racial policy based on Hitler's view that 'A State which in the epoch of race poisoning, dedicates itself to the cherishing of its best elements, must some day be master of the world.' The Nuremberg Laws for the 'Protection of German Blood and German Honour', 15 September 1935, forbade marriage or sexual relations between Jews and non-Jews, punishable by imprisonment and later death. Later regulations excluded Jews from the professions and the civil service.

ASEAN. Association of South-East Asian Nations, formed in 1967 to promote economic development and to increase political stability in South-East Asia. Its members are Indonesia, Malaysia, Singapore, the Philippines and Thailand.

Ashram (deriv. Sansk., near-religious exertion). Holy retreat frequented by Mohandas Karamchand Gandhi (1869–1948), the Hindu Indian national leader.

Asiento (Span.). Britain's 33-year monopoly to sell negro slaves to the Spanish colonies, secured by the Treaty of Utrecht in 1713 and managed by the South Sea Company. In 1748 the monopoly was renewed for four years by the Treaty of Aachen; in 1750, however, it was abandoned for a lump sum settlement.

Assassins (deriv. Arab. *hassāsīn*, eater of hashish). Sect of SHI'ITE Moslems, founded by the Persian Hasan i Sabbah c1090, which established a 200-year reign of terror over Persia and Syria. Members of a secret order, ruled over by a grand master, they were strictly organized into classes, graded by their degree of initiation. Devotees in the lower classes carried out assassinations under strict laws of obedience and in total ignorance of the objects and ritual of the sect. It is thought that the murderers were given to ecstatic visions induced by hashish. The Persian branch of the sect was destroyed by the coming of the Mongols in 1256; the Syrian branch met a similiar fate c1270 under the MAMELUK Sultan of Egypt.

Assephat Hanivcharim. The elected representatives of the Jewish community in Palestine under the British MANDATE which preceded the formation of the state of Israel.

assignats (Fr.). Interest-bearing Treasury bonds, issued by the French Constitutional Assembly in December 1789 to facilitate the purchase of Church lands which were to be expropriated by the revolutionary forces. In September 1790 they took on the role of a paper currency. The need to finance the revolutionary wars led to over-issue which, together with forgery by Royalists and others, caused depreciation in their value and was responsible for an inflationary crisis. They were superseded in 1796 by MANDATS.

assize (deriv. Lat. *assidere*, to sit together). Originally the jury summoned to judge a case; later the court which did the summoning. The term can also mean an ordinance or statute such as 'the Assize of Clarendon'.

Assize courts are of ancient origin in England and are defined in old law books as assemblies of knights and substantial men, together with the justice, meeting at certain times and places. They were regulated by MAGNA CARTA.

In recent times they have consisted of two or more commissioners, judges of assize, successors to the old justices in EYRE (*justiciarii in itinere*) who held special commission from the crown to travel the circuits of the kingdom and try matters under dispute.

assysthement. Under ancient Scottish law, the assessment of the value of the life of a murder victim, to be paid as compensation by the murderer.

Ataman (Russ., military leader). Cossack military title of the 16th century used by Zaporozhian Cossacks of the Ukraine. Also, the title given to the prince of the area east of the River Dnieper in the 17th and 18th centuries and to the elected commander of the Cossack hosts fighting in Russia (after 1723 only the lesser village ataman was elected).

The term was related to *hetman*, also a military title used in the Polish-Lithuanian state from the 16th to the 18th centuries. The *hetman wielk* (great *hetman*) was head of the armed forces and, in the king's absence, commander on the battlefield.

ateliers nationaux (Fr.). Government workshops founded in Paris in 1848 to provide the unemployed with work. They were not a success; within a year the workers rose against the government. Gen. Cavaignac's forces quickly suppressed the uprising and the ring-leaders were arrested and transported.

Atlantic Charter. Declaration issued by Churchill and Pres. Roosevelt following their mid-Atlantic meeting on the warships *Prince of Wales* and *Augusta* on 9–12 August 1941. It stated the principles on which the UK and USA wished to conduct international policy in the post-war world: no desire for territorial or other aggrandisement; no wish for territorial changes other than those freely approved by the peoples concerned; respect for the rights of all peoples to choose their form of government; desire for general economic development and collaboration; need to disarm aggressor nations; and the wish to construct a system of general security.

The statement's main achievement was a propaganda exercise to demonstrate the increasingly close links of the two countries. The US delegation resisted attempts by Britain to secure American commitment to specific post-war international obligations. A month later, the USSR and 14 other nations at war with the AXIS powers endorsed the Charter.

attainder (AFr., to convict). In medieval England, an act by which not only an offender was subject to forfeiture of his land and goods but also his descendants, so that he was thereby disinherited. Felons included those convicted of treason and jury members guilty of returning false verdicts. Acts of Attainder have been numerous; Strafford was executed under one in 1641 for treason. One passed by the Irish Parliament of 1689, summoned by James II after William III's landing in England, contained a list of over 2,000 names: it was the vehicle of many private vengeances, its authors hoping to dispossess personal enemies and their offspring. However, in 1695 the rolls and records of Acts of Attainder passed in James II's reign were cancelled. The last person executed by Act of Attainder was Sir John Fenwick in 1697. In 1814 and 1833 the severity of attainders was mitigated and the 1870 Forfeiture Act abolished the disinheriting of descendants (attaint of the blood).

Attalik Ghasi. Title given to Yakub Beg (c1820–77) a Moslem adventurer who took much of the Tarim Basin and proclaimed himself Beg (Chief) of an independent Moslem state in 1865. Britain urged his recognition by China in the hope that it would forestall Russian expansion in Turkestan, but the Chinese crushed him in 1877.

attrition, war of. Situation in which, as on the WESTERN FRONT in World War I, both sides appear equally balanced, are unable to break through to conduct a war of movement, and are restricted to wearing the enemy down militarily, industrially and psychologically.

audiencias (Span.). Higher courts in Spain and in colonial South America, which were important in the early modern history of the country. The three most significant domestic *audiencias* were Valladolid (established 1452), Ciudad Real (1494), and Granada (1505), and their task was to act as a final court of appeal in civil and criminal cases. In colonial South America they discharged an administrative and political function as the equivalent of regional parliaments in areas far removed from the seat of the Viceroy.

Augmentations, Court of. Institution established by Thomas Cromwell (1485–1540) in 1536 to collect revenues from the estates confiscated by the English Crown during the dissolution of the monasteries between 1536 and 1540. Some 800 institutions were dissolved and their lands possessed by the king; Henry VIII augmented his income by £90,000 a year as a result. The court was also responsible for selling former church property to the English gentry; in 1547 it was reconstituted and took charge of all crown lands until 1554 when it was abolished and its duties transferred to the EXCHEQUER.

aulnage (also alnage, ulnage; AFr., measurement by the ell). The Crown supervision of the size and quality of woollen cloths in medieval England. Standards were laid down in 1196 but only under Edward I were royal officers, aulnagers, appointed to enforce them. Faulty cloths were forfeited to the Crown. In 1381 the regulations regarding size were repealed but those remaining were still enforced until their abolition in 1699.

Ausgleich (Germ., compromise). The agreement reached in 1867 between the Austrian government and moderate Hungarian politicians, which transformed the Austrian empire into the dual monarchy of Austria-Hungary. It was an important achievement for Austria following, as it did, her defeat by Prussia in 1866 and Prussia's subsequent position as the leading German state. The Ausgleich remained valid until the collapse of the Habsburg monarchy in 1918, despite tensions which arose from the conditions of commercial union and the strong resentment felt by other nationalities in the empire at the privileged position of the Hungarians.

Austro-Marxists. A revisionist Marxist trend which emerged in Austria in 1907. Its main figures were Max Adler, who emphasized Marxism's scientific rather than ethical basis; Otto Bauer, who wrote on the national question and imperialism, and Rudolf Hilferding, who provided an economic analysis of imperialism which strongly influenced Lenin.

Autarky (deriv. Gk. *autarkeia*, self-sufficient). In economic terms, a policy aimed at total home-production to the exclusion of imported goods. Pre-World War II Germany's search for a blockade-proof economy provides a good example of economic autarchy.

auto da fé (*auto de fé* Span., act of faith). The ceremony accompanying the execution of condemned heretics during the INQUISITION in Spain and Portugal. Pope Sixtus IV first authorised the Spanish monarchy to name inquisitors in a bull of 1478. The Inquisition lasted until 1813, when it was suppressed by the Cortes de Cádiz. Restored by Ferdinand VII in 1814, it was suppressed again in 1820, only to be reinstated three years later. The last auto da fé took place in 1826; the Inquisition was finally abolished in 1834.

autogestion (Fr., self-management). A development of the concept of WORKERS' CONTROL stressing autonomy and arguing that self-management should extend to every aspect of economic, political and social life. Prominent in the 1968 French MAY EVENTS, autogestion as an aim was adopted by the non-communist trade union federation CFDT (Confédération Française et Démocratique du Travail) in 1970.

autonomy (Gk., self-law). Self-government, often used in a context where there are pressures which might alter this state or prevent its attainment.

Axis. Term first used by Mussolini in Milan on 1 November 1936 to describe the relationship between Nazi Germany and Fascist Italy that was established by the October Protocols of 1936. Mussolini said of the 'Berlin-Rome Line' that it was 'not a diaphragm but rather an axis'. Italy acceded to the German-Japanese ANTI-COMINTERN PACT of 25 November 1936; in May 1939 Germany and Italy entered a formal alliance (the 'Pact of Steel'). In September 1940 Germany, Italy and Japan signed a Tripartite Pact. During World War II the term 'Axis Powers' was therefore applied to the three countries plus their east European allies: Bulgaria, Hungary, Romania and Slovakia.

Ayankeeados. Mexicans who sympathized with America during the Mexican-American war of 1846.

ayatollah. Title given to the most renowned teachers and scholars of Islamic law in Shi'ite Iran. Demands for the return of Khomeini, an exiled ayatollah, sparked off the Islamic revolution in Iran in 1979. Since then real power has lain with the revolutionary council, composed of senior Shi'ite Moslem clergy. *See also* SHI'ITE.

Azania. Name used by some black nationalists to denote South Africa.

AZAPO. Azanian People's Organization. Black consciousness movement formed in South Africa (AZANIA) in 1977 following the banning of other similar organizations.

Aztecs. Indian tribe which ruled central Mexico and the neighbouring regions before the Spanish arrived in 1519. They entered the Anahuac valley in the 12th century and built the city of Tenochtitlan on an island in Lake Texcoco in the early 13th century. A martial race, they soon extended control over their neighbours, taking tributes and victims for sacrifice in their religious rituals. Aztec society was governed by a chieftain and a council representing the twenty clans of Tenochtitlan. The chieftain was elected by the Council but had to be a member of the royal family. The nobility were a military caste owning land individually with serfs to work it for them (while most land was owned communally by the clan). Slavery existed but the *macehual* or commoners did a great deal of the work. The Aztecs were defeated by Cortes and Tenochtitlan was destroyed in 1521.

B

Baader-Meinhof Group. Also known as the Red Army Faction, an anarchist group which emerged in West Germany from the wave of student protest in 1968. Named after two of its leaders – Andreas Baader (1943–77) and Ulrike Meinhof (1934–76) – the group conducted a terrorist campaign in the late 1960s and early 70s against German industrialists and politicians and US military personnel. Its aim was to expose the reactionary forces in West Germany and to oppose the US military presence in Europe. Its leaders were eventually captured and imprisoned in high-security gaols where they soon died in suspicious circumstances. The West German authorities maintain they committed suicide.

baaskap (Afrikaans, 'masterhood'). The underlying white supremacist ethos crudely expressing the ideology of APARTHEID.

Ba'ath Party (Arab., revival or renaissance). Arabic party founded (1910) by a Christian Syrian, Michel Aflaq, which adheres to his philosophy of pan-Arabism, the concept of 'one Arab nation with an external mission', and the principles of 'Freedom, Unity and Socialism'. In 1952 it united with the Syrian Socialist Party to become the Ba'ath Socialist Party.

However, the Ba'athists are not confined to Syria, and their 'pan-Arab' philosophy is influential in Iraq, Jordan, the Lebanon and the Persian Gulf states.

The Ba'athists were most influential in the 1950s, particularly 1956-59 when Egypt and Syria joined together in the United Arab Republic, but they were disillusioned by the authoritarian rule of the Egyptian premier Nasser. A military coup in 1961 preceded Syria's withdrawal from the Union the same year: the failure of this experiment in pan-Arabism was a severe blow to their cause, which has also suffered from the tendency of Ba'athist governments in Iraq and in Syria since 1963 to ignore democracy and to bypass the party's principles of free elections, free speech and free assembly. However, the Ba'athist desire to use socialism as a vehicle of Arab revival has been a significant factor in Arab affairs.

Babylonian Captivity. (1) The exile of the Jews in Babylon following the capture of Jerusalem by Nebuchadnezzar's Babylonian Empire in 586 BC, which according to tradition lasted for 70 years, although the Jews were allowed to return when Babylon fell to Cyrus of Persia in 538 BC.
(2) Metaphorically, the period

1309–78 when the papacy moved to Avignon and was under the control of the French monarchy.

bachelors. In 13th-century England, young knights and squires attached to the household of a great noble. They were forerunners of military retainers. *See* LIVERY AND MAINTENANCE.

backbenchers. *See* FRONT BENCHERS.

Baconists. The Liberal Party in the colony of Virginia who rose in rebellion in 1676 under the leadership of Nathaniel Bacon. The name was adopted by the Liberals in Maryland in 1678.

Bahai. Set of beliefs developed in 19th-century Iran from the teachings of the Bab (Mirza Ali Mohammed) and the Baha'u'llah (Mirza Husain Ali), emphasizing religious unity, universal peace and fellowship, and service to others. Its followers are led by an elected order, the Universal House of Justice. Persecuted by Ayatollah Khomeini's fundamentalist Islamic régime in Iran since 1979.

bail. The freeing of an arrested person upon others becoming sureties by recognizance for his appearance before a court at a certain time and place. It was a development of the medieval system of MAINPRISE.

bailli. In medieval France, a feudal representative of the Crown. He acted on behalf of the king in the territories of great lords, held a court and took cognizance of matters pertaining to the rights of the Crown and matters outside the jurisdiction of the feudal courts.

balanced ticket. A list of candidates designed to represent and to appeal to the regional, ethnic and gender make-up of an electoral unit.

balance of payments. Macroeconomic term to denote the balance between a nation's expenditure on imports and its receipts from exports, including invisible imports and exports. If the receipts from exports exceed the cost of imports the balance is said to be in surplus: if *vice versa* it is in deficit. It is possible, and is often the case in the UK, to have a deficit balance on visible trade and a surplus balance on invisible trade. The sum of the two balances is known as the 'balance on current account'.

A deficit can be financed by loans from abroad or by using national gold and foreign currency reserves to finance foreign payments which cannot be met any other way. However, if a deficit persists a government has to readjust permanently the pattern of trade. This may be done (1) by reducing the value of its currency, making exports cheaper to foreigners and imports dearer, thereby discouraging demand for them (2) by exchange controls, making it difficult to convert its own currency into foreign currency, thereby restricting investment of capital and spending abroad; (3) by import controls and tariffs to place foreign exporters at a disadvantage in competing with home producers, thereby decreasing demand for imports; (4) by deflating the home economy, by cutting employment and income and reducing the demand for both home-produced and imported goods.

balance of power. Diplomatic policy aimed at securing peace, particularly in Europe, by preventing any one state or alignment of states from attaining hegemony or military strength dangerous to the independence and liberty of the others. The policy is thus based on the maintenance of a counter-force equal to that of potential hegemonists. Britain had pursued such a policy for centuries to counter French predominance, but from 1904 to 1914 attempted to balance German power through the ENTENTE CORDIALE. A balance emerged between the Triple Entente of Britain, France and Russia and the TRIPLE ALLIANCE of Germany, Austria and Italy. Between the world wars, Britain at first attempted to balance French power by facilitating the rapid recovery of Germany, but later abandoned her balance of power policy in favour of APPEASEMENT. Since 1945, the predominance of the two super-powers, the USA and the USSR, has seen the demise of the old policy; a policy of deterrence, based on the threat of nuclear war, has now taken its place.

balance of terror. Mutual fear of commencing a nuclear war, a concept which postulates that no country will use nuclear weapons because of the fear of retaliation by the other side. Such a balance has been held because nuclear war, believed to be mutually destructive, would be non-productive to the aggressor. However, the concept is now questioned by proponents of a 'limited' nuclear war who believe that use of nuclear weapons can be closely controlled and restricted to certain areas without provoking massive retaliation. *See also* MAD.

Balfour Declaration. Written pledge made 2 November 1917 by Foreign Secretary A.J. Balfour to Lord Rothschild, chairman of the British Zionist Federation, that Britain supported 'the establishment in Palestine of a national home for the Jewish people, and will use their best endeavours to facilitate the achieve-

ment of this object', provided the rights of non-Jewish inhabitants were respected.

balkanization. Fragmentation of a geopolitical region into a patchwork of antagonistic states, often the clients of outside powers as in the pre-World War I Balkans, where two successive wars in 1912 and 1913 involved shifting alliances and mutual suspicion.

Ballila (Ital.). Youth movement of the Italian Fascist party (*see* FASCISM).

bamboo curtain. Term given to the physical and ideological barrier to movement across the frontiers of the Chinese People's Republic. At the Afro-Asian Conference at Bandung, Indonesia, in April 1955 the Chinese Prime Minister Chou En-lai denied its existence and invited delegates at the conference to visit China. Since 1971, when US embargoes on exports to China were suspended, the curtain seems to have been lifted. In 1971 the UN admitted the People's Republic as a member and Pres. Nixon visited China. In September 1975 official relations were established between China and the EEC. As China's relations with the USSR have deteriorated those with the West have improved.

bandeirantes (Braz. Port.). Explorers, usually of mixed blood, who opened up the interior of Brazil in the 17th century in their search for Indian slaves, gold and precious stones, greatly helping the country's development. Local churchmen condemned them for slavery, immorality and the destruction (1628–32) of Jesuit missions among the Guarani Indians on the Panama river.

Bandes d'Ordonnance (Fr.). Body of

3,000 cavalrymen which formed the standing army of the Netherlands in the mid-16th century.

banneret. Military rank in medieval England. In the late 13th century, bannerets were knights placed in command of other knights and men-at-arms. Receiving higher pay than their subordinates (who were eventually styled knights bachelor), they carried a distinctive rectangular banner, similar to that of a baron, consisting of a knight's pennon without the tail. By the 14th century banneret was a non-hereditary title of honour, usually conferred for military services; by the early 17th century it was synonymous with baronet. With the creation of the hereditary baronetcy by James I in 1611, the title of banneret ended.

banning order. Sanction used in South Africa to prohibit a person from engaging in any named activity, being quoted (even post-humously) or giving interviews to the media.

Bantu (people). Term derived from common dialect of numerous African tribes used by white South Africans to denote blacks. In the family of Niger-Congo languages, there are more than 200 Bantu languages with 60 million speakers.

Bantustan. A white South African term, derived from BANTU, denoting an area of land set apart for use and occupation by black Africans with limited powers of self-government. The best known of the eight Bantustans (which occupy a total of 14 per cent of the land area of South Africa) is the Transkei. *See also* APARTHEID.

banzai (Jap., ten thousand years, forever). The shout of Japanese soldiers during reckless massed frontal assaults in World War II.

Baptists. Members of an English Christian denomination founded by John Smyth (d. 1612), a minister of the Church of England who came under ARMINIAN influence in Holland. They base their doctrine upon the teaching of the apostles and hold that members can only be received into the faith by baptism as adults. The first Baptist church, built at Newgate in 1612, saw the start of the General Baptist Church which rejected CALVINISM in favour of the Arminian belief in redemption open to all. A later split caused the formation of the Particular Baptist Church which was Calvinistic. In 1891 the two bodies were reunited in the Baptist Union; today the church is spread all over the world and is particularly strong in the USA.

Barbarossa. Code-name given by the German Supreme Command to the invasion of Russia in 1941. Plans drafted in November 1940 were approved by Hitler on 18 December. The invasion, timed to begin on 15 May 1941, was delayed for nearly two months because troops had to be diverted to fight Greece and Yugoslavia. It finally began on 22 June when 79 German divisions together with Romanian and Finnish brigades crossed the frontier. British intelligence services had learned of the plan but Stalin (1879-1953) ignored their warning. The operation was the largest in history. However, only one of the three army groups kept to schedule, leaving the others caught in the severe Russian winter still trying to achieve their targets. As a result the USSR had time to recover from the initial shock and ultimately to defeat the invaders.

Barbary. Area of northern Africa – generally considered to comprise present-day Algeria, Morocco, Tunisia and Tripoli – previously inhabited by corsairs. Known as Barbary pirates, they collaborated with Turkish regular troops during the struggle between the OTTOMAN Empire and Spain in the 16th century. They established bases at Algiers, Tunis and Tripoli which became the capitals of new Ottoman states in 1518 when the corsair Khair ed-Din ('Barbarossa') placed himself and his bases under the protection of the Ottoman sultan Selim I. These new provinces became independent in the 17th century though piracy continued. In the 18th century, with the development of Europe, piracy at last began to decline. *See also* JIHAD.

barbette. Mound or platform of earth or stone or a carriage on which guns are mounted so that they can be fired over a parapet or wall rather than through a gun-port or opening. On a battleship, the term describes the armour protecting the rotating part of a ship's turret below the gunhouse.

Barbons (Fr.). Name given to Louis XIII's veteran counsellors Sillery, Jeannin and Villeroy, *c*1612.

Barebones Parliament. Assembly summoned by Cromwell on 4 July 1653, whose 140 members were selected by the army leaders from nominees of the INDEPENDENTS. Its name was a sneer at one of its members, Praise-God Barbon, a leather-seller and sectarian preacher. Proposals of radical reform alarmed conservatives in the assembly and they engineered its dissolution on 12 December 1653. The INSTRUMENT OF GOVERNMENT followed it.

barnburners. Bands of rural labourers who sought to force landlords to concede improved conditions by acts of arson against hay ricks and farm buildings between 1830 and 1833.

baronage (deriv. OFr. *barnage*, Lat. *baronagium*). In medieval England, the earls, tenants of feudal baronies and other important feudal tenants in chief; all the titled and landed nobility collectively, not merely those entitled baron.

Barons' wars. The conflict between Henry III of England and various barons led by Simon de Montfort, Earl of Leicester, between 1263 and 1265. In May 1258 Henry summoned a meeting of parliament to request taxes which he had promised to the pope; in return the pope was to make one of Henry's sons king of Sicily. The barons seized their opportunity to press the demand that the king should consult them regularly on matters of state rather than his own counsellors. They secured the appointment of a joint committee of twelve of their number and twelve of the king's supporters which produced the Provisions of Oxford. These demanded a council of 15 men to supervize the king's government; three parliaments a year of this council and twelve nobles elected by the community, and various other administrative reforms. In April 1261 Henry's financial problems eased; he persuaded the pope to absolve him of his oath to support the Provisions of Oxford and immediately dismissed the barons from their positions. War broke out in April 1264; de Montfort defeated the royalist forces at the battle of Lewes where he captured Prince Edward. He forced Henry to call parliaments in June 1264 and early in 1265. In May 1265 the prince escaped, quickly rallied the royalists and surprised the barons at Evesham on 4 August where they were defeated and de Montfort killed. Henry confiscated the lands of the dissident barons, but a milder policy was embodied in the dictum of Kenilworth (31 October 1266) after which the remaining rebels agreed to surrender. *See also* DISINHERITED, MONTFORTIANS.

Barrowists. Congregationalist sect active in the 16th century led by Henry Barrow and John Greenwood who preached views similar to those of the BROWNISTS. They held that, contrary to Elizabethan doctrine, the church had no relationship to the state; its only statute-book was the Bible; the Articles of Religion and Book of Common Prayer were mere acts of parliament and each congregation was independent with the power to choose its own ministers. Barrow and Greenwood were hanged at Tyburn in 1593 under an act of the previous year which sought to punish 'persons obstinately refusing to come to church'. Their followers fled in large numbers, first to Holland and later to America.

bashi-bazouks. Turkish irregular troops, recruited mainly amongst the Kurds and other Asiatic tribes of the OTTOMAN empire, who gained notoriety for their involvement in the massacre of some 12,000 Bulgarians, mostly unarmed, during the Bulgarian uprising against the Turks in 1876.

Bastille. Royal fortress commanding the eastern side of Paris. A pamphlet campaign by Radicals on the eve of the French Revolution gave it an exaggerated notoriety for its role as a state prison. It was destroyed on 14 July 1789 by workers from the Faubourg St Antoine. The date, known as Bastille Day, has been commemorated ever since as the national day of France and a symbol of the fall of royal despotism.

Battle of Britain. Period of aerial warfare over Britain between 10 July and 31 October 1940. The German airforce, numbering 1,400 bombers and 1,020 fighters at the outset, sought to achieve decisive air superiority over southern England as a prerequisite to the success of Operation Sealion, the planned cross-channel invasion of England. England's air defences consisted largely of 700 Hurricane and Spitfire fighters, although fighter production was running at 100 a month by the peak of the battle, to replenish losses. German air attacks began with attempts to disrupt shipping, then transferred first to fighter air bases and then to towns and cities. After suffering heavy losses in August (on 15 August, 75 German planes were lost to only 34 British), Germany seemed to have regained the tactical initiative in the first week of September. But in two separate engagements on 15 September 1940 they lost 56 planes, and on 17 September Operation Sealion was indefinitely postponed. 915 planes were lost in total by Britain and her allies in the three month battle; Germany lost over 1,700 aircraft. 'Battle of Britain Day' has since been celebrated on 15 September in memory of the British, Dominion, Polish, Czech, French and Belgian pilots engaged on the Allied side.

Bay of Pigs. Incident which occurred on 17 April 1961 at Cochinos Bay (Bay of Pigs), Cuba. Shortly after taking office Pres. Kennedy learned of a CIA proposal, accepted by the previous administration of Eisenhower, to land a force of Cuban exiles on the south coast of Cuba with a view to overthrowing the communist régime of Fidel Castro. Kennedy allowed the landing but vetoed the plan for US air support. It was mistakenly believed that the Cuban population would rally to the exiles and the invasion attempt rapidly became a fiasco. By 21 April all the exiles were dead or captured and Castro's popularity had increased. He strengthened his links with the USSR and by 1963 allowed Russian missile bases on Cuban soil. Kennedy had to accept responsibility for the disaster, which led him to try to tighten presidential control of CIA activities.

Bay State. Old nickname for the US state of Massachusetts, derived from its colonial name, Massachusetts Bay.

beatification. In the Roman Catholic Church, the prefixing of 'Blessed' to the name of one of the faithful departed, which usually preceeds CANONIZATION.

beauty contest. A primary election in which American voters demonstrate their support for a candidate but the result is not binding.

Bedouins. Wandering bands of Arabs, sometimes said to be the descendants of Ishmael (Genesis 25: 13-18), who profess a form of ISLAM and are governed by SHEIKS.

Beer Hall Putsch. Hitler's attempt to seize Bavaria on 9/10 November 1923 as a preliminary to overthrowing the WEIMAR REPUBLIC. The Nazis' headquarters were in a beer hall. The coup collapsed when police opened fire, killing 14. Hitler was sentenced to five years in prison.

beg. *See* BEY.

Beggars of the Sea. Dutch privateers, led by William de la Marck and commissioned by the Prince of Orange in the 1570s to attack Spanish merchant shipping.

beghards. In the 13th and 14th centuries, men who pursued a religious

life without rules or vows, similar to that of the female BÉGUINES.

Béguines (Fr.). Pious women who belonged to a sisterhood founded in Liège in the 12th century, pursuing a religious life without rules or vows. They lived singly or in convents which were often linked to the mendicant orders. The movement was popular from the early 13th century, but its growth was restricted in the 14th century by prejudice and accusation of heresy.

Belski. One of two factions of nobles, the other being the Choviski, who between them ruled Russia *c*1530 during the minority of Ivan IV ('The Terrible').

benefice (OFr. deriv. Lat., favour). An ecclesiastical living or preferment. Clerical benefices originated in the 12th century as an imitation of the lay system of FIEFS; until then priests had been supported by alms and oblations. The term refers now to vicarages, rectories, perpetual curacies and chaplaincies in the Church of England; bishoprics, by contrast, are termed dignities.

benefit of clergy. The right claimed by the medieval Church to withdraw its members from the jurisdiction of the secular courts to that of ecclesiastical courts. The term 'clerk', held to carry the right to ecclesiastical trial, was applied to all who could read. The spread of lay education consequent upon the RENAISSANCE brought increasing abuse and in 1532 the right to plead benefit of clergy in cases of felony was limited to the rank of sub-deacon and above.

Benelux (acronym). Agreement on economic collaboration between Belgium, the Netherlands and Luxembourg, which grew out of a convention in London in September 1944 and was manifested in a customs union established on 1 January 1948. In 1954 the three countries agreed that between 1 March 1954 and 1 March 1956 a common policy on trade and payments to non-Benelux countries would be established. Under the terms of the agreement no Benelux country would enter separate trade treaties with other states and steps were taken to increase the freedom of movement of capital between the three. A treaty establishing an economic union was concluded at The Hague on 3 February 1958 and came into force on 1 November 1960. This provided for free movement of capital, goods, traffic, services and population between the three member countries, a common trade policy and coordination of investment, agricultural and social policies.

benevolences (ME deriv. Lat., well-wishing). An arbitrary form of taxation, introduced by Edward IV of England in 1473, that was imposed without the consent of parliament. They were made illegal under Richard III in 1484 but Henry VII sought to reintroduce them in 1495. Henry VIII demanded them in 1528 and 1545 and James I in 1614, 1615, 1620 and 1622. The last, unsuccessful, attempt to raise them was made by Charles I in 1633.

Bennite. Supporter of the British Labour Party politician Tony Benn (b.1925), former minister (1966–70, 1975–79) and member of the Labour Party Executive Committee. Benn has always been a campaigner for party democracy and the injection of a stronger SOCIALIST element into Labour Party policy. The press tend to use the term 'Bennite' to describe the Labour left-wing in general and not just those persons who speci-

fically support Benn. The term has also been erroneously applied to members of the TROTSKYIST Militant Tendency of which Benn is not a member. Benn narrowly lost his seat in the General Election of June 1983, but was returned for Chesterfield in 1984. Unsuccessfully contested leadership, 1988.

bersagliere (Ital., sharpshooters). Corps of riflemen in the Italian army, founded by Victor Emmanuel II c1850.

Berserkers. Violent pre-medieval and medieval Norse and German warrior groups who worshipped Odin, wore skins, and acted as bodyguards to royal or noble courts. The word comes from the Old Norse for 'bearskin'.

Bethar. The youth movement of the Revisionist Party in Israel.

Bevanites. Members of the British Labour Party who supported the position taken by Aneurin Bevan (1897–1960) on defence policy during the early 1950s. In April 1951 Bevan (Minister of Health), Harold Wilson (President of the Board of Trade) and John Freeman (Parliamentary Secretary to the Ministry of Supply) resigned office in protest at the decision of the Labour cabinet to impose National Health prescription charges to meet the costs of defence. In May 1952, 57 Labour MPs voted with Bevan against the Labour Party line on a Conservative government motion on defence. They included those who had resigned in 1951, a remnant of the old 'Keep Left' group in the Labour Party and pacifists. They were mostly nominees of the constituency parties rather than of the trade unions, many being professional men, such as the journalists Michael Foot, Tom Driberg and

Richard Crossman. In April 1954 Bevan resigned from the shadow cabinet to organize opposition to German rearmament in defiance of the party conference decision to support it. In 1955 the Bevanites abstained in votes for Labour Party amendments to the defence White Paper outlining the decision to build a hydrogen bomb, demanding instead definite restrictions upon its use. At the end of 1955 Bevan was defeated by the reformist Gaitskell in a contest for the party leadership. In 1957, following the Suez crisis and his attacks on the Conservative government, Bevan was appointed shadow foreign secretary by Gaitskell; at the party conference of that year he opposed the Bevanites, arguing that Britain needed to retain the H-bomb as she could not go 'naked into the conference chamber'. *See also* GAITSKELLITES.

bey (Turk.) Modern spelling of a word found among the Turks since the earliest times, denoting the ruler of a tribal group, member of a ruling family or an important official. Under the OTTOMAN empire, the bey was the ruler of a province with his own flag; in Tunis, after 1705, the office was hereditary. Gradually the title became one merely of courtesy, similar to the English 'esquire'.

Bezaaygeld. Mid-18th century tax in Holland, levied on seed put into the ground.

Bianchi (Ital., white). (1) Members of a fanatical sect which appeared in Italy in 1399; they wore long white garments and ate only bread and water.
(2) *See* NERI AND BIANCHI.

biatagh (Gaelic). Tenant in Celtic Ireland who held his land in return for providing hospitality to travellers.

Bible Belt. Southern states of the USA where fundamentalist Christianity retains a strong popularity.

bicameral. Parliament with two chambers or houses, such as the US Congress with its Senate and House of Representatives, and the British parliament with its House of Commons and House of Lords.

'Big Five'. Permanent members of the UN Security Council: the USA, USSR, Britain, China and France.

'Big Four'. Representatives of the major victorious powers of World War I at the Paris Peace Conference of 1919. They were the British Prime Minister Lloyd George (1863–1945); the US President Woodrow Wilson (1856–1924); the French Prime Minister George Clemenceau (1841–1929) and the Italian Prime Minister Vittorio Orlando (1860–1952). Orlando is occasionally omitted from the group which is then known at the 'Big Three'.

'Big Three'. Leaders during World War II of the major Allied powers: the British Prime Minister Winston Churchill (1874–1965); the Soviet Marshal and dictator Josef Stalin (1879–1953) and the US President Franklin D. Roosevelt (1882–1945).

bilateral agreement. Agreement to which there are two parties as opposed to a multilateral agreement involving several parties.

billeting. The custom of requiring householders to provide accommodation for members of the armed forces. The system was widely abused in the 17th century under Charles I and protests against it were included in the PETITION OF RIGHT (1628). Despite the forbidding of forced billeting in 1679, it continued under Charles II and James II, ending only when parliament agreed to the building of permanent barracks in 1792.

Bill of Rights. (1) In the USA, the ten amendments to the constitution moved by James Madison in the House of Representatives in June 1789 and ratified by December 1791; they are generally regarded as a part of the original Constitution. The first prohibits CONGRESS from establishing any religion and from abridging the freedoms of speech, of the press, of assembly and of petition for redress of grievance. The second guarantees the right to keep and bear arms and the third prohibits quartering of troops without consent. The fourth to eighth amendments regulate the use of search warrants, trial for crimes and common law suits. The ninth states that 'the enumeration in the Constitution of certain rights shall not be construed to deny or disparage others retained by the people,' and the tenth that 'the powers not delegated to the United States by the Constitution, nor prohibited by it to the States, are reserved to the States respectively, or to the people.'

(2) In Britain, a Bill passed by Parliament in October 1689, incorporating the Declaration of Rights (*see* CONVENTION PARLIAMENTS) and condemning the actions of James II. The use of SUSPENDING and DISPENSING powers were attacked, as was the maintenance of a standing army in peace-time and the raising of money levies without parliamentary consent. The Bill's main purpose was to justify the accession of William of Orange and Mary to the throne and it placed little restriction on the new monarch's powers. But it did assert the principle of parliamentary supremacy, the right to free elections, freedom of speech within parliament and frequent meetings of parliament. It also excluded Roman Catholics from the succession to the throne.

Bilu. CHOVEVEI ZION members who were the first Jewish pioneers to form settlements in Palestine in the late 19th century.

bimbashi (Turk., head of a thousand). A colonel in the armies of the OTTOMAN empire.

bimetallists. Advocates of a monetary system which had considerable influence in the late 19th century as a potential remedy for Britain's 'Great Depression'. Gold and silver were to be placed on the same basis for coinage purposes by making silver a legal tender to any amount and establishing a fixed ratio between the two metals. Despite the advocacy of a number of leading politicians, including the future prime minister Arthur Balfour, the opposition of the City and the Treasury made the idea politically impracticable. An international conference held in Brussels in 1892 dissolved without making any recommendations because of the diversity of opinions displayed. Neither gold nor silver is now widely used for coinage purposes.

Birchers. Members of the US John Birch Society, a right-wing organization in the late 1950s and early 1960s with an obsessive belief that Christianity and American democracy were under threat from COMMUNISM.

biretta (deriv. Ital.). Square cap of black, red or purple worn by Roman Catholic priests.

Bishops' wars. Hostilities between England and Scotland 1638–1640, so called because they arose from Charles I's attempt to impose Anglicanism and the EPISCOPACY on the Scots. James I had re-established the episcopacy in Scotland and Charles I had at the beginning of his reign (1625–1649) sought to wrest back from the Scottish nobles the Church lands they had seized in the past. In 1637 he introduced a modified version of the English Prayer Book to Scotland which provoked the COVENANTERS into abolishing the episcopacy. An army was raised by the Scots and in 1638 war broke out. Charles raised an army to oppose them but did not have the finance to pay his troops. As a result he was forced to sign the Treaty of Berwick in June 1638 but he refused to agree to the abolition of the episcopacy in Scotland. He summoned the SHORT PARLIAMENT to secure finance, but it refused to vote supplies for a resumption of the war. He turned to the CONVOCATION who gave him £20,000 as a BENEVOLENCE. With further aid from the Irish parliament, war was resumed but the discipline and morale of the army was poor and it was routed near Newcastle. On 26 October 1640 Charles signed the Treaty of Ripon which was virtually a surrender. He was forced to summon parliament and had to pay £850 a day to the Scots who were to retain possession of Durham and Northumberland, until the religious issue was settled.

Black Africa. Those African states under majority or black rule. With the establishment of majority rule in Zimbabwe (formerly Rhodesia) in 1979, South Africa and the territories it controls remain the major states outside Black Africa.

Black and Tans. Special additional recruits of the Royal Irish Constabulary, first introduced in 1920, whose popular name – that of a common breed of Irish hounds – was derived from their uniform of dark green, almost black, caps and khaki tunics and trousers. Between March 1920 and January 1922 the Black and Tans were responsible for excessively severe reprisals against terrorist activity in suppressing Irish nationalist unrest and combating the Irish Republican Army. Their destruction of Balbriggan, near Dublin, and the killing of two Irishmen in September 1920, followed three months later by the firing of the library and county hall in Cork were acts of criminal irresponsibility which served to fuel republican resentment at British rule. The actions of the Black and Tans have been endlessly recounted and embroidered in poetry and song from Dublin to Boston; one legend has it that they were recruited from among protestant prisoners in Scottish gaols.

black bands. German mercenaries enlisted for service in the Italian Wars of the 16th century by Louis XII of France.

blackbirders. Ships engaged in the traffic in labour in the South Seas between 1847 and 1904, whose crews made a practice of kidnapping South Pacific islanders for slave labour on the cotton and sugar plantations of Queensland. The trade eventually died out as a result of a 1901 Act passed by the Australian Commonwealth which specified that all such islanders ('Kanakas' or 'blackbirds') be deported from Australia after 1906.

Black Circular. TUC General Council document issued in 1934 advising unions to exclude communists from responsible positions. Opposed by the mining, rail and engineering unions, it was a response to communist attempts to build a UNITED FRONT against fascism, rejected on the grounds that fascism and communism were equally totalitarian.

Black Consciousness. Movement in South Africa formed to re-establish black people's confidence and pride. It is banned by the South African régime and its leader Steve Biko died under suspicious circumstances while in police detention on 12 September 1977 at the age of 30. *See also* APARTHEID.

Black Death. Plague which swept Europe in the years 1348–50, transmitted to man by the fleas infesting black rats; the specific organism involved was *Bacillus pestis*. It began in the ports of ·Italy, being carried there on ships engaged in the Black Sea trade, and at least a quarter of the population of Europe died in the initial epidemic. It reached England in the winter of 1348 and Scotland in 1349. A third of the English population perished in recurrent epidemics in succeeding years, causing severe labour shortages which led to the STATUTE OF LABOURERS.

black economy. An underground economy, generally in the personal service industry, where transactions are made in cash without receipts, thereby avoiding payment of income tax, national insurance and – for individuals officially registered as unemployed – loss of benefits.

Black Friars. *See* DOMINICANS.

Black Friday. *See* TRIPLE ALLIANCE.

Black Hand. Common name for the Serbian secret society, *Ujedinjenje ili Smrt* (Unity or Death), formed in Belgrade in May 1911 with the aim of unifying the Serb minorities living in the Austro-Hungarian and OTTO-MAN empires with the independent state of Serbia. The leader of the society was Col. Dragutin Dimitrievic (known as 'Apis') and most of its members were young army officers. Black Hand members trained the Serbian student Gavrilo Princip (1894–1918) and gave him the weapons with which he assassinated the Austrian Archduke Francis Ferdinand and his wife in Sarajevo on 28 June 1914. Black Hand terrorists and the Serbian government were in conflict throughout World War I. In December 1916 Dimitrievic was arrested for complicity in the assassination and was shot with two others in 1917. The society was dispersed. In 1953, however, the supreme court of Serbia, now part of communist Yugoslavia, retrospectively quashed the sentences on the three Black Handers.

Black Hole of Calcutta. Suraj-ud-Dowlah, Nawab of Bengal, attacked a British garrison in Calcutta which surrendered on 20 June 1756 after a two-day battle. 146 prisoners were placed in a prison cell only 6 metres square; next morning only 23 remained alive.

black market. Illegal sale of goods for a high profit, usually those which are rationed or otherwise in short supply due to government action.

Black Monday. 19 October 1987, when the New York Stock Exchange DOW JONES Industrial Average fell by 22.6% and $500 billion was wiped off the value of shares, a fall which had a knock-on effect on the international stock market.

Black Muslims. Radical BLACK POWER movement in the USA which attained the height of its popularity in the 1960s under the leadership of Malcolm X. The world heavyweight boxing champion Cassius Clay changed his name to Muhammad Ali on joining the movement.

Black Power. Movement which emerged in the USA in the 1960s to express the dissatisfaction of black people with their position in a white-dominated society. Rejecting the belief that blacks should integrate themselves into white society, the movement stressed that blacks were equal to whites in intellect and culture. It was thus more radical than CORE or the NAACP and perhaps manifested dissatisfaction with the achievements of the CIVIL RIGHTS movement.

Black Power was at its most aggressive in the late 1960s and there were fears in the USA that inter-racial strife of civil war dimensions might erupt in the cities. However, the 1970s saw a great improvement in the position of American blacks and that, together with the deaths of Black Power leaders such as George Jackson and Malcolm X, appears to have muted the movement. In Britain RASTAFARIANISM appears to have superseded Black Power as the means of expressing black self-awareness.

Black Sections. Organization in the British Labour Party restricted to black members, advocated in the 1980s on the grounds that it would strengthen the ethnic minority voice in policymaking and overcome the neglect of black interests. Although overwhelmingly rejected at the 1984 and 1985 Labour Party Conferences, Sections were formed by 35 constituency parties.

Black September. Palestinian terrorist organisation, founded following the events in Jordan in 1970. In February 1970 King Hussein and his government sought to curtail the activities of the PLO, who responded with violence, and on 17-25 September general civil war broke out. The government forces eventually imposed their authority, and by July 1971 the last guerrilla camps in Jordan had been broken up and their occupants forced into Syria and Lebanon. Amongst other atrocities, Black September was responsible for a kidnap attempt at the Munich Olympic Games on 5 September 1972, which resulted in the deaths of nine Israeli athletes.

blackshirts. Members of fascist organisations, such as the Schutzstaffel (SS) of Nazi Germany who customarily wore black shirts; Mussolini's Fascisti in Italy; and Oswald Mosley's Union of Fascists in Britain. Their equivalents in Ireland were known as Blueshirts.

Black Thursday. 24 October 1929, the beginning of the Wall Street crash, when the first major fall in confidence in the US stock market occurred. Efforts to restore confidence failed and by Tuesday 29 October shares had become valueless. The Wall Street crash sparked off the DEPRESSION of the 1930s.

Blancs d'Espagne (Fr., whites of Spain). French ultra–royalist party who supported the claim of the Spanish Bourbons to the throne of France in the 19th century.

Blank Cheque. The verbal reply given on 5 July 1914 in response to a letter from Emperor Franz Joseph of Austria by Kaiser Wilhelm II to Count Hoyos, an Austrian Foreign Ministry official, guaranteeing German support if Austria attacked Serbia as punishment for the assassination of Archduke Franz Ferdinand in Sarajevo on 28 June 1914.

Blanketeers. Party of Lancashire textile operatives who, during the famine of 1817, attempted to march to London with the aim of demanding assistance from parliament. The leaders were arrested before they could start and the rank and file dispersed at Macclesfield. Their name arose from the blanket each marcher carried for shelter.

Blanquisme. Theory and practice of conspiratorial organization to foment mass uprising advocated by French professional revolutionary Auguste Blanqui (1805-81), who was active in the 1830 revolution, a Paris insurrection in May 1839, and the 1848 JUNE DAYS. His ideas influenced Lenin's views on BOLSHEVIK organization.

Blimp. Reactionary character who fails to face the facts of modern life. The term is derived from a cartoon character created by David Low (1891-1963). His Col. Blimp, an elderly British military gentleman, had extremely conservative views which he voiced in a somewhat unintelligent fashion.

blitz. *See* BLITZKRIEG.

blitzkrieg (Germ., lightning war). Penetration in depth by armoured columns, usually with preceding aerial bombardment to reduce enemy resistance; a technique perfected by Gen. Guderian in France in 1940. In Britain the term was abbreviated to 'blitz' and used to describe massive air attacks, particularly the night attacks on London and other cities between September 1940 and May 1941.

bloc. A cross-party coalition of American legislators who unite to vote on a single issue of common interest. More generally, a coalition or alliance of parties or states.

blockade. Action to prevent supplies reaching an enemy, either by placing ships outside its ports, troops outside a city or cutting off traffic across a country's borders. Under international law a neutral merchant vessel attempting to breach a blockade may be confiscated by the blockading country. The tactic was first attempted in the Napoleonic wars when Britain's navy blockaded France, Portugal and Spain. A recent naval blockade was imposed on 12 April 1982 by Britain on the Falkland Islands to cut off supplies to Argentine troops occupying them; it was lifted following the retaking of the islands by British forces in May and June 1982. *See also* CONTRABAND OF WAR.

blockbuster. Colloquial term for the demolition bombs used in World War II. Weighing from 2 to 11 tons, they were powerful enough to demolish a city block. On 17 April 1941 the RAF dropped the first blockbuster on Berlin: it contained more than a ton of explosive and air crews could feel the blast at an altitude of 14,000 feet.

Bloody Assizes. The 1685 summer assizes held by Lord Chief Justice George Jeffreys on the Western Circuit following the Duke of Monmouth's rebellion against James II, noted for its cruelty: Jeffreys sentenced over 300 rebels to death for treason, often with only the formality of a trial.

Bloody Sunday. (1) In Britain, Sunday 13 November 1887, when a mass meeting organized by the Social Democratic Federation to demand the release of the nationlist Irish MP William O'Brien was dispersed by the police and the Life Guards. Two people were killed and over a hundred injured, leading to increased mistrust between the labour movement and the authorities.

(2) 30 January 1972, when 13 civilians, demonstrating in favour of a united Ireland, were killed in Londonderry by British paratroops.

(3) In Russia, 22 January 1905, when troops on duty at the Winter Palace in St Petersburg fired on a procession of workers and their families, led by Fr. George Gapon, who hoped to present the Tsar with a petition calling for an eight-hour working-day, a constituent assembly and an amnesty for political prisoners. Over a hundred people were killed and several hundred wounded, helping to spark off the 1905 Russian Revolution.

bluejackets. In the British Navy, a name given to enlisted men below the rank of Chief Petty Officer.

Blueshirts. Irish fascists. *See* BLACK-SHIRTS.

Blut und Ehre (Germ., blood and honour). Nazi slogan, often inscribed on the daggers of members of the Hilter Youth Movement.

Blut und Eisen (Germ., blood and iron). Corruption of the phrase used by Otto von Bismarck on 30 September 1862 when he suggested that Prussia should unite Germany by military power because 'the great questions of the day will be decided, not by speeches and majority votes ... but by iron and blood'. This was a harsh comment on earliest attempts, especially in 1848-49, to achieve unification by liberal, democratic means. Bismarck's course was followed in wars with Denmark (1864), Austria (1866) and France (1870) which established Prussian hegemony over a united country to the exclusion of Austria.

boat people. Those persons, including numerous Chinese, who fled from Vietnam after the victory in 1975 of the communist North Vietnamese over the south in the Vietnam War. They were either political refugees, fearing reprisal from the communists for their part in the war, or were simply unwilling to live in a communist state. Forced to take to the sea in overladen small boats which tried to make land in Malaysia, Hong Kong or elsewhere, thousands of them drowned or fell prey to pirates. Their plight inspired international humanitarian action and severely damaged the prestige of the Vietnamese government.

bocca di leone (Ital., the lion's mouth). An opening in the wall of the ante-chamber in the palace of the DOGE at Venice, into which were dropped anonymous accusations against various citizens.

Boche (deriv. Fr.). Derogatory name for the Germans used by the Allies in World War I.

bocland. *See* BOOKLAND.

Boers (deriv. Dutch *boor*, peasant or small farmer). Name given to Dutch settlers, largely farmers, in South Africa since the 17th century. Discontented with British rule in the Cape after 1820, they emigrated northwards in 1835-37; after much fighting with the natives, they founded the Orange Free State (1836) and the Transvaal Republic (1848). The Transvaal declared itself independent in 1852 and proclaimed its constitution in 1858. In 1877, after war with the Zulus, it was annexed to the British dominions; in 1879 it was declared a Crown Colony. The

Boers, however, claimed independence and in 1880 proclaimed the establishment of the South African Republic under the presidency of Kruger. After some months' fighting against British troops in 1881, a peace settlement was reached with the help of the neutral Orange Free State. By a Convention of 1884 the South African Republic was to be recognized but to be under British suzerainty.

In the 1890s gold strikes attracted a large influx of non-Boers or UIT-LANDERS, mainly of British origin. The British government took up their demands for equality with the Boers; the failure of Kruger's government to fulfil these demands quickly precipitated the South African War (1899–1902). In 1902 the Boers unconditionally surrendered to the British at Vereeniging and the South African Republic was integrated into the British empire. Under the auspices of Alfred Milner, High Commissioner for South Africa (1897–1905) and Governor of Cape Colony (1897–1901) and his KINDERGARTEN, a serious attempt was made to reconstruct South Africa and integrate the Afrikaner population. In September 1910 the Union of South Africa was established (comprising the former Transvaal, Cape, Natal and Orange River colonies), in which British and Boers shared equal status. Its first prime minister, Botha, was a former Boer general.

Bogomils. Members of a heretical movement, founded by Bogomil, a 10th-century Belgian priest, which opposed the Greek Church and believed that all matter is evil. Initially active in Byzantium and the Balkans, they spread to western Europe and were responsible for founding the Cathari sect. The movement died out in the 15th century.

Bohemian Brethren. *See* UNITAS FRATRUM.

Bolshevik (Russ., member of the majority). Radical faction of the Russian Social Democratic Party after it split in 1903. Under Lenin's leadership the Bolsheviks opposed the moderate policies of the MENSHEVIKS. They seized power in the OCTOBER REVOLUTION of 1917; the name was retained by the Communist Party of the Soviet Union until 1952.

Bonapartism. (1) Support for the claims of the Bonaparte family to the French imperial throne, not now a factor of any political significance in France. The descendants of Prince Jerome, brother of Napoleon I (1769–1821) and one-time King of Westphalia, were admitted to the succession by Napoleon III (1808–73) and have the prior claim.

(2) Political system, in France or elsewhere, in the style of that existing under Napoleon I or III, that is, any popular military dictatorship or the popular dictatorship of an individual. Unlike a legitimate absolute monarchy, the system involves pseudo-democracy since there is a theoretical acknowledgement of the sovereignty of the people, as well as constant invocation of the popular will and the use of the PLEBISCITE, which can be manipulated. It is believed by some that there is a natural tendency towards Bonapartism following any revolution. MARXISM holds that Bonapartism occurs where no one class can dominate society and that it serves the function of protecting property owners from the working classes.

bond. Binding agreement, used as a means of compulsion as well as security; for example, to enforce a commercial contract or to ensure good behaviour. Bonds generally have two sections: the bond proper and the condition which, if ignored, causes a sum of money, specified in the bond proper, to be paid as a forfeit.

Bondevenner (Dan.). The Peasants' Friends, Danish political party formed in 1845 to pursue the interests of the rural population.

bondi. In feudal times (7th–12th centuries), freeholders of ODAL land among the Norsemen.

Bonus Marchers. US World War I veterans who travelled to Washington with their families in 1932 in an attempt to persuade the government to pay a promised postwar bonus. By this time the USA was suffering severely from the DEPRESSION; the government refused the payment and called the army in to disperse the marchers.

bookland (*also* bocland, deriv. OE). In Anglo-Saxon England, land from the public lands held privately by royal charter (*boc*). The holder of this privilege was exempt from many of the public services due from holders of FOLKLAND.

bordereau (Fr., memorandum). Term usually used for the forged document which led to the imprisonment of Albert Dreyfus (1859–1935) from 1894 to 1906. *See* DREYFUS AFFAIR.

borough (deriv. OE *burh*). Town holding legal liberties and privileges by charter of incorporation, formerly characterized by its right of sending a member to parliament. In Anglo-Saxon England there were some 50 *burhs* associated with the residence of the king where his special peace, the *burhgrith*, reigned. Some boroughs grew up as fortified towns for purposes of defence. Early boroughs were elevated above the status of other towns because of their markets, which made them nuclei of local trade. One characteristic of boroughs from the 12th century onwards was their position as places of industry and business; another was the existence of borough courts.

The land and dwellings of borough inhabitants were held under a special form of tenure and boroughs were free from Crown interference in financial matters due to the practice of farming revenues. By this process, the burgesses paid the Crown a fixed rent and collected in lieu the crown revenues such as TOLLS. From the 12th century onwards the Crown granted CHARTERS to boroughs which gave burgesses freedom from outside jurisdiction; power to elect MAYORS and other officers, and permission to form GILDS with aldermen, courts and codes of rules. Such gilds assumed great importance and often became governing bodies of the towns, their personnel becoming members of the township courts and their aldermen regulating trade.

At the same time, the communa appeared, with the mayor as its representative officer. In 1215 the citizens of London were granted the right to elect their mayor annually, a privilege gradually extended to other boroughs. By the 15th century a close corporation of mayor, aldermen and council had arisen from the amalgamation of the landowning community of the borough, the gild and the communa. Numbers and organization were defined by charter. Under Richard II (1377–99) corporate officers were made JUSTICES OF THE PEACE and each chartered borough was given the right to return members of parliament.

Between the 15th and the 18th centuries the parliamentary side of the borough came to the fore.

Municipal councils became partly self-elective and only the freemen of the borough, a small proportion of the population, had the franchise. This gave rise to ROTTEN BOROUGHS and pocket boroughs, electoral evils partly remedied by the 1832 Reform Act.

The Municipal Corporations Act of 1835 established a uniform system of government in 183 boroughs. Local government was placed in the hands of the mayor, aldermen and council, elected by the burgesses or resident ratepayers – freemen having no rights as burgesses but holding the parliamentary franchise. The borough franchise was based first on three years', later on one year's, payment of rates. This legislation was consolidated by the 1882 Municipal Corporations Act. Boroughs outside Greater London were abolished by the 1972 Local Government Act.

borough English. In England, a system of land and tenure dating from Anglo-Saxon to medieval times whereby estates passed at death to the youngest son. It was formally abolished by the Administration of Estates Act of 1925.

'boss'. Phenomenon often found in US politics, but not restricted to the USA, in which the archetypal 'boss' is a politician who achieves power locally by corrupt or devious means and then proceeds to strengthen the 'machine' (i.e. his supporters) that has helped him to power. His supporters will be nominated to public offices, including the judiciary and police force, and will receive lucrative public contracts. The 'boss', susceptible to bribery, will condone lawbreaking if it suits his purposes. He may assume high office himself or might prefer to remain in the background.

The most famous 'bosses' include Tweed of TAMMANY Hall, New York; Platt of New York, Huey Long of Louisiana, and Daley of Chicago. Flagrant examples of 'bossism' are now rare. It probably flourished largely because of political apathy and naivity among large urban immigrant communities and rural populations.

BOSS. Bureau of State Security, the South African secret police force, now known as the National Intelligence Service (NIS).

Boston Tea Party. Angered by the British government's insistence on levying a tax on tea in America after an equivalent tax had been repealed in Britain, a group disguised as Red Indians raided three tea ships in Boston harbour on 16 December 1773 and threw cargo valued at £18,000 overboard.

bōt (OE, amends). In Anglo-Saxon England, reparation either in the simple sense of repair (*see* BRIG-BŌT) or, more usually, a money payment as compensation for wrongdoing (*see* WEREGILD).

Boulangists. Supporters of Gen. Georges Boulanger (1837–91) who began a campaign in 1888 to revise the constitution of the Third French Republic with the aim of establishing a more authoritarian régime. He obtained a considerable following in the country by the denunciation of parliamentary abuses and was elected for three departments. But he failed to take the decisive step of overthrowing the government and his influence waned; he was forced to flee France in April 1889 and was condemned *in absentia* for treason. After the collapse of his movement, he committed suicide in Brussels in 1891.

Bourbons. (1) Members of the Bourbon dynasties which formerly reigned in Spain, France and Naples. The older French line was overthrown by the revolution of 1789 (Louis XVI was beheaded in 1793), restored in 1815 and ended again in 1830 when Louis Philippe ousted Charles X. Louis was of the younger line of Bourbon-Orleans. He in turn was deposed in 1848 and the royal dynasty was banned from France in 1871 when the Third Republic was established. French royalists were split between LEGITIMISTS (adhering to the older line) and ORLEANISTS, until the older line became extinct in the 1890s. Now most royalists accept the claim of the younger line which is headed by the Comte de Paris.

The Spanish Bourbons are descended from the older French line. In 1931 King Alfonso XIII (d. 1941) was deposed, but in 1947 Spain was declared to be a monarchy and in 1975 Prince Juan Carlos of Bourbon-Parma became king.

The Neapolitan Bourbons were a branch of the Spanish family who ruled Naples and Sicily from 1738 to 1860.

(2) Extreme reactionaries. The term arose in France after 1815 when many members of the Bourbon family and their supporters acted as if the 1789 revolution had not occurred.

bourgeoisie (Fr., citizen class). Term used by Marxists to indicate those persons other than the agricultural capitalist who do not, like the proletariat, live by the sale of their labour. They include, on the one hand, industrialists, financiers and members of the liberal professions; on the other, small artisans and shopkeepers who are described as the 'petty' bourgeoisie, although their standard of living may not be appreciably higher, and may even be lower, than that of the proletariat. According to Marxist theory, the bourgeoisie arose with modern industrialization, breaking feudal patterns of society and replacing the feudal lords as the ruling class; the petty bourgeoisie will gradually become proletarianized and the proletariat will then succeed its remaining members as masters of society.

Bourse (Fr., stock-exchange). Term used particularly to mean the Parisian stock-exchange.

Boy Pope. Benedict IX, a layman whose family purchased the office of Pope in 1032; reputedly aged 12, it is more likely that he was in his late twenties. Benedict held the office until 1044, in 1045, and again in 1047–8 when he was finally ousted for his vices.

bovate (deriv. Lat. *bovata*; also ox-gang). In feudal England, the measure of land that could be ploughed by one ox in a year, between 10 and 18 acres; eight times this measure was known as a carucate or hide.

Boxers. Popular term for members of the Society of Harmonious Fists, a secret organization opposed to European commercial interests in China at the turn of the 20th century, which had the tacit approval of the Chinese authorities and the dowager empress. Its members attacked Christians and workers on European controlled railways, prompting the European states to take steps to protect their nationals. British troops were fired upon at Taku; in an uprising in Peking on 19 June 1900, the European legations were besieged and the German minister assaulted. A six-nation expeditionary force relieved the legations in August

1900. Boxer outbreaks also occurred in Shensi province and in Manchuria, which the Russians then occupied in order to secure their railway interests. In 1901 the Peking Protocol imposed an annual monetary indemnity to be paid by China to the European powers in recompense for the uprising, furthering Chinese nationalism and helping to promote the republican movement.

Boyars (Russ.). Members of the nobility which emerged in 11th-century Russia when native Slavs began to join the retinues of the great princes. In the 15th and 16th centuries, the Boyars declined as a class and a new nobility of service was created. By the 18th century the Boyars and the new nobility were indistinguishable, since the Boyars had also accepted obligations of service.

boycott. Refusal by a body of people to have any dealings with a person or persons. The term is derived from Capt. C.C. Boycott (1832–97) who, having incurred hostility for a series of evictions, was made the victim of a conspiracy by the Irish Land League, preventing him from making any purchases or holding any social intercourse in his district.

braceros (Span.). Farm workers from Mexico who were legally admitted to the USA between 1942 and 1964 to take up work on temporary contracts; the scheme was designed to stop 'WET-BACKS' by regulating immigration and conditions of employment. In 1964, the last year of the programme, 180,000 entered. Admittance was stopped because it was felt that the scheme made it more difficult for native Americans to find jobs.

Braganza. The ruling house of Portugal from the reign of John IV, Duke of Braganza (1640–56), to the abdication in 1910 of Manuel II, when Portugal became a republic.

Brahmans, Brahmins (Sansk., priests). Highest or priestly class among Hindus, one of the four classes (*varma*) into which India is historically divided. It is not a true caste but is made up of numerous endogamous groups. Brahmans still have a disproportionate degree of influence in Indian society.

Brains Trust. Nickname given to a group of economists and business men in the USA who acted as advisers to Pres. Roosevelt (1882–1945) in formulating the NEW DEAL policy. The term has since been widely used to denote bodies of experts believed to have influence on government policy. In the UK the term 'brains trust' was extended to include groups of experts assembled to answer questions put to them by the public, especially the BBC's wartime panel of experts who broadcast on the wireless.

brainwashing. Treatment of a person in such a way as to alter his or her view of society, accomplished by physical or mental torture, propaganda and argument and the selective granting of 'rewards'. Originally the expression was used to denote communist treatment of prisoners in the Korean War (1950–53), designed to change their political views and lead them to question the prevailing morality of the West. The term is now more generally used to describe any change of attitude by a prisoner to one more sympathetic to that of his captors, or to any blanket acceptance and unquestioning allegiance to a particular code. In recent years it has been widely used to describe what are alleged to be the methods of religious cults in indoctrination of new converts, such as deprivation of sleep and privacy and constant criticism to break the will. It certainly appears to have occurred among the 911 followers of the People's Temple cult who committed mass suicide in Guyana on 18–19 November 1978. Methods of countering brainwashing involve similar techniques known as 'de-programming'.

Brehon (*also* Brethem; deriv. Gael. *breathamb*, judgement). A judge in pre-Christian Ireland. The office appears to have been hereditary and may have been connected with the Celtic priesthood. A change of religion in the mid-5th century led to a codifying of the traditional Brehon law in the *Benchus Mor* (411-438) when those aspects of ancient Irish law not inconsistent with Christianity were included alongside new laws. The *Benchus Mor* is said to have had nine authors: three kings, three Christian bishops and, most influential, three Brehons.

Bretton Woods. Town in New Hampshire, USA, where representatives of 28 nations attended a financial conference called by Pres. Roosevelt in July 1944 to organize a system of international monetary co-operation in order to prevent financial crashes such as those in the inter-war period which triggered the 1930s DEPRESSION. It was agreed that participants would establish a World Bank to provide credit for countries that required finance for major projects. An International Monetary Fund (IMF) was also set up for the purpose of operating cash reserves available to members facing BALANCE OF PAYMENTS deficits.

Bretwalda (OE, lord of the Britons). Term used in the earlier part of *The*

Anglo-Saxon Chronicle to describe certain kings as overlords of all England south of the Humber, and not just one of the kingdoms of the HEPTARCHY. Later the character of the title changed from one implying general military leadership to one denoting a strict control over subject rulers.

Brezhnev doctrine. The ideological basis of the WARSAW PACT invasion of Czechoslovakia in August 1968. Leonid Brezhnev, General Secretary of the Soviet Communist Party, pronounced a doctrine of 'limited sovereignty', denying East European states the right to divert widely from the Soviet model, and asserting the legitimacy of intervention. Soviet Party Secretary Mikhail Gorbachev's apparent rejection of this view in March 1988 has yet to be tested in practice. *See* PRAGUE SPRING.

brig-bōt (OE, bridge + *bot*). In Anglo-Saxon England, a tax levied on freemen for the repair of bridges. *See* BŌT.

brinkmanship. Term describing the policy of forcing a rival power to reach an accommodation by deliberately creating the risk of a nuclear war. The word comes from the statements of John Foster Dulles, US Secretary of State 1953–59, who told *Life* magazine on 11 January 1956 that to attain diplomatic goals statesmen needed 'the ability to get to the verge of war without getting into war' and that 'if you are scared to go to the brink you are lost'.

Brissotins. Followers of Brissot, one of the leaders of the GIRONDINS during the French Revolution. The name fell into disuse when the particular faction attached to Brissot merged with the larger body of Girondins.

British Commonwealth of Nations. Some 47 monarchies, dominions and republics in loose association with Britain and with each other. In the late 19th century the term British Commonwealth was occasionally used to denote the British Empire. During World War I it denoted the relationship existing between Britain and her self-governing dominions: the 1918 Imperial Conference used it in this way, as did the 1919 Paris Peace Conference, at which the dominions and India were separately represented.

In 1926 A.J. Balfour (1848–1938), speaking at the Imperial Conference, defined the dominions as 'autonomous communities within the British Empire, equal in status, in no way subordinate one to another in any aspect of their domestic or foreign affairs, though united by a common allegiance to the Crown, and freely associated as members of the British Commonwealth of Nations'. This definition was given statutory form in the 1931 Statute of Westminster.

Until 1947 the term commonly used was the British Commonwealth and Empire; when India and Pakistan gained independence, 'Empire' was dropped. The Dominions Office, established in 1925 to handle relations between Britain and the Commonwealth, was replaced in the same year by the Commonwealth Relations Office. In 1966 this merged with the Colonial Office to form the Commonwealth Office, which was in turn combined with the Foreign Office in 1968 to form the Foreign and Commonwealth Office. Since 1965, Commonwealth leaders have had the services of a permanent Commonwealth Secretariat in London, set up to promote economic, cultural and political cooperation.

All the members of the Commonwealth are independent and their leaders meet in conference at least every two years. Allegiance to the Crown is no longer required but it was agreed in 1949 when India became a republic that republics choosing to remain within the Commonwealth would acknowledge the British monarch as the symbol of their free association. Most ex-colonies chose to join; Burma was an exception. In 1949 Ireland left, followed by South Africa in 1961, Pakistan in 1972 and Fiji in 1987.

Brit-Shalom. 'Covenant of Peace'. An Israeli group formed by Dr Judah Magnes which seeks Arab-Jewish understanding and the creation of a bi-national state in Palestine.

Broederbond (S. Afr. brotherhood). Secret South African society founded shortly after the Boer War. Its members are of Afrikaner, as opposed to English, origin and its activities appear to be aimed at maintaining the predominance of Afrikaners in South African political, economic and cultural affairs.

brokered convention. An American political convention at which party leaders rather than delegates make the main decisions on candidates and issues.

Brownists. Followers of Robert Browne (1550–1633), an early CONGREGATIONALIST who rejected the authority of the EPISCOPACY. In 1580 he formed an independent congregation in Norwich but was forced to flee to Middelburg in Holland in the following year. He moved to Scotland, where for a time he was imprisoned by the church authorities; he returned to England in 1584.

Late in life he changed his views and reverted to Anglicanism. He was ordained in 1591 and died in gaol, having been charged with assault.

His reacceptance of the Episcopacy led to his being disowned by Congregationalists, who look rather to his successors Henry Barrow (*see* BARROWISTS) and John Greenwood as their models.

Brownshirts. *See* SA.

buccaneers (deriv. Fr. *boucanier*, to smoke meat). English, French and Dutch adventurers who preyed on Spanish colonies and shipping in the Caribbean and off the Pacific coast of America in the 17th century. Their name comes from the way they grilled meat on board ship, and their exploits were published in *Bucaniers of America*, an English translation of *De Americaensche Zee-rovers* by the Dutchman Alexander Esquemelin, published in 1684. They had many alternative names: the English preferred to style themselves privateers; the French *filibustiers* (*see* FILIBUSTERS) from the Dutch *vrijbuiter* (freebooter), and the Dutch *zeerovers*. Their Spanish victims called them *corsarios*.

The last great 'buccaneer' expedition came in 1685 when 3,000 men under John Eaton, Charles Swan and Edward Davis attacked the Spanish colony of Panama. In 1689 they gave up their freelance piracy and became legitimate privateers in the service of the nations fighting the War of the Grand Alliance.

Buchmanism. Beliefs of US evangelist Frank N.D. Buchman (1878–1961), which fall into three stages. He had a Lutheran background and was first associated with the First Century Church Fellowship, a Protestant fundamentalist movement. In 1920 he visited England and gave a series of lectures to Oxford undergraduates, thereby founding the Oxford Group. Buchman talked of the need for 'world changing through life changing' and his revivalist group adhered to his conviction that civilization was disintegrating and that the process could only be reversed by effecting a change in the hearts and minds of men. The group practised group confession of sin and set aside times when they would receive messages from God on current problems and behaviour.

The Oxford Group was superseded by the Moral Re-Armament campaign whose members stress the pursuit of four moral absolutes, honesty, purity, love and unselfishness, by which the world might be changed. Indeed, MRA claims to have helped solve racial, industrial and political disputes. The phrase 'moral rearmament', coined by the English scientist W.M. Bragg, received Buchman's approval. Interest in MRA reached a peak in the 1950s but the movement, lacking doctrine or intellectual content, suffered badly after the death of Buchman in whose personality and dynamism much of its appeal lay. The early death of his protegé and successor-designate, journalist Peter Howard, was a further blow and MRA is now of little importance.

Buddhism. Founded in North India in the 6th century BC by the real or legendary Hindu prince Siddharta Gautama, who was known as the Buddha ('Enlightened One'). He left no teachings but his followers formulated beliefs in which there was no universal god and liberation would come through ethics and discipline. The belief spread to Sri Lanka, Nepal, Tibet, Mongolia, Indo-China, Burma, Siam, China and Japan.

buffer state. Small state created or maintained between two larger ones, either to prevent their taking control of strategically important territory or to eliminate the possibility of an armed clash between them by removing their common border.

bull (deriv. Lat. *bulla*, seal). Seal affixed to a papal edict; by extension, the edict itself. Papal bulls have statutory authority within the Roman Catholic Church.

bullet vote. A ballot in which American electors confine their interest to a single issue or candidate.

Bull Moose Movement. Short-lived progressive party founded in 1912 by Theodore Roosevelt (1858–1919) after he failed to win the Republican nomination for the presidency against the incumbent president, Taft (1857–1930). He stood as an independent progressive or 'Bull Moose' candidate, won more votes than Taft, but split the Republican vote and allowed the Democrat Wilson (1856–1924) to win the presidency. His party's programme included extensive political and social reforms that were later introduced by the major parties.

Bummery. *See* IWW.

Bundesrat (Germ.). Federal council of West Germany, consisting of members of the government of the various states or Länder and elected by the ten Länder (Baden-Württemberg, Bavaria, Bremen, Hamburg, Hessen, Saxony, North Rhine-Westphalia, Rhineland-Palatinate, Saarland and Schleswig-Holstein). It has a limited veto of laws passed by the BUNDESTAG.

Bundestag (Germ.). Federal parliament or DIET of West Germany, established by the 'basic law' (the constitution) on 23 May 1949. Elected by universal suffrage for a four-year term of office, it passes federal laws and submits them to the BUNDESRAT.

Bundeswehr (Germ.). Federal armed forces, the army of West Germany. In the immediate post-war period the question of whether Germany should be allowed an army was highly controversial but the threat of the USSR and the obvious acceptance of democracy by Germany finally allayed fears of German militarism.

bunker. Bomb-proof shelter. The best-known is probably Adolf Hitler's Berlin bunker in which he spent the last days of World War II and where he committed suicide on 30 April 1945.

bureaucracy (deriv. Fr., office + Gk., rule). Originally a semi-ironic term analogous to democracy or aristocracy, originating in 18th-century France for officials given titles of nobility. Under Napoleon (1804–15) the country was run by units of centralized administration known as *bureaux*. The term now describes the rule of a body of high officials or the caste of officials itself, usually with connotations of lack of initiative and too strict an adherence to rigid rules.

burgage. Very old form of land tenure found in England and Scotland whereby a person held property within the lands of a borough, paying rent to the king or to some other lord. Terms of tenureship varied widely between boroughs. Roughly speaking it was a form of SOCAGE though the services provided were economic or agricultural in form. In Scotland the landlord was invariably the king and the service provided was military, being garrison duty in the burgh. Until 1874 burgage tenure in Scotland necessitated a special form of transference of title.

Burgfrieden. A German political truce in which the Social Democrats and Liberals united behind Kaiser

Wilhelm II at the outbreak of World War I.

burgrave (Germ. *Burg*, fortified town – *Graf*, count). Commander of a fortified town in medieval Germany. The title later became hereditary and carried with it the possession of land.

burh (OE). Fortified town or dwelling-place in Anglo-Saxon England between the 6th and 11th centuries. The most notable burhs were those constructed or strengthened by Alfred the Great (849–99) to resist Danish invasion.

Burschenshaften (Germ. deriv. *Bursche*, youth). German student organizations, the first of which was founded at the University of Jena in 1815. They spread quickly across Germany and expressed German nationalism in post-Napoleonic Europe. In their early years they were liberal and egalitarian in character and desired the political unification of Germany. They staged joint demonstrations at the Wartburg Festival of October 1817 which alarmed the governments of the German states, and in March 1819 Karl Saud, one of their members, assassinated August von Kotzebue, an aide of the Russian TSAR. The Carlsbad Decrees were promulgated the same year to provide for the suppression of the Burschenshaften. They subsequently met in secret until 1848, when they were active in the revolution in Germany. From 1871 they took an increasingly aggressive militaristic and nationalist stance, which included a belief in ANTI-SEMITISM. The Burschenshaften still exist but since 1945 have played only a minor political role.

bushido (Jap.). Strict traditional code of honour of the SAMURAI, dating from the 12th century and still a strong influence in Japanese society.

A military code similar in concept to the KNIGHTHOOD and chivalry of medieval Europe, it involves the formation of personal honour by pursuit of the principles of courage, honesty, justice and simplicity.

bussing. Policy introduced by the government in the USA to promote racial integration and increase social harmony. It became clear in the 1960s that whites had moved out of certain inner-city areas to the suburbs while blacks, who could not afford to move, remained in these poorer areas. As a result some schools were entirely white and others entirely black, leading to racial and social divisions. To combat this, children from both areas were 'bussed', that is, taken by bus, to schools in neighbourhoods other than their own where they would be taught alongside children from other racial backgrounds. The policy attracted great hostility and was condemned by many whites as an infringement of their right to choose schools for their children.

Butskellism. Term derived from Richard Butler, Conservative chancellor 1951–55, denoting the continuity of economic policy in the 1950s, despite a change of government from Labour in 1951. Both parties agreed on the need for limited state ownership and interference in industry and on the desirability of economic planning to maintain full employment. The term is a combination of the names of Butler and Gaitskell.

by-election. Election of a member to a representative body to fill a vacancy caused by the death or resignation of a former member during a normal term of office.

Byzantine Empire. The eastern half of the Roman Empire which, when it fell to the Turks in 1453, had survived the Western empire by a thousand years.

C

Caaba. The sacred sanctuary at Mecca, holy place of ISLAM, which every Muslim must visit once in a lifetime.

cabal. The name given to the ministry which took power in England in 1667 (when Charles II dismissed his chancellor, Clarendon), taken from the initials of its members: Clifford, Arlington, Buckingham, Ashley and Lauderdale. The term is also used generally to mean any close-knit group of persons, particularly those engaged in intrigue.

Cabala (*also* Cabbala; Heb., tradition). Originally a collection of Jewish doctrines about the nature of the universe, supposedly handed down by Moses to the Rabbis, which evolved into a mystical interpretation of the Old Testament dating from the 1st century AD. Students of the history of religious belief have found its origins to be extremely obscure, and some aspects of it to have been taken from ancient Egyptian sources. Cabalistic studies have flourished from the 13th century. Skilled Cabalists maintain that the system contains a key to biblical interpretation, based on the numerical values of the words and letters of the scriptures which reveal hidden depths of meaning behind the allegorical Old Testament stories.

caballerías (Span.). Small land grant (between 500 and 1,000 acres), made by the Spanish Crown to *caballeros* (gentlemen) during the reconquest of Spain from the Moors (11th–16th centuries) and during the conquest of South America (16th–17th centuries). The term is still used in some parts of Latin America as a unit of land measure.

Cabanagem (Span., cottagers). Rebels who overran the Amazon Valley and other areas of Brazil between 1833 and 1836 following the abdication of Pedro I.

cabildo abierto (Span., an open council). In South America from the 16th to the 19th centuries, meeting of all the householders in a Spanish colonial town called at a time of emergency by the governor of the council (*cabildo*).

cabinet noir (Fr., black cabinet). Government department established by Louis XIV (1678–1715) for the surveillance of the correspondence of suspected persons. It later became part of the French postal system, and was abolished in 1886.

Cabochiens. Guild of Parisian butchers, led by Caboche, who committed terrible atrocities against the ARMA-

GNACS in the early years of the 15th century. They were dissolved in 1416.

cacique (Amer. Ind., chief). In Latin America and Spain, an individual exerting great influence in local politics. In Spain, caciques were usually moneylenders in the north, and landowners in the south; they were mainstays of the corrupt electoral system known as CACIQUISMO.

caciquismo (Span./Amer. Ind.). Corrupt electoral system current in Spain from the 1830s to 1936, at its most prevalent from 1874 to 1923. The Conservative leader del Castillo and the Liberal Sagusta used it to secure office in rotation by 'fixing' election results. The Ministry of the Interior would send each provincial governor the names of candidates who were to win and sometimes would even determine their majorities. In municipal districts, officials who were dependent on the favour of the governor would falsify returns or provide him with blank returns to fill in as he liked. In country districts, the CACIQUES, who usually controlled the police and judiciary, secured the desired votes by promises of jobs or by threats of violence or of foreclosure on loans and mortgages. Stability of government was thereby ensured behind a semblance of two-party democracy. The system survived several attempts at reform and lasted until the outbreak of the civil war.

Cacos (Span., pickpockets). (1) Party in Guatemala which favoured complete separation from Spain and the establishment of an independent republic in 1820.
(2) Name applied to poverty stricken farmers in Haiti who hired themselves out for service in private armies and who bitterly opposed the American occupation forces in 1918–19.

Cadets. *See* KADETS.

cadres. Members of the Communist Party charged with the political education and organization of the proletariat.

Caesarism. Governmental system similar to that established by Julius Caesar (101–44 BC) in ancient Rome, that is, a semi-popular system of dictatorship, the dictator being enabled to seize power by the support of the army, a party or a section of the people. Once in power, the dictator preserves the outward democratic forms with impotent parliaments, rigged elections and manipulation of the PLEBISCITE. The property-owning class has its privileges and power curtailed, but is still protected from the poor. Egalitarian sentiments are expressed and the dictator claims to derive power from the people. BONAPARTISM is a variant of the model. Oswald Spengler (1880–1936), the German political philospher, held that Caesarism would replace democracy in the 20th century since it was a trend to emerge in all civilizations at a certain point in their development.

cahiers de doléances (Fr.). Lists of grievances drawn up in towns, villages and guilds for presentation at the meeting of the French ESTATES GENERAL in 1789. Demands were made for equality in legal matters, religious toleration, improvement in the condition of the parish clergy, an end to the sale of public offices and the abolition of seignorial judicial powers, such as the GABELLE and the CORVÉE.

caique (Fr.). A Levantine sailing vessel of the 16th century.

Cajuns. French-speaking inhabitants of the American state of Louisiana. The word is a corruption of 'Acadians', the Cajun ancestors who lived in Acadia (French Canada) until expelled by the British in 1755 for refusing to swear an oath of allegiance.

Caliph (deriv. Arab. successor). Title of Moslem rulers, successors of Mohammed. After Mohammed's death in 632, the first four acted as IMAMS of the Moslem world, but in 680 the Caliphate became hereditary when Mu'awiya passed it to his son Yazid I, and founded the Umayyad line which lasted until 750. The ABBASIDS then held it until 1258. At various times, particularly after the fall of the Abbasids, the title was assumed by minor potentates including those of the Fatimid Caliphate in North Africa (909–1171) and in Spain (923–1031), and by the MAMELUK Sultan of Egypt and Syria, Baybars (1260–77), who established a pseudo-Caliphate in Egypt which lasted until 1517. The title, revived for political reasons by the OTTOMAN emperors and used from the 18th to 20th centuries, was abolished in March 1924.

Calixtines (deriv. Lat., chalice). The more moderate of the two sections into which the HUSSITE sect was divided after the death of Jerome of Prague in 1416. Their name derived from their claim that lay communicants should be allowed to take the wine as well as the bread. The more fanatical Hussite group was that led by John Zisca, known as the TABORITES.

Calvinism. Branch of PROTESTANTISM founded on the teaching of the French reformer Jean Chauvin (1509–64), known as Calvin from the Latin form of his name. Calvin gave the first systematic justification of Protestantism in *Institutions of the Christian Religion* (1536) and thus became the intellectual leader of the Reformation. Calvinism is marked by its dogma of predestination, the belief that God has unalterably destined some souls to salvation and others to eternal damnation. Its harsh, logical beliefs inspired English PURITANS, French HUGUENOTS and some of the Dutch in their fight against the domination of Catholic Spain. The sect has been established in the Reformed or Presbyterian churches of France, Holland and Scotland; Calvinist rule was also ruthlessly enforced under Calvin himself in Geneva by the CONSISTORIUM. The Calvinist beliefs that labour is a command of God and material success a mark of his favour – contradicting the medieval ideas of the virtue of poverty and the evil of usury – may have contributed to the rise of CAPITALISM.

Camarilla (Span., a little room). Admirers and favourites of Ferdinand VII of Spain who effectively ruled the country after his restoration in 1814. They used their position to distribute public offices and justice to the highest bidders.

Cameronians. Scottish CONVENANTERS of extreme views who followed Richard Cameron in 1679. In 1689 they were formed into a regiment and were active in the Highlands against the JACOBITES. The regiment became the 26th Regiment of the Line and, later, the Cameronians (Scottish Rifles) Regiment.

Camissards. *See* ENFANTS DE DIEU.

Camorra (Ital.). Neapolitan secret society which for many years terrorized the kingdom despite Francis II's attempts to suppress it. Members of the Camorra who escaped deportation joined the GARIBALDINI and were largely instrumental in expelling the BOURBONS in 1861.

Camp David. Presidential retreat in Maryland, USA. Following the SADAT INITIATIVE it was the location of talks between Pres. Sadat of Egypt and Prime Minister Begin of Israel on 5–17 September 1978, chaired by Pres. Carter of the USA. It was agreed that a peace treaty between the two states would be signed within three months, to be followed by establishment of normal diplomatic relations within three years. Israel would withdraw from Sinai while UN troops were to guarantee Israel's security and access to the Red Sea. Israel agreed to stop settlement in the Gaza Strip and the West Bank and to enter negotiations with Jordan over the future of these areas: within five years Israeli military government was to be replaced by a government elected by the Palestinian inhabitants. But Israel was not required to give up the areas completely and no mention was made of the Golan Heights or East Jerusalem. The Syrians and the PLO, therefore, rejected the terms. Negotiations became bogged down over the ultimate future of the West Bank but on Pres. Carter's intervention a peace treaty was finally signed in Washington on 26 March 1979.

canaille (Fr., pack of dogs). Term of abuse for a crowd or mob of demonstrators.

Canal Zone. Area surrounding the 40-mile long Panama Canal in Central America. Work on the canal began in 1899 and the May-Pauncefote treaty gave sole control of it to the USA. In 1903 the Columbian Congress declined ratification of a treaty giving the USA control of the surrounding area as well. A revo-

lution was induced in Panama on 3 November 1903 and ten days later the USA recognized its independence from Colombia. Five days after this the new republic granted the USA sovereign rights in perpetuity over a zone five miles wide on each side of the canal. The USA paid $10 million for the rights, plus an annual payment of $250,000 which has been increased periodically since 1936. The canal was finally opened in 1914.

In 1936 a new treaty provided for the USA to consult the Panamanian government before using territory outside the zone for military purposes. During World War II the USA built 38 military bases outside the zone, but after Panama refused to extend leases on the sites in 1947 they withdrew into the zone. The zone is administered by a US governor appointed by the president and is under the control of the US army. In the 1960s Panama began agitating for retrocession of the zone, and broke off relations with the USA from May 1963 to April 1964. On 7 September 1977 Pres. Carter and the Panamanian leader Gen. Torrijos signed a treaty in Washington under which the zone is to be returned to Panama on 1 January 2000. Panama was not happy with the delay involved, while critics of Carter's foreign policy condemned it for weakening the US position in Central America.

canonization. Procedure for putting one of the faithful departed on the list of saints of the Roman Catholic Church. The rules which govern it were simplified by papal decree in 1969. Beatification, by which a person is called blessed, is usually, but not necessarily, followed eventually by canonization.

cantons (Fr. deriv. Lat., border). The twenty-two territorial units into which the Federal Republic of Switzerland is divided; sixteen of them were federated as early as 1513. Each has its own parliament and government and enjoys a high degree of regional autonomy. The Federal Assembly consists of two Houses – the Nationalrat, elected by direct vote; and the Ständerat, with 44 members, two from each canton. The Assembly elects the Bundesrat, or government, of seven members, each of whom must be from a different canton. German is the dominant language in 19 cantons, but Italian, French and Romansch (spoken in the canton of Graubünden) are also recognized as official languages.

cantred (*also* Cantref; Welsh, hundred towns). Administrative, judicial and fiscal unit in early Wales from about the 7th century. The cantred probably arose out of the older *gwlad* (country) or *tud* (tribe) which were bodies of tribesmen living within defined territorial areas. The larger *gwlads* such as Anglesey or Brycheiniog came to be divided into cantreds for the purposes of royal administration; while smaller *gwlads* such as Dyffrin and Clwyd would become cantreds themselves. The cantreds in turn were divided into manors. In the 12th century, the agricultural manor was replaced as the basic administrative unit by the *tref* (township) and the cantred by the COMMOTE. These subdivisions, detrimental to the establishment of a centralized political authority, were an inevitable consequence of the Welsh custom of partitioning inheritance between all sons.

CAP. Common Agricultural Policy of the EEC which dictates the farming and other primary production policies of the Community and allocates subsidies to the various sectors of European agriculture.

Capetian. Member or supporter of the royal house of France, founded by Hugh Capet in 987, and of its related branches. The main line of the dynasty came to an end in 1328 with the death of Charles IV when the throne passed to the related house of Valois; in 1589, Henry IV founded the BOURBON line which ruled France, except from 1792 to 1814, until 1848.

capitalism. Economic system in which control of the greater part of the means of production is in the hands of private individuals who are motivated to invest capital by a return of distributed profits. Supporters of the system believe that it provides the only rational basis for distribution of economic resources and that because of its flexibility it is the best method of satisfying economic needs. In the 19th century capitalism was equated with individualistic free competition, but in the 20th century there has been a tendency towards monopolization.

The capitalist system, though by no means synonymous with democracy, does imply a limitation of the functions of the state and the restriction of state interference in the economic field. MARXISM sees it as doomed to collapse.

A hybrid called 'state capitalism' is also said to exist, where the state takes a hand in organising production in order to make profits for distribution rather than to plan the economy on non-profit making lines.

capitania (Port.). Territorial division used in the Portuguese colonies, particularly in Brazil, dating from 1834 during the reign of King João III. The system was not a success and gradually the capitanias were reclaimed by the Crown. The Spanish term is also capitanía.

capitation (deriv. Lat., poll-tax from *capit*, head). Tax levied or grant given on the basis of population, that is, by a count of heads.

Capitol. Government building of the USA, situated in Washington, D.C.

capitulary. Term applied to the edicts of the early French kings; today used generally to denote a code of laws.

capitulation. Treaty under which the nationals of one state residing in the territory of another receive special privileges and immunities, most commonly the right to remain under the jurisdiction of their own government by means of local consuls. Such treaties were usually imposed by European states on Asian and African nations who were considered to be incapable of giving Europeans proper legal protection. They ceased in 1899 in Japan, 1923 in Turkey, 1928 in Persia, 1937 in Egypt and 1943 in China. With minor exceptions no capitulations now exist.

captain-general. (1) Title of the governor of colonial Brazil in the 16th and 17th centuries.
(2) An official of Spanish America charged with defence and, after the mid-16th century, with the government of an autonomous region.

Capuchin. Member of a mendicant order of FRANCISCANS founded in the 16th century with the aim of restoring the primitive and stricter observance of the rule of St. Francis; their name is derived from their capuces or pointed cowls.

Carbonari (Ital., charcoal burners). Italian secret society favouring national unity which attempted to overthrow the governments estab-

lished by the settlement of 1815. Instigators of unsuccessful revolts in Naples (1820) and Piedmont (1821) and of a wider series of risings in 1831, they were eventually absorbed into Mazzini's 'Young Italy' movement.

Carlists. Supporters of the claim of Don Carlos (1788–1855) and of his descendants to the throne of Spain, after the death of his brother, Ferdinand VII in 1833. Ferdinand had repealed the Salic Law, allowing his daughter Isabella to succeed him, with her mother Christina acting as Regent. Civil war lasted from 1834 to 1837, and disorder persisted throughout Isabella's reign. Two years after her death in 1868, open warfare again broke out and Carlist unrest continued into the late 19th century. *See also* CHRISTINOS.

Carmelites. Members of a body of mendicant friars founded at Mount Carmel in the Holy Land in the 12th century. Their severe original rule, requiring absolute poverty, abstinence from meat and an eremitical life was mitigated by Pope Innocent IV (1243–54). They are also known as White Friars on account of their white mantles. An order of Carmelite nuns was instituted in the 15th century.

Carolingians (*also* Carlovingians). Dynasty of Frankish kings, founded in the 8th century, which ruled, with interruptions, until 987 when it was replaced by the CAPETIANS.

carpet-baggers. Pejorative term for Northern Americans who migrated to the Southern States after the Civil War (1861–65) in the hope of advancement, such as being returned to Congress on the negro vote. The name implied that they had no interest in the South beyond their personal hand-baggage.

Carthusians. (1) Order of monks founded by St. Bruno in 1084 at Grande Chartreuse near Grenoble in France. The chief characteristics of the order are a separate dwelling-house for each monk and a general assembly in the church twice each day and once at night. The order invented and still holds the secret of the liqueur Chartreuse, from which it derives a large revenue. An order of Carthusian nuns was instituted in the 12th century.

(2) In England, also the name for members of the Charterhouse School which originally occupied the site in London of a Carthusian monastery built in 1731.

cartulary (deriv. Lat., paper). Register of title deeds to the lands, liberties and privileges of a landowner in medieval England. Cartularies first appeared shortly before the Norman Conquest for religious foundations, but later lay men and institutions adopted the practice of making them. They were usually in book form and often elaborately decorated.

carucage. In medieval England, a non-feudal tax on the land unit of CARUCATE, first levied in 1194 to ransom Richard I using assessments based on the Domesday Book. A further levy in 1198 met much opposition and led to new assessments. The last carucage was levied in 1224 to pay for the suppression of Fawkes de Bréauté's rebellion.

carucate (deriv. Lat., coach or plough; *also* hide). *See* BOVATE.

Casa de contratación (Span., house of trade). Principal body responsible for the organization and regulation of Spanish colonial commerce, founded by Ferdinand and Isabella in Seville in 1503. All trade from the colonies was required to pass through the customs house at Seville, the Casa dispensing licences for all shipping to and from the colonies and for migration there. It collected duties on trade; received the precious metals that accrued to the Spanish crown and also acted as a trade law court. It was moved to Cadiz in 1718 and abolished in 1790.

castlery (AFr., territory belonging to a castle). In feudal England, a district organized for the defence of a particular castle.

casus belli (Lat., occasion of war). Action taken by one state in order to justify declaring war on another.

casus foederis (Lat., occasion of treaty). Event that makes a treaty or alliance operative, thus enabling one party to it to call on the other parties for aid.

Cathars. Heretical Christian movement whose name derived from the Greek word meaning 'pure' and which spread from the Byzantine Empire to Italy and southern France in the 12th century. Persecuted for denying Christ's humanity and rejecting divine incarnation, the Cathars settlements in France were destroyed in the ALBIGENSIAN crusades of 1209–29.

Cathay (deriv. Chin. *Ch'i-tan*). Medieval European name for North China, derived from the name of a semi-nomadic Mongol tribe who conquered Manchuria and North China in the 10th century. Under Ghengis Khan (d.1227), the Mongols began referring to North China as Kitai and South China as Mangi; the former is still current in Russia as a word for China as a whole. The name Cathay was brought to Europe by two Franciscan friars who visited the Mongol capital of Karakorum in 1246 and 1254, but it was Marco Polo (1254–1324) and his published accounts of visits to the court of Kublai Khan (d.1294) which brought the name and the country to prominence in Europe.

Cathays Park. The buildings housing the Welsh Office in Cardiff.

Catholic emancipation. Movement in Britain and Ireland to secure full political and civil rights for Roman Catholics. Unlike Protestant Dissenters, Catholics had received no freedom of worship under the 1689 Toleration Act. Though in practice they did receive a degree of toleration, they were formally excluded from ministerial and administrative office, commissions in the armed services and from universities under a series of acts known collectively as the PENAL LAWS. A Roman Catholic Relief Act applying to England and Wales was passed in 1778 and one applying to Scotland in 1793. But for most of the 18th century, opinion remained fiercely anti-Catholic (*see* GORDON RIOTS).

From 1807, when Sydney Smith, Canon of St Paul's, took up the Protestant Dissenters' cause, agitation grew for the repeal of the Test and Corporation Acts of Charles II. In 1828 they were repealed and the remaining discriminatory legislation against Catholics was shown to be an anachronism. There were only 60,000 Catholics in England but the majority of the Irish population was Catholic and was beginning to refuse to accept the Protestant ascendancy.

In May 1823, Daniel O'Connell (1775–1847) revived an old Catholic association which raised a rent of 1*d* a month from the Irish Catholic community. Within the year it had £22,700 to fight for emancipation. Its aim was to promote Protestant MPs sworn to Catholic emancipation. In 1829 the association was suppressed. O'Connell was elected an MP but as a Catholic could not take his seat. In the face of constitutional deadlock and increasing agitation, the Prime Minister, Wellington and the Home Secretary, Peel, renounced their opposition and in 1829 steered the Catholic Emancipation Act through parliament. In 1832 a Roman Catholic Charities Act regularized the position of Catholic charities.

caucus. Term originating in the USA to denote private meetings of members of political parties, usually called to decide party policy or to adopt candidates.

caudillismo (Sp. deriv. *caudillo*, leader). In Spanish American politics, a system whereby the CAUDILLO as leader or head of state exercises almost absolute authority at all levels of government and has the personal loyalty of his supporters. It arises from the social system of Latin America in which politics are seen as an extension of the HACIENDA at national level. Transition from one caudillo to another is often violent and there is no guarantee that a caudillo will reach the end of his elected term of office. It is related to 'personalismo', the Latin American practice whereby a single leader is glorified at the expense of party interest, ideology and the constitution. Juan Domingo Perón, President of Argentina 1946–1955, was such a caudillo. But the caudillo can be a simple military dictator, such as Gen. Juan Gomez who ruled Venezuela between 1909 and 1935.

Caudillo, El (Span., the leader). Title assumed by Gen. Francisco Franco (1892–1975) in 1937 following his leadership of the right-wing Spanish revolution of 1936 and his victory over the Republicans in the civil war. In July 1947 his authority was strengthened by the declaration that he should remain head of state for life. He nominated Prince Juan Carlos (b. 1938) as his successor, who became king in 1975.

Cavalier (deriv. Fr., horseman). Member of the Royalist party during the English Civil War (1642–49); also, loosely, any knightly, imperious or gallant personage.

Cavalier Parliament. The parliament which met on 8 May 1661 and was dissolved in 1679. It succeeded the CONVENTION PARLIAMENT and took its name from its strongly royalist and Anglican complexions which led to its passing the CLARENDON CODE. The first leader was the Earl of Clarendon who fell from power in 1667, largely as a result of the reverses in the Second Dutch War (1665–67). He was succeeded by the CABAL under whom Charles II pursued a dual foreign policy: open alliance with the Netherlands and Sweden and a secret treaty (signed at Dover in 1670) of alliance with their enemy France. In return for French subsidies he promised to declare himself a Catholic. In March 1673 the Third Dutch War broke out and Charles issued a Declaration of Indulgence for Catholic and Protestant dissenters. Parliament responded by reasserting its policy of Anglican exclusiveness in a Test Act (1673). The Cabal broke up and fell from power. Sir Thomas Osborne (Earl of Danby) became Chancellor in 1674 but during most of his administration the King, financed by French subsidies, could afford to prorogue parliament. Danby was anti-French and in 1677 secured the marriage of Mary, daughter of the Duke of York, to the Protestant William of Orange. When the POPISH PLOT was discovered a movement began to exclude the Catholic James from the succession and the Cavalier Parliament was dissolved on 24 January 1679.

CBI. Confederation of British Industry, formed in 1965 from the merger of the Federation of British Industries (established 1916), the British Employers' Confederation (established 1919) and the National Association of British Manufacturers. Its purpose is 'to provide for industry the means of formulating, making known and influencing general policy in regard to economic, fiscal, commercial, labour, social and technical questions, and to act as a national point of reference for those seeking industry's view; to develop the contribution of industry to the national economy; and to encourage industry's efficiency and competitive power and to provide advice, information and services to British industry to that end.' Its members include private companies and employers' organizations who look to the CBI to act as a political pressure group on matters of interest in any sphere of industry.

Cento (acronym). The Central Treaty Organization, the basis of which was laid by the Baghdad Pact of Turkey and Iraq, signed in February 1955, providing for economic co-operation and mutual defence. Britain, Iran and Pakistan acceded, while the USA, though not a member, became 'associated' with the organization – it was in any case linked with individual members by various treaties. Iraq withdrew on 24 March 1959 and Pakistan ceased to be an active member. Iran's Islamic revolution in early 1979 and her subsequent relations with the West have been a further blow to the organization. It was designed specifically to counter communist aggression and the provisions relating to defence are inoperable if members are in conflict with non-communist countries.

centralism. Political system in which a country is governed from the centre with no autonomy for regions; it is the opposite of federalism. France is a good example of centralism. Britain is less typical because of extensive delegation of powers to popularly elected local authorities such as county councils.

Centralists. Members of the Mexican Party founded in 1823 to support the centralized Republican government and to oppose any undue extension of the autonomy of the various states.

Central Office. Headquarters of the British Conservative Party in Smith Square, London.

Central Powers. Before 1914, members of the TRIPLE ALLIANCE concluded by Bismarck in 1882: Germany, Austria-Hungary and Italy. On the outbreak of war in 1914 Italy remained neutral; the term was then applied to Germany, Austria-Hungary, their ally Turkey, and later Bulgaria.

ceorl (OE). In Anglo-Saxon England, originally a freeman owning his own land independently of any feudal overlord. The class was subdivided into GENEAT, GEBUR and KOTSETLA. Ceorls were liable for military service and public duties such as attending the MOOT and bridge-building. The general unrest of the 11th century eroded their economic position and led many to hold land from nobles in return for labour. After the Norman Conquest, ceorls lost their freedom and became part of the VILLEIN class. The name

was corrupted to form the derogatory 'churl'.

cession. Act by which one state cedes territory to another, the citizens inhabiting such territory then becoming citizens of the new owner unless arrangement is made specially for them to retain their original nationality. Cession may be peaceful, as with Denmark's sale of the Danish West Indies to the USA in 1916, or it may be forced by defeat in war, as with Spain's cession of the Philippines to the USA in 1898.

Cetnik. *See* CHETNIKS.

CGT (Fr., Confédération Générale du Travail). The largest French trade union federation, formed in 1906 on a non-political syndicalist platform. A Communist minority broke away in 1921, the two sections reuniting in 1935, since when the CGT has been Communist-led.

Chamber. In medieval England, a financial department of the royal household, probably the centre of finance in the 11th and 12th centuries before being superseded by the EXCHEQUER. As a department of the CURIA REGIS it provided the king with ready cash and freed him from financial and administrative control. Endowed with the revenues from forfeited estates such as those of the TEMPLARS, it declined in importance after the transfer of many of its lands to the Exchequer in 1322, but survived as a household office. Under the Tudors it regained importance and was endowed with revenues from new bodies such as the Court of Augmentations, but in 1554 these were also incorporated into the Exchequer and the Chamber lapsed into obscurity.

chamberlain. In 11th-century

England, a member of the king's household and later a financial officer; the precursor of the modern Lord Chamberlain of the Household. The holder of the office today is responsible for appointments to the Household and for all ceremonials at the palace except for coronations and openings of Parliament. Until 1968 he was also censor of plays. The Lord Great Chamberlain, an hereditary office held for each reign by a descendant of the de Veres, Earls of Oxford, attends the monarch at the coronation and state opening of Parliament and is custodian of the Palace of Westminster.

Chambre Ardente (Fr.). Court of devout Roman Catholics, charged with the trial of heretics, established by Henry II in the PARLEMENT of Paris in 1551.

Chambre Introuvable (Fr.). Louis XVIII's name for the French Assembly convened in 1815. Of extreme royalist sympathies, it consisted of 402 deputies, many young and inexperienced, and 176 nobles of the ANCIEN RÉGIME. They favoured reprisals against Bonaparte's followers and condoned the reactionary WHITE TERROR. Their extremism proved unpopular with the countries which had restored Louis to the monarchy and the assembly dissolved in September 1816.

chancellor (deriv. Lat. *cancellarius*, a clerk who sat at the railing, *ad cancellos*). Chief minister of state, as for example in Germany. In England, office which originated in the reign of Edward the Confessor (1003–1066) of chief secretary of the king. He kept the GREAT SEAL of state and was head of CHANCERY; in the 14th century he became a judge in the COURT OF CHANCERY. He also sat in the EXCHEQUER and his deputy there became CHANCELLOR OF THE EXCHEQUER.

Chancellor of the Exchequer. In England, office dating from the 13th century when the name was given to the clerk to the CHANCELLOR in EXCHEQUER business. The office grew in importance in the 16th century as a result of reforms of the Exchequer in 1554 and the personal chancellorship of Sir Walter Mildmay (1566–89). In the 17th century the Chancellor of the Exchequer was given the post of second Lord Commissioner of the Treasury. Since the first Lord Commissioner assumed the function of Prime Minister, the chancellor became responsible for the national purse. With this increased financial responsibility, the post's judicial functions were abolished in the 19th century. The Chancellor of the Exchequer now has responsibility for national revenue and expenditure, meaning in effect that he has charge of economic policy.

Chancery (ME). In medieval England, originally the writing office of the CURIA REGIS, which later occupied permanent quarters of its own. By the 13th century it dealt with petitions to the king and its significance lay mainly in specialist administrative work, such as that performed by the CLERK OF THE HANAPER. Chancery clerkships later became sinecures, the duties being performed by deputies. In time, most of the clerical work was transferred to the Supreme Court of Judicature, the Crown Office and the Patent Office. As Chancery's political importance declined, it undertook new legal functions and its clerks became experts in the law; by the mid-14th century it was acting as an equity court. *See also* CURSITOR.

Chancery, Court of. In England, a court with the professed object of making justice complete by mitigating the rigour of other courts which were bound by the letter of the law. Claimed in legend to have originated in the reign of Alfred (871–901) or William I (1066–87), its power was initially probably derived from the CURIA REGIS. It gradually gained in independence and became divided into two tribunals: the 'ordinary' being a common law court and the 'extraordinary' being a court of equity. Its acts were the source of frequent complaints by the HOUSE OF COMMONS in the 14th and 15th centuries. Delays in Chancery proceedings proved a source of dissatisfaction and eventually during the 1850s and 1860s acts were passed to amend its practice. By the Judicature Act of 1873 it was superseded by the Chancery Division of the High Court of Justice. What had been its extraordinary jurisdiction – the execution of trusts, partnership disputes, redemption and foreclosure of mortgages, etc. – became the ordinary jurisdiction of the Chancery Division.

chantry (ME deriv. AFr., singing). Endowment founded to celebrate masses for the souls of the founder and others; also the place – an altar in a specially reserved chapel or a separate building – where masses were sung for the dead. From the 13th century onwards, chantry foundations to intercede for both the living and the dead were common. They often had independent financial provisions and were sometimes linked with the founding of schools (for example Winchester and Eton). In England the chantries themselves, though not their associated institutions, were dissolved in 1545–47.

Chaperons Blancs (Fr.). The White

Capes, the popular party of Ghent in 1379, led by Jan Yoens.

Charge of the Light Brigade. Incident during the Crimean War at the Battle of Balaklava, 25 October 1854. Lord Raglan ordered his cavalry commander Lord Lucan to retrieve Turkish guns captured by Russians. Misunderstanding the order, Lucan deployed the Light Brigade in a frontal attack on the main Russian position, and a third of the Brigade were killed or wounded in its capture.

charter (deriv. Lat. *carta*, paper). Written evidence of a transaction between two parties. Such documents, recording the actions of private persons, serve as deeds and instruments under seal for the conveyance of lands, etc. A royal charter records the grant of lands and privileges, usually in perpetuity, from the Crown – either to persons (letters patent for title, for example) or to corporations giving them sovereign rights, as in the case of the British South Africa Company or the British North Borneo Company.

Charter 77. Group of Czechoslovakian DISSIDENTS formed in Prague early in 1977 (a 'human rights year') to monitor abuses of civil rights by the authorities. Throughout 1978 and 1979 it was subjected to official harassment and many of its members were imprisoned or driven into virtual exile.

Chartism. Movement for political, and later social, reform in Britain between 1838 and 1858, which took its name from the PEOPLE'S CHARTER. It gradually became an expression of working-class unrest against the POOR LAW, economic conditions and the difficulty of developing effective TRADE UNIONS. In July 1839 Thomas Attwood, MP for Birmingham and head of the Birmingham Political Union, failed to persuade parliament to accept a petition with 1,200,000 signatures. A division then arose between the three leaders: Lovett, a moderate; O'Brien, who saw the Charter as the means to bring about a social revolution; and O'Connor, who in 1842 renounced the original Charter and pursued instead a Utopian concept of agricultural social reform.

A proposed general strike never materialized though there were sporadic outbreaks of violence such as that at Newport in 1839. A second petition, with three million signatures, was rejected by parliament in May 1842 and for a time the movement seemed near collapsing. However, in April 1848 O'Connor managed to revive interest, threatening a mass procession to parliament to deliver a third petition. When the government began assembling troops to resist the demonstration it was called off and though vestiges of the movement survived until 1858 it was of no further political importance. Its main significance was the proof that the working classes could be organized on a massive scale.

Chauffeurs (Fr., stokers, firemen). Brigands who roamed northern and, later, central France in 1793. They roasted the feet of their victims to force them to disclose the whereabouts of their valuables.

chauvinism (Fr.). Excessive patriotism; also, by analogy, excessive commitment to any cause. The word is derived from the name of Nicolas Chauvin, whose exaggerated devotion to Napoleon exposed him to ridicule.

checks and balances. Feature of constitutions in which the powers of each part – executive, legislative and judicial – are counterbalanced by those of the other parts to prevent one part from becoming too powerful. The constitution of the USA is the best example of an attempt to implement checks and balances.

Cheka (Russ., acronym). Extraordinary commission, or secret political police force, established by the BOLSHEVIKS in post-revolutionary Russia to defend the regime against internal enemies.

Chequers. Official country residence of the British Prime Minister, situated in the Chilterns, about 35 miles from London. The house is a Tudor mansion given to the country in August 1917 by Viscount Lee of Fareham (1868–1940); it first came into use as an official residence in 1921.

Chetniks. Originally, guerrillas from Serbia seeking to liberate their country from Turkish domination between 1907 and 1912. During World War I they were active in raiding German supply lines in the Balkans. The organization survived in inter-war Yugoslavia; at first it opposed the German occupation in World War II and received British aid until 1944. But the Chetniks were Serbian rather than Yugoslavian nationalists and were strongly opposed to communism. Thus some Chetnik commanders collaborated with the Germans and Italians against Tito's PARTISANS.

Chicago Martyrs. Eight anarchists arrested after a policeman was killed by a bomb in a demonstration on 4 May 1886. Found guilty on circumstantial evidence, four were hanged in November 1887, one committed suicide and three were imprisoned. Pardoned on grounds of miscarriage of justice in 1893, the eight were the American left's earliest political martyrs.

Chiltern hundreds. Three HUN-DREDS in the Chiltern Hills – Stoke, Burnham and Desborough – whose stewardship is now a nominal office under the Chancellor of the EXCHEQUER. Since *c*1750, MPs have been enabled to resign their seats by nomination to the stewardship, which is held to be an office of honour and profit under the Crown. A similar symbolic post is the stewardship of the Manor of Northstead in Yorkshire, which has been used in this way since 1841.

Chindits (deriv. Burm. *Chinthé,* a mythical winged beast of great ferocity). The force raised by Gen. Wingate to operate behind Japanese lines in Burma in 1943 and 1944. They raised morale by demonstrating that Western troops could operate in the jungle and inflict defeats there on the Japanese who had previously seemed invulnerable.

Chônin (Jap., deriv. *cho,* city ward). In Japan, a city-dwelling merchant class which emerged in the early 17th century and flourished throughout the Tokugawa period (1603–1867), receiving government sponsorship. When the Meiji Emperor Mutsuhito ascended the throne in 1868, Japan began a period of rapid industrialization. Old feudal institutions were abolished, sponsorship of the Chônin ceased and the class declined, to be replaced in commercial prominence by SAMURAI entrepreneurs who were no longer bound by feudal duties.

Chouans (Breton Fr., screech owl). A band of peasants, mainly smugglers, in western France who joined the royalists in 1793 in revolt against the revolutionary forces. Led by Larochejaquelin and Cadoudal, they held out in La Vendée and other parts of Brittany until 1799. Their name is derived from their signal of the hooting of an owl.

Chovevei Zion (Isr. 'Lovers of Zion'). Late 19th-century movement originating in Russia to encourage Jewish settlement in Palestine, which pre-dated and later joined forces with the Zionist Organization.

Choviski. *See* BELSKI.

Christian Socialism. (1) In Britain, a movement which began in the mid-19th century with the object of emphasizing the social principles found in the New Testament. It opposed 'LAISSEZ-FAIRE' and sought to establish industrial co-operatives (*see* CO-OPERATIVE MOVEMENT). To further the education of the poorer classes it founded the Working Men's College in 1854. The movement's leaders were John Malcolm Forbes Ludlow (1821–1911), Charles Kingsley (1819–75), F.D. Maurice (1805–72), and Thomas Hughes (1822–96) whose novel *Tom Brown's Schooldays* displays many of the tenets of the movement.

(2) Name given to the beliefs of many political parties in Europe, founded in response to the challenge of SOCIALISM. The first was formed in Austria in the late 19th century. Two papal ENCYCLICALS (*Rerum novarum* and *Quadraqesimo Anno*), anti-socialist but in favour of a Christian corporate state with protection for labour, encouraged their efforts. Today the Christian Socialist parties are essentially conservative but may have quite advanced programmes of social reform. After World War II the Austrian Christian Socialist Party was renamed the People's Party.

Christinos (strictly **Cristinos**) (Span.). Spanish party which supported the Regency of Queen Cristina in opposition to the CARLISTS in 1833.

church scot. In early Anglo-Saxon England, payment of grain and hens to support parish priests, levied on all free men according to their holdings; it was originally known as 'food rent'. The peasantry found it a heavy burden and although it continued after the development of the TITHE, it gradually declined to a modest payment of eggs and hens.

churl. *See* CEORL.

CIA. US Central Intelligence Agency, established in 1947 to co-ordinate and analyze foreign intelligence reports for the President. Its Director was also Chairman of the National Security Council and the Agency was to be responsible solely to the President. Under the directorship of J.F. Dulles (1953–61) its original purpose was altered to the planning of covert operations designed to topple unfriendly foreign governments, for example, those in Guatemala and Iran (1953–4). The policy resulted in the BAY OF PIGS fiasco of 1961, when Cuban exiles unsuccessfully attempted to invade Cuba.

Under a new Director, John McCone (1961–65) these operations were curbed and intelligence-gathering emphasized instead. However, covert operations, such as plans to assassinate Fidel Castro of Cuba, continued without McCone's knowledge; under Presidents Johnson and Nixon, they were fully resumed, with Richard Helms as Director (1966–73). The WATERGATE scandal revealed a proliferation of CIA agencies which had infringed civil liberties. The activities of the CIA in the 1980s, particularly in Central America, have continued to cause controversy.

ci-devants (Fr., heretofore). Name given during the French Revolution to those who, as a result of the abolition of titles of honour, were no longer known by title but by family name. Marie Antoinette, for example, was tried as Widow Capet.

Científicos (Span.). Pejorative name for an influential group of politicians, intellectuals and financiers in Mexico during the dictatorship of Porfirio Diaz (1876–1911). The name was a reference to their belief in POSITIVISM, which they mistakenly interpreted as a form of social Darwinism.

Cinquecento (Ital., 16th century). In Italy, the later period of the RENAISSANCE.

Cinque Ports (Fr., five ports). Originally Hastings, Romney, Hythe, Dover and Sandwich; Rye and Winchelsea were added later. They were brought into association by Edward the Confessor (1044–66) to provide coastal defence in return for certain privileges. In 1265 they were summoned to send Barons to Parliament by Henry III; their earliest known charter was granted by Edward I in 1278. Their privileges were abolished by the 1835 Municipal Corporations Act.

Circumspecta agatis (Lat.). Royal writ issued by Edward I in June 1286, directing the justices to 'deal circumspectly' with the Bishop of Norwich and his clergy and to allow the Church to hear certain pleas such as moral offences, TITHE disputes and cases of defamation of the clergy. The writ, Edward's response to complaints by the clergy that royal courts were encroaching on matters which properly related to ecclesiastical jurisdiction, provided a much needed definition of the judicial sphere of Church courts and came to be regarded as a statute. It was repealed by the 1963 Ecclesiastical Jurisdiction Measure.

Cisalpine Republic (south of the Alps; deriv. Lat. *cis-*, on this side of). Republic formed by Napoleon comprising the provinces he had conquered in 1796–1797: Lombardy, the old Venetian territories west of the River Adige and south as far as Modena, Reggio nell'Emilia, Ferrara and Bologna.

Cispadane Republic (south of the Po; deriv. Lat. *cis-*, on this side of). Name given to the republic comprising the province of Emilia (capital Bologna) which Napoleon formed in Italy in 1797.

Cistercians. Religious order for men and women founded at Cîteaux, near Dijon, in 1098, noted for the rigidity and uniformity of its rule. The golden age of the order was the 12th century when its fortunes were closely tied to those of St Bernard of Clairvaux (1090–1153). Bernard entered Cîteaux as a novice in 1112 and in 1115 left to found a Cistercian monastery at Clairvaux. He was extremely active in encouraging the foundation of further houses and monks from Clairvaux alone were responsible for establishing 68 houses by the end of the century; by the time of his death the order had 338 abbeys from Sweden to the eastern Mediterranean.

Between 1130 and 1145 Bernard was a member of numerous ecclesiastical and civil councils, had been advisor to five popes and was instrumental in launching the SECOND CRUSADE. In theological matters he combined a Christian mysticism with a desire to serve others but he remained a strong adherent to the institutionalized church. His beliefs brought him into direct conflict with the rationalist dialectics of Peter Abelard (1079–1144), a founder of scholastic moral theology, whose rationalism led him to publish *Sic et Non* ('Yes and No'), a collection of quotations aimed at showing inconsistencies in the position of the church, and whose *Theologia* was declared to be heretical in 1121. Bernard was canonized in 1174.

The architectural achievements of the Cistercians in the 12th century are considerable, many monasteries showing the preferences of Bernard himself for massive but simple lines in keeping with the gravity and austerity of the order. The uniformity of the rule was mirrored in the uniformity of the architecture, and Cistercian abbeys were markedly similar in appearance. Usually in remote situations, the abbeys were often of benefit to the local agricultural economy. Notable buildings were constructed at Pontigny, Burgundy (1140); Rievaulx and Fountains (1131 and 1135); Kercz, Hungary (1202); Beirut, Lebanon (1155); Alcobaca, Portugal (1158); Vieta, Sweden (1100) and Fossanova, Italy (1187).

From having been noted for their austere and strict rules, the Cistercians were notorious for laxity and greed by the 15th century. After the REFORMATION they disappeared from northern Europe and were struggling to survive elsewhere. However, the 17th century saw successful attempts at reform. In 1664 Armand Jean Le Bouthillier de Rancé became abbot of La Trappe and commenced restoration of a rule of seclusion, silence, prayer and manual labour: his followers became known as Trappists. Trappists adopted the title 'Order of Cistercians of the Strict Observance' (OCSO). The rest of the order which underwent moderate reform in 1666, are known as Cistercians of Common Observance. In the 1960s the Second Vatican Council called for greater diversity and individuality in the OCSO; their rule was moderated and is no longer strictly uniform to each establishment.

Citizen King. Louis Philippe (1773–1850), King of the French 1830–48, so called because he was an ostensibly constitutional monarch, sharing the political and social attitudes (and the sartorial style) of his middle-class supporters. He fled to England after the February 1848 revolution.

citoyen (Fr., citizen). Name given to those loyal to the ideals of the French Revolution – *liberté, fraternité, egalité* – and thus to the Republic. The term implicitly excluded sympathy for aristocratic or clerical titles and refusal to be called by it could result in execution.

Civilistas (Span.). Late 19th-century civilian party in Peru, organized to oppose the administration of Balta, a corrupt soldier closely associated with Henry Meiggs, an unscrupulous American speculator who was active in Chile and Peru.

Civil List. Payments from the CONSOLIDATED FUND for the upkeep of the British royal household. The Civil List Act, first passed in 1697, originally also covered government expenses, thus giving the Crown substantial powers of patronage. In 1761 George III relinquished the revenues from Crown lands to parliament in return for an annual payment on the 'civil list'. In 1831 government expenses were removed from the civil list.

Members of the royal family other than the monarch have received monies on the Civil List since 1901, leading to some controversy in recent years. Certain members of the Labour Party have argued that only the immediate family of the monarch should receive money at a time when it has been necessary to reduce public expenditure.

civil rights. Social freedoms and privileges possessed by a citizen, denial of which is a denial of citizen status. The nature of civil rights varies among societies. Where they are infringed it should be the duty of the courts to resolve disputes but where they are insufficient it is necessary for the legislature to amend them. A basic list of civil rights is given in the UN Declaration of Human Rights.

In Britain, civil rights have arisen mainly through custom and tradition as opposed to statutory declaration. In France, the constitution names the Declaration of the Rights of Man (1789) as the source of the country's civil rights.

In the USA, the various articles and amendments of the Constitution (see BILL OF RIGHTS), together with judicial decisions, form the basic source of civil rights but legislation has been necessary to implement them. In June 1963 Pres. Kennedy submitted a Civil Rights Bill to the US Congress specifying that voting qualifications including literacy tests should be identical for all, regardless of colour; that employment, pay and promotion prospects be equal and that racial discrimination on public transport, in public places, private shops and restaurants be made illegal. Despite a FILIBUSTER by Southern politicians, the bill passed the Senate on 19 June 1964. In 1966 a bill was introduced by Pres. Johnson to stop racial discrimination in the housing market, but it was rejected by the Senate. On 11 March 1968 the Senate passed a bill to protect civil rights in housing, civil order and riot control; it also protected the rights of American Indians. *See* CIVIL RIGHTS MOVEMENT.

On 30 July–1 August 1975 the Helsinki Conference on Security and Co-operation in Europe, in response to calls from Pres. Carter, agreed to a statement concerning 'respect for human rights and fundamental freedoms'. The USSR was present at the conference but has not secured the civil rights of DISSIDENTS in eastern Europe. *See* 'CHARTER 77' and HELSINKI HUMAN RIGHTS GROUP.

Civil Rights Movement. Movement to secure implementation of the 14th and 15th amendments to the American constitution, made in 1868 and 1870, by which the citizenship and voting rights of negroes were established. As early as 1909 the National Association for the Advancement of Coloured People was established, but no real progress was made until the 1950s and 1960s. This was because in 1883 and 1896 the Supreme Court decided in favour of Southern states practising segregation of whites and blacks, holding that states' rights to make their own laws could not be overriden. By manipulation of the voting qualification tests, blacks were also excluded from voting in the Southern states.

However, in May 1954 the Supreme Court ruled in the case of Brown v Board of Education of Topeka that in public education there was no room for a concept of 'separate but equal' because segregation necessarily imposed inequalities. Federal enforcement of 'desegregation' and other rulings required the presence of troops at Little Rock, Arkansas in September 1957. In 1957 and 1960 two acts established a federal agency of six commissioners to look into allegations that black citizens were being denied the protection of the law. Violent white reaction in the South, and the impatience of blacks at the slow progress of desegregation led in 1960 to sit-ins, boycotts of stores and numerous demonstrations.

Under the leadership of Dr Martin Luther King (1929–68), the movement culminated in a peaceful demonstration of 250,000 people in Washington on 28 August 1963. Legislative progress was made under the Kennedy and Johnson administrations (*see* CIVIL RIGHTS), but outbursts in Harlem (July 1964) and Watts, Los Angeles (August 1965) revealed a black militant movement which remained dissatisfied. The black movement began to splinter, a process speeded by the murder of King in April 1968.

The Nixon adminstration (1968–74) did little for civil rights and with the onset of depression in the late 1970s it has been widely felt amongst American blacks that their civil rights in the spheres of employment and education have again been eroded. Nor were there significant developments during the Reagan years.

Clann na Talmhan (Ir.). The Farmers' Party in the Republic of Ireland.

Clapham Sect. A strand of the Anglican Evangelical Movement, stressing the importance of good works, moral earnestness and salvation by faith. The Sect – whose leading members worshipped in Clapham Parish Church, South London – was involved in the campaign to abolish the slave trade, missionary work in India and ameliorating the plight of the poor.

Clarendon Code. Series of acts

passed in the English parliament between 1661 and 1665 with the aim of destroying the power of the Protestant dissenters by restricting their religious freedom and excluding them from secular office. Edward Hyde, 1st Earl of Clarendon (1609–74) was not in fact the driving force behind the legislation, more accurately it was the extremist Anglican House of Commons that was returned in 1660. In 1661 the Corporation Act was passed, barring dissenters from municipal office; in 1662 the Act of Uniformity excluded them from church offices. Finally the Conventicle Act of 1664 and the Five Mile Act of 1665 restricted their freedom of public worship.

class against class. Policy imposed on communist parties by the COMINTERN in 1928–34 which claimed that capitalism was undergoing decisive crisis and that reformist socialist and labour parties (with which the communists had hitherto attempted to work) were the main obstacle to revolution. Its roots lay in the struggle within the Soviet Party over Stalin's COLLECTIVIZATION programme.

Clause IV. Clause in the constitution of the British Labour Party, drawn up in 1918 by Arthur Henderson (1863–1935) and the FABIAN Sidney Webb (1859–1947), which commits the party to 'secure for the producers by hand or by brain the full fruits of their industry and the most equitable distribution thereof that may be possible upon the basis of the common ownership of the means of production and the best obtainable system of popular administration and control of each industry or service'. This clearly commits the party to a socialist policy but it is not a Marxist party and does not seek to achieve its ends by revolution.

In accordance with the clause, the Labour government of 1945–51 nationalized the Bank of England, the coal, gas, electricity and railway industries. In the late 1950s there was an unsuccessful attempt to remove Clause IV from the constitution by the GAITSKELLITES. In the 1980s the party reaffirmed its commitment to SOCIALISM, but under Kinnock also recognized that the party must respond to market forces.

Cleargrits. Extreme democratic party in Canada in 1850 which favoured secession from Britain and union with the USA. Its name is derived from its claim to political purity: 'all sand and no dirt, clear grit all the way through'.

Clericos Laicos (Lat.). BULL issued by Pope Boniface VIII in 1296 forbidding the clergy to pay tribute to temporal sovereigns without papal assent on pain of EXCOMMUNICATION. In England the clergy complied with the bull and were outlawed by Edward I in 1297 and their property confiscated. However, the pope allowed Philip IV of France the right to levy taxes on the clergy in cases of emergency. This precedent, together with the Scottish victory at the battle of Stirling in 1297, led the English clergy to agree to a subsidy for Edward I, though only for use against the Scots. The king consequently abandoned his claim to tax the clergy as of right.

Clerk of the Hanaper. Chancery official charged with the task of recording the payment of fees on the writs which commenced every action at common law. Those writs having exclusive reference to the affairs of the subject were kept in a HANAPER (*in Hanaperio*); those relating to matters involving the Crown were kept in a bag (*in parva baga*). The office was abolished in 1852.

closed shop. Compulsory trade union membership for all employees, accepted by management where unions are in a strong bargaining position. Attacked as an infringement of individual liberty, unions argue that all workers sharing gains arising from negotiation should contribute to maintenance of union machinery.

close rolls. In England, grants from the Crown, directed to particular persons for specific purposes. Because they are not for public inspection, they are closed up and sealed on the outside. The first close rolls, dating from 1204–5, dealt with most government business of transitory importance, but as new types of roll developed for recording special documents the range of business covered by close rolls diminished. Private deeds (e.g. enclosure awards, deeds poll, etc.) were first copied onto the backs of close rolls in the late 14th century; from the early 16th century they have been their sole content. They ended in 1903.

closure. Stopping of parliamentary debate by the process of bringing to a vote the question under discussion. Originally designed to prevent obstruction of parliamentary business, it is now used to speed the passage of government business even where there is no obstruction. In Britain it takes three forms in the House of Commons: by a member moving that the question be now put (to a vote); by the guillotine or closure by compartments whereby a bill's passage is limited according to timetable; or by 'kangaroo' closure, where a member moves to put the question, thus ruling out amendments not already moved.
    In the USA the procedure for curtailing debate works easily in the House of Representatives (*see* CON-GRESS). In the Senate, however, there is extensive freedom of debate and great scope for FILIBUSTER.

cloture. *See* CLOSURE.

Clubmen. Bands of armed men who assembled in various parts of England in 1644, mainly in the West Country, for the purpose of protecting their districts and property from the ravages of the Civil War. They attacked both Royalists and Parliamentarians impartially.

Cluniacs. Monastic order founded by the Benedictines at Cluny, near Mâcon in Burgundy, in 910, marking the first real attempt at closer organization of the Benedictine order. The order had a strict rule and observed exacting liturgical services. Cluny abbey was increasingly approached for advice on the reform of other monasteries and a succession of Cluniac abbots developed a network of client monasteries throughout western Europe. The monks were usually nobles and the order prided itself on the eminence of its princely patrons and the numerous former Cluniacs who became bishops and even popes.

Clydesiders. Members of the Independent Labour Party elected to represent west-coast Scottish constituencies in the 1922 general election. Noted for their left-wing views and strong commitment to SOCIALISM, their ranks included James Maxwell, David Kirkwood and John Wheatley, Minister of Health in the 1924 Labour government.

CND. The Campaign for Nuclear Disarmament, launched on 17 February 1958 by Bertrand Russell and Canon L. John Collins, to demand the abandonment of nuclear weapons and a large reduction in British defence expenditure. It grew out of protest demonstrations at Aldermaston Atomic Weapons Research Establishment during Easter 1956. The annual Easter 'Aldermaston' march, culminating in a demonstration in Trafalgar Square, London, drew large support between 1958 and 1964.

At its peak in 1960–61 CND had more active supporters than any British mass movement since the Anti-Corn Law League in the 1840s and in 1960 the Labour Party conference passed a resolution in favour of unilateral disarmament. But from 1961 to 1979 CND's fortunes were on the wane.

The revival of CND in recent years dates from 1979 and is echoed in the peace movements developing in Germany and the Netherlands. In that year NATO ministers agreed on a 'twin-track' strategy involving the siting of a new generation of nuclear missiles (Cruise and Pershing) in Europe. From 1980 the membership of CND rose dramatically and demonstrations attracted hundreds of thousands of supporters. CND also enjoyed growing support in the USA where the 'Freeze' campaign declared its intention to oppose in CONGRESS the siting of Cruise and Pershing missiles. The momentum, however, has been difficult to maintain, especially in the face of little tangible success; by the late 1980s CND's membership was again falling.

cniht (OE, youth). In Anglo-Saxon England, the retainer of an important noble, attached to the household to perform administrative and military duties. After the Norman Conquest, the word was used to denote a follower of a Norman lord; it developed into the modern 'knight'.

CNT (Sp., Confederación Nacional del Trabajo). National Confederation of Labour. Spanish anarcho-syndicalist union federation formed in October 1910, strongest in industrial Catalonia and rural Andalusia, with two million members by the mid-1930s. The CNT resisted Franco's rising in 1936, encouraging industrial and agricultural collectivization. Weakened by growing communist influence in the Republic and driven underground by Nationalist victory in 1939, it re-emerged in the 1980s. *See* FAI.

Codini (Ital., pigtails). Name given to the papal party by the House of Savoy in the late 19th century, implying that supporters of the papacy were reactionary and conservative.

Cod War. Popular term given to the diplomatic dispute between Britain and Iceland from September 1972 to June 1976. It was occasioned by Iceland's unilateral extension of her 12-mile fishing limit to 50 miles (i.e. the area of sea around the Icelandic coast within which foreign fishing was not permitted). At times the argument was expressed in incidents on the high seas when Icelandic gunboats attempted to intercept British civilian trawlers within its 50-mile limit and Royal Naval frigates intervened. The dispute was ended when a compromise agreement was reached by which a maximum of 24 British trawlers would be allowed within a 200-mile zone claimed by Iceland as hers.

Somewhat ironically, the extension of British fishing limits in the North Sea following EEC agreements resulted, in January 1983, in Danish fishing ships denying Britain's right to such a zone, entering it and being intercepted by the Royal Navy. Amidst great publicity a Danish Member of the European Parliament hired a ship and entered the zone in order to be arrested so that he could force the matter either to the Court of International Justice at The Hague, or back to the EEC to secure a revision of the limit.

coexistence. The 'living together' of states with ideological or foreign policy conflicts, such as the USA and USSR, or East and West Germany. Coexistence might not involve friendly relations but denotes a situation well short of armed aggression.

coif. *See* SERJEANTS AT LAW.

Cold War. Protracted state of tension between countries falling short of actual warfare. The term was first used in a US Congress debate on 12 March 1947 on the doctrine expounded by President Harry S. Truman (1894–1972) promising US aid to 'free peoples who are resisting attempted subjugation by armed minorities or by outside pressures'. A direct product of the civil war in Greece (1946–49), the doctrine bore the wider implication that the US would actively respond anywhere in the world to what it saw as an encroachment by the USSR. The grant of US aid to Europe under the MARSHALL PLAN was outlined on 5 June 1947 and, not surprisingly, any hope it held out of economic collaboration with countries behind the IRON CURTAIN was rejected by the USSR who instead founded COMINFORM and COMECON.

In February 1948 the Communist Party seized control of Czechoslovakia and on 30 March the USSR imposed traffic restrictions on Berlin. The tension implied in the term was thus significantly increased within a year of its being coined. The establishment of NATO (1949–50) and the signing of the WARSAW PACT (1955) completed the division of Europe into hostile camps bound by military alliances. A summit meeting in Geneva in July 1955 of US, USSR, British and French leaders promised some easing of tension but the Hungarian rising against Russian domination (October–November 1956) and Britain's invasion of Suez (31 October 1956) put an end to these hopes. The construction of the Berlin Wall (13 August 1961), symbol of the city's division between communism and Western democracy, reflected hardening attitudes on both sides. In October 1962 the discovery of Russian missiles on Cuba and President Kennedy's demands that they be removed brought the Cold War to its highest peak of tension and a real war appeared for a brief time to be imminent.

For a period in the early 1970s OSTPOLITIK and Strategic Arms Limitation Talks (SALT) looked like replacing the Cold War with a permanent DETENTE. In May 1979 a further SALT treaty was agreed in principle between the USA and the USSR, but in December Russian troops entered Afghanistan following a Soviet-backed coup. This act, internal domestic politics and a genuine belief that the USSR had not adhered to the terms of previous SALT treaties but had established military superiority, led the US Senate to refuse to ratify the treaty. Moreover, alarm at what appeared to be Soviet superiority in nuclear weapons caused the USA to seek bases in Europe for its Cruise missiles; in June 1980 the British government announced that these would be sited in the UK. This decision, together with Western support for the independent Polish trade union, SOLIDARITY, served to heighten tension again. Disarmament talks between the USA and the USSR began in Geneva in 1981, but 1982 saw only offer and counter-offer, usually on the basis not of reducing nuclear missiles overall but simply on their levels of deployment in Europe. With the advent of Gorbachev in Russia, however, a whole new climate in US–Soviet relations has begun, as instanced by the agreement reached in 1987 to reduce intermediate nuclear forces. *See also* DISARMAMENT, MCCARTHYISM.

collaboration. The relationship between sections of the population and World War II German occupation forces in Europe. Collaboration ranged from active political, administrative and economic support for PUPPET GOVERNMENTS, through unavoidable co-operation, to reluctant acquiescence. *See* QUISLING.

collective leadership. Leadership by a group rather than an individual. *See also* COLLECTIVE RESPONSIBILITY.

collective responsibility. Concept applicable to countries with parliamentary government (e.g. Britain), under which the government as a whole is responsible for the actions of each of its members unless a member resigns, and each member is responsible for the acts of the government as a whole, unless he or she resigns.

collective security. Term widely used in international diplomacy between the two world wars, first coined at the 1924 Geneva Conference, denoting a policy whereby the security of individual countries was guaranteed jointly by others. It was the basic principle of the LEAGUE OF NATIONS and required acceptance by individual members of collective decisions backed up, if necessary, by military action. The term was also applied to attempts to establish a system of multilateral alliances for defence against NAZI Germany in the 1930s. Under the Charter of the UN, power to meet threats to peace

is vested in the Security Council of the USA, USSR, Britain, France and China. As the Council cannot act if any member dissents, the principle of collective security is not present in its full form.

collectivism. Politico-economic system which incorporates a degree of central planning and co-operation implying some expression of collective thought, assent and action. The term is applied not only to socialist systems but also to looser economic systems such as corporatism and co-operativism.

collectivization. Process of transferring land from private to state or communal ownership. Small peasant farms in the USSR were amalgamated in this way to form agricultural collectives. Strictly the term denotes only the formation of a KOLKHOZ, but it is sometimes loosely used to describe the SOVKHOZ system.

Colonels, Greek. Military junta which seized power in Greece on 21 April 1967. Led by two colonels, George Papadopoulos and Stylianos Pattakos, they claimed to be protecting Greece from a communist takeover and suspended the democratic constitution. The regime collapsed in July 1974 following its intervention in Cyprus (*See* ENOSIS). Twenty of its rulers were tried in August 1975 following the re-establishment of constitutional government; Papadopoulos and Pattakos received death penalties which were subsequently commuted to life imprisonment.

colonialism. The process which began about 1500 with European conquest, settlement and exploitation of territories in America, the East and Africa. The first wave of colonialism was undertaken by England, France, the Low Countries, Portugal and Spain, followed in the 19th and 20th centuries by Belgium, Italy, Japan, Russia and the United States.

colons (Fr.). French colonists, for example those in Algeria who supported the OAS.

colour bar. Separating of peoples according to race, usually by prohibiting coloured peoples from entering public places frequented by whites.

Combination Acts. Two Acts of Parliament passed in 1799 and 1800 during a period when it was widely feared that the French Revolution would spread to Britain. They made it illegal for two or more persons to combine in pursuit of higher wages, improved working conditions, etc. They were repealed in 1824.

Comecon. Acronym of Council for Mutual Economic Assistance, an organization established in Moscow in January 1949 with the aim of improving trade between the USSR and other eastern European socialist states. It was used by Stalin as an instrument for enforcing a commercial boycott of Yugoslavia between 1948 and 1955, but was later adopted to serve as a Soviet response to the growing economic interdependence of western European nations. Original members were Albania (expelled in 1961), Bulgaria, Czechoslovakia, Hungary, Poland, Romania and the USSR. East Germany joined in 1950, Mongolia in 1962 and Cuba in 1972.

Cominform (acronym). Communist Information Bureau established in Warsaw in October 1947 following a conference of communist leaders from the USSR, France, Italy, Bulgaria, Yugoslavia, Czechoslovakia, Hungary and Poland. Formed to co-ordinate communist party activities throughout Europe, its headquarters were in Belgrade until June 1948, when they were moved to Bucharest on the expulsion of Yugoslavia. In April 1956 it was dissolved by Khruschev as a gesture of reassurance to the West and to Yugoslavia.

Comintern (acronym). The Communist International, established by Lenin in March 1919 with the aim of promoting revolutionary MARXISM. Its stated aim was world revolution but it was always a tool by which the USSR maintained control of the international communist movement. It was formed by the socialist parties which had opposed the war efforts of their national governments between 1914 and 1918, accepting instead Lenin's call for a class war. At the 1920 Congress nationalism was repudiated and adherence to the class war sworn. A structure similar to that of the Soviet Communist party was adopted, with a small praesidium having the real power. By 1928 it had become a vehicle for Stalinist theory. It was dissolved by Stalin in May 1943 as a good-will gesture towards Russia's Western allies.

Comisco. Committee of the International Socialist Conference which met between 1947 and 1951 and called for socialist unity. In 1948 it declared that socialism was incompatible with suppression of democratic rights and approved the concept of a united Europe. It denounced the socialist parties of Hungary, Bulgaria, Czechoslovakia and Romania for uniting with communists, expelled the pro-communist wing of the Italian socialists led by Nenni, and admitted exiled social democrats from eastern Europe, the German social democrats and Italians under Saragat and Lombardo. The heir to the 'Second International', it was superseded in 1951 by the 'Socialist International' to which 40 social democratic parties affiliated.

Comité des Forges. French iron and steel combine formed in 1864 which exerted strong influence over French inter-war domestic and foreign policies, discouraging government controls, the creation of state monopolies and graduated taxation; sought to preserve close economic links with German industry after the Nazi rise to power.

Comitia Paludata. (Lat., cloaked or armed assembly). In medieval Poland, a DIET attended by the whole body of nobles which met during an INTERREGNUM.

Comitia Togata (Lat., peaceful assembly). In medieval Poland, an ordinary DIET of representatives of the nobles which was summoned by the king.

commando (Port., command). Military system established by the Afrikaners in South Africa in 1806. The country was divided into districts, each under a commandant whose duty it was to summon the burghers when they were required for military service. Compulsory military service for males between the ages of 16 and 60 was abolished in Cape Colony in 1834, but the independent Dutch states maintained the system until 1902. The term is now used generally to describe specialized units of fighting men.

commendation (deriv. Lat., entrust). In medieval England, the act of personal submission to a feudal lord, by which a man became his lord's vassal.

commissar (Russ.). Head of a government department in the USSR. Political commissars are also attached to the RED ARMY where they hold responsibility for the political education of the armed forces.

Common Agricultural Policy. *See* CAP.

common land. Fields around villages in which villagers had the rights to graze livestock, collect wood, fish and dig turf. These rights were removed as common land was increasingly enclosed in the agrarian revolution, limiting the independence of cottagers and forcing them to become paid labourers. See ENCLOSURE.

Commonwealth. Generally, the period between the execution of Charles I on 30 January 1649 and the RESTORATION on 8 May 1660; specifically, the period from the declaration of the English republic on 19 May 1649 to the establishment of the PROTECTORATE by the INSTRUMENT OF GOVERNMENT on 16 December 1653, which made Cromwell Lord Protector. Under the Commonwealth, severe censorship was enforced by a high court of justice which conducted treason trials without a jury. Revenues were derived from taxation, victimization of royalists and the sale of Crown and Church lands.

The basis of commercial policy was laid in 1650 and 1651 with the passing of the Navigation Acts, designed to weld the colonies into a cohesive unit by establishing tight trading links between themselves and Britain. Trade between the colonies and other nations, especially the Dutch, was prohibited. The re-exportation of colonial produce from London, facilitated by these acts, shifted the centre of west European trade from Amsterdam to London, saw an increase of 200 ships in the British navy, and marked the birth of an 'old colonial' system of trade which lasted a century.

The Navigation Acts, together with the English desire to exclude the Dutch from trade with the declining Portuguese empire, led to the Dutch War of 1652–54. Victory in the war gave Britain 1,700 'prize' ships taken from the enemy which were used to swell the mercantile fleet and gave English merchants a monopoly of trade in the Portuguese empire. It was thus under the Commonwealth that the basis of Britain's future strength in international trade was laid.

Common Market. *See* EEC (European Economic Community).

commote (Welsh *cymwd*, neighbourhood). In Wales between the 10th and 16th centuries, a subdivision of the CANTRED which performed the same functions. Each commote was self-contained as regards civil relations and within its boundaries an hereditary chief had a status akin to that of a ruling prince. It had a court of justice and the administrative machinery to supervise the unfree in its bond villages.

Communard (Fr.). Member of the short-lived Paris Commune formed on 26 March 1871, a socialist-democratic rising opposed to the peace with Germany and the conservatism of the new Third Republic. Paris had been the centre of opposition to both the Third Empire and the government of national defence; unrest was encouraged by the decision of the Bordeaux Assembly to end the moratorium on debts and stop the wages of the National Guard. When Adolphe Thiers attempted to withdraw artillery from the city, trouble flared and the Commune was established. In May, government troops under Mac-

Mahon entered the city; after bitter street fighting the Commune was suppressed with 25,000 Communards killed. Many more were later executed or deported.

communism. Social system in which property is communally owned by all the people, functioning on the principle 'from each according to his ability, to each according to his needs'. The political system would, ideally, be non-hierarchical though people would fulfil tasks for which they were best equipped. Communal ownership would remove the need for money, and labour would be directed to the communal rather than the private interest.

There are examples of communism in the writings of Plato (427–347 BC), the DIGGERS and some French socialists of the 1840s. For most of the 19th century communism was synonymous with SOCIALISM, but the main exponents of modern communism were Karl Marx (1818–83) and Friedrich Engels (1820–95). Their *Communist Manifesto* of 1848 remains the credo of parties calling themselves either communist or socialist, but MARXISM interpreted as MARXIST-LENINISM implies a distinction between the two.

The *Manifesto* advocated expropriation of landed property by the community and the use of its income to meet state expenditure; a progressive income tax; the abolition of rights of inheritance; the establishment of a state bank and centralized credit; nationalization of transport; redistribution of land and state ownership of industries; a legal obligation on all to work, and the provision of state education. Communism was to be the final synthesis in the process of DIALECTICAL MATERIALISM. Lenin (1870-1924) interpreted the dialectic to show that there would be two stages following revolution, the socialist and the communist. What both Marx and Lenin saw more clearly than earlier communists was that revolution would be necessary, since the possessor classes would use the state to defend their position by violence. It is arguable whether or not a truly communist society exists, though many states claim the title, including the USSR, China and Cuba. Interpretation of Marxist doctrine varies between each.

community politics. Concentration on the local interests of voters rather than on national issues, based on the belief that the average voter is more concerned with matters that directly affect him, such as the condition of roads, the state of schools and the number of hospitals in his area, than on great national questions such as defence or foreign policy. The Liberal Party developed 'community politics' in Britain in the 1970s, probably because it had too few members of parliament to make a real impact on national policies. The support which the Liberals won by this tactic convinced the major parties that they too had to give consideration to local issues.

Compagnies d'Ordonnance (Fr.) French cavalry and mounted infantry units, established 1445–46 by Charles VII and his constable Artur de Richemont, to regularize the crown's relationship with the bands of mercenaries (*routiers*) who ravaged the countryside in times of peace. The best military commanders and mercenaries were placed under permanent contract, billeted in towns and maintained by a new system of taxation; in effect, they formed a standing army. They contributed to French success in the HUNDRED YEARS' WAR, helped keep internal order in the royal dominions and provided the core of the permanent royal army.

Compounders. Name given in 1692 to the more moderate section of the English JACOBITES who wished to see the Stuart dynasty restored, but were prepared to countenance a general amnesty for all opponents of the Stuart claims. However, it was the Non-Compounders, opposed to an amnesty, who were more powerful at the Stuart court in exile at St. Germains.

Compte Rendu (Fr., report). Manifesto drawn up by Odilon Barrot in May 1832 on behalf of the Moderate Party in the French Chambers, criticizing the Ministry for continuing the Restoration and not the Revolution and attacking hereditary peerages, the excessive civil list and the large sums spent on the army. It claimed that the weakness of the Ministry was leading to the abandonment of Poland to Russia and of Italy to Austria.

compurgation (deriv. Lat., purge). Anglo-Saxon practice by which an accused person could be acquitted if twelve or more persons took an oath testifying to the validity of his statement. Found in very early Anglo-Saxon laws, compurgation was later incorporated into common law as a defence in both criminal and civil cases and was widely used in ecclesiastical courts. Its use was severely curtailed by the Assize of Clarendon in 1166 although the principle was still retained in certain actions until 1833.

Comrades. The radical black militants in the black townships of South Africa (e.g. Soweto). Distinguished from the more moderate 'Fathers'.

concentration camp. Name originally applied to the camps organized by the British under Gen. Kitchener in the Transvaal and Orange River Colonies during the South African War of 1899 to 1902. Unable to defeat the BOERS, Kitchener found it necessary to deny them supplies and support by interning the rural civilian population. Poor hygiene and maladministration resulted in the deaths of about 20,000 of the 120,000 internees, although a commission of investigation dismissed charges of mismanagement as absurd.

In NAZI Germany, camps were established at Dachau and Oranienburg in 1933 for the detention of political and 'racial' enemies. By 1939, six such camps existed in Greater Germany, holding 20,000 prisoners. As part of Hitler's 'FINAL SOLUTION', these 'preventive detention camps' were increased in number and converted into extermination camps for Jews. Bogus and sadistic medical experiments were often conducted in them and some provided slave labour. Among the most notorious were Belsen, Buchenwald and Ravensbruck in Germany; Auschwitz and Treblinka in Poland. The total number killed in them, both Jews and non-Jews, is believed to be more than five million. *See also* 'HOLOCAUST'.

conclave. Assembly of the cardinals of the Roman Catholic Church, meeting in seclusion for the purpose of electing a new pope. A conclave must be convoked within three weeks after the death of a pope. All cardinals are invited, but only half need to be present for the conclave to act. Each accompanied by a secretary and attendant, they meet in the Vatican – usually about 300 persons are present and they are pledged to secrecy for life as to what occurs. They have no communication with the outside world until a pope is chosen. A two-thirds majority is needed for the papal election and if this is not

achieved the ballot papers are burned with straw thus producing black smoke. The process is repeated until a two-thirds majority is obtained. The papers are then burnt without straw producing white smoke, the signal that a pope has been chosen. The oldest Cardinal-Deacon then proclaims to the world '*Habemus papam* (we have a pope)'.

concordat (deriv. Lat. *pactum concordatum*, agreed pact). Agreement between the Pope and a secular government regarding the status and rights of the Roman Catholic Church within that country. Where state-church relations preclude a concordat, a MODUS VIVENDI may be reached instead.

concurrent power. In a FEDERATION, the power of both the federal and the state or regional legislatures to legislate on the same subject.

condominium (Lat., joint rule). Joint government of a territory by two or more states. Examples have been the government of the Sudan by Britain and Egypt; of the Phoenix Islands by Britain and the USA and of the New Hebrides by Britain and France.

condottieri (Ital). Mercenary captains who hired themselves out to various warring Italian states in the 15th and 16th centuries. The most successful, the Sforzas, rose from minor origins to become dukes of Milan.

Confederacy. The independent republic formed under the presidency of Jefferson Davis in 1861 by eleven of the Southern States of America who seceded from the UNION following the election of Abraham Lincoln. The secession led to the Civil War of 1861–65.

confederation. Association of states for mutual defence or co-operation, involving the institution of a government of the territorial area encompassing several previously autonomous states. The states vest specific and limited powers (e.g. over trade) in the government or other authority, but retain separate identities and are independent in relation to powers not so vested. The government body of the association has no direct power over the citizenry of the individual states, unlike the central government of a FEDERATION and, whereas a federal union is usually indissoluble, the ties of confederation are often fragile. Though territorial contiguity is not essential, its absence is a major practical obstacle.

Examples include the Confederation of the Netherlands (1580–1795); the Germanic Confederation (1815–1866); the North American states (1781–1789), i.e. between the Articles of Confederation and the writing of the Federal Constitution of the USA; and the Confederation of Southern States (1861–65).

Confederation of British Industry. *See* CBI.

confessional party. Political party declaring a relationship, either formal or intentional, between its principles and its religious faith, creed or denomination. The Italian Christian Democrats profess a connection between their politics and Catholicism, while several Lebanese parties revolve around their adherence to Christianity. The opposite of a confessional party is a secular party where no such relationship is recognized, for example, the Labour Party in Britain and the Republicans and Democrats in the USA.

confirmation. The formal agreement by the US Senate to the appointment of a Cabinet officer, the signing of a treaty, or other Presidential action.

Confucianism. System of cosmology, politics and ethics derived from the philosophy of Confucius or K'ung-Fo-tzu (551-478 BC). A contemporary of Buddha, Confucius hailed from the feudal state of Lu (part of modern Shantung province); like Buddha, he had little interest in the supernatural or in gods, but there the similarity ends. Confucius was concerned with practical affairs and the desire to reform the feudal system existing in China, a goal which he believed would increase the happiness of the Chinese people. He made much of etiquette and courtesy to inferiors and believed that subjects followed the example of their rulers. He spent much of his life trying to convert local rulers to his belief in a past golden age and to the concept of a 'golden mean'. Unimpressed by great men or unusual acts, he had an abiding belief in destiny, holding that nature decided a man's station in life. If a man accepted his destiny, he could find in nature what he chose and by his own will determine all things. His conservative view of the universe was incompatible with MAOISM and he was denounced by the Chinese communist party as 'a forefather of all reactionaries'.

congé d'élire (A Fr., permission to elect). In England, a royal writ to a cathedral chapter inviting it to elect the person named to the vacant see of the DIOCESE. First introduced as part of the process of Reformation in 1533, it marked the victory of the state over the chapters and the papacy in determining the outcome of episcopal elections.

Congregationalism. In England, the oldest tradition of NONCON-

FORMISM, originating with the BROWNISTS and the BARROWISTS and represented in the ranks of the INDEPENDENTS, which was finally given liberty of worship under William III in 1689. Common to its various manifestations is the insistence on the right of each local congregation to choose its own minister and forms of worship independently of a central church government. In 1833 its members formed the Congregational Union of England and Wales but this was without prescriptive powers over its component congregations and ministers remained responsible to their own churches and to no one else. The sect is widespread in England and the USA, where it is held in special honour since Congregationalists were among the PILGRIM FATHERS who set sail for America in 1620 in search of religious liberty. In 1972 the Congregational Church in England and Wales and the Presbyterian Church of England formed the United Reform Church; the majority of members who did not join comprise the Congregational Federation.

Congress. Two chambers of the legislature of the USA: the Senate, the more powerful body, composed of two members from each state, and the House of Representatives with 435 members elected by district. Members of both chambers are elected by popular vote, senators for 6 years with one-third standing for election every 2 years; and members of the House of Representatives (usually referred to as Congressmen) for 2 years.

Congress House. Headquarters of the Trades Union Congress in London.

Congressman. Member of the US House of Representatives (*see* CONGRESS).

Congress System. System established at the Congress of Vienna in 1815 by Britain, Russia, Austria and Prussia (the victors of the Napoleonic Wars 1804–1815), with the intention of establishing a series of regular diplomatic conferences, to maintain peace in Europe. Congresses were held at Aix-la-Chapelle in 1818, Troppau in 1820, Laibach in 1821, Verona in 1822 and St Petersburg in 1825. The system collapsed when Britain broke with it, due to growing disapproval of her partners' desire to interfere in the internal affairs of other countries. With George Canning (1770–1827) as Foreign Secretary, Britain strove to pursue a more liberal foreign policy and rejected the restrictive and conservative aims of Russia and Austria. Britain did not attend the final St Petersburg Congress, but left the other members trying to use the system to halt the spread of European liberalism.

conquistadores (Span., conquerors). The Spaniards who participated in the conquest of America between 1492 and the 1550s.

conscientious objector. Person who refuses to enlist for military service on moral or religious grounds. He or she may merely refuse to serve as a combatant and act instead in a medical capacity, or refuse to act in any way helpful to the war effort. The position of conscientious objectors has become more significant since the introduction of CONSCRIPTION. In Britain and the USA their position is accepted and they are exempted from military service if they can convince a tribunal that their objection is sincere. Political objection is not recognized. During the Vietnam War (1965–73) many Americans refused to serve in the forces for political reasons. An AMNESTY was later granted to them. In 1988, a movement began amongst some white South Africans to refuse military service. The Government responded harshly.

conscription (deriv. Lat., levying of troops). Recruitment for military service by compulsory enlistment. Modern conscription dates from the French *levée en masse* of August 1793, introduced by the Revolutionary government. During the 19th century most European countries introduced conscription; Britain, after much debate, finally instigated it by the National Service Act of February 1916 which remained effective until 1920. In April 1939 a new National Service Act conscripted men aged 20 to 41; this was extended in September 1939 to men between the ages of 19 and 41 and in December 1941 to men aged between 18 and 41 and single women of 20 to 30. When peace returned women were exempted and the period of service for men reduced to 18 months (2 years during the KOREAN WAR of 1950–53). Conscription was ended in Britain in 1960. In the USA 'selective service', a form of conscription, was introduced in May 1917, ending in 1919. In 1940 peacetime conscription was introduced for the first time by the Selective Service and Training Act, which was extended in 1942. In 1948 the Act was replaced by the Universal Military Training Act, operative in both the Korean War and Vietnam War (1965–73). New Zealand introduced conscription in August 1916, but it met great opposition; Australia twice rejected conscription in popular referendums during World War I, but the threat of Japanese invasion led both countries to introduce it in World War II. Canada introduced conscription by the Compulsory Military Service Act of 1917, but here again opposition was strong and remained so in World War II, particularly in Quebec.

Consistorium (deriv. Lat., hold firm). Tribunal established by Calvin in Geneva in 1541 to maintain religious and moral standards. It acted with great severity, proscribing all amusements and vigorously repressing criticism of Calvinist doctrine. Within 5 years it was responsible for 58 executions and 800 imprisonments.

Consolidated Fund. Fund established in 1787 by Pitt the Younger (1759–1806), combining or 'consolidating' previously separate customs and excise revenues in one fund. The revenues are held by the Bank of England in an EXCHEQUER account and are used to finance the national debt and the CIVIL LIST.

constable. In medieval England, the chief military officer of the royal household. The first identifiable constable was Walter of Gloucester during the reign of Henry I (1068–1135). In the 12th century lesser constables were also appointed but as they appear to have enjoyed only short-lived appointments their office was probably a political expedient. Since Tudor times the Lord High Constable has been appointed by the sovereign to serve on coronation day.

The title was more widely applied to lesser officers of the Crown of two types: the high constable, whose main task was to keep the peace within the HUNDRED; and the petty constable, subordinate to him, found in every town and parish, whose main function was to maintain the peace in the parish. Gradually the duties of serving summonses and executing warrants issued by justices of the peace devolved upon the petty constable. The emergence of the police force as we know it today made the office redundant and no petty constable has been appointed since 24 March 1873.

In the modern police force, the Metropolitan and City police are each under the orders of a Commissioner, but outside London each police force is under a Chief Constable. The term constable is also applied to the basic rank of policeman. In addition, special constables act as voluntary auxiliaries to the established police force, though magistrates retain the power to press people into service as special constables in emergencies.

constituency. Area represented by a British Member of Parliament, US Congressman, etc., after election by the voters, or constituents.

Constitutions of Clarendon. Enacted in 1164 at Henry II's hunting lodge of Clarendon, near Salisbury. Drawn up by a committee of barons and bishops, the Constitutions reasserted the Crown's supremacy over the Church and the jurisdiction of civil courts over ecclesiastical courts.

constructive engagement. United States policy towards South Africa under President Reagan, based on the argument that APARTHEID could be ended through preserving relations with the white regime rather than by imposing trade sanctions and diplomatic ostracism.

Consubstantiation. The belief of German Protestant reformer Martin Luther (1483-1546) that although the bread and wine remain unchanged at the Eucharist, Christ's body and blood are physically present, a concept that divided the reform movement.

consulados (Span.). Merchant gilds in Spain and, from the 16th century onwards, her South American colonies. They survived until the 19th century and attained great power; in Mexico City, for example, the consulado had influence enough to secure the removal of the viceroy and to choose his successor.

Consulate. Government of the French republic between November 1799 and 1804 established when Napoleon overthrew the DIRECTORY. It had three legislative chambers with an executive headed by three consuls. In practice Bonaparte, the First Consul, dominated the entire government throughout its life; it was dissolved when he declared himself emperor.

Consulta (Span.). Committee of three members – the Bishops of Arras, Barlaymont and Viglius – which was part of the Council of State of the Netherlands in the regency of Margaret of Parma (1559–1567).

containment. Policy adopted by the USA in 1947 in response to Russian expansion after the end of World War II, with the aim of containing communist influence to its existing territorial limits. Its clearest exposition was given by George Kennan, using the pseudonym 'X' in *Foreign Affairs* (July 1947). He argued that the USSR was more likely to be deterred from expansion by a resolute stance than Hitler had been but not by a single defeat. The need was therefore for 'patient but firm and vigilant containment of Russian expansive tendencies'. This policy has been pursued by economic assistance such as that given to Europe under the MARSHALL PLAN and by armed intervention as in Korea and Vietnam.

Continental System. Attempt by Napoleon Bonaparte (1769–1821) to exclude British trade from Europe between 1806 and 1813. He hoped that such economic warfare would bring Britain to her knees, but British naval superiority enabled her to break the system and it eventually collapsed. British retaliation included seizure of neutral ships trading with France and was one of the causes of the Anglo-American War of 1812.

contraband of war (deriv. Lat. *contra bannum*, against the ban). Goods which may not be supplied by a neutral to a belligerent party. The law of contraband permits the seizure of supplies destined for an enemy even if they are consigned to neutral ports and also permits belligerents to search neutral vessels. If contraband constitutes more than one half of the total cargo, the vessel itself may be seized. The London Declaration of 1909 was signed by representatives of every major power though it was never ratified. Under it, contraband was divided into two types, 'absolute' (arms and ammunition) and 'relative' (goods normally used for peaceful purposes, but which may also be used for war). The law of contraband covers only ingoing shipping since the stopping of enemy exports is covered by the law of reprisals. In both world wars, the law of reprisals has been invoked by both sides – by the Allies in retaliation for German submarine attacks and by the Germans in respect of *de facto* British BLOCKADES.

contracting in. Suggested reform of the relationship between British trade unions and the Labour Party, by which subscriptions would no longer automatically include political levy to the Labour Party. Trade unionists would have to elect positively that part of their subscriptions should be so used. Those in favour of

the idea argue that this would ensure that only true supporters of the Labour Party would be required to help finance it.

contracting out. Process whereby members of British trade unions must positively elect not to pay the political levy given by the trade union movement to the Labour Party, such payment otherwise being automatically included in their subscriptions. The system is much criticized, since under it apathetic trade unionists who do not bother to contract out finance a party of which they might not approve.

Contra-remonstrants (*also* Gomarists). Opponents of the ARMINIANS in early 17th-century Netherlands. The name is derived from their presentation to the States General of a counter-remonstrance against the five articles set out in the 1610 Arminian remonstrance.

Contras. Nicaraguan exiles in Honduras who supported the former right-wing régime of Anastasio 'Tachito' Somoza Debayle. Despite Somoza's death in Paraguay, they continue to oppose the government of the Sandinistas and have been responsible for large-scale armed incursions into north-west Nicaragua. The present Nicaraguan government claims that they are receiving military and financial aid on a massive scale from the USA and that the USA is helping them to plan an invasion of Nicaragua. However, the refusal of the US Congress to continue large-scale aid to the Contras suggests their cause is doomed.

conventicle (Lat., assembly). In Scotland, an open-air meeting for public worship held by ministers dispossessed when the RESTORATION established the Episcopal Church in

Scotland in 1660. Conventicles were declared illegal in 1662, then permitted by Indulgence in 1664, before being finally declared illegal and suppressed.

In England, the Conventicle Act of 1593 penalized those persons who declined to attend Church of England services and went to conventicles. An act of 1664 (part of the CLARENDON CODE) was more lenient, prohibiting only those conventicles attended by more than five persons not from the same household. The act expired in 1668, was renewed in 1670, but moderated by the Declaration of Indulgence in 1672 and 1688.

convention. (1) Meeting of the delegates of US political parties to formulate policy, nominate candidates for office, etc. The most important are held in the summer of every fourth year and at these the party's candidate for the presidential election the following November is chosen. The conventions are characterized by exuberant demonstrations of support and hard bargaining by the various candidates for nomination.

(2) International agreement concluded between two or more governments as opposed to two or more heads of state.

conventional warfare. Hostilities involving the use of non-nuclear weapons only.

Convention parliaments. (1) Parliament called in 1660 by General Monck (1608–1685), commander of the army in Scotland, when he and his men took control of London in February. Siding with the city against the RUMP parliament which the English army had reinstated, he forced the Rump to dissolve itself and replaced it with the MPs excluded in PRIDE'S PURGE. They dissolved themselves after organizing the elections which returned the Convention parliament. The Convention met on 25 April 1660 and was Presbyterian and Royalist in character. It restored the House of Lords and accepted Charles II's Declaration of Breda, outlining the terms on which he would assume the throne. Following Charles's return, an Act of 1 June 1660 was passed finally dissolving the LONG PARLIAMENT and recognizing the Convention as a lawful parliament. Having established the basis of financial and judicial continuity after the RESTORATION, the Convention was dissolved on 9 December 1660 to be succeeded by the CAVALIER PARLIAMENT.

(2) Parliament summoned in 1689 by William of Orange to consider the constitutional and practical problems caused by the flight of James II to France. It sat from February 1689 to February 1690. Many of its members had been MPs in the reign of Charles II and it reaffirmed in its composition the role of the country gentry as rulers of the nation. On 13 February 1689 it offered the crown jointly to William and his wife Mary. With the offer went a Declaration, later embodied in the BILL OF RIGHTS passed in August 1689, which determined the succession to the throne of Anne, daughter of James II; and made it illegal for a Catholic to take the throne or for the monarch to marry a Catholic. The Declaration of Rights contained a statement of the nation's case against James II and the assertion that 'the election of members of Parliament ought to be free', but the bill's negative provisos against suspension of legislation by the monarch and use of the DISPENSING POWER were something of an irrelevance following the overthrow of James. More important was the requirement that parliament approve the mainte-

nance of a standing army, which was reinforced by the Mutiny Act.

conventions of the constitution. In Britain, constitutional rules which are followed, though they do not have the force of law. Such rules are of vital importance to the functioning of the political process in a country which has no written constitution. For example, two conventions – that ministers are collectively responsible to parliament for the actions and policies of the government as a whole, and that ministers are individually responsible for the work of their departments – ensure the accountability of the government.

convocation. Assembly summoned to deliberate upon ecclesiastical affairs. In the Church of England the provinces of Canterbury and York each have their own convocation, whose history dates back to Archbishop Theodore's occupation of office (668–690). Under the ANGEVINS, convocations dealt not only with ecclesiastical affairs but also acted as a clerical parliament, claiming the right to tax the clergy and make payments to the royal exchequer. From the 15th century both convocations have had two houses, an upper house of the archbishop and diocesan bishops and a lower of inferior clergy. In 1533 the Act of Submission of the Clergy prohibited convocations without the king's permission; in 1660 the clergy renounced its claim to the right to tax itself and since 1663 has been taxed by parliament. For a time after 1688 the convocations displayed an independent turn of mind which proved an embarrassment to the government. In 1716 the convocation censured Benjamin Moadly, Bishop of Bangor, for his work *A Preservative against the Principles and Practices of the Non-Jurors both in Church and State*, defending

the secular power's right to deprive the NON-JURORS of office. The following year, George I suspended convocation which then met only rarely until the mid-19th century.

Since then they have met two or three times a year and are concerned mainly with reform of the canons of ecclesiastical law.

convoy. Naval tactic by which merchant ships travel in groups under the protection of warships.

co-operative movement. Movement with the aim of conducting economic activities through co-operating associations rather than through the business processes of CAPITALISM, avoiding consumer exploitation by abolishing profit. Consumers' 'co-ops' run a shop or chain of shops, buying goods wholesale and selling at current prices, and redistributing profits to members. Producers' 'co-ops' run a factory which is the joint property of the members who divide the profits; they may work in it themselves or hire labour. Farmers' 'co-ops' buy farmstuffs cheaply for members, guarantee loans and help market produce.

Co-operativism was one of the early forms of SOCIALISM and was strong in Britain between 1837 and 1934. In 1844 the modern pattern of co-operativism, run on business lines and created by workmen, emerged at Rochdale. In 1863 the Co-operative Wholesale Society was founded in Manchester to become one of the world's largest trading organizations. In 1917 the co-ops founded their own political party, closely associated with the Labour Party. The Scottish CWS, founded in 1868, collaborates with its English counterpart but is distinct from it.

In Germany, the reformer Raiffeisen was responsible for a widespead agricultural co-operative movement in the late 19th century, with the primary aim of guaranteeing members credit, thereby securing cheaper finance. Similar urban lending associations were formed at the same time, the brainchild of Schultze-Delitzsch.

The movement is common throughout Europe and is particularly widespread in Scandinavia. For many years a nominal agricultural co-operativism was the hallmark of Soviet agriculture (*see* KOLKHOZ). Canada, Australia and New Zealand all have important co-operatives, particularly in agriculture, but the USA has only a small movement.

Copperheads. Name given by the FEDERALISTS to the 'Peace Party' in the Northern states during the American Civil War (1861–65). It derives from the venomous and deadly copperhead snake which does not provide a warning rattle before striking.

co-prosperity sphere. Name given by Japan to eastern and south-eastern Asia in the period between World War I and World War II. The area which Japan hoped to control and develop extended from the USSR's Pacific coast to Timor and from New Guinea to Burma. In World War II Japan did succeed for a time in controlling the whole area except for parts of China and New Guinea and the Soviet territory.

copyhold. In late medieval England, tenure held by service, as opposed to leasehold or freehold, although generally the service was commuted in favour of a small annual payment. It developed from the VILLEIN system following the BLACK DEATH of the late 14th century and the PEASANTS' REVOLT of 1381, but the copyholder was freer than the villein had been and subject to a diminishing number of manorial customs. He held a written title to his land and a copy of his admission was kept on the manorial COURT ROLL. The property of copyholder dying intestate and without issue reverted to the lord of the manor. Copyhold tenure was abolished in 1926.

Cordeliers (Fr.). Members of a Parisian revolutionary club during the early days of the French Revolution, largely followers of Georges Jacques Danton (1759–94). The name derived from the regular meeting place of the club, an old monastery of the Franciscan Cordelier order.

cordon sanitaire (Fr., sanitary line). Term applied to the chain of states created along the borders of France following the defeat of Napoleon in 1815 whose purpose was to provide a zone in which any recurrence of revolution or aggression on France's part could be contained. The same was done on the western borders of Russia in 1918 with the purpose of containing communism.

CORE. Congress on Racial Equality, founded in the USA in 1942 to obtain CIVIL RIGHTS for blacks.

cornage (O Fr., horn). In medieval England, rent for cattle paid by freemen, common in the north of England; in Cumberland it was known as *notegeld* (from OE *neat*, cattle).

Corn Laws. Regulations controlling Britain's import and export of grain, recorded as early as the 12th century but only of major political importance in the late 18th and early 19th centuries. An act passed in 1791 to restrict the import of foreign grain was not unusual, but the French Wars (1792–1815) meant that domestic production could not match demand. As prices rose there were food riots (1795) and the protective legislation became a focal point of grievance. When the war ended prices began to fall and the landlords clamoured for greater protection from imports.

In 1815 a Corn Law was passed prohibiting the import of corn until the domestic price had risen to eight shillings a quarter. This measure failed to stabilize prices: dealers kept corn off the market to force prices up above eight shillings, then flooded the market with imported grain causing price slumps. Furthermore, the high cost of bread, a staple of the popular diet, meant that less was spent on other agricultural produce causing an agrarian recession. In 1828 a sliding scale was introduced, by which high duties replaced total prohibition, the duties on imports being lowered as home prices rose. Again speculators stored imported corn until the duty fell to its lowest point, and then flooded the market at the point where domestic prices were highest.

Because the Corn Laws protected the interests of the landed class, they drew the opposition of the emerging industrial middle class and in 1839 the ANTI-CORN LAW LEAGUE was founded, soon gathering working class support. A series of bad harvests up to 1842 and a trade depression between 1839 and 1843 swelled the League's ranks: in 1842 Sir Robert Peel, the Prime Minister, reduced the duty on corn. However, it was the failure of the Irish potato crop in 1845 and the outbreak of widespread famine in Ireland that persuaded Peel and parliament of the need to repeal the Corn Laws. In 1846 the duty was very greatly reduced and in January 1847 it was suspended until March 1848. After 1848 duty was fixed at one shilling a quarter and abolished in 1869 by the Chancellor, Robert Lowe.

corporate state. State whose economic and political life is based on trade and on professional corporations rather than territorial units. Thus members of parliament would be elected by vocational corporations instead of by geographical constituencies and would regulate industrial production and working conditions. The arguments in favour of such a system are that it would exclude party politics, prevent the state from growing too powerful and correspond to the links which truly bind people (professional ties, fellowship in the workplace and shared economic interest) rather than haphazard territorial association and that it would end class warfare. Believers in the theory have no particular bias to right or left although the societies which have come closest to being corporate states were Italy under FASCISM and Portugal under the dictator Salazar (1928-74). The Catholic Church has tended to favour the idea and NAZI Germany toyed with plans for it.

Corresponding Society. Organization founded by a London shoemaker, Thomas Hardy (1752–1832), in January 1792 which he led with the philologist and radical politician John Horne Tooke (1736–1812). It advocated annual parliaments and universal male suffrage and established 'corresponding committees' in several provincial cities. From the start it attracted the hostility of a government scared that the French Revolution might spread to Britain, and at a meeting in Edinburgh in 1793 it was thought prudent to organize a way for the society to work secretly. Several of its members were arrested and sentenced to TRANSPORTATION; Hardy and Tooke were tried and acquitted of treason. The society was finally banned in 1799 and thereafter disbanded.

cortes (Span., courts). The various parliaments of medieval Spain and latterly the national legislature of modern Spain. The cortes developed from the right of elected representatives of free cities to attend and participate in the deliberations of the king's court, the curia regis. By the early 13th century, cortes with similar procedures and functions existed in Leon and Castile and when the two kingdoms were united in 1230 they began holding joint assemblies. Other cortes were established in Catalonia (1218), Aragon (1274), Valencia (1283) and Navarre (1300).

The cortes consisted of three estates: the nobility, clergy and procuradores, who were town clerks or attorneys elected by fortified boroughs and given written instructions by the electorate. By the 14th century the procuradores were the dominant estate as it was only they who could consent to the extraordinary taxes required by the crown. The cortes did not meet as of right, but were convened when and where the king wished. Their power declined in the 16th and 17th centuries as Spain's growing empire overseas relieved the monarchy of the need for extraordinary taxes. By the early 18th century their authorizing of royal actions was merely a formality.

After the French invasion of Spain in 1808, the cortes had a brief new lease of life but was suppressed when Ferdinand VII returned from exile. It was restored again between 1820 and 1823 but from 1823 to 1833 ceased to function during the general suppression of liberalism in Spain.

Its history in the 20th century has been equally turbulent. In 1923 it was suppressed by the dictator Primo de Rivera and was only reconstructed by Gen. Franco in 1942 to serve as a mere cypher to his dictatorship. Members were appointed by FAL-ANGIST agencies to acknowledge legislation prepared by Franco.

With Franco's death in 1975 the monarchy was re-established and on 15 June 1977 Spain held its first free election since 1936. In 1978 a democratic constitution was introduced under which there is a bicameral parliament, the Cortes General. The lower house, the Congress of Deputies, has 350 members elected by universal suffrage every four years. The upper house, the Senate, has four members from each of Spain's provinces and autonomous communities, again elected every four years.

corvée (Fr.). Term originally applied to regular work owed by freed men and serfs to their feudal lords. Feudal obligations disappeared in France in the 15th and 16th centuries after which the term became synonymous with forced labour on public projects, periodically revived when state revenues were too low to hire sufficient labour. From 1726 the corvée was used in France to provide free labour on roads; it was abolished following the revolution of 1789. Today the word denotes an unpleasant task or drudge and, in military parlance, fatigue duties.

In Egypt, the term was applied to the centuries-old system of forced labour whereby peasants removed mud from the bottom of canals that was caused by the seasonal rising of the Nile. The soilworkers (*fellahin*) were freed from this obligation by the British administration in 1882.

Cossacks (Russ., adventurers). A distinct social group inhabiting the lands between Lithuania and Muscovy and the lands of the Crim TARTARS in the 15th century, who were originally runaway peasants. By the 16th century they had established themselves principally in the river basins of the Dnieper and the Don.

They entered military service under the grand dukes of Muscovy and Lithuania but dissatisfaction with the central government in Muscovy led to numerous revolts in the 17th and 18th centuries. They maintained a degree of independence until the reign of Catherine II; their last rising as a 'free' race failed in 1773–1774. Catherine razed their territories, extended serfdom to the Ukraine and destroyed the form of government they had developed, based on the ATAMAN. Cossacks continued to serve in the armies of Imperial Russia and harried Napoleon's army in 1812. In December 1917, led by Generals Kornilov and Kaledin, they revolted against the BOLSHEVIK government and were engaged in the civil war against the communist RED ARMY until they were defeated in 1918.

cottereaux (Fr.). Mercenaries employed by the French kings in the 12th century.

Council Communism. Influenced by workers' councils activity in the 1917–20 European revolutionary upheavals, Council Communism rejected BOLSHEVIK party-led socialism. Marxist, but with strong anarchist undertones, it advocated economic and social organization based on a network of factory councils. Its leading theorist was a Dutch astronomer, Anton Pannekoek (1873–1960).

Council of Europe. Organization set up on 5 May 1949 by Belgium, Britain, Denmark, France, Ireland, Italy, the Netherlands, Norway and Sweden; it was also joined by Greece, Iceland and Turkey later in 1949, West Germany in 1951, Austria in 1956, Cyprus in 1961, Switzerland in 1963 and Malta in 1965. Independent of the EUROPEAN COM-MUNITY, its purpose is discussion between members of areas of common interest except national defence. It seeks to achieve greater European unity based on common heritage and to promote human rights. Any European nation which recognises the basic rights embodied in individual freedom, the rule of law and political liberty may join.

It functions through two main institutions: an executive Committee of Ministers which meets on average twice a year (deputies meet up to ten times a year) and a European Assembly which meets but cannot legislate for one week three times a year in Strasbourg. This advisory and consultative body normally debates reports on matters of common concern. In April 1955 the Council set up a Commission and Court of Human Rights which hears complaints made by individuals against their national governments, or by member states against others. It has also sought ways of substituting a system of European Federalism for the present collection of national sovereign states.

Council of State. In England, body in which executive power was vested during the INTERREGNUM of 1649–1660, elected by the RUMP parliament. It had 40 members, 31 of whom were MPs and the remainder army officers. The INSTRUMENT OF GOVERNMENT concentrated a great deal of power in its hands. Under the PROTECTORATE, the executive was comprised of a council of 22 members and the Lord Protector: there was then no procedure for removal of council members so parliament was effectively deprived of control. Following the HUMBLE PETITION AND ADVICE its powers were curbed and in 1660 it was abolished.

coup d'état (Fr., stroke of state).

Sudden change in the government of a state, brought about by force or illegally, by a person or persons already in a position of political or military power, as opposed to a revolution, which involves mass participation of those without powerful individual positions. Examples include the overthrow of the French Republic in 1851 by Louis Napoleon who then became emperor. In recent years Africa and Latin America have been the regions where coups are most common.

coupon (Fr., detached piece or slice). Name given to the letter of approval signed by Lloyd George, leader of the Coalition Liberals, and Bonar Law, leader of the Conservatives, which was distributed to candidates in the 1918 or 'Coupon' election. 531 coupons were issued (150 going to Liberal candidates) to signify that the holders had the approval of the wartime coalition leaders and were not to be challenged by candidates of the other party in the coalition. 362 'coupon holders' were returned, the majority of whom were Conservatives. Thus the 1918–22 coalition government had a Conservative bias, although Lloyd George was the Prime Minister.

Cours d'heritage (Fr.). Ancient feudal court in Jersey whose jurisdiction extended to all disputes over landed property.

Cours plénière (Fr., plenary court). In medieval France and England, an assembly of the BARONAGE called on great festivals of the year.

court roll. Written record of proceedings in court, usually concerning manorial proceedings such as wills, grants, the surrenders and admissions of tenants and the regulations of common land. Regarded as the property of the lord of the manor, they are kept by his steward or agent, but are of the nature of a public book held also for the benefit of tenants. In an issue between two tenants the law courts will grant an inspection of the court rolls.

Covenanters. Name given to supporters of the National Covenant of 1638, drawn up by the TABLES in opposition to Charles I's attempts to Anglicanize the Scottish church by enforcing the use of a new prayer book. In 1581, the Scottish Protestant leaders, the Lords of the Congregation, had entered into a covenant designed to protect the Protestant religion which was signed by James VI. The National Covenant led to the BISHOPS' WARS and, in 1640, the calling of the LONG PARLIAMENT.

On 25 September 1643, Parliament adopted the Solemn League and Covenant between the English and Scots parliamentarians in opposition to Charles I. This attempted to pledge the signatories to the establishment of PRESBYTERIANISM in England, although a sentence added by Sir Henry Vane to the effect that the form of religious organization to be adopted should be 'according to the word of God' allowed greater religious liberty than was originally intended. Under the terms of the Covenant, the Scots received £30,000 a month and in return undertook to provide an army to fight the Royalists. The Covenant was accepted by Charles Prince of Wales in the early 1650s in his efforts to secure Scots help to put him on the English throne. After his restoration in 1660 the Covenant was declared illegal by parliament in 1661 and all copies of it were ordered to be burnt.

cowboys. Name originally applied to British marauders on the banks of the Hudson River during the American War of Independence (1775–81). The term later came to denote the cattlemen of the mid- and far-west of the USA.

Creoles (Fr.; *also* Span. *Criollos*; Port. *Crioulos*). Whites born in the Spanish or Portuguese colonies of America, whose social and political position was below that of European-born whites, creating antagonism between the two groups. Creoles provided the leaders for many of the 19th-century independence movements. Today the word is used in connection with the old French, Spanish and Portuguese American colonies; it is often taken, wrongly, to mean a person with some negro blood.

Cristeros (Span.). Right-wing Mexican terrorist movement, active in the late 1920s, led by militant Roman Catholics who opposed the anti-clerical regime of Plutaco Elias Calles. The name derives from the battle cry *Cristo Rey* (Christ the King).

Croppies. Name given to Irish rebels in 1798; also, a rare name for the Roundheads during the English civil war.

crossbencher. A member of the House of Lords who demonstrates political neutrality by not taking a Party whip.

CRS (Fr., Compagnie Républicaine de Sécurité). A highly trained nationally controlled riot police force used for public order duties, prominent in the 1968 MAY EVENTS and in industrial disputes.

crusade (deriv. Lat. *cruciata*, cross). Generally, a fight, either spiritual or physical, against evil, anti-Christian beliefs or the enemies of Christianity. More specifically, the military campaigns of feudal Christendom against the Islamic peoples in the Near East between 1096 and 1254 AD. The continuous warfare between Spanish Christians and Islamic Moors on the Iberian Peninsula between the 7th and 12th centuries and the actions of the TEUTONIC KNIGHTS in East Prussia might also be called crusades. Finally, in 1208 AD, a crusade was launched against the heretic ALBIGENSIANS.

Religious fervour pervaded all these activities. Popes promised that Christians killed on crusade would go to heaven and St Bernard of Clairvaux (*see* CISTERCIANS) urged criminals to join the crusades and thus gain forgiveness for their sins. The crusades were also the result of social-economic conditions in western Europe: the feudal system was becoming more rigid and lands in the East were available for conquest by the younger landless sons of the European nobility. The prospect of trade with the East drew many merchants to the Holy Land in later crusades while plunder and higher living standards were also an attraction. Finally, in these years the concept of the knight carrying out 'great deeds' was emerging to capture the imagination of the feudal nobility, making adventure and chivalry further reasons for 'taking the cross'.

Cuban missile crisis. Period of extreme tension in the COLD WAR from 22 to 28 October 1962. Intelligence agencies in Washington, aware of increased Soviet interest in Cuban affairs, discovered on 16 October from aerial reconnaissance photographs evidence that Soviet ballistic missiles capable of delivering nuclear warheads on US cities were being installed in Cuba. During the previous month the Soviet government had admitted supplying arms to Cuba but denied that they were offensive in nature. On 22 October Pres. Kennedy declared that the US navy would blockade Cuba and requested the USSR to remove its missiles. The Soviet reply on 26 October was that they would be removed if NATO missiles were removed from Turkey. Pres. Kennedy found this offer unacceptable and the world faced a real threat of imminent nuclear war. Khrushchev, the Soviet premier, realising perhaps that the USSR had 'overplayed its hand', agreed on 28 October to remove the missiles. Castro, the Cuban premier, would not allow UN observers into Cuba to check that they had been dismantled, but the US Defense Department accepted by the first week in November that they had been. The blockade was ended on 20 November following Soviet promises to remove bombers and missile technicians by the end of the month. Kennedy's resoluteness and calm during this period of great tension marked him as a leading statesman on the world stage.

Cultural Revolution. Name given to the period of reassertion of Maoist doctrine in China between 1965 and 1968. On 3 September 1965 Marshal Lin Pao urged students to emphasize the fundamental principles of the Chinese revolutionary movement and to adopt a critical attitude towards liberal and 'Krushchevian' elements within the Chinese Communist Party. Criticism led by the RED GUARDS found expression in giant parades and wall-posters, party apparatus was purged and criticism extended even to the nominees of the President, Liu Shao-Chi. A personality cult centred on Mao Tse-tung was also inaugurated. But the activities of the Red Guards and the excitement they generated closed schools and colleges and threatened the Chinese economy. By late 1966 the Prime Minister Chou En-lai, who had earlier encouraged public criticism of party members, sought to restore normality. The Revolution may be said to have ended in October 1968 with the dismissal of Liu Shao-Chi from all his posts.

Curia Regis (Lat., king's court). Term denoting two different, but related, institutions. It referred to the place where the king resided with his chief officials and household and also to the supreme central court where government business was transacted. Under the Norman kings the term denoted the assembly of feudal magnates in whose presence every royal measure of importance, legislative, judicial and financial, was taken, such as the CONCORDAT of London in 1170 resolving the investiture conflict between the crown and papacy. However, as the king's followers became settled on their own estates they ceased to travel with him and the Curia Regis was only assembled three times a year, at Christmas, Easter and Whitsun – the three 'crown hearings'.

This system of convening the Curia proved cumbersome and its defects were rectified by an inner council, the nucleus of which was drawn from the royal household. Initially there was no distinction between the two bodies, the assembly of all the magnates merely being the Curia Regis in full session. But the growth of governmental business gradually left the inner council and the household as the effective instruments of government and it was from this inner council that later administrative institutions stemmed. In early days the EXCHEQUER was the counting house of the king, CHANCERY his writing office, etc. Eventually such departments detached themselves from the household and the Curia

Regis. By 1172 the Exchequer Court had been established by Roger le Poer, Bishop of Salisbury, with the Barons of the Curia Regis sitting for financial purposes as Barons of the Exchequer. In 1178, during the reign of Henry II, five specially selected judges were appointed to hear crown pleas – the origin of the King's Bench division; following MAGNA CARTA a third court was added to hear 'Common pleas'.

The executive and advisory role of the Curia, as opposed to its administrative functions, was also developing. During the reign of Edward I (1271–1307) a secret council met to advise the king, consisting of the more important and experienced members of the nobility and probably those committed to the king's cause (*See* PRIVY COUNCIL). During the 13th century the barons began to claim attending the Curia as a right, arguing that laws could not be changed or annulled without their consent. By the 14th century the Curia Regis had been replaced by the elements which later grew into the full English parliamentary system.

cursitor (Old Fr.). Junior clerk of CHANCERY charged with writing out formal common-form writs. By the 14th century their number was fixed at 24. They lived at the Inns of Chancery, each dealing with the business of one or more assigned counties. Incorporated in 1573, they occupied an office and adjoining hall in Chancery Lane, London. The advent of printed forms signalled a decline in their usefulness and they were abolished in 1835.

Cursitor Baron. An office formerly attached to the EXCHEQUER Court, abolished in 1856.

Custos Rotulorum (Lat.). Keeper of the Rolls or the records of the sessions of the peace, originally appointed by the LORD CHANCELLOR, and later (1545) by a bill signed by the King. He is always a JUSTICE OF THE PEACE. By the Local Government (Clerks) Act of 1931 the CLERK OF THE PEACE has custody of all county records and documents subject to his power.

Cymru am Byth (Welsh). 'Wales forever!'; slogan of the Welsh nationalists. *See* PLAID CYMRU.

Czar. *See* TSAR.

D

dacoity (Hindi). Violent gang robbery, especially brigandage and highway robbery, prevalent in India during the British RAJ.

In 1772 Warren Hastings decreed that every convicted dacoit should be executed in his own village, his family enslaved and the village fined; in 1782 the Zemindars, who were often in league with dacoits, were made responsible for crime in their districts. In 1852 over 30 bands of dacoits were still active around Calcutta alone and between 1905 and 1915 dacoity became even more common. In remote regions of India it still poses a problem today.

Dáil Éireann (Ir., assembly of Ireland). The House of Representatives in the Irish OIREACHTAS, with 144 members elected for five years by adult suffrage on a system of proportional representation. The name is often abbreviated to Dáil.

daimyō (Jap., great name). Title of the feudal lords who emerged in Japan in the 14th and 15th centuries. By the 16th century – a period of intense, continuous warfare and successive convulsions of the social order – they were in control of almost the whole country. The older daimyō families (*shugo* daimyōs) were replaced by lesser lords (*sengoku* dai-

myōs) who were in turn overthrown by their vassals (*shokuhō* daimyōs). In the 17th century many daimyōs were dispossessed but a third of the country remained in the hands of about a hundred of them. Although they owed nominal allegiance to the Emperor and in some cases to the SHOGUN, daimyōs were virtually independent sovereigns whose power was only reduced after 1867 by the modernizing Meiji government's establishment of central control.

Dalai Lama (Tibetan, chief priest). Spiritual and temporal leader of Tibet, held always to be a reincarnation of a previous Dalai Lama. He delegated his temporal powers of government to the DES-RI. From 1715 to 1913 Tibet was under Chinese suzerainty and he was a vassal. In 1951 Chinese troops again occupied Tibet and following a major rebellion in 1959 the Dalai Lama and some 9,000 of his subjects fled to India.

Dambusters. 617 Squadron, Royal Air Force, which carried out a precision bombing raid on the Moehne and Eder dams in the Ruhr industrial belt, the centre of German munitions production, 16/17 May 1943, using 'bouncing bombs' developed by Barnes Wallis, releasing 330 million tons of water, killing 1,294 civillians, destroying or badly damaging 125 factories and 46 bridges.

Danelaw (OE, Danes' law). In 9th- and 10th-century England, the law of the Danish invaders. Also the area in which it was enforced: the kingdoms of Northumbria and East Anglia and the Danish boroughs grouped around Leicester, Nottingham, Stamford and Lincoln.

Dark Ages. The period between the decline of the western Roman Empire in the 4th century and the creation of a new west European empire under Charlemagne, crowned Emperor of the West in 800. 'Dark' generally refers to the lack of sources available to historians rather than the period's culture.

dark horse. A candidate for political office who makes an unexpected appearance or rapidly achieves unforeseen prominence.

Darwinism. The evolutionary theories of Charles Darwin (1806–82) set out in *On the Origin of Species by Means of Natural Selection* (1859) and *The Descent of Man* (1871). Darwinism's central concepts are the struggle for existence, the survival of the fittest, and natural selection. *See also* SOCIAL DARWINISM.

Dauphin (Fr.). Title borne by the eldest sons of the French kings from 1349 to the revolution of 1830.

Dawes Plan. Plan presented by American banker Charles G. Dawes (1865–1951) to the Allied Reparations Committee in April 1924, involving an annual payment by Germany of REPARATIONS according to a fixed scale. Simultaneously the German State Bank was to be re-organized and foreign loans made to Germany in order to stabilize her currency. Between 1924 and 1929 the plan enabled Germany to meet the harsh treaty obligations imposed on her by the Allies at the Paris Peace Conference (1919–20).

D-Day. Code name for the first day of Operation Overlord, 6 June 1944, which saw allied troops land on the coast of Normandy between the river Orne and the Cotentin peninsula, in the largest ever seaborne invasion. Three divisions from the Canadian and British army landed on 'Gold', 'Juno', and 'Sword' beaches west of the Orne and two divisions of the American First Army at 'Omaha' and 'Utah' beaches one on either side of the Vire estuary. After a fierce battle on 'Omaha' a substantial beach-head – 24 miles long and 4 miles deep – was established by nightfall, at a cost of 10,000 casualties.

decade (Fr.). Ten-day week introduced by the revolutionary government in France in 1793.

Decembrists (*also* Dekbrists). Conspiracy of army officers in St Petersburg who attempted to overthrow the Tsarist government in December 1825. They were severely punished by Nicholas I whose reign proved particularly repressive. The attempted coup is sometimes referred to as the 'first' Russian Revolution.

decimation (deriv. Lat., tenth). In ancient Rome a military punishment (for mutiny, etc) in which one man in ten, his name drawn by lot, was executed. Also, in England, an arbitrary income-tax of ten per cent levied by Cromwell's MAJOR GENERALS on royalist sympathisers in 1655–56.

decolonization. The post-World War II withdrawal by the European powers from their overseas possessions. Britain left India and Pakistan in 1947 and had freed the majority of its African colonies by the 1960s while Belgium, the Netherlands and Portugal had decolonized by the 1970s. France was forced out of INDO-CHINA, Tunisia and Algeria in the 1950s following protracted wars.

deed poll (deed + ME *poll*, to cut even). A deed made by one party needing no duplicate or parts, which was cut straight at the upper edge. (Where there was more than one party to a deed it was indented, i.e. each part was cut at an acute angle on the upper edge). In medieval England, deeds poll were usually grants in perpetuity, but today they are restricted, usually to instruments signed, sealed and delivered for changing personal names.

de facto recognition (Lat., in fact). Actions which imply acceptance of a political change but which fall short of formally recognizing it. A new government or state emerging from a civil war, for example, might thus be recognized as possessing effective authority over its territory but DE JURE RECOGNITION will not be granted until such time as it has shown itself to be enduring or ready to honour commitments.

Defenders. Name adopted by agrarian bands of Irish Roman Catholics, largely living in Ulster, formed in the 1780s for self-defence against the PEEP O'DAY BOYS.

Defensor fidei (Lat., defender of the faith; *abbr*. Fid. Def.). Title conferred on Henry VIII of England by Pope Leo X in 1521 for his defence of the seven sacraments in opposition to Luther. After Henry broke with Rome and assumed headship of the Church of England in 1534, Pope Paul III withdrew the title but Parliament confirmed it in 1544 and it has been used ever since by English monarchs, who are the heads of the Church of England.

Defenestration of Prague. Incident at the start of the THIRTY YEARS WAR. When the Austrian monarch Ferdinand II threatened the religious liberties of Bohemian Protestants, Count von Thürn led Protestant nobles to the palace in Prague on 23 May 1618 and threw two Roman Catholic governors and a secretary out of a window. Their fall was broken by a rubbish heap.

deflation. Opposite of inflation, that is, a reduction in the volume or velocity of circulation of money causing prices to fall and credit to be restricted. Since limitation of purchasing power reduces demand for both imports and domestic goods, deflation may ease a deficit in the BALANCE OF PAYMENTS but can result in lower output and unemployment. An increase in interest rates normally diverts money into savings and reduces circulation, thereby causing deflation.

de jure recognition (Lat., according to law). Formal and binding recognition of a political change by a government, such as occurs with the emergence of a new government or state after a civil war. *See also* DE FACTO RECOGNITION.

Delinquents. Term applied generally to royalists after a declaration by Parliament on 6 September 1642 that it would not disband its armed forces until King Charles I delivered to it all 'delinquents' and other 'malignant and disaffected persons'. By 1648 the king himself was being referred to as the 'chief delinquent'.

demagogy (deriv. Gk., people + leader). Derogatory term for a popular leader who appeals to the baser instincts of the masses by pandering to prejudice and passion.

demesne (AFr., of or belonging to a lord). In medieval England, lands that were not conferred to feudal tenants after William I had laid claim to all the land in the kingdom. Known as the Ancient or Royal Demesne, they were managed by stewards of the crown. From 1689 the revenues from such land that remained in the direct possession of the crown were surrendered to parliament in return for annual votes of money to the crown known as the CIVIL LIST.

Demilitarized Zone. Zone that roughly follows the 38th parallel dividing North from South Korea, established in 1953 following the invasion of South Korea by the communist North in 1950. Acting for the UN, US and British troops helped the South expel the invaders. No military forces of either side are allowed to enter the Zone, although in 1974 the first of a series of North Korean tunnels beneath it were discovered.

democracy (deriv. Gk., people + power). Government by the people, originally as practised in the city states of ancient Greece where popular assemblies of the people, or plebiscites, held control over all questions of legislation and policy. Indirect democracy, in which the people control legislation via representative institutions such as parliaments, has proved more suitable to western Europe, the USA and the BRITISH COMMONWEALTH OF NATIONS. It involves, as a rule, certain common principles. There is a separation of powers, with each branch of the legislative, executive and judicial functions of government being prevented from interfering with the others and being exercised by different persons. Legislation originates in a freely elected parliament and executive power lies either with a government responsible to the legislature (as in Britain) or with a president answerable to the people (as in the USA). Elections are held at regular intervals offering the electorate a free choice between two or more parties. The rule of law applies, under which people are free from arrest unless charged with a specified crime, at which time they are fairly tried before an independent tribunal. There is freedom of speech, opinion and association.

The system began to evolve in Britain in the 17th century and was established in France and the USA, following revolutions, in the 18th century. In communist countries these principles of democracy are not generally practised, but it is claimed nonetheless that communist societies are truly 'democratic' since the state owns and controls the means of production, and uses them for greater benefit of all citizens, ensuring that the common good is placed before private interests.

Democrats. Members of one of the two major US political parties. The Democratic Party began between 1787 and 1792 as a group of voters supporting Thomas Jefferson in his opposition to the FEDERALISTS and his argument for restriction of the powers of the Federal Government. It was called Democratic-Republican or Republican to emphasise its anti-monarchist views. In the mid-1820s its name was the National Republican Party; during the administration of Andrew Jackson (1828–36) it adopted the name Democratic.

Despite being a powerful force in CONGRESS it was not until 1801 that its candidate, Jefferson, became President. Between 1817 and 1825, the 'era of good feeling', it was the only party. It was split in the 1850s over the issue of slavery, with the northern Democrats siding with the REPUBLICANS. In the 20th century the southern states have continued to vote Democrat on most occasions; the party has also attracted support from the northern industrial cities and ethnic groups.

denazification. Process undertaken by the Allies after World War II of locating NAZIS and removing them from private and public positions. Both party members and those who merely prospered under them were sought, to be punished or requalified for professional work. Special courts, *Spruchkammern*, were established which were empowered to confiscate property, disqualify people from practising professions and impose sentences of up to 10 years' hard labour.

The system failed: minor officials were victimised while leading Nazis escaped. Higher courts often quashed the sentences of the *Spruchkammern* and the German population on the whole sympathized with the Nazis. Judges hostile to the Nazis were frequently removed from their posts. Many Nazis returned to public life and in the 1950s over 70 per cent of the German civil service were ex-Nazis. *See also* EPURATION.

Dengism. The modernizing programme introduced in China by Deng Xiaoping in 1984 which attempted economic advance through decentralization, individual enterprise, market forces, and foreign investment. Agricultural collectivism was weakened to boost pro-duction, while in industry managerial authority was strengthened and factories were allowed to retain their profits. The reforms were intensified at the 13th Communist Congress in 1987 but were threatened in late 1988 by inflation and fears of mass unemployment.

deodand (deriv. Lat., gift to God). In early medieval England, any object used to bring about a person's death, which was believed somehow to share in the guilt. The object itself or, more usually, its equivalent value in money, was forfeited to the Crown and applied to charitable purposes. Deodands were abolished in 1846.

depression. Decline in economic activity, manifested in a falling off of trade and of general prosperity. The term is often used specifically to describe the word slump of 1929–35 (*see* GREAT DEPRESSION), which began with overproduction and consequent price collapse in primary products and was worsened by a general financial collapse beginning on WALL STREET and spreading to Europe in May 1931. The Depression had various consequences: mass unemployment by 1932, 13.7 million in the USA, 2.9 million in Britain, 5.5 million in Germany; increased economic planning in many countries; tariff walls to protect domestic industries which led to a further decline in world trade; the undermining of the WEIMAR Republic and the accession to power in Germany of Hitler.

The world moved back into depression in 1979. During that year the Islamic revolution in Iran halved Iranian oil production while at the same time other OPEC states sought to raise the price of oil. The cost of a barrel rose first from $13 to $25; by 1980 it was at $32. The fuel shortage led to a fall in industrial output, high inflation and BALANCE OF PAYMENTS deficits in industrialized countries. A rise in interest rates and a fall in investment led to further falls in production and rising unemployment.

Britain and the USA were particularly badly affected and the fall in their demand for imports created difficulties for Japan, Germany and other exporters. There followed a general falling off of world trade and threats to the GATT. The fear of encouraging inflation led both the Conservative government in Britain and Pres. Reagan in the USA to resist demands for increased public expenditure to stimulate the economy. Estimates of the true level of unemployment varied but in 1983 it was thought that some 4 million people were out of work in Britain and 10 million in the USA.

descamisados (Span., the shirtless ones). Urban poor in Argentina who supported Juan Domingo Perón (1895–1974) and his wife Eva. As Minister of Labour and Social Security in the government of the 'Group of United Officers' which seized power in June 1943, Perón made generous decrees regarding wages and welfare. When he was imprisoned in October 1945 by resurgent democrats backed by US agents, the descamisados thronged the streets of Buenos Aires threatening civil war until he was released. Perón became a dictator after victories in the 1946 and 1951 elections but the death of his wife Eva in July 1952 and a conflict with the Catholic Church lost him much support. Following an attempted uprising in June 1955 he was forced into exile. His cause recovered strength in the early 1970s and he returned as President in October 1973 until his death in July 1974. *See also* PERONISMO.

'Desert Fox'. Erwin Rommel (1891–1944), so nicknamed for his intuitive strategy in leading the German Afrika Korps during World War II.

'Desert Rats'. Nickname for the British Eighth Army which fought in North Africa under the leadership of Gen. (later Field Marshal) Bernard Montgomery (1887–1976) between 1942 and 1944.

Des-Ri (Tibetan). Political ruler of Tibet to whom the spiritual and nominal political ruler, the DALAI LAMA, delegated the functions of government.

destalinization. Process which commenced at the 1956 20th Party Congress in the USSR, following the death of Soviet Marshal and Prime Minister Josef Stalin (1879–1953). Nikita Khruschev (1894–1971), First Secretary of the Communist Party, criticized Stalin's 'cult of personality' and the purges instigated by him. The 22nd Congress in 1961 had Stalin's body removed from Lenin's mausoleum and placed in a plain grave alongside the Kremlin. Statues of Stalin were removed and place names changed: Stalingrad, for example, became Volgograd.

Stalin's reputation has come under renewed attack in the more open atmosphere instituted by Gorbachev. It seems likely that there will be further official revelations about the extent and human cost of Stalin's purges.

détente (Fr., relaxation; also Ital. *distensione*). Diplomatic term signifying the diminution of strained relations between states. The term is usually applied to the improved relations, beginning November 1969, between the WARSAW PACT countries (led by the USSR), and the West (headed by the USA), which were inaugurated by SALT (the Strategic Arms Limitation Talks). These ended in agreement on arms reductions in May 1973. Further SALT talks began in November 1974 and an agreement reached in May 1978, but the continued build-up of Soviet arms and the invasion by the USSR of Afghanistan in December 1979 called into question the validity of détente. The tension has decreased significantly, however, since the changes instituted by Gorbachev. *See also* COLD WAR.

Deutsche Arbeiterfront (Germ., German labour front). NAZI organization founded in November 1933 following the dissolution of the trade unions, professing to represent the interests of every German and to unite employers and workers. Wage rises were to be paid only for increased production and 'class warfare' was to be ended. The organization used the contributions of members (30 million by 1939) and confiscated trade union funds to finance members' holidays and to develop its own industrial and commercial enterprises such as the Volkswagen motor company. *See also* KRAFT DURCH FREUDE.

Deuxième Bureau (Fr., second bureau). Military intelligence department of the French government; the equivalent of MI5 in Britain.

devaluation. Reduction in the value of a country's currency, often done deliberately by a government to rectify BALANCE OF PAYMENTS deficits. As the value of the currency is reduced, imports become relatively more expensive; after an initial rise in money leaving the country, demand for imports falls off in favour of domestic goods. Britain, for example devalued in 1949 and 1967.

Development Loan Fund. American agency established by the Mutual Security Act of 1958 to supply financial aid for the assistance 'on a basis of self-help and mutual cooperation' of 'the efforts of free people abroad to develop their economic resources and to increase their productive capacities'. It made loans for specific developments planned either by government or private organizations, provided the project was commercially viable. In November 1961 the Fund was replaced by the AGENCY FOR INTERNATIONAL DEVELOPMENT.

Devil's Decade. A largely discredited view of Britain in the 1930s which portrays the decade from the 1929 Wall Street Crash to the outbreak of war in 1939 as one of unrelieved misery, marked by mass unemployment, the MEANS TEST, the clash between extremes of left and right and the humiliating foreign policy of Appeasement. *See* HUNGRY THIRTIES.

devolution. Decentralization of political power to a region. An attempt to create a Scottish Assembly failed when on 1 March 1979 only 32.85% voted in favour in a referendum on the issue, failing to meet the requirement that 40% of the electorate should show support. In a Welsh referendum on the same day 46.9% opposed devolution, 11.9% expressing support.

devshirmeh (deriv. Turk., levy of boys). The 'tribute of children' levied on Christian people, particularly the Slavs in the Balkans who were subject to OTTOMAN rule, established by Bayezed I (1389–1403). It lapsed after the battle of Ankara (1402) but was revived by Murad II (1421–1451). Many became JANISSARIES while the most able were trained for high administrative posts. The devshirmeh was only intermittently applied in the 16th and 17th centuries and was last imposed in 1705.

Dewline (acronym). Distant Early Warning Viewing Line, established in 1957 by the North American Air Defence Command (NORAD). It forms a section of a comprehensive radar system built to detect the approach of nuclear missiles or enemy aircraft. It stretches across the Aleutian Islands, Alaska, North Canada, South Greenland to Iceland and its main purpose is to detect a surprise 'first strike' by the USSR against North America. The equivalent in the USSR is the Tallinin Line. Though obviously still of importance, the value of the line has perhaps been altered in recent years by the development of 'spy satellites' in space, the construction of multi-targeted nuclear warheads and the shift in military thinking towards limited nuclear war in Europe.

dialectical materialism. Philosophical system developed by Karl Marx (1818–83) and Friedrich Engels (1820–95). Marx, pre-eminently a German philosopher, was greatly aware of the work of Hegel (1770–1831) who had developed the theory of the dialectic. For Hegel history was a logical process, a work of reason, in which conflicting views (thesis and antithesis) were reconciled in a third state, synthesis. This system is deeply imbued with metaphysical, even mystical, overtones but its relevance to Marx's dialectical materialism is easily apparent. For Marx, each state of economic production is a synthesis, but also a thesis with an antithesis. It produces a class to organize production, but the techniques outgrow their social shell and a new class emerges, interested in the new mode of production and at odds with the older class.

Capitalism represented the penultimate stage of the process. Marx took the classical economic view of Ricardo (1772–1823) that only labour creates value and that capital is 'stored' labour, alienated from the proletariat. Workers are forced to accept low wages because, as the capital they produce increases, they are replaced by machines. There is thus an ever-increasing surplus pool of labour; thesis and antithesis are heading towards synthesis. Eventually, when productive power has outstripped demand and prices have fallen, the pool of unemployed and impoverished grows until revolution occurs with the workers taking control of the means of production. The state, which has existed in the past only because of conflicting economic interests, will wither and die. The means of production can be organized on the basis of COMMUNISM and the historical process will have unfolded.

The most obvious criticism of the theory is that revolutions have not in fact occurred in highly developed capitalist countries but in agrarian ones. There is widespread criticism of the economic value of labour claimed by Marx: investment in capital is today seen as having a role of its own in the economic process, and the laws of demand and supply are seen as the prime factor in determining wages. Marx was extremely vague on the details of the proletarian revolution and withering of the state, but some explanations of his apparent discrepancies are offered by MARXIST-LENINISM.

diarchy (deriv. Gk., two+rule). Joint rule, a constitutional mechanism widely used in the British Empire, under which the government of a territory was split into two. One part was administered by imperial officials appointed by the governor of the territory and responsible to the British parliament; the other by ministers chosen from and responsible to a locally elected legislature.

diaspora (Gk., dispersion). Term applied to the scattering of the Jews among the Gentiles, taken from Deut. 28:25. The first dispersal of Jews came in 586 BC when the Babylonians conquered Judah and carried many Jews into exile in Babylon. In 538 BC Cyrus the Great of Persia conquered Babylon and allowed them to return home, although some chose to remain. From the 4th century BC Jews were leaving Palestine to settle in Alexandria in Egypt and Antioch in Syria. By the 2nd century BC they had spread throughout Asia Minor and North Africa. The largest community of the diaspora in the 1st century was in Alexandria where almost half the population was Jewish. In 55 BC Cicero refers to Jews becoming Roman citizens and living in Rome. By the 1st century AD Jews in the diaspora outnumbered Jews in Israel. Five million Jews lived outside Israel, four million of them within the Roman Empire. In 70 AD the Jewish rebellion against Roman rule ended with the capture of Jerusalem. Many Jewish prisoners were taken into slavery by the Romans but there was no policy of deportation. In John 7:35 there is a reference to the diaspora before 70 AD.

Over the centuries, the chief centres of Judaism have varied and have included Persia, Egypt, Spain, France, Germany, Poland, Russia and now the USA. The various communities developed distinctive cultures and languages, partly absorbed from their host nations. Yiddish, widely spoken even by Jews in the USA, was originally a form of German.

To the Jews of the diaspora, Israel has religious, philosophical and political connotations. Orthodox Judaism has always looked towards a 'gathering in' of Jews to Israel and it has been argued that only Jews returning to Israel can be truly Jewish. Those who do not will eventually assimilate the culture of their host nations. At the same time, however, many orthodox Jews consider the state of Israel in practice to be secular and godless. Three million of the world's fourteen million Jews reside in Israel, fewer than in the USA (5.7 million) and only slightly more than in the USSR (2.7 million).

dictatorship (deriv. Lat.). In ancient Rome, the system of appointment of a man by the senate to hold absolute power for seven years in times of emergency. At the end of his term he had to retire, at which time constitutional rule was reinstated and conventional republican forms restored. Today, the term denotes absolute rule by a person or group who are under no constraint to retire. They are not answerable to the people although democratic forms might be loosely preserved. Seizure of power, either by the army or a party, often takes place prior to a dictatorship, but rule is usually embodied in a single individual, either holding true power or acting as a figurehead.

dictatorship of the proletariat. Marxist description of working-class rule between the collapse of capitalism in revolution and the birth of a classless, communist society. Developed by Lenin after the 1917 BOLSHEVIK seizure of power, dictatorship was exercised by a centralized party. The concept was abandoned by West European communist parties in the 1970s and was replaced in the 1977 Soviet Constitution by the 'state of the whole people'.

'Diehards'. Extreme Conservatives (also known as 'stand-patters' and 'ditchers'); the term was first used in British politics in 1911 to describe those Conservative peers in the House of Lords who swore to 'die in the last ditch' or 'die hard' rather than allow the passage of the Parliament Bill which would remove the power of the Lords to reject legislation passed by the Commons. The Bill was passed despite their opposition.

Diet (ME deriv. Lat. *dies*, day). In German history, an assembly of dignitaries or delegates called together on a particular day to decide important political or ecclesiastical questions. The most famous Diets were those held at Worms (1521), Speyer (1529) and Augsburg (1530) to settle matters of religious conflict arising from the REFORMATION.

Dieu et mon droit (Old Fr., God and my right). Motto of the monarchs of England. It was the password which Richard I gave to his army at the battle of Gisors (9 September 1198) in which the French were heavily defeated. The phrase appears to have been adopted as a motto by Henry VI (1422–1461).

Diggers. One of the radical movements which proliferated in England during the INTERREGNUM, whose name was derived from their attempts to dig or cultivate untilled land. Their leader Gerrard Winstanley (c1609–c1660) taught the need for social and economic equality. In various pamphlets, including *The True Leveller's Standard Advanced* (1649), he advocated the abolition of private property and castigated the clergy for upholding society's class structure while receiving tithes from the poor.

In April 1649, 20 or so diggers occupied the common on St George's Hill in Surrey and commenced cultivation of it, demanding that common land should be turned over to the poor. This pleased neither the COMMONWEALTH government nor local landlords. Legal actions and violent attacks against them followed and in March 1650 their settlement was dispersed by force. They spread throughout Kent, Essex and Buckinghamshire and for a time made converts, but their influence rapidly waned. Winstanley continued to pursue a career as a pamphleteer, arguing for a crude type of communism and making rationalist attacks on clericalism.

diktat (Germ., order). Diplomatic or military settlement forcibly imposed on a defeated enemy, often applied to the 1919 TREATY OF VERSAILLES.

dilution. The introduction of unskilled labour in areas traditionally restricted to skilled tradesmen to meet the wartime needs of engineering, shipbuilding and munitions. The March 1915 'Shells and Fuses Agreement' guaranteed British unions that pre-war conditions would be restored, but resistance to dilution encouraged the growth of a shop stewards' movement, notably on Clydeside.

dime (Fr.). French tithe or tenth.

diocese (deriv. Lat., governor's district). Territorial area administered by a bishop in the Roman Catholic and Anglican churches, and by a Patriarch in the Eastern Orthodox churches of Greece and Russia. It was initially an administrative division of the Roman Empire, itself being subdivided into provinces. The early Christian church reversed this order: they made the province the larger unit, under the control of a metropolitan bishop, and the dioceses subdivisions of the province. From the 9th to the 13th centuries, church organization was in a state of flux but by the 13th century two distinct patterns had emerged. In the Orthodox Church the basic unit of administration was and is the parish, administered by a bishop. The diocese is a larger area comprising a number of parishes and under the control of a patriarch. In the Catholic Church dioceses are administered by bishops but are also subdivided into parishes (each having its own church) or into rural deaneries containing several parishes. The Pope alone can abolish, merge or create new dioceses. In the Church of England, parliament has created new dioceses (in the 16th, 19th and 20th centuries) by dividing existing ones. Dioceses are subdivided into rural deaneries which are in turn divided into parishes.

diplomat de carrière (Fr.) A professional career diplomat.

diplomatic immunity. Immunity from legal prosecution given to foreign diplomats by the country in which they are stationed.

diplomatic recognition. Process by which the government of one state formally recognizes and accepts as legitimate a new government taking power in another state.

direct action. Slogan used by the advocates of revolutionary SYNDICALISM in the early 20th century to denote strikes, industrial sabotage, occupation of factories by workers and even political uprisings in place of parliamentary action. The phrase was revived by the French Communist Party in 1947 in an attempt to provoke strikes and civil unrest.

direct primary. A method of party

voting in the United States by which members directly nominate candidates and convention delegates.

Directory (Fr. *Directoire*). The executive power in France between 1795 and November 1799, established following the fall of Robespierre. Power was vested in five Directors assisted by a council of 500, and a council of 250 known as the Council of Ancients. The Directory presided over a period of chaotic provincial administration. Renewed revolt in La Vendée and defeats in the War of the Second Coalition resulted in the alienation of the majority of the population, and there was little resistance when Napoleon overthrew the Directory on 9 November 1799 and established the CONSULATE.

dirigisme (Fr.). State intervention in the economy, within a system of fundamentally free enterprise rather than one of socialist planning. The subject of much debate in the 1930s, dirigisme became an established practice in post-war France.

dirigiste (Fr.). Advocate of state planning (*see* DIRIGISME).

Dirty War. The brutal and successful counter-insurgency campaign conducted by the Argentine military government under General Jorge Videla between 1976 and 1978 against marxist MONTENEROS and People's Revolutionary Army guerrillas.

'Disappeared ones'. People in Latin American countries who have disappeared without trace as a result of government action. It is thought that up to 90,000 may have died, 30,000 of them in Argentina alone.

disarmament. Reduction or abandonment of armaments. The concept of disarmament first rose after World War I. The Covenant of the LEAGUE OF NATIONS expressed a desire for reduction in armaments and over 60 members of the League, plus non-members such as the USA and USSR attended a Geneva Conference in 1932–34. The conference failed because of insistence by France that COLLECTIVE SECURITY be assured before armaments were reduced and because of the increase in international tension arising from the accession to power in 1933 of the NAZIS in Germany. In Britain the policy was adopted in 1925 by the Conservative government and was supported by the Labour and Liberal parties until the mid 1930s.

The ATLANTIC CHARTER of 1941 referred to an intention on the part of the Allies to 'lighten for peace-loving peoples the crushing burden of armaments'. In October 1943 a joint 'Moscow Declaration' was issued by the USA, USSR, Britain and China expressing desire for 'a practical general agreement with respect to the regulation of armaments'.

The Charter of the UN makes provision for the Security Council to explore means of regulating armaments. In 1946 the UN established the Atomic Energy Commission to end the use of atomic energy for military purposes, and in 1947 the Commission for Conventional Armaments to regulate and reduce armaments and armed forces. Neither Commission made much progress and in 1952 they were combined in the UN Disarmament Commission. After the explosion of hydrogen bombs by the USA in 1952 and by the USSR in 1953, the USA proposed joint attempts to use nuclear power for peaceful purposes only, in response to Russian suggestions for the prohibition of nuclear weapons and a general reduction of conventional forces. Between May 1954 and November 1957 talks were held on disarmament but broke down at the USSR's insistence on a one-third reduction of conventional forces, which would have left her with superiority over the West.

In 1963 a partial TEST BAN TREATY was attained and between January and August 1966 the UN Commission sponsored a disarmament conference in Geneva. On 1 July 1968 the USA, USSR, Britain and 57 other states signed a Non-Proliferation Treaty to restrict the spread of nuclear arms. On 10 April 1972 an agreement to ban germ warfare was signed by 46 states. SALT produced two treaties signed by the USA and USSR agreeing a reduction in the number of nuclear weapons but the US Senate refused to ratify the second treaty. On 30 November 1982 new talks began between the USA and USSR at Geneva, and on 18 November Pres. Reagan made his zero-option proposal. With the advent of Gorbachev and GLASNOST a new disarmament climate has appeared. *See also* CND.

discoverers. In early 17th-century Ireland, those who undertook the investigation of some of the older titles to land on behalf of the Crown. If a flaw was discovered, the land was confiscated by the Crown and the discoverer received a percentage of the value.

disestablishment. The removal from a Church of its entitlement to state recognition and aid. In 19th-century Ireland, the special position accorded to the Anglican Church was a source of great resentment to the Roman Catholic majority, as it was in Wales to the NONCONFORMIST majority. Consequently the Church of Ireland was disestablished by Gladstone in an Act of 1869 which took effect in 1871, and the Church of Wales by

Asquith in an Act of 1914 which took effect after World War I. Both churches lost their special position in the state along with some of their endowments.

disinherited. Name given to the MONTFORTIANS who continued to wage the BARONS' WAR after the Battle of Evesham (1265), and against whom a decree of FORFEITURE had been issued in 1266 by Henry III.

dispensing power. In England, ancient prerogative right of the sovereign to exempt individuals from the operation of the law. The power was useful to ensure smooth and effective administration under a feudal monarchy, but later was used to protect royal officials and to license trade, worship, etc., contrary to statute. With the growth of PARLIAMENT, opposition to it grew, the LONG PARLIAMENT (1640–53) being particularly vigorous in opposing Charles I's use of it. Charles II tried, and failed, to get Parliament's approval of the dispensing power in his Declaration of Indulgence; he continued to use it nevertheless in connection with matters of trade and the TEST ACTS. James II used it to promote Roman Catholics who were debarred from holding certain military and civil offices by the Test Acts. In 1689 it was declared illegal by the BILL OF RIGHTS.

displaced persons. People estranged from their homelands before and during World War II, including those forcibly taken from their own countries to work in another, particularly Germany; those who had fled before invading armies during the war; and those obliged to leave their homes before the war, for example, German Jews and Spanish Republicans. At the end of the war there were some 8 million displaced persons in Europe, 6 million of whom were in Germany. Between June and December 1945 some 5.5–6 million persons were returned home, others were housed in special camps under the auspices of the United Nations Relief and Rehabilitation Administration (UNRRA). Some 2 million could not be sent home because they refused to live in communist-dominated eastern Europe. New classes of displaced persons also arose in the late 1940s including Jews on their way to Palestine from the USA and people fleeing from Russian-held territories. There were some 15 million displaced persons in Asia by 1949, mainly in China but also in India and Pakistan.

In mid-1947 the care of displaced persons in Europe, who numbered just over 1,600,000 was transferred from UNRRA to the International Refugee Organization (IRO) who organized mass migration via camps, hospitals, training centres, sponsors and agencies. By December 1951 it had managed to settle some 1,100,000. Its responsibilities were then transferred to the UN High Commissioner for Refugees who in 1954 had 350,000 refugees on their books. The majority of these, however, were not those originally displaced in the war but persons who had since fled from Soviet-dominated eastern Europe.

dissenters *See* NONCONFORMISTS.

dissidents. Those who refuse to conform with the prevailing political and social mores in their countries. In the USSR the term is used pejoratively of individuals and groups who criticize abuses of human and CIVIL RIGHTS. The most famous is probably the Nobel Prize-winning novelist Alexander Solzhenitsyn who was expelled from the USSR in 1974. His works (*One Day in the Life of Ivan Denisovich, The Gulag Archipelago*) highlight the conditions in which political prisoners were held in 'special' camps in the USSR. In 1976, several appeals were made by groups of dissidents for an AMNESTY for political and religious prisoners (*see* HELSINKI HUMAN RIGHTS GROUP). In December of that year the Soviet authorities released Vladimir Bukovsky from prison and allowed him to leave the USSR in return for the release of a Chilean, Luis Carvalan, held by the Chilean right-wing JUNTA. Almost immediately, dissidents were accused of causing an explosion on the Moscow underground and persecution of the Helsinki Human Rights Group was intensified. The USSR has persistently denied Western claims that healthy dissidents are declared mentally ill and incarcerated in mental hospitals. However, with the advent of Gorbachev the situation appears to have altered and in 1988 Moscow appeared willing to release all 'political' prisoners.

distress (deriv. Lat. *distringere*, to distrain). Process by which a person may seize and detain a chattel or item of personal property from a wrongdoer in order to procure satisfaction for a wrong or performance of a legal obligation. Now usually necessitating court action, it is most commonly used by landlords to seize goods following non-payment of rent. Because the process is open to abuse it is not favoured in the USA where some states have refused to recognise it.

'Ditchers' *See* 'DIEHARDS'.

divide et impera (Lat., divide and rule). The imposition of authority by keeping subject peoples divided amongst themselves.

Divine Right of Kings. Doctrine which holds that monarchs in direct line of succession have a divine or God-given right to the throne and that rebellion against their will is a sin. The doctrine originated in France where it reached its apogee in the 17th century. In England it first appeared in 1569 in a 'Homily against Wilful Rebellion'. The English clergy accepted the doctrine on the whole, and were prepared to comply with the ecclesiastical canons of 1640 that required them to remind their congregations of the doctrine four times a year. The doctrine was most popular during the reign of Charles I (1625–1649). Where obedience was impossible NON-RESISTANCE was prescribed. The civil war (1642-46) broke the doctrine, though the position of the NON-JURORS reflected a late manifestation of it.

Dixie. Southern states of the USA. The name is derived from the Mason-Dixon line, the boundary between Pennsylvania and Maryland, drawn up by two English surveyors, Charles Mason and Jeremiah Dixon, between 1763 and 1767. The boundary had for some time previously been a matter of dispute. Later the line marked the boundary between the southern states which practised slavery and the northern states which did not.

Dixiecrats. Name given to those US DEMOCRATS who insisted on continuance of racial segregation and of white domination in the Southern states. The origin of the name is obscure and may be either a reference to the Mason-Dixon line (*see* DIXIE) or to the bank notes issued by the Confederacy (*see* CONFEDERACY), known as dixies because they had *dix* (French for ten) printed on them. Dixiecrats attempted to block CIVIL RIGHTS legislation by means of FILIBUSTERS in the early 1960s.

dixième (Fr., tenth). French tax of 10% of all gross incomes imposed by Louis XIV in 1710 to finance the War of the Spanish Succession. Regarded as an attack on their financial privileges by the nobility, it was opposed and abandoned in 1717. It was revived as a wartime emergency measure in 1733 and again in 1741 and 1746.

doctrinaires (Fr.). In France, name given after 1814 to philosophic liberal politicians, such as Guizot, Molé and the Duc de Broglie, who upheld constitutional principles in opposition to arbitrary monarchical power. They came into office under Louis Philippe in 1830 and fell with him in 1848.

In England, the term was applied during the 1820s to certain writers in the *Westminster Review*, such as Bentham and Molesworth.

Doge (deriv. Lat. *dux*, leader). Chief magistrate in and ruler of the former republics of Venice (1697–1797) and Genoa (1339–1797, 1802–1805).

dole (ME, that which is distributed). English colloquialism which became current in the 1930s for unemployment benefit, the weekly payments to unemployed workers under the National Insurance Act and related legislation. The principle that the genuinely unemployed should receive assistance from the state separate from the old POOR LAW payments was first recognized in Britain in 1905; a partial system of compulsory unemployment insurance was introduced in 1911 and extended in 1920. Germany and Australia had had such a system for a considerable time prior to 1911. Modern unemployment benefits are based on the principles embodied in the 1946 National Insurance Act.

dollar-diplomacy. Term originally applied to the policy of the US Pres. Taft (1909–13) in China, though it had been foreshadowed by the policy of Pres. Roosevelt (1905–09) in the Caribbean. Taft stated in December 1912 that his policy was that of 'substituting dollars for bullets' and that it was 'one that appeals alike to idealistic humanitarian sentiments, to the dictates of sound policy and strategy and to legitimate commercial aims'. In effect it is the policy of using the great wealth and commercial influence of the USA as a factor in the pursuit of US foreign policy. It can be either positive, by lending or giving money and aid to potential allies and encouraging US industry to trade with them, or negative, by denying aid. The policy was criticized and fell into disrepute, but has been revived and again attacked, both by domestic critics and more prominently by communist and third world states opposed to US foreign policy.

US policy in Latin America has been alleged to be an example of dollar-diplomacy. Since the Cuban revolution in 1959, the USA has been particularly keen to use its wealth as a tool to combat communism in South America. Under the Alliance for Progress proposals, the USA was to provide $20 billion for the development of South American countries prepared to resist communism. More recently Pres. Reagan was accused of pursuing dollar-diplomacy in El Salvador though the issue was clouded by the supply of arms as well as finance.

The application of SANCTIONS by the USA on grain exports to the USSR, on British firms participating in the supply of technology to the USSR for the Soviet-European gas pipeline, and on Argentina following her occupation of the Falklands have all been criticized as examples of dollar-diplomacy. The term is thus now being used more generally to describe any economic action by the USA if taken in pursuit of foreign policy.

Domesday Book (ME, day of judgement). A comprehensive record of property in England compiled in 1086 on the orders of William the Conqueror (1027–1087) so that he could compute the maximum possible yield from land tax. The name has various explanations: one that it arose in the 12th century when it was decided that there was no appeal against the book, another that it is derived from Domus Dei in Winchester Cathedral where it was deposited.

Commissioners were sent into each county to establish the name of each place, the number and rank of its inhabitants, the names of possessors of land and the size of their holdings, their value, their number of mills, fish-ponds, etc. The survey was extremely detailed and one chronicler reported that 'there was not a single hide, nor one vintage of land, nor even ... an ox, nor a cow, nor a swine that was not set down.' However, it did not take in Cumberland, Westmorland, parts of Lancashire, Durham and Northumberland. Juries were called to swear to the accuracy of the facts reported. The survey was comprised in two volumes, the Little Domesday which held details of Essex, Norfolk and Suffolk and the Great Domesday dealing with other counties. The Book is now kept at the Public Record Office.

Dominicans. Order of mendicant preaching friars founded by St. Dominic in Languedoc in 1215 and confirmed by the Pope in 1216. Their official name is Friars Preachers; they are also called Black Friars on account of their long black mantles.

dominion. State which was a member of the British Empire or British Commonwealth of Nations but which also had autonomy in foreign and domestic affairs. Canada received dominion status in 1867; Australia, New Zealand, the Irish Free State, Newfoundland and South Africa in 1931. There are almost 30 dominions, although many have never actually claimed the status and the term has fallen into disuse since 1945.

domino theory. Belief prevalent in US foreign policy in the early 1960s that if South Vietnam was allowed to become communist as a result of North Vietnamese aggression, other countries in south-east Asia would follow suit in a chain reaction. If the communists seized control of the whole of Vietnam, they could then seize Laos and Cambodia; from there they could take control of Thailand and Malaysia and so on throughout Asia. US troops were therefore sent to the aid of South Vietnam from 1965 until 1973; in April 1975 it fell to the northern communist troops. The domino theory has not since been proved correct. Rather than expanding its influence, communism in south-east Asia has split into two camps, pro-Soviet Vietnam and the Chinese-backed Khmer Rouge of Kampuchea (Cambodia).

Donatists. Members of a heretical sect in Numidia (modern Algeria) from the 4th to the 8th centuries who originally called themselves the Church of the Martyrs, but were more commonly known after Donatus, the bishop they elected in Carthage in 312. Their strength lay in powerful and rigid organization and the simplicity of their dogma, the main tenets of which were that God's church was a society of saints which no sinner could enter and that only the priests of this pure church had the power to administer the sacraments. In 412 they were crushed as an organized church by the Emperor Honorius but their influence persisted until ISLAM reached Africa in the 7th and 8th centuries. Their most lasting influence on Christianity stems from the reaction they provoked. St Augustine of Hippo (354–430) spent many years combating the heresy and, though he was initially hostile to secular intervention in church affairs, he eventually recognized the need for the state to interest itself in the church and vice versa.

doodlebug. Nickname for the German V1 rocket used in 1944–45, also known as the 'buzzbomb'. The rockets were jet-propelled, unmanned and each carried a warhead packed with high explosive. The V1 and V2 rockets, regarded as 'vengeance weapons' by the NAZIS, were designed for indiscriminate use on British cities.

doom (OE dōm). In Anglo-Saxon England the judgement given by a court or MOOT.

Doppers (Afrikaans). Members of the strict Calvinist Separatist Reformed Church in the Orange Free State and Transvaal, established in 1859.

Doukhobors. Russian religious sect, founded in the mid-18th century, who sought direct communication with God, believed in an 'inner light' and were given to religious ecstasies, shaking and speaking in strange tongues. Liturgy, ritual and ceremony were non-existent. They maintained that God alone had power over them and therefore refused to recognize state authority; they were consequently persecuted in Tsarist Russia. In 1898 Leo Tolstoy used his influence to have them removed to Canada, where the government settled 8,000 of them in previously uninhabited land in Saskatchewan. Recently their difficulties have again increased as the Canadian government is finding it difficult to tolerate their rejection of state authority, including their refusal to pay taxes.

doves *See* HAWKS.

dower (ME deriv. Lat., endowment). In medieval England, a proportion of a married man's estates – usually a third or a half – given to his wife at the wedding and assigned to her for life when he died. The aim of the practice, adopted in the 12th century, was to secure the wife's claim to the tenures her husband held from his lord and so to discourage secret marriages without the lord's knowledge. However, 13th-century court records show that it remained difficult for widows to get control of their dowers. The law of dower gradually declined as new forms of marriage contract developed.

Dow Jones. The WALL STREET index compiled by the Dow Jones Company which since 1897 has been used as an indicator of trends in United States stocks and bonds prices.

Dragonnades (Fr). Persecution of the HUGUENOTS in Poitou and other parts of France in 1684 by the dragoons of the minister, Louvois. The persecution culminated in the revocation of the Edict of Nantes on 22 October 1685, with the result that 50,000 Protestant families emigrated.

Drang nach Osten (Germ., thrust to the east). German desire to seek territorial gains in eastern Europe.

Dreadnought. The class of 'all-big-gun' battleships whose construction was inaugurated by HMS *Dreadnought*, laid down in October 1905, launched in February 1906 and at sea by October 1906. She carried 10 12–inch guns, whereas no other extant battleship carried more than 4; she was the fastest battleship in the world with a speed of 21 knots and the first large battleship to be turbine-powered. Able to outrange and outpace all other battleships, she represented a revolution in naval shipbuilding, sparking an international naval armaments race. In July 1907 Germany began construction of her *Nassau* class ships, similar to the *Dreadnought* class. By 1914 Britain had 19 *Dreadnought* class ships at sea, with a further 13 under construction; Germany had 13 at sea and 7 under construction. France and the USA both had 8 such ships afloat, Japan 4 and Austria-Hungary 2.

dream ticket. A political leadership combination which appears to offer the best prospect for party unity and electoral victory. Term used in Britain in 1983 when Neil Kinnock and Roy Hattersley became Labour leader and deputy leader, balancing left and right in the Labour Party.

Dreikaiserbund (Germ., league of three emperors). Informal alliance between the three emperors of Germany, Russia and Austria-Hungary, dating from a personal meeting in 1872. By 1879, when the foundation of the TRIPLE ALLIANCE was laid, it had effectively ceased to exist.

Dreyfus Affair. Scandal in France between 1894 and 1899 surrounding Alfred Dreyfus (1859–1935), a French army officer and a Jew. Charged with treason and convicted – on what was later proved to be false evidence – of passing information to Germany, he was deported to serve a life sentence on 'Devil's Island' in French Guiana. Liberals took up his cause and 'J'ACCUSE' helped play a part in exposing the truth, which was that evidence damaging to a Major Esterhazy had been suppressed by the authorities. ANTI-SEMITISM was believed to have played a part in the authorities' actions and Dreyfus's friends persuaded a Major Hubert Henri to confess to the forgeries which had led to Dreyfus's conviction. Henri then committed suicide. France was for a time in a severe state of shock. At a second trial in 1899 Dreyfus was acquitted, although it was not until 1906 that he was completely exonerated. He was then made a Chevalier of the Legion of Honour and restored to his army rank.

Dreyfusards. Supporters of Alfred Dreyfus (*see* DREYFUS AFFAIR).

'dries'. Members of the British Conservative Party who are prepared to pursue a strict monetarist policy, resist calls for increased public spending to alleviate unemployment, approve of PRIVATIZATION, pursue a vigorous defence policy and desire curtailment of the power of TRADE UNIONS. Their ranks include the party leader and prime minister, Margaret Thatcher, Norman Tebbit and Sir Geoffrey Howe (*see also* 'WETS').

droit du seigneur (Fr., right of the lord). Also called *jus primae noctis* or 'right of the first night', a feudal right by which a lord could sleep with the bride of a vassal on her wedding night. All the evidence of it in medieval Europe is negative (i.e. there are only records recalling payments made by vassals in lieu of it). Many feudal rights related to marriage (e.g. the lord might select a bride for his vassal) but duties were invariably paid to redeem them and the droit du seigneur was probably a tax of this sort.

Druidism. The religion of Celtic Britain and Gaul, of which the Druids were the priesthood. Little is known of their practices but from Roman sources it appears that they worshipped the powers of nature in sacred oak groves and that their ceremonies included human sacrifice. Attempts to link Druidism with the stone circles at Stonehenge and Avebury or with early Christianity are fallacious. Druids may have used the circles but recent evidence suggests that the megalithic stones belong to a pre-Druid Bronze Age culture (2100–1600 BC). The religion was finally wiped out in its last stronghold of Anglesey by the Roman general Suetonius Paulinus in 58 AD.

In Wales, the name survives in the Eisteddfods, the annual festivals of Celtic poetry, music and drama, whose semi-religious leaders have the title of Druids. The romantic associations of Druidism mean that even today 'Druidic' ceremonies are practised by devotees at appropriate times of year, with varying degrees of seriousness.

Druzes. National and religious minority in Syria and the Lebanon whose religion is of mixed origins but bears a close resemblance to ISLAM. When France received Syria as a MANDATE she favoured the Christian Maronites and the Druzes turned to Britain for support. In 1925 they revolted and extracted certain concessions from the French and when Syria was given independence in 1941 they were awarded a measure of autonomy.

Dual Entente. Alliance between Russia and France, cemented in 1893, which lasted until the BOLSHEVIK seizure of power in 1917.

dual-key. System whereby the governments of both the USA and the host country have to assent to the launching of American-owned nuclear missiles based abroad. The system's functioning is ensured by a mechanical check in the firing system which can only be removed by the use of two keys – the president of the USA retains one, the premier of the host country the other. The main check on independent launching of US missiles in Britain since World War II has been the long-standing trust between the two countries but in 1958 Prime Minister Macmillan secured dual-key control of 60 US 'Thor' nuclear missiles stationed in the UK. A similar arrangement was employed for the Lancer Battlefield Missiles System based in West Germany in the early 1960s. In the 1980s, growing opposition to the siting of Cruise and Pershing missiles in Europe has led to suggestions that they should be under dual-key control.

dual mandate. MANDATE jointly administered by two nations.

Dual Monarchy. Name given to the Austro-Hungarian Empire and, by extension, to its system of government.

dual power. Rule by two groups, for example that in Russia after the FEBRUARY REVOLUTION when both the Provisional Government and the Soviets vied for control of the state.

dual-track. Policy adopted by NATO ministers in December 1979 to deploy 572 medium-range missiles under US control in western Europe, while at the same time seeking bilateral negotiations between the USA and USSR with a view to fixing an overall ceiling on the number of such missiles deployed by both sides in Europe. There were thus to be two tracks to NATO policy in responding to the targetting of Soviet SS–20 missiles on western Europe.

Duce (Ital. leader). Name adopted by Benito Mussolini (1883–1945) who was appointed Prime Minister of Italy in October 1922, as head of a coalition of Fascists and Nationalists.

Duma. Russian parliament established by Tsar Nicholas II in 1905 as a response to the revolution of that year. Its achievements were largely confined to reforms in the areas of justice and administration. Suspended for much of World War I because it criticized the conduct of the war, it met in November 1916 to give the Tsarist régime warning of the danger of revolution.

durbar (deriv. Pers. *darbar*, audience, court). In India, either a council for administering affairs of state or a purely ceremonial gathering. The word was applied to great occasions such as Lord Lytton's proclamation of Victoria as Queen-Empress in 1877.

E

ealdorman (OE). In Anglo-Saxon England, a national officer of noble rank appointed by the king and his council and removable at the king's pleasure. Placed in charge of the SHIRE, his duties were to maintain law and order, to preside over and enforce the judgements of the MOOT and to raise the LAND FYRD. From the early 9th century, when the SHERIFFS began to assume control of individual shires, ealdormanries expanded beyond their borders but remained homogeneous units. At the time of Cnut (1017–1037) the term was replaced by the Anglo-Scandinavian EARL and ealdormanries by earldoms.

earl (OE deriv. ON *jarl*). Originally a non-royal military leader in 9th-century Denmark; later a royal officer in the DANELAW who performed duties similar to those of the EALDORMAN. In the 11th century, earls replaced ealdormen throughout England but the earldoms, created by King Cnut for political rather than administrative reasons, lacked the local unity of the former ealdormanries. The earl shared the presidency of the MOOT and led the LAND FYRD, but many of his routine duties soon devolved upon the SHERIFF; from the 12th century the title was one of nobility and not of office. Earls received the 'third penny' – a third of the shire courts' judicial profits and payments made by towns – and may also have had the profits of certain manors connected to the office.

East India Company. Company incorporated by royal charter in 1600 to capture the far eastern trade of the declining Portuguese empire. Initially trade centred on the Dutch East Indies, but the Dutch drove the British out in the 1620s. In 1633 the Company based itself at Bengal. In the 18th century commercial rivalry with the French escalated into open warfare in the Seven Years' War (1756–63) in which the Company's army, led by Robert Clive (1725–74), was successful in expelling the French. The Company then enjoyed a great increase in trade and wealth (*see* NABOBS). With wealth went corruption and maladministration and there were demands for reform of the Company's administration of the subcontinent. Acts of 1784, 1813, 1833 and 1853 gradually limited its powers; in 1858, following the Indian Mutiny (1857–58), the Crown assumed full administrative responsibilty for the subcontinent. The Company was wound up in 1873.

Easter Rising. Armed insurrection in central Dublin between 24–29 April 1916 with the aim of achieving immediate independence for Ireland. Patrick Pearse led 5 battalions of the Irish Republican Brotherhood and James Connolly 200 of the SINN FEIN Citizen Army. They seized the general post office in Sackville Street (which became their headquarters), the Four Courts, St Stephen's Green and Boland's Flour Mill. A south Dublin workhouse was captured but attempts on the castle and the arsenal in Phoenix Park failed. Pearse proclaimed an Irish Republic with himself president of its provisional government.

Heavy street fighting began on the first day (Easter Monday) and after five days the British army forced the rebels into unconditional surrender. Connolly, Pearse and 12 others were executed in Kilmainham Gaol; 3,000 more were interned but were granted an AMNESTY in June 1917. Though many Irish people regarded the uprising as a treacherous attack because Britain was heavily engaged at the time in World War I and many Irish troops were serving in the British army, the courage of the rebels made a deep impression and the subsequent executions increased sympathy for their cause. The rising is now an epic feature in Irish history, much celebrated in patriotic song.

Eastern bloc. Communist states of eastern Europe including the WARSAW PACT countries, Yugoslavia and Albania.

Eastern Front. Battlefront between Russia and Germany in World Wars I and II. *See also* BARBAROSSA.

Eastern Question. Term used to denote the many problems arising in south-east Europe due to the decline of the Turkish OTTOMAN empire. The late 19th century saw continuous manoeuvring, with Russia and the Austro-Hungarian empire seeking to benefit territorially at Turkish expense. Until 1897 Britain sought to bolster the Turkish position as a means of preventing Russia from gaining control of the Dardanelles and Bosphorus. However, the Ottoman empire's failure to reform itself and the ARMENIAN MASSACRES lost them Britain's sympathy.

In 1898, the German Kaiser William II (1859–1941) visited Constantinople and Turkey began to draw closer to Germany, giving her valuable railway and commercial concessions and receiving in return a German military mission. The question became more complicated following the independence of various Balkan states, particularly Serbia and Romania who in 1912 combined to fight against Turkey in the Balkan War. The Eastern Question was ended by World War I when the Ottoman empire, which was Germany's ally, finally collapsed and a Turkish national state emerged.

Economic Co-operation Administration. *See* EUROPEAN RECOVERY PROGRAMME.

economic penetration. Process by which a country establishes economic dominance in another country, making that country dependent upon it for its continuing economic survival or well being, thereby gaining control over it. Attainment of economic dominance usually requires large-scale capital investment such as road and rail construction; the purchase or foundation of industry, or monopoly of the country's foreign trade. In the 19th century a number of European powers, including Britain, Germany and Russia, were successful in penetrating China in this way, thereby obtaining massive political influence in the running of the country. More recently, the degree of economic penetration by the USA into the economies of Central and South America has given it considerable political influence in those regions. In 1982, the USA expressed concern that the construction of a gas pipeline between the USSR and West Germany would give the USSR undue political influence in western European policy-making.

Economists. Philosophical school, founded *c*1761 in France by the physician Quesnay, who believed in a natural order of human institutions, divinely ordained, which, if adhered to, would lead inevitably to prosperity. He also argued that agriculture was the sole true source of wealth. Turgot, finance minister of Louis XVI, was greatly influenced by the doctrines of the Economists.

ecorcheurs (Fr., flayers). Bands of brigands who ravaged France during the Hundred Years' War (1337–1453).

Ecosol (acronym). Economic and Social Council of the UN.

EDC. European Defence Community proposed in 1952, intended to be supranational, embracing states with common institutions, which was to have an international army and budget, be more coherent than NATO and mutually guarantee the security of its members. Membership was open firstly to members of the European Coal and Steel Community (France, Italy, West Germany and BENELUX), but it was hoped that other European states including Britain would join. A draft treaty was produced after negotiations in Paris between February 1951 and 8 May 1952: it was initialled by the members of the Coal and Steel Community and signed by the respective foreign ministers on 27 May 1952. However, it had to be ratified by the national parliaments before taking effect; the French parliament refused and the idea was abandoned.

Edwardian. Properly, the reign of Edward VII, 1901–1910. More commonly used to describe the period between the turn of the century and the outbreak of World War I in August 1914. The popular image of these as innocent, carefree years before the horrors of the WESTERN FRONT ignores the political and social turmoil of the Edwardian period.

EEC. European Economic Community, also known as the Common Market, first envisaged in June 1955 when the foreign ministers of the members of the European Coal and Steel Community (France, Italy, West Germany and BENELUX) met at Messina. The Belgian minister Paul-Henri Spaak was instructed to make proposals for an expansion of the existing community to one based on free trade, free movement of labour and capital, common social and economic policies and the removal of restrictive trade practices.

On 25 March 1957 'the Six' signed the Treaty of Rome and the EEC came into being on 1 January 1958. Under the agreement any member could veto the admission of a future applicant, a device which Spaak had hoped would exclude the dictatorships of Franco's Spain and Salazar's Portugal. In fact Pres. De Gaulle of France used it to veto applications made by Britain on 10 August 1961 (vetoed January 1963) and again in May 1967 (vetoed 19 December), when negotiations on British entry were stopped but the application was not withdrawn.

Following De Gaulle's resignation

in April 1969 an invitation to join the EEC was extended to Britain, Ireland, Denmark and Norway in June 1970. These four countries signed a treaty of accession in Brussels on 22 January 1972, but in September Norway withdrew after a referendum had shown that most Norwegians opposed entry. The other three became members from 1 January 1973. On 5 June 1975 a referendum in Britain (called as a result of left-wing Labour Party opposition to the EEC) showed more than 67 per cent of the public to be in favour of membership. In January 1981 Greece joined, but the Panhellenic Socialist Movement (Pasok) which came to power in October 1981 favours withdrawal. On 24 February 1982 Greenland, part of the kingdom of Denmark, voted to leave. Spain and Portugal joined in 1986.

In 1973 the EEC agreed to free trade in manufactured goods between its members and those of EFTA and on 28 February 1975 it signed the Lomé Convention giving 46 developing countries access to the EEC market.

EFTA. European Free Trade Association, at one time commonly known as 'the outer seven', formed in 1959 in opposition to the EEC. In July 1965 the Council of Ministers of the Organization for European Economic Co-operation initiated a report on the feasibility of an association in which members would abandon tariffs and other trade restrictions between themselves but preserve individual tariffs and commercial policies in relation to non-members (the EEC in contrast had a common tariff policy regarding non-members).

On 20 November 1959 the Stockholm Convention established the association with Britain, Denmark, Norway, Sweden, Austria, Switzerland and Portugal as founder members. Britain secured the omission of foodstuffs from the tariff agreements since many members of the BRITISH COMMONWEALTH OF NATIONS were dependent on her for their exports of foodstuffs. In addition, Denmark and Britain both wished to protect their domestic agricultural sectors. On 1 July 1960 a 20 per cent cut in tariffs on industrial goods was implemented. By 1 January 1966 duties had fallen by 80 per cent and by 1 January 1967 all duties on industrial goods had been removed. Only Britain, in 1966, broke the tariff agreements, putting an import surcharge on manufactured goods to correct a BALANCE OF PAYMENTS deficit. On 1 January 1968 the Faroe Islands, a dependency of Denmark, joined; Iceland applied in 1969 and became a member in 1970. On 31 December 1972 Britain and Denmark left to join the EEC, and EFTA agreed to free trade in industrial products between itself and EEC members.

EGP. *Ejercito Guerrilero de los Pobres*, a left-wing guerrilla group active in North Guatemala and responsible for the assassination of senior policemen and army officers. It co-operates closely with ORPA and many of its members fought for the SANDINISTAS.

Eighth Army. *See* DESERT RATS.

Einkreisung (Germ., encirclement). Term coined by the German chancellor Prince Bernhard von Bülow (1849–1929) in 1906 to denote the policy embodied in the Anglo-French-Russian alliance, ascribed to Edward VII of England because of his various visits to European courts. In Germany's opinion her neighbours to east and west were joining hands to encircle her in a hostile alliance aimed at preventing German expansion, thus stopping her from taking a place in the front line of developed nations. The term was again used in 1939 when Britain guaranteed the security of Poland, Greece, Romania and Turkey after Germany's annexation of Czechoslovakia. *See also* LEBENSRAUM.

'Ein Reich, Ein Volk, Ein Führer'. (Germ. 'One, nation, One people, One leader'). Slogan of the NAZIS which embodied their belief in ARYAN supremacy and the FÜHRER PRINZIP.

Einsatzgruppen (Germ., special service squads). Task force selected to maintain law and order in German occupied territory between 1941 and 1945 and, more particularly, to murder Jews, partisans, communists and other 'dangerous elements' opposed to NAZI ideology. When the directive was issued for the FINAL SOLUTION, 3,000 men were assembled in Pretzch and Düben in Saxony in May 1941 to begin training. Formed into four squads, they were drawn from the SD (*see* SS) and WAFFEN SS, the GESTAPO, Kripa (*Kriminal polizei*, the criminal police working with the Gestapo) and Stapo (the State police). They later recruited Ukrainians, Letts, Lithuanians and White Russians to help them. Attached to the army groups of BARBAROSSA they supervised the murder of two million Jews in eastern Europe and Russia.

ELAS. In wartime Greece, the National People's Army of Liberation, founded by the communist wing of the resistance EAM, after the German army occupied Greece in April 1941. By 1943 it had liberated more than a third of the country, but Britain and the USA lent their support to the pro-monarchist resistance groups, the X-bands, led by Gen. Zervas. Clashes between the two sets of partisans led to the expulsion of Zervas in 1943 and the despatch of British troops to Greece in 1944 to prevent a civil war. It was by then clear that ELAS wished to achieve a communist revolution in the way Tito's Yugoslavian PARTISANS had done.

Further clashes in the winter of 1944–45 were ended by the Truce of Varkiza (12 February 1945) between the royalists and ELAS under which ELAS received control of two-thirds of the country. In October 1946, after the return of King George II, remnants of ELAS led by Gen. Markos Vafiades established a 'Democratic Army of Greece' in the northern rural areas and sought support amongst the rural population. At the request of the USA, British troops remained in Greece until 1950 with the UN Security Council rejecting Soviet demands that they leave.

Civil war broke out, with the USA backing the royalists and Yugoslavia, Albania and Bulgaria aiding Vafiades. The split between Yugoslavia and the USSR consequent on the former's expulsion from COMINFORM closed supply routes through Yugoslavia. Seriously weakened, the Democratic Army was largely destroyed in August 1949 in a battle around Mt Grammos. Vafiades was murdered by his followers on the orders of the USSR.

El Dorado. *See* MANOA.

electors. In the medieval Holy Roman Empire, members of the Electoral College formed by the efforts of a group of prominent German princes who established the convention that their votes alone could elect the emperor. In the 1198 election a great many princes voted but by the 13th century a group of six had monopolized the right: the Archbishops of Mainz, Trier and Cologne, the Imperial Steward (the Count Palatine of the Rhine), the Chamberlain (the Margrave of Brandenburg) and the Marshal (the Duke of Saxony). Later in the century the Imperial Cup-bearer (the King of Bohemia) joined the college and only these seven voted in 1257. In 1356 the GOLDEN BULL of Emperor Charles IV established this group as the permanent and sole constituents of the electoral college and assured its secular members that their electorates would never be divided.

Elizabethan. The period of Elizabeth I's reign from 1558 to 1603, an era of developing English self-confidence, domestic stability, and a flowering of literary expression by, among others, Shakespeare, Spenser and Marlowe.

emigrés (Fr., emigrants). Term applied to the opponents of the 1789 French Revolution who were forced to flee France. Many were members of the nobility and some actively worked to promote a coalition of European sovereigns against the Revolution. The revolutionaries themselves enacted various punitive decrees against the emigrés.

éminence grise (Fr., grey eminence). One who wields power behind the scenes; nickname of François du Tremblay (d. 1638), secretary to Cardinal Richelieu.

Empire Crusade. Press baron Lord Beaverbrook's campaign begun in 1930 advocating Empire Free Trade, with Britain supplying industrial goods and the Dominions providing food and raw materials, with a tariff wall excluding outsiders. Unpopular in the Tory Party through fears of the charge that tariffs were a tax on food, and among Dominion leaders keen to forward their own industrial development, the cause was effectively abandoned by 1933. *See* TARIFF REFORM.

Enabling Law. Act passed by the German Reichstag in 1933 giving the NAZI Chancellor, Adolf Hitler (1889–1945) the power to pass laws without parliament's consent, signifying the end of the WEIMAR republic.

Encilhamento (Braz. Port.). Period of great financial speculation in the first years of the Brazilian republic from 1889 to 1892.

encirclement. *See* EINKREISUNG.

enclosures. Originally the fencing in and appropriating of waste and moorland, but later of open fields and common pastures. After 1500, complaints regarding the enclosures of former common land became frequent, particularly in the north and midlands where open-field farming was widely practised. Designed to promote agricultural specialization and efficiency at a time of rising prices, enclosures were usually effected by agreement, but disputes often arose when landlords disregarded commoners' rights. Enclosures became more numerous in the 17th century and in the 18th century landowners began to secure them by private bills in parliament. The movement reached its height in the reign of George III (1760–1820) and was completed by the Enclosure Acts of 1801, 1836 and 1845. The technical efficiency of farming was improved, but land was accumulated in fewer hands, driving the 'small man' off and denying labourers valuable customary rights of access to common and waste land.

encomiendas (Span.). In colonial South America, concessions of the labour services of Indians granted by the Spanish Crown to colonists who were in theory to care for their welfare and Christianize them. In practice the system, common in the early 16th century as a means of supplying labour on HACIENDAS and for the mines, caused abuses and hardship for the Indians. The Spanish Crown came to oppose the system as it threatened to give the colonists sufficient economic strength to seize independence. It also reduced the supply of labour for the Crown's own needs. A moral crusade by the DOMINICANS led the Crown to decree new laws to abolish the system in 1542 but the laws were revoked when the colonists threatened revolt. The system was finally abolished in 1720 but by then debt PEONAGE and other devices had replaced encomiendas in most regions as ways to secure permanent labour.

encyclical (deriv. Lat. *bulla encyclica*, circular letter). Letter defining papal policy from the pope to the Catholic bishops on matters of religious and political doctrine or discipline. The contents do not have the status of dogma, but nonetheless carry great authority and influence. Issued only on matters of importance, they are known by their opening words, e.g. Leo XIII's *Rerum Novarum* ('on new matters') which criticized the idea of a socialist state; Pius XI's *Mit Brenneder Sorge* (written in German and criticizing NAZI excesses) and John XXIII's *Pacem in Terris* on nuclear weapons and the need for peace.

END. European Nuclear Disarmament, a British-based movement formed in 1980 and headed by E.P. Thompson who is also a leading figure on the national council of CND.

The initial objective of END was to secure the removal of all nuclear weapons from Europe, but it has since developed into a pressure-group fighting for a re-united Europe free from domination by either the USSR or the USA. In this capacity END has established links with peace groups behind the IRON CURTAIN, such as the Moscow-based Group to Establish Trust, which has suffered greatly from official persecution. The divergence of approach between END and CND became apparent at the CND national conference in November 1982 when Prof. Thompson lost a debate in which he argued against CND's long-standing policy of British withdrawal from NATO.

Enfants de Dieu (Fr., children of God). Name used by the Camissards, the Protestants of the Cevennes whose 1702 rebellion against the French Crown was suppressed in 1704.

Engagement, The. (1) Agreement signed by Charles I and the Scots COVENANTERS on 26 December 1647, marking a change of allegiance on the part of the Scots. Charles, having lost the English Civil War, was forced to seek aid north of the border. He agreed to accept the 'Solemn League and Covenant' and to establish the PRESBYTERIAN church in England for three years. England and Scotland were to enter closer ties of unity and the 'engagers', moderate covenanters and some royalists, were in return to restore Charles to power. A Scottish army accordingly invaded England but was defeated by Cromwell in the Battle of Preston (17–18 August 1648); the 'Kirk Party' of extreme covenanters seized power in Scotland. Charles's actions led English parliamentarians to demand his death and he was beheaded on 30 January 1649.

(2) A controversial oath of allegiance imposed in 1650 by the COMMONWEALTH on all English men over 18, demanding loyalty to government rulings.

enlightened despotism. Form of ABSOLUTISM in which the government acts for the good of the governed rather than for its own self-interest. In the 16th and 17th centuries European absolutism was called by its supporters benevolent or enlightened. Strong monarchies increased the power of central government, initiated the abolition of feudalism, reduced the power of the nobility and protected the rising citizen class of the towns. This process unified the countries of Europe and laid the foundations of the modern national state.

Enlightenment, the. A broad term for 18th-century philosophical movements in which the power of human reason was stressed and obscurantist religious and political practices criticized. Fed by scientific as well as philosophical discoveries, the Enlightenment had a profound effect throughout Europe upon economic and political development, by creating a climate conducive to research and innovation; its influence can be seen in both the French and American revolutions.

Enosis (deriv. Gk., to unite). Greek Cypriot movement for the political union of Cyprus and Greece, dating from the late 19th century. When Britain assumed administration of Cyprus in 1878 the country remained under Turkish sovereignty. But Greeks formed 80 per cent of its population and they requested that the British grant union with Greece. Until the 1930s the question re-mained academic, but in 1931 severe rioting broke out between the Greek and Turkish populations of Cyprus and again demands for enosis came to the fore. In 1954 the movement was revived under the leadership of Archbishop Makarios III, Patriarch of the Orthodox Church in Cyprus. At the same time demands were made for the right of the island to determine its own future and terrorist activities began, led by EOKA.

In 1956 the British government accepted the need for a new and liberal constitution but by December 1957 the Turkish population, afraid of enosis, were demanding partition of the island. After an unsuccessful intervention by NATO, the Greek and Turkish governments reached a proposed solution at a conference in Zurich in February 1959. There was to be a new republic pledged not to participate in political or economic unity with any other state and not subject to partition. Tension between the Greek and Turkish communities persisted, however, and in 1964 the UN sent a peace-keeping force to the island. Violence, including political kidnappings and assassinations, continued and in 1967 Turkey came near to invading the island in support of the minority Turkish population. A coup by EOKA sympathizers in the National Guard on 15 July 1974 finally prompted Turkish invasion. The Turks occupied two-fifths of the island and in February 1975 declared that region a Turkish federated state, thereby partitioning Cyprus.

Enragés (Fr., the angry ones). Extremist French political group, led by Jacques Roux, originating amongst the Parisian SANS-CULOTTES in 1793, whose main demand was for economic control of the price of food.

entail. System of land tenure, introduced into England by the Statute *De Donis* in 1285, under which the holder of land had only a life interest and was precluded from alienation of the land or from any act which diminished its capital value. The land passed to the male heir on death. Legal entail was abolished by the Law of Property Act in 1925.

Entente Cordiale (Fr., cordial agreement). Term often abbreviated to Entente, originally used in the 1840s to denote the special understanding between Britain and France. It was revived as a designation of mutual goodwill in the Anglo-French Entente of 8 April 1904. Based on the resolution of outstanding colonial differences, the Entente was cemented by the efforts of both powers to remain neutral during the 1904–05 Russo-Japanese war. In August 1907 Britain concluded a similar Entente with Russia. The Anglo-French Entente was frequently strained, e.g. in 1923 by French occupation of the Ruhr and in 1940 when the British Navy sank the French fleet at Oran to prevent it falling into German hands. In 1947 attempts were made to revive the friendship by the Treaty of Dunkirk. Between 1907 and 1917 the term 'Entente powers' was applied to Britain, Russia and France, the Anglo-French and Anglo-Russian Ententes being transformed into military alliances in September 1911.

entrada (Span., entry). Term used in Spain's South American colonies to denote a military expedition into previously unexplored or unconquered regions; in Brazil, any exploratory expedition into the interior and also, occasionally, the conversion of Indians to Christianity by military force.

entrenched provisions. Provisions in the 1909 South Africa Act which can be amended or repealed only by a bill passing both houses of the parliament sitting together. On third reading such a bill must receive the approval of two-thirds of the total membership of both houses. Section 152 states that certain other sections can only be altered in this way and is itself subject to the process. The relevant sections of the Act are 33 and 34 (concerning the system of proportionate representation of the original four South African colonies); 35 (giving and protecting the right to vote of Cape 'coloureds'), and 137 (securing equality of the English and Dutch languages).

The 1931 Statute of Westminster gave the South African parliament the power to repeal any act which formed part of the country's law; nationalists concluded that this gave them the power to repeal the entrenched provisions. Section 35 was altered in 1951 and coloured voters were removed from the common electoral roll and placed on a separate one. The Supreme Court, however, ruled that this was unconstitutional. Section 152 had to be adhered to, or could itself only be altered according to the prescribed process. The nationalists then altered the method of electing senators and increased their number from 48 to 89 (later reduced to 54). In this way they obtained the requisite two-thirds majority, and altered entrenched provision 35, removing coloureds in Cape Province from the common electoral roll.

EOKA (Gk., *Ethniki Orgánosis Kypriakoú Agónos*, National Organisation of Cypriot Struggle). Anti-British Greek-Cypriot guerrilla movement founded by Col. George Theodoros Grivas to drive the British out of Cyprus by terrorism. Grivas adopted the nom de guerre of Digenes or Dighenes, a folk hero who had saved the Greeks from Arab attacks. Between 1955 and 1959 EOKA were responsible for a number of murders and in March 1956 the British deported Archbishop Makarios III, Patriarch of Cyprus and the Bishop of Kyrenia under the mistaken impression that they were EOKA leaders. Makarios was allowed to return a year later after which EOKA suspended its activities for a short time. Despite Makarios's wishes, Grivas was given command of the Greek Cypriot National Guard when a new Cypriot Republic was established in 1960. Between 1964 and 1967 Grivas and other EOKA veterans used their offices in the Guard to launch attacks on the Turkish-Cypriot community. An outrage in November 1967 nearly provoked invasion by Turkey and Grivas had to leave for mainland Greece. In 1971 he secretly returned to co-ordinate the activities of 'EOKA-B'. Makarios, considered a traitor for taking Cyprus into the Commonwealth, was the victim of murder attempts in 1970 and 1973. Grivas died in hiding in January 1974 and on 15 July EOKA members in the National Guard overthrew Makarios in a coup. Their action provoked the Turkish invasion of Cyprus five days later and the subsequent partition of the island. *See* ENOSIS.

eorl (OE). A Kentish noble in Anglo-Saxon England. The term, peculiar to Kent, possibly signifies an original nobility by birth rather than by service. The equivalent rank in the rest of England was GESITH.

episcopacy (deriv. Lat., bishop). The government of the church by bishops, a form of organization which was retained in England by Elizabeth I (1558–1603) distin-

guishing the Anglican from most other 'reformed' churches. Archbishops Parker and Whitgift checked early attempts by Calvinists to introduce a PRESBYTERIAN system but the struggle continued under James I and Charles I when the PURITANS attacked episcopacy. It was abolished by Parliament in 1643 but reinstated at the Restoration and confirmed at the Savoy Conference of 1661. The episcopacy was not seriously questioned again until the rise of METHODISM in the 18th century. The Scottish Reformation created a Presbyterian system after 1560. Despite James I's gradual reintroduction of episcopacy, it was abolished by the COVENANTERS in 1638. Reinstated in 1661, it was finally abolished in the Scottish Church in 1689.

épuration. The purge of collaborators following the liberation of France from Nazi occupation in 1945. Officially, 767 individuals were executed after trial, including Pierre Laval, the leading figure in the VICHY regime. Unofficially, 30,000 were executed in spontaneous acts of vengeance.

equal time. A legally enforceable right of American political candidates to claim equal time on radio or television to answer opposing statements made in the course of a campaign.

Erastianism. Theory, wrongly attributed to Erastus of Switzerland (1524–83), that the state has the right to decide the religion of its members. The term has usually been used in a derogatory sense: the Scottish churches, for example, held that the 'call' of the congregation was the only way to elect ministers and considered that the advocates of EPISCOPACY were practising Erastianism.

ersatz (Germ., substitute or make-shift). Substitute goods usually produced during shortages in wartime; for example, World War II ersatz coffee was made from acorns.

escheat (OFr. deriv. Lat., fall away). In feudal and medieval England the reversion to the Crown of an estate held in VASSALAGE if the vassal failed to produce heirs.

escheator. Royal officer who administered ESCHEATS and forfeited goods and lands. The office, which first appeared in 1195, was partly designed to reduce the powers of the SHERIFF. It lapsed in 1660 with the abolition of feudal tenures. In some LIBERTIES, officers styled feodaries performed similar duties.

escutage. *See* SCUTAGE.

esquire (OFr. deriv. Lat., shield-bearer). Originally the armour-bearer or attendant of a knight. An esquire was created by the king bestowing on him a pair of silver spurs, but in *c*1389 John de Kingston was created esquire by patent. Later it became legal to be made an esquire by birth, by creation or by holding certain offices. Today the term is widely used as a courtesy title.

essoin (OFr. deriv. Lat., lawful excuse). In medieval England, an excuse for failure to attend the king's court when summoned. Designed to overcome genuine difficulties of attendance, essoins were used unscrupulously to delay court actions for anything between three weeks to an almost indefinite period. Two of the more common pleas were *de malo lecti* ('ill in bed') and *de malo veniendi* ('mishap en route').

estates-general. *See* STATES-GENERAL.

Estatuto Real (Span., royal statute). Constitution promulgated by Bermúdez, Minister of the Queen-Regent Cristina of Spain in 1834, which replaced the despotic system which had existed under Ferdinand.

ETA. Militant Basque separatist movement responsible for numerous acts of violence against the government authorities in northern Spain. Its aim is the re-establishment of the short-lived Basque republic, Euzkadi, founded 7 October 1936 which ceased to exist 18 June 1937 when the right-wing forces of Gen. Franco (1892–1975) captured Bilbao in the Spanish civil war.

etas (Jap.) In Japan from the 8th century to 1868, outcasts (believed by some to have been descended from Korean prisoners of war) who performed all the most degrading trades such as scavenging, tanning, executions, etc.

étatisme (Fr.). The extension of the power of the state over the individual citizen.

états generaux (Fr.). *See* STATES-GENERAL.

ethel (OE). In early Anglo-Saxon England, land held on the original allotment made at the time of the Anglo-Saxon invasion of Britain, as opposed to BOOKLAND which was land held by a later grant or charter.

eugenics. A development of SOCIAL DARWINISM chiefly, eugenics is the science of racial improvement. Influential in Britain in the early decades of the 20th century, and later utilized by the NAZIS in their policy of ARYANIZATION, eugenicists prophesied catastrophic racial degeneration as a result of continued breeding by physically and mentally 'corrupt' sections of society, e.g. the insane, criminals and even the urban poor. At their most extreme, eugenicists advocated the elimination of the 'degenerate' by extermination or sterilization.

Euratom. European Atomic Energy Community, established by the Treaty of Rome in March 1957, which came into existence on 1 January 1958. Its original members were Belgium, France, Italy, Luxembourg, the Netherlands and West Germany and its membership remains identical with that of the EEC. Member states are pledged to co-operation in the development and application of nuclear power for peaceful purposes.

Eurocommunism. Communist policy pursued by western European communist parties since the war, by which they seek power within the framework of their own national political systems independently of the USSR. Unlike pre-war communists who tended to be dominated by the USSR via COMINTERN, Eurocommunists have often been openly critical of Soviet actions and policies.

euro-dollars. Dollars held on bank deposit in Europe (including Britain) originally either lent on loan by Americans seeking interest or as a result of US economic aid to Europe after World War II. Euro-dollars are the main part of markets for bank deposits in foreign currencies. The market grew rapidly in the 1960s when banks realized that, when handling large units of money, they could make a profit by borrowing in one country and lending in another, while still paying rates of interest above average in the first and charging rates below average in the second. The growth was helped by the continuing deficit in the US BAL-ANCE OF PAYMENTS which caused an overflow of dollars from the US to banks who were willing to hold or lend them. Since 1973 funds from the OPEC countries, called 'petro-dollars', have made their way onto the market because OPEC states have had trade surpluses with the USA. The future of the market became uncertain in 1983 following the US recession, the difficulties of OPEC and the prospect of various countries in Africa and South America defaulting on loans from foreign banks.

European Community. Organization established in July 1967 which combines the executive bodies of the EEC, EURATOM and the European Coal and Steel Community. Membership is identical with that of the EEC. The main decision-making body of the Community is the Council of Ministers (established December 1974) which consists of representatives of member states. The European Commission in Brussels presides over a large BUREAUCRACY, makes proposals to the Council of Ministers, implements its decisions and exercises powers of its own in the community's interest. It has 13 members, pledged to act independently of their own national interest; they are appointed for four years on the agreement of member states.

The European Parliament, originally set up in 1952 along with the ECSC, was later expanded to consider matters arising from the functioning of the EEC and Euratom. It has general supervisory and consultative powers and meets in Luxembourg or Strasbourg. The Parliament can dismiss the Commission and has a degree of control over the Community budget. In July 1976 it was decided that the 198 members nominated by the members' national parliaments would be replaced by 410 members directly elected by the voters of member states; the first direct elections were held in June 1979. The European Court of Justice (originally an ECSC body) is responsible for the interpretation and application of Community treaties; its decisions are binding on member states. It has nine judges, nominated by member governments, who serve for six-year renewable terms. In 1958 a European Investment Bank was established to provide capital for investment in economically backward areas of the EEC and to fund large-scale projects.

European Economic Community. *See* EEC.

European Free Trade Association. *See* EFTA.

European Monetary System. European Economic Community attempt introduced in March 1979 to create currency stability by providing for central bank intervention to keep member states' currencies within 2¼% band of the par exchange rate. It is seen as a move towards European monetary union.

European Nuclear Disarmament. *See* END.

European Recovery Programme. Four-year programme presented to the USA on 22 September 1947 by 16 European nations – Austria, Belgium, Denmark, France, Greece, Iceland, Ireland, Italy, Luxembourg, the Netherlands, Norway, Portugal, Sweden, Switzerland, Turkey and Britain. It called for increased production by each nation, internal financial stability, economic co-operation and planning and a means of rectifying the trade deficit between Europe and the USA by increasing European exports to the latter. These countries formed the Organization for European Economic Cooperation (OEEC) in response to Truman's offer of 'MARSHALL AID', administered by the Economic Cooperation Administration. West Germany joined the OEEC in 1955 and Spain in 1959. Canada and the USA were associate members and Yugoslavia had limited participation. On 30 September 1961 it was replaced by the Organization for Economic Co-operation and Development (OECD).

Euzkadi. Basque national homeland in northeast Spain, granted autonomy in October 1936. Euzkadi was occupied by Franco's forces in June 1937 and Basque political and cultural nationalism was repressed until his death in 1975. The formation of a Basque parliament in March 1980 has not prevented continued militant agitation, particularly by the ETA terrorist organization, for full autonomy from Spain.

evangelism (deriv. Gk., gospel). Preaching of the gospel with emphasis on the need for a new birth or conversion. In England, the evangelistic fervour of John Wesley and George Whitefield (*see* METHODISM) aroused the great missionary spirit of the late 18th and the 19th centuries. George Fox, founder of the Society of Friends, (*see* QUAKERS) was also an evangelist.

ex cathedra (Lat., from the throne). Term used to describe pronouncements made by the pope in consistory (*see* PAPAL INFALLIBILITY).

exchange control. Prevention of foreign currency from leaving a country, usually imposed to arrest depletion of central reserves when there is a BALANCE OF PAYMENTS deficit. The cost of imported goods cannot be met by the receipts earned on the sale of exports but has to be met instead from reserves of foreign currencies or gold. In the early post-World War II period, when there was a world-wide shortage of dollars, strict exchange controls were imposed in Britain to prevent conversion of sterling into dollars for private purposes. British residents were forbidden to travel in the USA (which would have required dollars) for other than business purposes.

In 1967 a deficit forced the British government to restrict the amount of foreign currency which could be taken out of the country for non-business purposes to £50. By imposing such restrictions on convertibility, governments can impede the movement of capital, such as private foreign investment and restrict current foreign spending. In October 1979, after 40 years of restrictions, the Conservative government lifted all remaining exchange controls.

Exchequer. Financial department originating in the CURIA REGIS, established in the reign of Henry I (1100–35), which takes its name from the chequered cloth on which the accounts were calculated. Under the supervision of the king or the treasurer it dealt with the collection and expenditure of Crown revenues. In the 12th century royal officials such as SHERIFFS had to render their accounts to the exchequer. Unlike departments such as the WARDROBE, the Exchequer maintained its functions for 700 years. It was abolished in 1833, and the name is now applied to the public funds.

exclusion crisis. English political crisis 1679–1681 which grew out of the movement arising from the POPISH PLOT to exclude the Catholic James, Duke of York (brother of Charles II) from the succession to the throne. The Parliament which met in March 1679 drew up the first Exclusion Bill and to counter it Charles first prorogued and then in July 1679 dissolved it. A new parliament met in October 1679 and the Commons passed a second Exclusion Bill, threatening to cut off supplies to the Crown until it was passed. Again Charles dissolved parliament. Opponents of the court organized petitions against prorogation or dissolution and were given the name PETITIONERS. Opponents of exclusion expressed abhorrence of the petitions and were known as ABHORRERS. These groups later formed the bases of the WHIG and TORY parties respectively.

In March 1681 another parliament was summoned, a third Exclusion Bill passed, and parliament dissolved within a week. From 1681 to his death in 1685 Charles was forced to rely on French subsidies rather than monies voted by parliament. In early 1682, James returned from voluntary exile abroad, the notorious Jeffreys was made Lord Chief Justice and Robert Spencer, 2nd Earl of Sunderland, was asked to oversee legal terrorizing of Whigs and dissenters. Because he could rely on French finance and was therefore independent of parliament, Charles was able to withstand the pressure for exclusion until enthusiasm had waned.

excommunication. Censure by most Christian churches, by which someone is excluded from the communion of the faithful according to canon law. It does not exclude a person from church membership, but from the sacraments and from church burial. An excommunicant can be absolved if he confesses his sin and does penance. In the Roman Catholic Church there are two types of excommunication: *toleratus* ('tolerated') and *vitandus* ('to be avoided'). Only the gravest sins are punished by vitandus excommunication, which is announced in public, usually by the Vatican.

exterritoriality. Legal device by which foreign diplomats and diplomatic agencies, such as embassies and legations, are considered to be outside the country of their residence despite their physical presence in it. They are for legal purposes 'foreign islands' in the territory of the host state. The custom stems from the principle of inviolability of envoys. Its practical effect is that foreign diplomats are not subject to the laws of the host nation; their embassies may not be entered, even by the police, nor may their private apartments or vehicles. Diplomats cannot be arrested and must receive goods free of all taxes and duties. A breach of exterritoriality is a grave offence of international law.

extradition. Process by which a state can remove a resident to another state where he or she is alleged to have committed a crime or has been convicted of doing so. There is no rule of international law compelling a state to extradite; the process has been brought into effect by a vast system of treaties whereby one or more states have mutually agreed on extradition in cases of serious crime. Political crimes are not usually a reason for extradition.

eyre (OFr. deriv. Lat., journey). Justices in eyre (also known as justices *in itinere*) developed from the journeys made by the king and his court throughout medieval England. As legal work increased and the importance of central government grew, Henry II (1154–89) selected judges from his own court, the *aula regia*, delegated power to them and sent them 'on eyre' around the country. They heard both criminal and civil pleas and dealt with questions of finance and administration in the shire court. They received the records of the sheriff, one of a number of supervisory functions linking local and central government and occasionally received special commissions such as undertaking an enquiry into the role of sheriffs in 1170. In 1215, Magna Carta directed them to be sent into every county once a year to take the verdicts of jurors. They were superseded by the justices of ASSIZE and NISI PRIUS established in 1280 and finally lapsed in the mid-14th century.

F

Fabian. Member of the socialist Fabian Society founded in London in January 1884 with the aim of reorganizing society 'by the emancipation of land and capital from individual and class ownership, and the vesting of them in the community for the general benefit'. The name is taken from the Roman general Quintus Fabius Maximus who sought to weaken Hannibal during the second Punic War by harassing operations while avoiding pitched battle. The name is meant to imply the rejection of revolutionary methods and the belief that universal suffrage will eventually result in SOCIALISM after a process of educational and legislative advance. The Fabian Society was one of the constituent elements responsible for the foundation of the Labour Representation Committee (later the Labour Party) in 1900. For most of the 20th century the society has acted as a specialized research agency for the Labour Party. Notable Fabians have included Sydney and Beatrice Webb, George Bernard Shaw and Graham Wallas.

FAI (Sp. *Federación Anarquista Iberica*). Iberian Anarchist Federation, formed in July 1927 to maintain anarchist ascendancy in the CNT labour movement. 30,000 strong at the outbreak of Civil War in 1936, the FAI led resistance to Franco's rising in Barcelona and Valencia and its leaders accepted government posts. Weakened by internal divisions and communist influence in the Republic, the FAI maintained a nominal existence in exile following the Nationalist victory in 1939. *See also* CNT.

Fair Deal. Policy adopted by Pres. Truman (1894–1972) when running for a second term as US President in 1948. He was faced by an ex-colleague, Wallace, who claimed to be the true representative of Democratic thinking as exemplified in the NEW DEALS as well as the Republican candidate. Truman denied the need for a planned economy but, like Roosevelt, accepted the necessity of using executive influence to prevent deflation or inflation. Presidential influence would also be used to promote housing, health and educational programmes and to extend social justice by labour legislation and civil rights measures. Finally, the Fair Deal envisaged programmes of foreign aid, military and economic, and the development of backward areas of the world.

fakir (Arab., poor man). Moslem friar or religious mendicant.

Falangist. Member of the former official FASCIST party of Spain, founded in 1933 by José Antonio Primo de Rivera, son of Gen. Primo de Rivera, Spain's dictator from 1923 to 1930. De Rivera, whose aim had been to emphasize national tradition rather than a narrowly fascist ideology, was shot by the Republicans on 20 November 1936 shortly after the outbreak of civil war. By 1937 the Falangists were showing signs of social radicalism and Franco merged them with other right-wing groups to form the Falange Española Tradicionalista ('the traditional Spanish Falange') which replaced the CORTES (parliament) between 1939 and 1942. The Falange was the only political party allowed in Spain during the Franco era although in later years its influence declined rapidly and considerably as Franco sought to free himself from dependence on it.

Falk laws. Series of laws introduced in Prussia by the Minister of Public Worship, Dr. Falk, between 1872 and 1879, which were extremely oppressive to Roman Catholics. Passed in pursuance of the KULTURKAMPF, the more important of them date from May 1873 and are known as the May laws.

Family Compact. A conservative group in Upper Canada which provoked a rebellion in 1837 arising from charges by political reformers that the Compact monopolized the acquisition of land and was overfavourable to the Church of England.

FAR. Guatemalan revolutionary group active in rural areas. In the 1960s it was nearly destroyed by the military régime (which governed until 1966), but it is now reorganized and has recovered its strength to oppose the military dictatorship of Gen. Lucas García which was established in July 1978.

farthing (deriv. OE *feōthping*, a fourth part). In England, from the 8th to the 13th centuries, literally a quarter of the silver penny, which was the only coin minted. After the Norman Conquest the penny bore a cross design which facilitated its division into farthings and half-pence. Regular minting of round silver farthings began in 1279 under Edward I. The coins were called 'Londoners' because they were first minted in London. In 1821 copper farthings were introduced and in 1860 bronze ones. The minting of farthings was discontinued in 1961.

fascism (deriv. Lat. *fasces*). Nationalist, authoritarian and anticommunist political creed, the antithesis of liberal democracy, which takes its name from the ancient Roman symbol of state authority, a bundle of rods wrapped around an axe. Its roots lie in Hegel's exaltation of the state, the mystical irrationalism of Nietzsche and Schopenhauer and Sorel's concept of a 'myth' as the focal point for emotion and action. It emphasizes the right of a self-constituted élite to rule, a disciplined party apparatus to replace parliamentary democracy and expounds the virtues of war and aggression as a means of furthering a nation's interests. Opposition, political or religious, is illegal.

Fascism, founded by Benito Mussolini in Italy in 1919, arose in the interwar period out of disillusionment with the ability of existing régimes to meet economic and social problems, to counteract BOLSHEVISM and to increase national grandeur. The Fascist Party claimed to be neither capitalist nor socialist but advocated a corporate state; it became the only recognized party when Mussolini came to power in 1922. Its members wore black shirts, were organized in military formations and used the Roman greeting of a straight outstretched arm. Their slogan was 'Mussolini is always right'. Mussolini, as IL DUCE, was the head of government and Parliament was allowed only to approve his decrees. Private enterprise was protected but strictly controlled, strikes were forbidden and some industries such as mining, shipping and armaments became largely state-owned.

Italian fascism served as a model for Spain (*see* FALANGIST), Germany (*see* NAZIS) and Japan. In Britain it was imitated by the British Union of Fascists, founded in 1933 and active until the outbreak of war; and in France by the *Croix de Feu* established in 1927 which attained some influence in the early 1930s. Since 1945 the term fascist has usually been used in a pejorative sense.

Fatah, Al. The Syrian wing of the Palestinian movement led by Yasir Arafat which became the dominant force in the Palestine Liberation Organization following the 1967 Arab-Israeli war. *See* PLO.

Father of the House. Either the oldest or the longest serving member of a parliament; the usage may vary between different parliaments.

fathers. *See* COMRADES.

faubourg (Fr., deriv. Lat., false city). Term dating from c15th century for part of a town that lay outside the walls. As cities expanded, these became what are now the inner suburbs.

favourite son. An American state political leader nominated as Presidential candidate in preference to declared candidates to enable his state party to wield bargaining power at the nominating convention.

FBI. Federal Bureau of Investigation, an agency of the US Department of Justice, founded in 1908 by the Attorney General Charles J. Bonaparte. It was known as the Bureau of Investigation until July 1935. Its longest-serving director was J. Edgar Hoover who held the post from 1924 until his death in 1972.

The FBI is charged with investigating alleged violations of federal law and as such it is responsible for dealing not only with inter-state crimes but also with acts of espionage and sabotage and general internal security. The history of the FBI is not a happy one. In 1956 Hoover set up a counter-intelligence programme, Cointelpro, to fight domestic subversion. Subsequently, the FBI, as part of Cointelpro, was responsible for illegal telephone tapping, burglaries, kidnapping, production of anonymous and fictitious materials to create internal tension in suspect groups, and of informing employers of their workers' political activities in order to get them dismissed. Hoover, angry at criticism of the FBI by CIVIL RIGHTS leader Martin Luther King, had King's telephone and rooms tapped, and produced tapes of him in allegedly compromising circumstances which he sent to King's wife. He also suggested that King should commit suicide. A Senate Committee said in 1976 that such acts were 'indisputably degrading to a free society'.

Hoover was succeeded by L. Patrick Gray who resigned in 1973 after admitting that he had destroyed papers found in the safe of one of the WATERGATE burglars. Clarence Kelly, ex-FBI agent and Chief of Police in Kansas City, replaced him and helped bring the FBI more under the control of the Justice Department. In 1978 he was succeeded by William H. Webster.

The FBI has 16,000 employees

(7,200 of whom are agents and the rest clerical and technical staff); offices in 60 major cities; 526 residencies in the USA and in Puerto Rico, and liaison offices in 11 foreign countries. Its headquarters are in Washington, DC.

FDR. (1) Revolutionary Democratic Front of El Salvador, a pluralist political movement opposed to the ruling military junta. Its president, Guillerma Ungo, resigned from the junta in 1980 in protest at its policies and abuse of human rights. The FDR is part of the FMLN in its military capacity. Mexico and France have offered to negotiate with the junta on FDR's behalf, but the USA continues to supply financial and military aid to the government which in turn refuses to negotiate.

(2) Common appellation for Franklin Delano Roosevelt (1882–1945), 32nd US President (1933–45).

fealty, oath of. Oath sworn by a man to his lord or employer by which he promised faithful service. In medieval England, feudal tenants were required to take such oaths when doing LIEGE HOMAGE. At the RESTORATION, the homage was abolished but oaths of fealty are still administered.

February Revolution. First revolution in Russia in 1917. Disenchantment with the war together with food shortages resulted in strikes and riots in St Petersburg on 8 March 1917 (February in the Julian Calendar). Troops joined the rioters and the DUMA was obliged to appoint a provisional government under Prince Lvov. On 15 March Tsar Nicholas II was forced to abdicate and real power passed to the liberal intelligentsia inside and outside the Duma. However, the BOLSHEVIKS under Lenin (1870–1924) revived the SOVIET that was established in the 1905 Revolution and criticized every act of the provisional government. On 16-17 July they made an abortive attempt to seize power but lost ground after their failure and Lenin went into hiding.

The new prime minister of the provisional government, Alexander Kerensky (1881–1970), pressed for vigorous prosecution of the war against Germany – a highly unpopular policy with the people and the army. Moreover he found it impossible to work with the commander-in-chief, Gen. Kornilov, who led an abortive coup in September 1917. These factors and the continuing food shortage enabled the Bolsheviks eventually to seize power in the OCTOBER REVOLUTION.

February Strike. 25 February 1941. A general strike in Amsterdam organized by Communists in protest against the arrest and transportation to concentration camps of 425 young Jewish men by German occupation forces on 23 February. In response the NAZIS imposed a state of siege which remained in force throughout the war.

Fedayeen (Arab., those who risk their lives for a cause). Palestinian terrorists who carried out guerrilla raids in Israel under the leadership of the GRAND MUFTI. Dispossessed of their homeland by the Israelis in 1948–49, they were forced into refugee camps in Jordan. With the decline of the Mufti's influence, the direction of the Fedayeen was eventually subsumed in the PLO.

Federal Bureau of Investigation See FBI.

Federalists. US party which in the early days of American independence in the late 18th century, favoured a concentration of power in the central government. Their opponents, the anti-federalists (later the DEMOCRATS) were supporters of the rights of individual states.

federal republic. State whose system of government is republican, as opposed to monarchical, but which is a FEDERATION. The USA and West Germany are examples.

federation. Political unit consisting of several smaller units, usually termed states, involving a central government and regional or state governments. The states or provinces devolve certain powers over themselves and their citizens to the larger unit, such powers being embodied in a written constitution which can only be amended with the consent of a fixed percentage of the states. The constitution specifies the powers devolved to the federal or central government and the restrictions placed on its interference in the internal affairs of the states. Given the possibility of disputes as to the spheres of competence of federal and state governments, machinery such as a 'supreme court' is established to interpret the constitution. Examples of federations include the USA, Canada, Australia, India and West Germany. *See also* CONFEDERATION.

Fédérés (Fr.). Young revolutionaries from Marseilles led by Barbaroux, who marched to Paris in 1792 to aid the Revolution.

fee (ME deriv. Lat. *feodum*). In England, a feudal term originally denoting a payment in cash or kind as a retainer; but later the term was extended to cover a number of miscellaneous payments.

fee farm rents. In medieval England, a group of miscellaneous crown revenues of which the most important were borough rents. The right to collect the revenues was sold for a fixed sum paid to the EXCHEQUER. The system excluded the SHERIFF from the revenue process and therefore encouraged the independence of boroughs. The first borough to receive the privilege was Lincoln in 1130. In the 12th and 13th centuries the privilege was given only on a temporary basis, but from the reign of Richard I it was granted in perpetuity. In 1670 Charles II, in need of money, agreed to transfer the fee farm rents to trustees for sale, thereby raising £700,000.

Fehden (Germ.). In medieval Germany, private wars between semi-independent barons and knights.

feitoria (Port.). Trading posts in 15th- and 16th-century Portugal, during its early period of overseas expansion; the largest were in Brazil and the East Indies.

Feldgrau (Germ., field-grey). Traditional dark bluish-grey uniform of the German armies.

fellow traveller. Term applied to someone who sympathizes with the ideals of a political party or group but who is not an official member. It is usually used with reference to the Communist Party

feminism. The belief that women's subordination to men should end and the practice of achieving this. Three main strands have appeared historically. Liberal feminism believes equality can be achieved through reform and legislation without altering the social structure. Socialist feminism argues for the overthrow of capitalism to create a society in which class and gender divisions are abolished. Radical feminism, the Women's Liberation Movement which emerged among women active in the 1960s New Left, views women's oppression as the root of all oppression and stresses its confrontation as a priority.

Fenian Brotherhood (deriv. Ir. *fianna*, body of warriors). Irish revolutionary society established *c*1858 by James Stephens. The Fenians became an organized institution during the US Civil War and occupied headquarters in New York. Their objective was to foment disturbances in Ireland in order to render English government there impossible. In 1866 they mounted an unsuccessful raid into Canada; a planned general uprising in Ireland in 1867 was also a failure. Further unsuccessful attempts were made on Canada in 1870 and 1871, after which the society's activities were restricted to minor outrages.

feodary *See* ESCHEATOR.

feormfultung (OE). In Anglo-Saxon England, a tax paid in kind levied on the land for the support of the royal household.

fermiers généraux (Fr.). System of tax gathering initiated by Francis I whereby persons, often royal favourites, obtained the right to collect taxes in return for payment of a fixed sum. The GABELLE was farmed out in this way in 1546. The system lasted until the Revolution.

Festung Europa (Germ., fortification of Europe). Term applied to Hitler's plans for an impregnable REICH during World War II.

feudalism. Social, military and political system which lasted in Europe, generally speaking, until the late 13th

century. It was organized on the basis of land tenure. Society was divided into three estates: the clergy, the nobility (including kings and emperors) and the mainly agricultural workers. Each was dependent on the others in a web of mutual responsibilities. In theory, God had given spiritual charge of men to the pope and secular power over them to the emperor from whom kings held their kingdoms, whilst dukes, counts etc. in turn received their land from the king. Thus the members of the second estate (the nobility) held their lands on condition of fulfilling certain obligations to those above and below them. When a noble received a FIEF or piece of land he became the VASSAL of the lord who bestowed it and owed him military service, advice and attendance. In return the lord offered his vassal protection and justice, received his sons into his own household and educated them for knighthood. Large fiefs were frequently subdivided and the clergy often governed church lands held in fief from nobles. The toiling class (VILLEINS or serfs) dwelt on the land of a noble or the church, rendered service by working on it or by pursuing a craft for the manorial lord in return for protection, justice and security. Villeins were given a share in the common lands or pastures to provide for their own needs. Feudal tenures were abolished in England in 1660 long after they had become inoperative. In Japan a feudal system existed up to 1871; in Russia until 1917.

Feuillants (Fr.). Members of a French club formed in 1791 by the moderate majority of the JACOBINS. They took their name from their meeting place – an old monastery near the Tuileries in Paris previously used by the Feuillants, monks of a reformed branch of the CISTER-

CIANS. They left the name Jacobin to the minority of extreme revolutionaries who gained control of the revolution.

Fianna Fail (Ir., soldiers of destiny). Party formed by Eamon de Valera (1882–1975) in 1926 from moderate members of SINN FEIN, reflecting a reversal of his previous hostility to the acceptance of DOMINION status for Ireland. In the election of February 1932 Fianna Fail emerged in a position to form a government in alliance with Labour members. Over the next 16 years de Valera, as prime minister, set about cutting the links binding Dublin to British rule, and in June 1937 a new constitution made Eire a sovereign democratic state. The party lost the 1948 election but was returned in 1951 (until 1954), 1957 (until 1973), June 1977 (until 1981) and 1982–1983. Its leaders have been de Valera, Sean Lamass, Jack Lynch and Charles Haughey. In 1982 it was accused of financial corruption and in 1983 suffered from fresh scandals including accusations of illegal tapping of telephones by Haughey's government.

fidalgo (Port.). Nobleman under the monarchy, equivalent to the Spanish *hidalgo*.

fief (ME deriv. Lat. *feodum*). Feudal term denoting the land or some other tenure held by a VASSAL in return for the provision of military service to the lord.

Field of the Cloth of Gold. Site near Calais where, in June 1520, Henry VIII of England (1491–1547) met Francis I of France (1494–1547) in an extravagant but insincere show of friendship. An enormous amount of money was spent on pomp and entertainment, including fountains running with wine, but a year later England signed an alliance against France with the German emperor Charles VI.

Fifth Amendment Communist. Term of abuse to denote suspected communists who plead the Fifth Amendment of the American constitution before civil courts or congressional committees to avoid admitting their sympathies. The Fifth Amendment provides that 'No person shall be compelled in any criminal case to be a witness against himself'. In the early 20th century it was pleaded by businessmen and politicians in anti-trust cases and was much criticized by American liberals.

fifth column. Secret enemy sympathizers who would rise if necessary to assist attackers. The term was first coined by Gen. Mola during the Spanish Civil War (1936–39). He advanced on Madrid with four military columns but claimed to have a 'fifth column' within the city itself. The term gained wide usage during World War II particularly as a popular means of explaining Germany's rapid conquest of the Low Countries and Norway.

Fifth Monarchy Men. Members of a 17th-century fanatical sect with great influence among the supporters of Cromwell in the English civil war. They believed that the COMMONWEALTH signalled the coming of the fifth monarchy, prophesied in Dan.2:44, which they identified with the MILLENNIUM as predicted in the Apocalypse.

Fifth Republic. Established in France on 6 October 1958, it has a strong Presidency and a weak legislature, with the President nominating the Prime Minister, dissolving parliament, and having power to rule by decree and appeal directly to the electorate through referenda. The Republic emphasizes independent economic and foreign policies, a commitment to nuclear weapons, and support for the European Economic Community with a vigorous defence of French interests.

filibuster (deriv. Fr., freebooter). (1) In the 17th century, a term applied to a buccaneer or pirate, owing no loyalty to any government who occupied a small island or isolated stretch of coast and used it as a base of operations. In the 18th and 19th centuries, it denoted a man taking part in an expedition with the aim of seizing and settling a tract of land in disregard of prevailing international law. The best examples of the latter type are Narciso Lopez who seized part of Cuba (1850–1851) and William Walker in Nicaragua (1855–1860). Both were later captured and executed.

(2) In the USA, a tactic of 'talking out' a bill by obstructing its passage by endless speechmaking or other legitimate means. It does not work well in the House of Representatives since a simple majority may end a debate, but in the Senate a filibuster may continue if more than one-third of those present and voting object to the ending of the debate. Long filibusters can disrupt the legislative programme by forcing the amendment or abandonment of a bill. They were widely used by opponents of the CIVIL RIGHTS legislation of the early 1960s.

filioque (Lat., and from the Son). Clause in the Nicene Creed claiming that the Holy Ghost proceeds from the Son as well as the Father. It is not accepted by the Eastern Orthodox churches.

fille de régiment (Fr., female camp-follower). An army prostitute.

Final Solution. Euphemism applied by the NAZIS to their genocidal policy against the Jews (*see* HOLOCAUST; CONCENTRATION CAMPS). In preparation for Operation BARBAROSSA, Field Marshal Keitel issued a secret directive to his staff on 13 March 1941 which spoke of 'the final struggle that will have to be carried out between two opposing political systems'. As it also spoke of the SS having 'special tasks' in 'political administration', he clearly referred to the battle between Nazism and 'Jewish Bolshevism'. In the summer of 1941 Himmler, head of the GESTAPO and SS, summoned Höss, commandant of the Auschwitz concentration camp, to Berlin and told him that 'the Fuhrer had given the order for a Final Solution of the Jewish Question' and that the SS must carry out that order. On 31 July 1941 Göring sent a directive to Himmler's deputy Heydrich authorizing him to prepare the logistics 'for a total solution of the Jewish question in the German sphere of influence in Europe'. It is clear therefore that the invasion of the USSR was to coincide with a deliberate attempt to eliminate all the Jews in Nazi-occupied territory.

Fine Gael (Ir.). Moderate nationalist party in the Republic of Ireland which in recent years has posed a real challenge to FIANNA FAIL, winning national elections in 1973, 1982 and 1983.

fire eaters. Extremist supporters of slavery and 'States Rights' in the Southern States of the USA in the years leading up to the Civil War. The name was given to them by their political opponents.

fireside chats. Wireless talks given by US Pres. Franklin Roosevelt (1882–1945) in which he discussed the NEW

DEAL and sought to restore commercial confidence during the DEPRESSION. The term derives from Roosevelt's relaxed and expert manner of utilizing the new medium.

firman (Pers.). Official edict of the government of the OTTOMAN empire, issued in the sultan's name, but not necessarily carrying his signature.

First International. Federation of socialist and communist parties founded in 1864, largely on the initiative of Karl Marx. Membership was of individuals, not parties, allowing a number of ANARCHISTS into the body, led by Michael Bakunin (1814–1876). In 1872 conflict between the anarchist and socialist/communist factions ended in the collapse of the International, and it was formally dissolved in 1876. *See also* INTERNATIONAL.

First Reich *See* THIRD REICH.

first strike. Tactic of nuclear warfare in which the aim is to destroy an enemy's missiles while they are still on the ground, thereby forestalling retaliation.

Five Members. MPs and leaders of parliamentary agitation for reform whom Charles I tried to arrest on 4 January 1642. They were John Pym, John Hampden, Denzil Holles, Sir Arthur Heselrig and William Strode. Charles's intention to impeach the five, together with Lord Mandeville, was frustrated by the House of Lords. Charles attempted to arrest them by force but they escaped to the City of London which would not surrender them. Resolutions in their support came from all over the country. Charles left London and a week later the five returned to parliament in triumph. The episode, in uniting Lords and Commons against the king, was instrumental in bringing nearer the civil war.

five-year plans. Method of planning economic policy over limited periods, adopted in a number of socialist states and the basis of national planning in the USSR, where it originated under Stalin (1879–1953). The first plan covered the years 1928–32 and was aimed at developing heavy industry in Russia. It also envisaged a centralized system of agriculture based on collective principles, causing great suffering to the KULAKS. The second plan (1933–37) aimed at increased production of consumer goods but the third (1938–42) revised this trend, concentrating productive resources on armaments.

flagellants. Members of the fanatical medieval religious movements, usually laymen, who engaged in mass public flagellations as a form of penance. They were stimulated in Italy from 1260 by the spread of the prophetic works of Joachim of Fiore which were often distorted to predict the coming of the end of the world. In the following century, the BLACK DEATH again produced flagellant movements, particularly in Germany. They were condemned by Pope Clement VI in 1349, and again by the Council of Constance in 1411–18.

flapper vote. Term used to describe the enfranchisement of British women between the ages of 21 and 30 in 1928, deriving from the contemporary slang word 'flapper' meaning a fashionable and modern young lady.

Fleet Street. Until the mid-1980s, the centre of the British national press, most of which, with modern technology, has now moved to new premises in London's former docklands.

Flemings. The majority community in Belgium, Roman Catholics speaking a language close to Dutch. A late 19th-century cultural revival encouraged agitation for Flemish autonomy and German occupation forces in both wars used their grievances in an attempt to divide Belgium. Constitutional amendments in July 1971 guaranteed the political and cultural rights of the Flemings and the minority community, the French-speaking WALLOONS.

Floating voter. Term applied to members of the electorate who do not vote consistently for one party or another.

Flotterverein. The German Navy League, founded in 1898, which agitated for an expansion in German naval power. Its propaganda was financed by Rhenish steel manufacturers, northern shipbuilders and mine-owners, all of whom would benefit financially from an enlarged fleet, as well as conservative nationalists who sought to rival British naval supremacy.

FMLN. Farabundo Marti Liberation Front of El Salvador, named after a national patriot of the 1930s. It is a military alliance of the various parties opposed to the ruling military junta. In early 1981 it began a protracted offensive in the Chalatenango area and around the capital, San Salvador. Over 1,000 members of the government forces were killed in combat in the first half of 1981 and by July the FMLN controlled a third of the country from Matapan in the north to north-east Morazan. During the mid-1980s guerrilla activity by them continued.

FNLA. National Front for the Liberation of Angola, an independence movement which for a time shared the aims of the MPLA and UNITA. In the Angolan civil war which began in 1975, however, the FNLA fought alongside the UNITA against the MPLA. It received support from China and initially from the USA and Zaire.

foederati (Lat., allies). Name given by the Romans to those barbarians who were granted land on which to settle within the frontiers of the empire. The foederati were expected to protect that part of the frontier against attacks by other barbarians.

folkland (OE). In Anglo-Saxon England, land on which FOOD RENT and customary duties were owed to the king. It was a rare term, denoting an early stage of society in which all land bore common burdens.

folkmote (OE). In early Saxon England, the gathering of the tribe in arms.

fonctionnaire (Fr.). A minor civil servant or petty official.

food rent. In early Anglo-Saxon England, an obligation to provide sufficient provisions to maintain the king and his household for 24 hours. Villages on royal estates were grouped together for this purpose, each group having to provide food rent once a year. Later many food rents were commuted to money payments or were granted away by the Crown. *See* PURVEYANCE.

foral (Port.). In colonial Brazil, a contract between the Portuguese crown and recipients of captaincies to regulate their actions and their treatment of the colonial population.

Forbidden City. (1) Fortress within the inner city of Peking which contained amongst other buildings the imperial palaces of the emperors, built between 1421 and 1911. Only the higher echelons of Chinese imperial society were allowed entry. Communist China has converted the palaces to museums open to the people. (2) Lhasa, capital of Tibet, which earned the name in the late 19th century both because of its inaccessibility and the hostility of its Buddhist monk inhabitants towards Westerners.

force de frappe (Fr.). Term for France's nuclear striking force.

Foreign Operations Administration. Body established in August 1953 to supervise and administer non-military US aid to foreign countries friendly to the USA. It replaced the MUTUAL SECURITY AGENCY and assumed the functions of the Technical Co-operation Administration, the Institute of Inter-American Affairs and a number of smaller bodies concerned with the provision of foreign aid. It was replaced by the INTERNATIONAL CO-OPERATION ADMINISTRATION in 1955.

Forest Laws. In feudal England, laws protecting forests of the crown, areas where wild beasts were maintained for hunting purposes (not necessarily woodland). They were mainly passed between 1066 and 1189 and infringement of them could result in mutilation or capital punishment until 1217. They were rarely enforced after 1688 and abolished in 1817.

forfeiture (deriv. OFr., crime). From medieval times, the practice whereby outlaws, the specially disinherited and those convicted of high treason forfeited their lands and goods. Felons' goods went directly to their lords but their lands were held first for a year by the Crown. Those convicted of high treason forfeited all possessions immediately to the Crown. The goods of heretics were divided between the Crown and the Church. Forfeiture is now governed by an act of 1870 and is severely restricted.

fouage (Fr.). Tax on chimneys imposed by Edward, the Black Prince, in Gascony during the HUNDRED YEARS' WAR.

Four Freedoms. Freedoms enumerated as basic human rights by Pres. Franklin D. Roosevelt (1882–1945) in his annual message to the US Congress in January 1941. They are the freedoms (1) of speech and expression, (2) of religion, (3) from want and (4) from fear.

Fourierism. System of communism devised by the French socialist Charles Fourier (1772–1837) who proposed the establishment of communes of 1,800 persons each, known as phalanxes, which were to be united under a central government. The gains of each phalanx were to be subject to common ownership. An unsuccessful attempt was made to establish the system near Versailles.

Fourteen Points. Peace programme outlined by Pres. Woodrow Wilson to the US Congress on 8 January 1918. The Fourteen Points were: renunciation of secret diplomacy; freedom of the seas; removal of economic barriers between states; general reduction of armaments; impartial settlement of colonial claims; evacuation of Russia by Germany and her allies; restoration of Belgium; German withdrawal from France and the return of Alsace-Lorraine to France; readjustment of the Italian frontiers; autonomous development for the nationalities in Austria-Hungary; evacuation of occupying forces from Romania, Serbia and Montenegro, with Serbia to have access to the sea; free passage of the Dardanelles and self-determination for non-Turkish peoples in the Ottoman empire; creation of an independent Poland, having access to the sea; and the creation of a general association of nations to guarantee the independence of all states. With the amendment of the tenth point to read 'complete independence for the people of Austria-Hungary', Germany and Austria-Hungary accepted the fourteen points as the basis of their request for armistices. Later many Germans held that the Paris Peace Conference violated the principles of Wilson's points by denying self-determination, especially in regard to ANSCHLUSS.

fourth estate. Name occasionally given to the Press, which implies that they have as much political power as the other three estates, the nobility, the clergy and the commons. *See* ESTATES GENERAL.

Fourth International. Formed by Trotsky in 1934 because of his rejection of the Stalin-dominated COMINTERN. A small foundation congress held near Paris in September 1938 agreed to Trotsky's 'Draft Programme' and his description of the Soviet Union as a 'degenerated' workers' state ruled by a bureaucratic stratum. Since Trotsky's death in 1940 various splinter groups have asserted claims to constitute the Fourth International.

Fourth Party. Nickname of a radical group of British Conservative MPs – Lord Randolph Churchill (1849–95), Sir Henry Drummond Wolff (1830–1908), J.E. Gorst (1835–1916) and

A.J. Balfour (1848–1930) – who first started working together in 1880. They were particularly active in opposing the Liberal government of 1880–85 and in attempting to democratize the Conservative Party; they also founded the PRIMROSE LEAGUE. Their nickname arose in conversation when it was remarked that there were two great parties in parliament; someone said there were three, including the Irish Nationalists and Churchill, the leader of the group, said there were four, including themselves. In 1884 the group began to split up when Churchill challenged Balfour's uncle Lord Salisbury (1830–1903) for leadership of the Conservative Party; Balfour sided with Salisbury. The final split came in 1886 when Churchill resigned his post as CHANCELLOR OF THE EXCHEQUER, plunging the government into crisis. Neither Wolff nor Gorst condoned his action.

Fourth Republic. Formed in France, 24 December 1946, its constitution created a figurehead President, a National Assembly and a weak second chamber. Despite some economic and industrial success, the Republic was racked by political division and weakness (23 governments in 12 years) and harried by colonial wars in INDO-CHINA and Algeria. It collapsed with France near civil war in October 1958, opening the way to the Gaullist FIFTH REPUBLIC.

francfief. A tax imposed by Louis IX of France in 1260 on commoners who came into possession of a fief. Designed to compensate the lord for their inability to render military service, it was abolished by Louis's successor Philip III.

franchise (ME, deriv. Lat., freedom). In medieval England, the body of freemen in a borough or manor; later, the rights and duties of those freemen, particularly the right to vote. Since universal suffrage the term franchise has come to be used chiefly with reference to the right to vote, particularly in parliamentary elections.

Franciscans. Order of mendicant friars, founded by St. Francis of Assisi, authorized by Pope Innocent II in 1215. Unlike earlier orders they were not confined to monasteries but lived amongst the community caring for the poor; in addition to their ordinary monastic vows they took a vow of poverty.

Francistes. A blue-shirted French fascist movement founded in 1934 by Marcel Ducard initially funded by Italy and which, although never strong, was supported financially by Germany during the Nazi occupation of France.

francs archers. A French militia first raised by Charles VII in 1448. Every parish was forced to select and equip one man who was relieved of all taxation in return for his military service.

francs-tireurs. French peasants who waged guerrilla warfare against the Germans in the Franco-Prussian War of 1870. At first the Germans treated them as brigands and shot them when captured, but in the later stages of the war they were organized by the French authorities and accorded the status and rights of belligerents.

frankalmoin (A Fr., free alms). In England, feudal tenure by which land granted to the Church by laymen was not subject to the burdens of ESCHEAT, RELIEFS, etc. It was usually granted in perpetuity in return for prayers or a CHANTRY for

the soul, but occasionally it was granted for rent. *See* MORTMAIN.

frankpledge (A Fr., trans. of OE *frithborh*, peace pledge). In later Saxon and early Norman England, a system under which the free population of England was divided into groups of ten men, TITHINGS, each member of which was responsible for the actions of the others. In this way, the policing of the country was carried out with the HUNDRED court supervising the system.

Franks. A tribe of Germanic origin settled east of the Rhine in the 3rd century, divided into three branches, the Salians, Ripuarians and Hessians. In the late 4th and early 5th centuries many settled in Roman Gaul with federate status. Following the fall of Rome, the Salians under Clovis ruled Gaul, forming a kingdom under the Carolingians which dominated most of the Germanic peoples.

Fraticelli (Ital., humble friars). Spiritual FRANCISCANS in Italy who left the order and attempted to follow a rigorous observance, with an exaggerated emphasis on the role of poverty in religious life. They were condemned for heresy by Pope John XXII in 1317. The name was also given generally to orthodox members of religious orders and to hermits.

Frauendienst (Germ.). The medieval code of courtly love.

free city. City under an international administration, not that of one state, such as Danzig between 1919 and 1939 which was under the control of the League of Nations.

free companies. Bands of mercenaries employed by the French and English during the Hundred Years'

War (1337–1453). After the treaty of Brétigny (1360) they were disbanded; finding themselves unemployed, they chose their own leaders and proceeded to freeboot in France and later in Italy.

free fire zone. Military concept developed by the American forces fighting in the Vietnam War (1965–73) against the communist North Vietnamese and VIET CONG. Tracts of the difficult Vietnamese countryside were designated to be clear of friendly Vietnamese and anyone in the zone could be fired on at will. It is not clear that all of those in the zones subjected to 'free fire' were in fact communists and the policy attracted some criticism.

'Free French'. The *Forces Françaises Libres*, partisans who continued hostilities against Germany after the fall of France in the summer of 1940 in opposition to the policy of the VICHY régime. They were drawn from French troops and naval units in Britain and French pre-war exiles living in Britain. In October 1940 Gen. de Gaulle (1890–1970) established a Council of Defence of the Empire after Free French troops had fought alongside the British against the Vichy French in Syria. In September 1941 he created the *Comité National Français* (French National Committee) as a rival government to the Vichy régime. Free French naval forces seized the islands of Saint-Pierre and Miquelon off Newfoundland because in December 1941 they were loyal to Vichy, embarrassing the USA who was not at war with the Vichy régime. At the same time de Gaulle's claim that he embodied French sovereignty and his demands for total control of links with the RESISTANCE in France annoyed the British.

On 19 July 1942 the Free French changed their name to *Forces Françaises Combatantes* (Fighting French Forces) as a display of solidarity with the Resistance. Gradually the British and Americans came to accept de Gaulle's movement as the true representatives of French liberation and in June 1943 the *Comité Français de Libération Nationale* (French Committee of National Liberation) was established in Algiers under de Gaulle and Gen. Henri Giraud. De Gaulle assumed supreme control of the French war effort in spring 1944 and in August he and Free French regular forces drove into Paris to mark its liberation following the uprising in the city of resistance groups acting as the *Forces Françaises de l'Intérieur*.

freehold. Originally, land held in free tenure, such as FRANKALMOIN or SOCAGE as opposed to COPYHOLD, tenancy at will or tenancy for some fixed period. The latter was the normal landlord-tenant relationship under FEUDALISM. In 1215 MAGNA CARTA recognized persons holding freehold estates as having the rights of freemen. The term is used today to denote land held at least for life, and occasionally indicates land which the owner is free to do what he likes with, as opposed to leasehold land which is subject to restrictions. The concept of land held entirely free of duties, however, is alien to English common law.

Freemasons. Widespread and influential secret society. In medieval England and Scotland, itinerant working masons were organized in lodges with secret signs for mutual recognition. But modern freemasonry arose in England in the early 18th century. The first Grand Lodge was opened in 1716 and the Freemasons' Hall in 1776. With clubs for discussion and social enjoyment from which women were excluded, freemasonry spread quickly in England and abroad. It has a graded lodge structure, confers social prestige and indulges in much ritual, ceremony and symbolism. In some European countries it has been held to have links with the occult.

In late 18th- and 19th-century Europe, freemasonry was associated with political radicalism, especially in countries agitating for national independence. As such, it came into conflict with the established political order and the Roman Catholic Church, and attempts were frequently made to suppress it.

Until quite recently, membership conferred definite business and social advantages, comprising as it did a high middle-class element, but this has now markedly declined and the society is mainly a charitable organization. Fear of its secret nature has led the Roman Catholic Church to condemn it, FASCIST dictators to ban it and the COMINTERN to denounce it.

Free Officers. Egyptian radical nationalist and republican movement of young army officers, nominally led by Mohammed Neguib but Gamal Abdul Nasser (1918–1970) was its most influential figure. Egypt's military failure against Israel in 1948 encouraged growing support and the movement mounted a bloodless coup against King Farouk on 23 July 1952. Neguib became President but was deposed by Nasser in November 1954.

Freesoilers. US party formed in 1848 with the aim of preventing the extension of slavery to the Territories; absorbed in 1856 by the REPUBLICAN Party.

Free Staters. Supporters of the Irish Free State which excluded six counties in Ulster, created 15 January 1922, following the 6 December 1921 Treaty of London, Arthur Griffiths becoming President and Michael Collins Prime Minister. De Valera's Irish Republican Society rejected the Free State and, defeated in the June 1922 elections, mounted an armed struggle against it until May 1923, during which Griffiths and Collins were killed.

free trade. Free interchange of commodities, unrestricted by the imposition of duties by government, except perhaps for revenue purposes. The principle, first advocated by Adam Smith in *Wealth of Nations* (1776), became a matter of practical politics in Britain in 1846, mainly as a result of its advocacy by Cobden and the MANCHESTER SCHOOL, and of the agitation of the ANTI-CORN LAW LEAGUE. The opposite of protectionism, it is held that removal of protective tariffs and monopolies allows 'natural competition' between countries and produces considerable benefits to world trade and economy.

Free Traders *See* FREE TRADE.

free world. Term used by Western politicians to describe non-communist countries.

Freeze. Peace movement in the USA campaigning for a 'freeze' of expenditure on nuclear weapons (that is, maintenance of the present number and technology of such weapons). It is believed that further or increased expenditure will lead to a dangerous ARMS RACE with the USSR. The movement's popularity has increased rapidly and it has staged several mass demonstrations involving hundreds of thousands of people.

freikorps (Germ., free corps). Counter-revolutionary volunteer forces recruited by the German government in December 1918 to restore internal law and order, to prevent revolution and to protect German frontiers after the collapse of the monarchy and dissolution of the imperial army. They suppressed left-wing revolutionary movements, including the SPARTACIST rising of January 1919 and the Bavarian SOVIET. Further units fought on the eastern frontiers, mainly against Poland and the RED ARMY in the Baltic states, until the Allies demanded their disbandment. Mostly young, middle-class nationalists and veterans of World War I, many were unable to adjust to civilian life. When disbanded in 1919 some joined the REICHSWEHR, the state armed forces; others, expressing a common resentment against the WEIMAR republic, plotted to overthrow it. The involvement of freikorps members such as Erhardt and Lüttwitz in the abortive Kapp Putsch signified the end of the force apart from a brief revival in 1921 due to the war in Upper Silesia. Large numbers of the freikorps who were anti-semitic and anti-communist later joined the various right-wing para-military organizations active in Weimar Germany.

Freisinnige (Germ.). A coalition party of advanced radicals and seceders from the National Liberals, formed by Richter in 1884, who sat in the German REICHSTAG.

Frelimo (abbrev.). The Frente de Libertação de Moçambique, a Marxist liberation movement which waged a guerrilla war against the Portuguese in Mozambique from 1964 to 1974. Upon decolonization, Frelimo became the dominant political force in the People's Republic of Mozambique.

frérage (Fr.). In feudal France, a system of tenure whereby land passed to the eldest son who retained part of it but passed the rest to his brothers who paid him HOMAGE. The system was similar to SUBINFEUDATION in its form and results.

Fretelin. The independence movement in the former Portuguese colony of East Timor, illegally seized and occupied by Indonesia.

friars. Members of certain mendicant orders of the Roman Catholic Church. The four main orders are FRANCISCANS (Grey Friars); DOMINICANS (Black Friars); CARMELITES (White Friars) and Augustinians (Austin Friars).

Friars Preachers *See* DOMINICANS.

Frisians. Inhabitants of the northern Rhine and Schleswig areas of Germany in the 5th and 6th centuries, some of whom settled in East Anglia. Their expansion south was checked by the Franks who defeated and dissolved Frisia Magna in 734.

frith (OE, peace). In medieval England, a code of behaviour generally acceptable to the community, transgression of which led to punishment determined by the community at the MOOT. Originally a supplement to the King's Peace, it was later replaced by it.

frithborh *See* FRANK PLEDGE.

frith-guilds. In 12th- to 14th-century England, societies formed in the towns based on conditions of mutual responsibility similar to those entailed in the FRANK PLEDGE. They may later have combined to form the merchant guilds which came to regulate conditions of labour and the price of commodities.

Fronde (Fr., sling). Party which rose against Mazarin during the minority of Louis XIV. Its contention was that the royal prerogative was not above the law. The initial outbreak caused the court to vacate Paris in 1648; it was ended in 1649 by an arrangement known as the Treaty of Ruel, but the fronde was not finally suppressed until 1652.

front benchers. In the British House of Commons, members of the government and the opposition who sit on the two facing benches nearest the centre of the House. Other MPs are termed 'back-benchers'.

fudai (Jap.). Vassal DAIMYŌS or nobles of the SHŌGUN.

fueros (Span.). In Spain and later in colonial Spanish America, the charters and special privileges granted by the Crown to individuals and corporate bodies, e.g. town guilds or the Church, in return for services. The earliest known fuero was granted to the town of Léon by Alfonso V in 1020. They were revoked in the 19th century.

Führer (Germ., leader). Title assumed by Hitler when he became Chancellor of Germany in 1933.

Führer Prinzip (Germ., leadership principle). Basis of Hitler's organization of the NAZI state, arising from the doctrine of the aristrocratic idea of Nature. Führer Prinzip was to replace democracy as a system of the authority of every leader downwards and the responsibility upwards, with Hitler at the pinnacle of the system, having supreme authority and ultimate responsibility for Germany's destiny. The Führer, and not a parliament, was the ultimate decision-maker in affairs of state. Hitler described the principle in *Mein Kampf* as 'absolute responsibility unconditionally combined with absolute authority' which would 'gradually breed an élite of leaders such as today, in this era of irresponsible parliamentarianism, is utterly inconceivable'.

full employment. Economic condition defined by Lord Beveridge (1879–1963) in *Full Employment in a Free Society* where there are 'more vacant jobs than unemployed men'. The definition does not include those incapable of work or unwilling to take a job, but it should be noted that there can still be men unemployed, even under 'full employment'. In the UK Beveridge considered that a limit of three per cent of the work force unemployed was compatible with full employment.

fundamentalist. One who believes that the Bible contains only literal truths which need not be the subject of interpretation: the description of creation in Genesis, for example, leads to a refusal to accept the Darwinist theory of evolution. Fundamentalism is popular in the southern states of the USA, hence the description of those states as the 'BIBLE BELT'.

Moslem fundamentalists, such as the AYATOLLAH Khomeini in Iran, desire that their countries be ruled in strict accordance with Islamic law and reject non-Islamic Western or communist influences.

Furstenbund (Germ., bond of princes). League of German princes, formed in Berlin in July 1785 between Prussia, Saxony and Hanover under the auspices of Frederick the Great; it was later joined by most other German states. Its purpose was to reduce Austrian power in Germany and, more immediately, to thwart the attempt by the Austrian Emperor Joseph II to gain possession of Bavaria by agreement in exchange for the Austrian Netherlands.

fusillades (Fr.). Wholesale massacres in Lyons in 1792 when the city surrendered to the Revolutionary troops.

fyrd *See* LAND FYRD.

G

gabelle (Fr.). French tax on salt, first levied in the 14th-century. Nobility, clergy and certain towns and provinces were exempt while elsewhere it was strictly imposed and proved both burdensome and unpopular. It was abolished in 1791.

Gahal. The party formed by the merger in 1965 of the Herut and the Liberal Party in Israel.

Gaitskellites. Members of the British Labour Party who supported the moderate and reformist policies of Hugh Gaitskell (1906–1963) in the late 1950s and early 1960s. In 1955 Gaitskell was elected party leader, defeating Bevan. His supporters, many of whom came from the trade unions and their sponsored MPs, represented the social democratic tradition in the party and found themselves in conflict with the more left-wing BEVANITES, particularly over defence policy. Labour's defeat in the 1959 general election led Gaitskell to try altering the party's image. He suggested dropping CLAUSE IV of the constitution which demanded 'common ownership of the means of production, distribution and exchange', but was forced after a sharp controversy to abandon the idea. In 1960 the Gaitskellites were defeated over defence at the party conference which passed a resolution in favour of unilateral nuclear disarmament. Gaitskell resigned the party leadership but was re-elected by the parliamentary party.

galleon. Mediterranean sailing vessel developed from the galley and later adapted for ocean waters by 15th-century explorers. Also, part of the Spanish fleet which annually sailed from Seville to the isthmus of Panama and Cartagena.

Gallicanism. Term coined in the 19th century for the position opposed to ULTRAMONTANISM in France, also denoting a more general complex of doctrines favouring restriction of papal power. It has three main strands: the assertion of the independence of the French king from the papacy; the collaboration of clergy and secular powers to limit papal intervention in the French state; and the superiority of an ecumenical council over the papacy. It first manifested itself in a 13th-century dispute between Philip IV and Pope Boniface VIII; by the 16th century a conciliar theory of church hierarchy had arisen which held that the Pope is subject to the general council of the Church. In 1398, following a national synod of French bishops, Charles VI withdrew his obedience to Benedict

XIII, the Pope at Avignon, yet did not recognize his rival Boniface IX in Rome. In 1438 Charles VII issued the *Pragmatic Sanction of Bruges*, stating that the Pope's secular jurisdiction was dependent on the king and that the Pope was subject to a general council of the Church. The papacy secured its revocation in 1516.

The best exposition of Gallicanism was the *Gallican Articles* issued by a synod of the French clergy in 1682. These held (1) that the pope has no secular power though he is spiritually supreme; (2) that he is subject to ecumenical councils; (3) that papal infallibility in matters of doctrine is conditional on confirmation of the papal position by the whole church, and (4) that the pope must recognize the inviolability of the immemorial customs of the church in France, such as the right of the crown to appoint bishops and receive the revenues of vacant bishoprics. The articles were condemned by Pope Alexander VIII in 1690 and revoked by Louis XIV in 1693. However, not all the French clergy accepted the Gallican position. The French Jesuits did not and Napoleon took no real interest in the matter. The first Vatican Council (1869–70) formally declared the Ultramontanist position to be the correct one, but by this time the emergence of the modern state had rendered disputes about papal intervention anachronistic.

galloglasses (deriv. Ir., *gallóglach*, foreign soldiers). Mercenary troops (also known as KERNS) from the Hebrides and north-west Scotland who first appeared in Ireland in the service of a native chief in 1258. Many settled in Ireland, particularly in Ulster, forming an hereditary élite fighting corps for Irish chiefs. They served in Irish armies until Elizabethan times when they were rein-forced by more Scottish mercenaries from the Isles, called Redshanks by the English. Galloglasses took part in Tyrone's rebellion but disappeared after his defeat at Kinsale in 1601.

game theory. An approach to understanding individual and group human and animal behaviour which proposes that life is a strategic game following complex rules which can be mathematically analysed and calculated.

gamonal (Span. colonial, large land-owner). Owner of a large estate in Peru, Ecuador or Bolivia. *Gamonalismo* denotes a system in which such local landowners dominate the economic, political and social life of the region to the detriment of the Indians.

Gang of Four. (1) Those Chinese political leaders – Wang Hongwen, Zhang Chungqiao, Yao Wenyuan and Jiang Qing – who were publicly denounced following the triumph of the moderates in 1976. There has been a constant division between moderates and radicals in the Chinese Communist Party though the doctrines of MAOISM have given support to the latter. Amongst the moderates might be counted Chou En-Lai (1898–1976), Prime Minister from 1949 to 1976, and his deputy Deng Xiaoping: both had great reservations about the CULTURAL REVOLUTION. Following the death of Chou En-Lai and of Mao Tse-tung, a power struggle broke out in the party and for a time Deng Xiaoping fell from favour. A group of radicals, centred in Shanghai and supported by Mao's widow Jiang Qing, argued the case for ideological purity and continued revolution at the expense of internal development. The moderates wished to pursue Chou En-Lai's old pragmatic economic policy, arguing that political development would result from economic progress.

The moderates regained control of the party and a vicious propaganda campaign against the Gang of Four commenced through the medium of street posters. The Gang were arrested and accused of planning to take control of the army. During 1977 Deng Xiaoping was rehabilitated and given charge of a modernization programme. Demands for greater freedom were tolerated for a time, but stopped after violent outbreaks by radicals in Shanghai. To aid industrialization China strengthened links with the West and on the thirtieth anniversary of the foundation of the People's Republic, the Cultural Revolution was denounced as a calamitous mistake. A show trial was held of the Gang of Four and a suspended death sentence was passed on Jiang Qing in January 1981.

(2) In Britain, name popularly given to four ex-Labour Party members – Shirley Williams, David Owen, William Rodgers and Roy Jenkins – whose decision to leave the party coincided with the attacks on the Chinese Gang of Four.

On 25 January 1981 the 'Gang' published the 'Limehouse Declaration' announcing the establishment of a Council for Social Democracy. Originally this was not to be a separate party, but a pressure group within the Labour Party to fight for moderate left-wing policies. However, in March 1981, David Owen, William Rodgers and ten other MPs said they would not seek re-election as Labour MPs and the same month the Social Democratic Party (SDP) was formed. Most Social Democrats merged with the Liberals in 1988 to form the Social and Liberal Democrats. Dr Owen continued to head an emasculated SDP.

garde nobile (Fr.). Corps of militia.

Garibaldini (Ital.). Democratic Italian party at the turn of the 20th century which wished to realize Garibaldi's dream of a united republican Italy.

Garter, Order of the. Noble order founded in 1348 by Edward III: the premier order of knighthood in Great Britain and the most ancient in Europe. Its emblem, a dark blue garter and its motto, 'Honi soit qui mal y pense' ('shamed be he who thinks evil of it'), are associated with an occasion on which either the Countess of Salisbury or the Countess of Kent dropped her garter at her ball and had it returned to her by Edward with those words. The order was modelled on the fellowship of King Arthur and the Knights of the Round Table and was originally limited to the sovereign and twenty-five knights. The number has been considerably extended and now includes royal personages and leading representatives of the peerage. Members wear the velvet garter (with a gold motto) on the left leg below the knee, a mantle of blue velvet with white silk lining, a surcoat and hood and a gold and enamel collar; women wear a sash across the left shoulder.

Gastarbeiter (Germ. 'Guestworker'). Overseas labour – predominantly Turkish – recruited to meet the needs of West German industry in the 1960s and 1970s which was denied citizenship rights and often forced to return home when its services were no longer required. *See* MIGRANT LABOUR.

GATT. General Agreement on Tariffs and Trade, administered since 1955 by the Organization for Trade Co-operation. Aimed at reducing tariffs and other trade restrictions with a view to moving towards FREE TRADE, it has grown out of a series of major negotiations since World War II: at Geneva (10 April–30 October 1947); Annecy (April–October 1949); Torquay (September 1950–April 1951) and Geneva (1956; 1964–1967).

By 1951 some 374 bilateral agreements had been concluded with reference to 58,700 trading items. Individual bargains on tariffs between pairs of countries have been extended widely by operation of the MOST FAVOURED NATION principle. Britain insisted on applying differential rates of import duties between members and non-members of the BRITISH COMMONWEALTH; the USA insisted on retaining high tariffs, and there remained opportunities to practise discrimination or restriction of imports even without tariffs because of the way agreements were phrased.

After 1951 the emphasis was on preventing such discrimination. The 1964–67 talks, the 'Kennedy Round' (named after Pres. J.F. Kennedy), ended when the US Trade Expansion Act expired, allowing the USA to make very large reductions in its tariffs. Agreement was also reached on cereals and an 'anti-dumping' code was adopted.

Four-fifths of world trade is now covered by GATT which attempts to preserve tariff concessions by prohibiting other forms of protection, such as internal taxes, too strict a customs administration and sudden changes in safety standards.

Gauchistes (Fr. 'Leftists'). Political groupings to the left of the French Communist Party, including anarchists, Maoists and Trotskyists, usually with a large proportion of student members, active in the 1968 MAY EVENTS and the early 1970s.

Gauchos (Span.). Argentinian shepherds, inhabiting the pampas or plains of the interior, who supported Ortiz de Rosas, effective dictator of Argentina 1835–52.

Gauleiter (Germ.). High ranking NAZI official in a *Gau* (a territorial division of the Nazi party), who was responsible for political and economic activity in the division as well as the mobilization of labour and civil defence.

Gaullist. Generally, a follower of Gen. Charles de Gaulle (1890–1970), although Gaullism does not lend itself to precise definition. Under the Fourth French Republic Gaullism proved to be a short-lived mass movement, although de Gaulle himself retained an important following. In 1947 he launched the Rassemblement du Peuple Français (RPF) which appealed to anti-communist fears and exhibited authoritarian and even fascist tendencies. The RPF reached the peak of its power in 1948 and won a large number of seats in the 1951 election, but was dissolved in 1955 following internal dissensions and electoral setbacks. De Gaulle always saw it as a national movement rather than a political party but many RPF deputies had wished to be actively involved in parliamentary politics. After 1953 Gaullist deputies sat as Social Republicans until the end of the Fourth Republic, their leaders joining various coalitions. With the establishment of the Fifth Republic in 1958, the Union pour la Nouvelle République (UNR) was formed from various Gaullist movements (including the Union for French Renewal, the Republican Convention and the Workers Committee for the support of General de Gaulle). It won 234 seats in the 1958 election, but soon found itself divided on questions of leadership, organization and policy, being united only by loyalty to de Gaulle and belief in the need for national renewal. However, during the 1960s it became more homogeneous and developed some of the reflexes of a political party. Gaullism survived the retirement of de Gaulle in 1970 and provided a basis of support for his presidential successor Georges Pompidou.

gavelkind (ME deriv. OE, tribute). System of land tenure in Saxon and early Norman England, under which inheritance was equally divided among the sons at death. A similar system of tenure also existed in Kent whereby, in cases of intestacy, estates passed equally to all sons and not wholly to the eldest. *See also* SOCAGE.

gebur (OE). In Saxon England, a subdivision of the CEORL class, being free peasants each working a yardland (usually 30 acres), who were liable to burdensome dues and services to their feudal lords. Their economic position was similar to that of the later VILLEIN. The name gave rise to 'boor' as a derogatory description of a peasant.

Geddes Axe. Economies in government expenditure, recommended by a committee appointed by Lloyd George in August 1921 in response to pressure from right-wing members of the Liberal-Unionist coalition. Chaired by Sir Eric Geddes, its other members were Lord Inchcape, Lord Farringdon, Sir J.P. Maclay and Sir W. Guy Granet; they were charged with investigating the scale and nature of government spending. They reported in February 1922, proposing economies of £86 million, few of which were actually made.

geld (OE). Extraordinary tax assessed on land, first levied in 9th-century England to buy peace with the Danes but only nationally imposed under Ethelred II (978–1016). From *c* 990 to *c*1010 it was again used to buy off the Danes but under Cnut it went to maintain the HOUSECARLES and was known as here-geld (OE, army-tax). Later it became known as danegeld for whatever purpose it was levied.

Gemeinschaft (Germ.). Association or community.

gemot *See* MOOT.

geneat (OE, companions). In Saxon England, a subdivision of the CEORL class, being freemen who constituted a form of peasant aristocracy. Originally members of the warband, they were of lower status than GESITHS.

generalissimo (Ital., Span.). Supreme commander of a combined military/naval force.

general strike. An attempt to bring an economy to a standstill through a nationwide stoppage of work, often with political objectives. The concept arose in Britain in the 1830s as a 'Grand National Holiday' but aroused little trade union interest. The French CGT's Charter of Amiens of 1906 advocated a general strike and factory occupations as the means by which the industrial working class could seize power. The SECOND INTERNATIONAL debated the possibility of a Europe-wide strike to prevent war before 1914. Although never seriously undertaken, the theory of the general strike coloured labour movement thinking between 1906–26. The General Strike in Britain in May 1926 proved a disastrous failure.

geopolitics. Study of the relationship between geographic environment and national and international politics. The earliest exponent of geopolitical theories was the Swede, F. Ratzel, in his work *Political Geography* (1897); the term was coined by his pupil Kjellen. Many geopolitical theories arose in the early 20th century, among them those of Sir Halford Mackinder, Karl Pearson and Fairgrieve in Britain; Admiral Mahan and Brooks Adams in the USA and Vallaux and Demangeon in France.

In *Democratic Ideals and Reality* (1919), Sir Halford Mackinder explained that the three contiguous continents (Asia, Europe and Africa) form a 'world island'. America and Australia are other 'islands' of less importance and the smaller far eastern islands are satellites of other 'islands'. On the 'world island' is a 'heartland' – the area between the Volga and East Siberian mountains, between the Arctic and the Himalayas. Its 'glacis' is eastern Europe, from the Volga to the Hensburg-Trieste line. Russia thus occupies much of the 'heartland' while Austria and Germany are on the glacis. Mackinder argued: 'Who rules East Europe commands the Heartland: who rules the Heartland commands the World-island: who rules the World-island commands the World'.

Mackinder's theories had great influence in Germany. German geopolitics sees nations or states as organisms engaged in a perpetual struggle to survive. The 'spaces' into which the earth is divided determine, independently of human will, their areas of struggle. All nations are subjected to the same forces depending on the 'space' affecting them. The theory envisages perpetual struggle and accounted in the 1920s for Germany's feelings of being 'boxed in' and therefore prevented from ever being a world power. The influential Institute of Geopolitics was founded in Munich in 1923 by Gen. K. Haushofer who coined the term LEBENSRAUM. Many geopolitical theories were reflected in the rhetoric of the NAZIS; they have undoubtedly emphasized the effect of geographical factors on international affairs.

Geraldines. Clansmen of the Norman family the Fitzgeralds (later of Desmond and Kildare) who settled in Ireland in the mid-12th century at the time of the conquest under Henry II. An exceedingly turbulent clan, they were involved in Tudor times in numerous intrigues with Spain and rebellions against English rule. They rose in 1569 and were not suppressed until 1580 when the clan was broken up and its influence in Irish politics ended.

Germania. A revolt in the kingdom of Valencia in 1519 against the privileges of the nobility. It had no support from Charles V.

gerrymandering. Manipulation of boundaries of electoral divisions in such a way as to give one political party an undue advantage; derived from Elbridge Gerry, Governor of Massachusetts in 1812.

Gesellschaft (Germ.). Society created for a particular purpose, e.g. a commercial company.

gesith (OE). Members of the king's warband at the time of the Anglo-Saxon conquest of England; they later became the aristocracy of England. Their title was replaced in the 9th century by that of THEGN.

Gestapo (Germ., abbrev. Geheime Staatspolizei). Secret State Police established in Prussia by Goering on

26 April 1933, replacing the Prussian political police. Originally a personal instrument of terror to arrest and murder opponents of the NAZI régime, in April 1934 the Gestapo was rapidly expanded under Himmler and eventually became an arm of the SS.

Gevey, Les. Confederacy formed in 1566 by patriotic nobles and gentry of the Netherlands, led by Count Louis of Nassau and Brederode. It was broken up in 1567 and many of its members executed.

ghazi (Arab., raid). One who makes a raid, particularly as part of a JIHAD, notably during the expansion of the Moslem OTTOMAN empire in the 14th and 15th centuries. Raids were carried out from Transoxania against the non-believers of the Steppes in central Asia and from the Syria-Mesopotamian border against Byzantium. More loosely, the term has been used to denote the Moslem fanatics who spearheaded attacks in Asiatic warfare.

Ghibellines (Ital., deriv. Germ. *Waiblingen*). Party in medieval Italian and German politics, whose name is said to be derived from that of an estate belonging to the Hohenstaufens. Their feud with the GUELPHS, occurring during the campaigns of Emperor Frederick I, developed in 13th-century Italy into a bitter conflict between the Ghibellines supporting the Emperor, and the Guelphs, supporting the Pope.

GI. US soldier in World War II; derived from 'Government Issue', the standard stamp on US army equipment.

gilds (*also* guilds; deriv. OE, payment). In medieval England, associations for religious and social purposes. In the late 11th century merchant gilds arose which combined these functions with defence of commercial interests; they succeeded in controlling trade within a town's boundaries by establishing monopolistic privileges. In the 12th century craft gilds which regulated and protected particular trades arose. In the 13th century the apprenticeship system developed whereby entry to a trade was restricted by high fees, with day workmen or journeymen providing extra labour. In the 14th century London gilds were incorporated as livery companies, some of which still exist. Gilds were undermined from the 17th century onwards by the disintegration of the apprenticeship system and the growth of large capitalist enterprises, although many survived to the 18th century and later.

Girondins (Fr.). Middle-class republican group led by Brissot, Roland, Petion and Vergniaud, which sat in the Legislative Assembly of 1791 and the Convention of 1792; their name derived from the Gironde region of south-west France. Having rushed France into war in early 1793, they found themselves in conflict with the JACOBINS over its conduct, which led to their overthrow and the execution of their leaders in 1793.

glasnost (Russ., 'openness'). The liberalization of the Soviet intellectual climate following the emergence of Mikhail Gorbachev as Communist Party Secretary in March 1985. As well as encouraging greater discussion of contemporary Soviet society and of the role of the Party, glasnost appeared to open the way for an honest appraisal of post-revolutionary history, particularly the role of Stalin. Inseparable in Gorbachev's view from PERESTROIKA.

glebe (deriv. Lat., land). In medieval England, an area of land held by the incumbent of a parish church as part of its endowment. Parish priests usually participated in the system of open-field agriculture.

Gleichberechtigung (Germ.). Equal status, for example, in armaments.

Gleichschaltung (Germ., coordination). Term taken from the vocabulary of electrical engineering which was applied to the process of official subordination of all political and social organizations in Germany to NAZI control. The term was first used in March 1933 with the introduction of a law establishing Nazi majorities in the government of each federal state; later it referred to the subordination of many institutions, e.g. trade unions, youth clubs, etc. Its aim was to deprive Germans outside the Nazi party of a political or social focal point in their daily lives. The term fell out of usage after 1939.

Glippers. Netherlanders who supported the party of the Spanish king c1570.

Glorious Revolution. Series of events of 1688–89 which led to the exile of James II (1633–1701) and the accession to the throne of his daughter, Mary (1662–94) and her husband William of Orange (1650–1702). James's unconstitutional rule and pro-Catholicism led seven men, including the Bishop of London, Danby (1631–1712), Sydney Russell and Cavendish, to invite William to invade England. As William prepared, James frantically tried to rescind his previous policies, but to no avail. On 5 November 1688 William landed at Torbay with 11,000 infantry and 4,000 cavalry. The English peerage and gentry rallied to him and James was allowed to flee to France. William and Mary became joint sovereigns after accepting the Declaration of Rights and the BILL OF RIGHTS.

godos (Span., Goths). In colonial South America, name given to upper-class Spaniards.

gold bugs. Name used in the USA in the 19th and early 20th centuries to describe supporters of the GOLD STANDARD.

Golden Bull. (1) In Hungary, a charter of liberties extorted from Andrew II by his nobles in 1222; among other concessions it provided for annual meetings of the DIET.
(2) In Germany, an edict issued by Emperor Charles IV in 1356 which settled disputes as to which ELECTORS should form the electoral college.

Gold Coast. Region of West Africa which attracted European traders from the late 15th century because of the large quantities of gold mined in the Akan forest and went on to become a prime source of slaves. British rule was established in the 18th century, gradually extending to the interior. The colony achieved independence as Ghana on 6 March 1957.

Golden Fleece. Order of chivalry, founded by Philip the Good of Burgundy at Bruges in 1430, which became a Spanish order when the Netherlands became a Spanish province. However, since Emperor Charles V was also emperor of Germany, it was claimed as an Austrian order by his Habsburg successors and thus developed two branches under two sovereigns.

Golden Horde. The Mongol kingdom established by Batu, grandson of Genghis Khan, and ruled over by his descendants throughout its existence from 1256 to 1502. The regime centred on Old (later at New) Saray on the lower Volga. Internal dynastic disputes and defeat by the Russians in 1380 weakened the state and after 1419 breakaway independent khanates were established in the Crimea, at Astrakhan and Kazan. What remained of the Golden Horde led a precarious existence, threatened by Russians, Poles and Lithuanians, until its demise in 1502.

Golden League. League formed by the Catholic states of Switzerland in 1586 to defend their faith.

Golden Temple. The Sikh temple in Amritsar stormed by the Indian Army in 1984 because of the presence of armed SIKH militants who favoured a separate state. The attack provoked the assassination of Indian prime minister Indira Gandhi, which in turn caused riots in which thousands were killed.

gold penny. English gold coin, first minted on a regular basis in the mid-14th century. Various Saxon kings had occasionally minted coins and in 1257 Henry III minted a gold coin modelled on the Florentine florin, called variously the gold penny and the bezant (after a Byzantine coin then current in Europe). Originally worth 1s 8d, it quickly rose to 2s. Too high in value to be of use for most of the population, it was withdrawn from circulation in 1270.

Gold Standard. Currency system in which money is held in the form of gold or in paper notes which are convertible to gold on demand. General in Europe and the USA before 1914, the system involved keeping a gold reserve large enough to meet all likely demands and to back the issue of notes. During World War I the gold market could not function freely and Britain went off the Standard in 1919. When she returned to it in 1925, the restoration was incomplete, as the gold reserve was too small, but both political parties felt that the prosperity of the City of London as a centre of international finance depended on maintaining the Gold Standard. In September 1931 Britain again abandoned the Standard in response to the international financial crisis. France was forced off it by World War I, returned to it in 1926 and finally abandoned it, together with Belgium, the Netherlands and Switzerland, in 1936. In the USA the 1900 Gold Standard Act made the gold dollar the standard unit of value, but the system was abandoned by the Roosevelt administration in 1933. Since 1945 economic theory has tended to discount the reliability of gold as a stable unit of currency.

Golkar. The ruling political party in Indonesia under President Suharto in the 1970s and 1980s.

Gomarists. Followers of Gomarus, professor of theology at Utrecht, and opponents of the ARMINIANS. Gomarus favoured the severe doctrine of Calvin, Arminius a milder and broader form of religious belief. In 1604 their differences divided the Dutch church and led to the convening of the Synod of Dort in 1618.

good neighbour policy. Foreign policy stance adopted by US Pres. F.D. Roosevelt (1882–1945) involving a cautious move away from ISOLATIONISM and a positive effort to establish better diplomatic relations with other countries, especially those in South America.

goosestep. Straight-legged form of marching used by the troops of the USSR and numerous South American countries. It was made infamous by the NAZIS and FASCISTS of Europe.

gôshi (Jap.). In Japan from the 8th century up to 1868, a social class, ranking between the SAMURAI and the agricultural class, whose members farmed their own lands and owed no allegiance to feudal lords.

Gosplan. Soviet State Planning Commission, a centralized unit set up to administer the economic policies of the USSR during the Stalin era (1924–53).

Goths. A Teutonic people who invaded and settled in parts of the Roman empire from the 4th to the 6th centuries. *See* OSTROGOTHS and VISIGOTHS.

Grágás (ON). Codification of Norse laws made by Magnus the Good, King of Denmark and Norway (1035–1047).

Grand Coalition. West German government formed on 26 November 1966 to confront growing economic problems, with Christian Democrat Kurt Kiesinger as Chancellor and Social Democrat Willy Brandt as his deputy and Foreign Minister. Ended by federal elections of 27 September 1969, when Brandt formed a Social Democratic government with Free Democrat support.

Grande Armée. (Fr., great army). Army organized and commanded by Napoleon between 1804 and 1814, particularly the force of *c* 350,000–400,000 troops who participated in the Russian campaign of 1812.

Grand Monarque (Fr., great monarch). Sobriquet of Louis XIV of France (1643–1715).

Grand Mufti. Title applied by the British to the MUFTI of Jerusalem, supreme religious leader of Moslems in the third most important city of ISLAM. Muftis in all important cities command great respect, but there is no hierarchy and Islam recognizes no 'Grand Mufti'.

Mohammed Said Maj Amin el Husseini (b. 1890), last Mufti of Jerusalem 1921–36 blamed the British for the arrival of ZIONISTS in Palestine; he led the anti-Zionist movement and formed the Palestine Arab Party (the 'Mufti Party'). The authorities deposed him in 1936 for fomenting disorder in Palestine and issued a warrant for his arrest. He fled to Syria and during World War II actively supported the NAZIS. After the war he escaped from Paris to Egypt where the ARAB LEAGUE appointed him the 'spiritual leader' of the Palestine Arab Committee.

After the Israeli-Arab war of May 1948 – January 1949 he installed himself at Gaza where an Arab 'All-Palestine Government' was set up under Egyptian auspices. He was made chairman of the national council and the supreme council, i.e. head of state, and encouraged FEDAYEEN ('fanatics') from the Palestine refugee camps to make guerrilla raids on Israel. After 1956 his influence declined. The PLO and Syria-dominated AL FATAH replaced him as leaders of the Palestinian struggle.

'Grand Old Party'. Republican Party of the USA, so named by itself.

Grand Remonstrance. Statement of Parliament's demands of King Charles I prepared in 1641 by John Pym (1584–1643) and other parliamentary leaders. It was largely a propaganda exercise, listing reforms enacted by the LONG PARLIAMENT, accusing 'Jesuited Papists' of a 'malignant and pernicious design' for subverting the constitution, and demanding resolution by the king of parliamentary grievances, the appointment of Crown ministers approved by parliament, the curbing of the powers of the EPISCOPACY and Protestant reform of the clergy. The highly controversial proposal was passed only by eleven votes and rejected outright by Charles. Its real significance lay in its startling assertion of parliamentary demands and it drove many moderates into Charles's camp, marking a hardening of lines as civil war approached.

Grand Siècle (Fr., great century). Period of the reign of Louis XIV (1643–1715); the classical age of French literature.

Great Crash. The WALL STREET stock market collapse, 24 October 1929. A two-year speculative boom faltered when 132 million shares were offloaded in panic trading. As selling continued banks and finance houses collapsed, leading to an American business slump with drastic effects on European financial stability, ushering in the 1930s Depression.

Great Depression. Popular name for the DEPRESSION of the 1930s which, initiated by the GREAT CRASH, brought economic hardship to most capitalist countries.

Great Exhibition. Initiated by Prince Albert, Consort to Queen Victoria, the Great Exhibition was the first of many such exhibitions displaying chiefly the products of industrialization and celebrating the period's faith in progress and human ingenuity. Held at the Crystal Palace in London, the Great Exhibition opened on 1 May 1851, featured more than 13,000 exhibitors and attracted six million visitors.

Great Fire of London. Conflagration of 1666 which consumed most of the City of London. Its chief effects were to eradicate the insanitary conditions which had encouraged the GREAT PLAGUE and to clear the way for rebuilding, the most notable examples of which are the cathedral and churches built by Sir Christopher Wren.

Great Leap Forward. Chinese slogan denoting a series of radical changes in social and economic policy between 1958 and 1961 intended to hasten the establishment of a truly communist society. Private consumption was cut and material incentives withdrawn in order to allow diversion of resources to other sectors; massive agricultural communes were set up with light industry and construction projects being established to service them. The effort failed because of natural disasters such as bad harvests and the withdrawal of technical aid by the USSR. Managerial difficulties also arose and in 1962 a more regular system of economic planning was restored.

Great Plague. Outbreak of bubonic plague which began in London in late 1664 and reached its peak in the autumn of 1665. It was the last and the worst of a series of outbreaks that had recurred throughout the century. Over 68,000 Londoners died and a further 30,000 people in the rest of Britain.

Great Powers. Britain, France, Russia, Germany, and Austria-Hungary before 1914. The USA was not included because prior to 1917 ISOLATIONISM had prevented her from taking a full role in international politics, despite her powerful industrial base.

Great Schism. The election of Pope Urban VI in 1378 was disputed by the

French party in the Catholic church which elected a rival in Clement VII. Papal rivalry continued until 1417 when the election of Martin V as Pope in Rome proved acceptable to both parties.

Great Seal. Premier seal of state in Britain by which the greater part of the royal authority is exercised. It is double sided and round, with the sovereign portrayed mounted on one side, crowned and enthroned on the other. All public acts of state are sealed by it. Edward the Confessor (1003–66) introduced the seal which alone could issue those orders requiring full legal backing, such as land grants and foreign treaties, although a warrant from the PRIVY SEAL or SIGNET was usually also required first. The Act of Union between England and Scotland (1603) provided that there should be one great seal for the whole of Great Britain; it is delivered into the custody of the LORD CHANCELLOR.

'Great Society'.. Phrase used by the US Pres. Lyndon Johnson (1908–73) to describe the America his administration (1963–68) hoped to create by its CIVIL RIGHTS legislation, implying that the USA, and not the USSR, would be the ideal to which free peoples would aspire.

Great Sophy. The ruler of Persia in the 16th and 17th centuries.

Great Trek. Mass emigration of BOER settlers from Cape Colony in 1836 and 1837, caused primarily by the inadequate compensation received when Britain emancipated the black slaves. It resulted in the first colonization of southern Africa beyond the Orange River. Other Boers crossed the Drakensberg into Natal and established a republic there in 1838.

A second trek occurred in 1844–45 when Boer farmers left the area between the Orange River and the Vaal and founded the South African Republic, in order to avoid British rule established in 1848 in the Orange River Sovereignty.

Great War. World War I, which began when Austria-Hungary declared war on Serbia on 28 July 1914 and ended on 11 November 1918 when Germany agreed an ARMISTICE on the WESTERN FRONT.

greenback. Slang expression for the US dollar, arising from the colour of currency notes.

Green Book. *Land and the Nation*, published 1925 by the Liberal Party under the inspiration of Lloyd George (1883–1945). The book was largely his brainchild and took its name from the colour of its cover and its agricultural subject matter. Its most controversial recommendation for the rejuvenation of British agriculture was the establishment of a 'cultivating tenure': the appropriation of cultivable land by the state to be given to small farmers and agricultural labourers for their own use, with compensation paid to the landlord.

green line. *See* HOT LINE.

Green Mountain boys. Organized band of settlers from Vermont, formed in 1773 to resist encroachment by New Yorkers who claimed Vermont as part of their state territory under a charter of Charles II of England.

Green Revolution. Post-1945 upswing in agricultural production in developing countries, the result of the application of pesticides, chemical-based fertilizers and high-yield crop seeds.

Not all scientists approve of modern agricultural techniques because of their effect on the ecosystem, while economists have suggested that patterns of international primary production have been disadvantageously disturbed by the 'revolution'. Cynics doubt that any real revolution has in fact occurred, and point to the continuing problems of over-population in relation to the food supply.

Greens. Ecology party of West Germany which first emerged as a political force in the Bremen elections of October 1979, when the 'Green List' candidates, representing a number of environmentalist and anti-nuclear groups, won 59 per cent of the votes for the Land Parliament. In the Bundestag elections of October 1980 this vote fell away, but they have remained a force in West German politics. Green parties have also made headway in Scandinavia and Italy. In Britain, the Green Party fielded 133 candidates in the 1987 General Election, polling 89,854 votes but losing their deposit everywhere.

Green Socialism. A strand within socialism emerging in the 1980s which attempted to reconcile environmentalist concern over the threats of industrialization to the future of the Earth with the traditional socialist aim of a general improvement in the overall standard of living. *See* GREENS.

Gregorian. (1) Religious chant named after Pope Gregory I (560–604) which added extra tones to the hitherto traditional Ambrosian chants.
   (2) The modern calendar introduced by Pope Gregory XIII (1502–85) on 24 February 1582 to replace the Julian Calendar. (*See also* OLD STYLE *and* NEW STYLE).

Grenzgänger (Germ., one who crosses a frontier). Term often used to denote those who escape west from east Germany.

groat (ME, great). Also known as the gross penny, English coin first issued in 1279 worth 4*d*. Modelled on the French *gros* and the *groot* of the Low Countries, it was the first multiple of the penny. Minting was soon suspended, but *c*1340 Edward III started to re-issue groats for use in his European dominions. In 1351 regular coining in England was commenced of silver groats (worth 4*d*) and half-groats (2*d*). Issue ceased in 1662.

Grondwet. Constitution or fundamental law of the Republic of South Africa adopted in 1849 by the BOER communities north of the Vaal.

Gründerzeit (Germ., time of building). Term applied to the period of rapid expansion in the German economy following the foundation of the German empire in 1871. It was fuelled by the French 'war contribution' of 2.2 million gold marks; the redemption of war loans and state debts; and the standardization of the monetary and banking system on a federal basis. New businesses proliferated, promoted by nearly 50 new banks and joint stock companies and a rise in production of 30 per cent. This over-production resulted in a slump in 1873, the liquidation of more than 60 credit banks, a sharp decline in the number of enterprises operating and a 5 per cent fall in production. The slump led to monopolies being formed in the banking and heavy industries.

guchupin (Am. Ind., one with spurs). Term used in Mexico to refer disrespectfully to PENINSULARES who in

South America were called *chape-tónes* (tender-feet). Spanish-born colonialists held special favour in the eyes of the Crown and occupied the leading secular and ecclesiastical posts. They received preferential treatment in commerce whereas restrictions were placed on the businesses of the CREOLES. They sided with the Spanish government during the wars of independence fought by the Spanish colonies in the early 19th century and were later expelled by the Creoles.

Guelph (Ital., deriv. Germ. *Welf*). Party in medieval Italian politics, whose name is said to be derived from that of the founder of the House of Brunswick. *See also* GHIBELLINES.

guerre à outrance (Fr., war to the death). Another term for TOTAL WAR.

guerrilla warfare (from Sp., little war). Irregular warfare involving popular support, a high degree of politicization and tactical flexibility. Mounted by Spanish peasants against Napoleon in the early 19th century and by the BOERS against Britain, 1899–1902. It has been successfully used in 20th-century revolutionary and national liberation wars; by the Chinese Communists against Japan and the Nationalists in the 1930s and 1940s; by anti-Nazi Yugoslav PARTISANS in the 1940s; by the Algerian National Liberation Front against France in the 1950s; in the Cuban revolution; by the Vietnamese against France in the 1950s and the United States in the 1960s; and by the Afghan rebels against Soviet occupation in the late 1980s.

Guesdist. After Jules Guesde (1845–1922), journalist and leader of the *Parti Socialiste de France*, founded in

1899, marxist with strong SYNDICALIST influence. He formulated a programme committing Socialist deputies to take the class struggle into Parliament and to refuse co-operation with non-Socialists. Elected to the Chamber of Deputies in 1893, Guesde became a Cabinet minister under the UNION SACRÉE. *See* POSSIBILISTS.

Guided Democracy. Ideological underpinning of President Sukarno's Indonesian regime from July 1959 until his overthrow by an army coup in October 1965. Sympathetic to the left and with Communist support, Guided Democracy involved strong executive government and an attempt to institute Nasakom, a union of national, religious and communist forces.

Guillotine (Fr.). (1) Instrument of execution (decapitation by a falling blade) named after its inventor, the French physician Joseph-Ignace Guillotin, and first used in revolutionary France.
(2) In parliamentary vocabulary, the device whereby a government imposes a time limit on discussions of legislation. *See* CLOSURE.

guinea. English coin, originally a guinea pound or sovereign (20*s*), which replaced the unit in 1663, minted from gold from the coast of Guinea in West Africa. By 1700 its value had risen to 30*s* but in 1717 it was fixed at 21*s*. The last guinea coin was minted in 1813. It was replaced as the standard gold coin by the sovereign (20*s*) minted between 1817 and 1925. The term is still used, to mean the sum of £1.05, equivalent to 21*s*.

gunboat diplomacy. The use of naval power to achieve foreign policy ends – invariably by a stronger against a weaker state – associated particularly with Lord Palmerston's second period at the Foreign Office from 1846 to 1851 and with American policy towards the Caribbean.

Gurkhas. Properly, the royal family of the small kingdom of Gurkha and their followers the Thakurs, Khas, Magars and Gurwngs. However, the term is loosely applied to the inhabitants of Nepal (conquered by the Gurkhas in 1768–9) who are famous for their fighting prowess. The Gurkhas have been allies of Britain since 1816 and gave military aid during the Indian mutiny and the two world wars. Their brigade still forms part of the British Army.

gutter press. The most widely read British newspapers which specialize in crime, sexual titillation and an exaggerated patriotism.

H

habeas corpus (Lat., you shall have the body). Writ ordering the body of a person under restraint or imprisonment to be brought into court for a full inquiry into the legality of the restraint. Although nominally in existence since MAGNA CARTA, the right was ignored on numerous occasions; the first Habeas Corpus Act put it on a statutory basis in 1679. In times of public peril the privilege of habeas corpus may be suspended, an occurrence common in Ireland during the two world wars and under INTERNMENT.

habitans. Canadian farmers of French descent living in the province of Quebec.

Habsburg. (often misspelt Hapsburg). House of Habsburg-Lorraine, Austrian royal dynasty which ruled from 1282 to 1918. It was in fact of Swiss origin. The family held the title of Holy Roman Emperor 1438–1740 and 1745–1806; when the Empire was dissolved it took the title Emperor of Austria. Its rise to power was based on a series of fortunate marriages and reached its zenith in 1521 when Emperor Charles V divided his empire into two branches, part ruled by Austrian Habsburgs and part by Spanish Habsburgs. In 1526 the Hungarian and Bohemian crowns were united with the Austrian to form the Habsburg Danubian Monarchy.

The murder of the heir to the Habsburg throne, Francis Ferdinand, on 28 June 1914 caused World War I. The last Habsburg Emperor, Charles I, abdicated in November 1918 and died in 1923. Various movements in the 1930s sought to restore the Habsburg monarchy and to place Charles's son Otto on the throne; these were crushed by the NAZIS following the ANSCHLUSS.

hacienda (Span. deriv. Lat., wealth, or treasury). Great rural estates of the LATIFUNDIA type which have dominated the Spanish and South American land tenure systems since the 16th century. The owner (*haciendado*) is typically portrayed in the style of a feudal lord who controls all aspects of the lives of his labourers (*peones*), in South America often Indians. From the 19th century onwards it has been known for various South American nations to be governed by *ad hoc* alliances of haciendados. Although the hacienda might sell some of its produce, one of its main purposes has been to achieve self-sufficiency, resulting in inefficient land use since most of the territory is only partially used.

Hadith (Arab., traditions). The record of the words and actions of the prophet Mohammed, which provides a corpus of information to act as an authoritative guide for the conduct of Moslems.

Haganah (Heb.). Protective force secretly formed by the Jews in Palestine in 1936 for the defence of their communes against Arab attacks. In April and May 1948 the Haganah fought pitched battles with Arab forces in order to keep open communications between Tel Aviv and Jerusalem. They later became the nucleus of the Israeli army, as opposed to the purely terrorist organizations, the Stern Gang and IRGUN ZVAI LEUMI, whose activities the Haganah leadership publicly condemned.

hajji (*also* hadji; Pers., pilgrim). A Moslem who has made the *hadj*, the pilgrimage to Mecca.

Hakenkreuz (Germ.). A hooked cross, either the SWASTIKA or its mirror image.

Haleuca *See* MAMELUKS.

Half breeds (*also* Featherheads). Name given by the STALWARTS in New York State in 1881 to those Republicans who supported Pres. Garfield in his campaign for reform of the civil service.

ham (OE, home). In Anglo-Saxon England, an enclosure or farm. In modern English place names, it denotes the original existence of an Anglo-Saxon settlement smaller than a TUN.

hammer and sickle. Symbol on a red background, the flag of the USSR, denoting the unity of the peasantry and industrial proletariat and emphasizing the equal importance of industry and agriculture to Soviet Russia.

hanaper (deriv. A Fr., drinking vessel). Box of wood, leather or wicker in which documents were kept. Attributively, in medieval England, a department of CHANCERY which collected the fees due from documents passing the Great Seal. *See* CLERK OF THE HANAPER.

handsuppers. BOERS who surrendered to the British during the Boer War (1899–1902), regarded with contempt by those who fought on to the bitter end.

Hang Seng. The shares index on the Hong Kong Stock Exchange.

Hanoverians. Royal dynasty which ruled Great Britain and Ireland, from 1714 to 1901. From the Brunswick-Lüneburg branch of the GUELPH family, they took their name from the German state of Hanover where they were ELECTORS of the Holy Roman Empire. Their succession to the English, and later British, crown was secured by the 1701 Act of Settlement. In 1837 the crown of Hanover went to the uncle of Queen Victoria, Ernest, Duke of Cumberland and the personal union of the Hanoverian and British crowns ceased.

The British Hanoverian monarchs were George I (ruled 1714–27); his son George II (1727–60); George III, grandson of George II (1760–1820); his eldest son George IV (1820–30 and Prince Regent from 1812); William IV, third son of George III (1830–37) and Queen Victoria, granddaughter of George III (1837–1901). The succession then passed to the Saxe-Coburg line through Victoria's son, Edward VII (1901–10).

Hanoverian   Succession   *See* HANOVERIANS.

Hansard. In Britain, the official reports of parliamentary debates, named after Luke Hansard, a partner in a firm of printers to the House of Commons in the 1770s. His son T.C. Hansard was first the printer and later the publisher of an unofficial series of parliamentary debates, inaugurated by William Cobbett in 1803. Production of the reports was taken over in 1909 by H.M. Stationery Office; today's volumes contain full, substantially verbatim reports of debates in both Houses of Parliament.

Hanseatic League (deriv. OHG *hansa*, company). A confederation of north German towns established *c*1241 for mutual protection in the pursuit of international commerce. As middlemen they formed an integral part of the medieval trading system, acquiring a monopoly of the Baltic trade and predominance in North Sea routes. They came thus to dominate the foreign trade of Norway, Sweden, Denmark and, to some extent, London. By the mid-14th century, the League comprised a loose association of nearly a hundred towns headed by Lübeck, but from 1380 onwards competition from the Low Countries and England began to herald its decline. It survived to the mid-17th century, its last meeting being in 1669. To this day, Lübeck, Hamburg and Bremen retain, by commercial courtesy, the name of 'Hanse Towns'.

Hapsburg *See* HABSBURG.

hara-kiri (*also* SEPPUKU; Jap., cutting of the belly). Method of suicide adopted by the Japanese SAMURAI from the 12th century when they faced no alternative but death or disgrace: it could be either a voluntary act or the penalty for a crime on the order of a feudal lord. In the case of an order it was, effectively, execution and was surrounded by an elaborate ritual, particularly in the case of a DAIMYO.

Hardshell Democrats *See* HUNKERS.

harijan (Hind., children of God). Term used by Mohandas Gandhi (1869–1948) to describe the untouchables.

Hartal (Hind., shop + bolt). Ceylonese general strike of 1953, organized by Marxists in protest at the rapid rise in the cost of living and particularly of the staple, rice. From 1945 onwards the Ceylonese government had rationed rice and subsidized production to keep the price down. By 1952 subsidies were equal to 20 per cent of the market value. In 1953 the Prime Minister of the United National Party government, Dudley Senanayake, drastically reduced the subsidies and prices rose by up to 300 per cent.

To end the strike the government introduced very repressive measures; in clashes with government forces ten people were killed. Senanayake was forced to resign and his successor partially restored the subsidies. The Hartal reflected national dissatisfaction with the government. The Sri Lanka Freedom Party drew great propaganda value from it and won the 1956 election.

Hashemites. Arab descendants of Mohammed (570–632), Prophet of ISLAM, either directly or by marriage. Mohammed was a member of the House of Hashim, a subdivision of the Quraysh tribe whose senior branch descended from Hasan, son of Mohammed's daughter Fatimah and her husband 'Ali. Hasan was the last member of the line to be CALIPH but his descendants were hereditary amirs of Mecca and continued to be so under OTTOMAN rule. In 1916 Husayn ibn Ali became amir of Mecca and King of Hejaz, a position he held until 1924. His sons Faisal and 'Abd Allah became kings of Iraq and Jordan and are the founders of the modern Hashemite dynasty.

hashomer. Self-defence units established by the first Jewish settlers in what is now Israel, necessary because of the Arab hostility to Jewish settlement. See GRAND MUFTI.

Hashomer Hatzair (Isr. 'The Young Watchmen'). Israeli Marxist socialist group, the main element in MAPAM, strongly organized in the KIBBUTZIM.

Hasidim (deriv. Heb. *hasid*, pious one). Reforming movement in Judaism, founded in 18th-century Poland by Israel ben Eliezer, a lime digger. Called by his followers Ba'al Shem Tov ('Master of the Good Name'), he grew famous for his spiritualism, expositions on theology and the reports of his ability to heal the sick. He accepted Judaism but gave it a new emphasis, claiming that true religion was to see how God lived and dwelt in all creation and that true worship can be expressed in every action.

The most important early leader of the Hasidim was the scholar Dov Baes ('Great Preacher') who in the early 18th century succeeded in converting many rabbis to the beliefs of the movement. He gave fellow-leaders the title Kzaddiqim ('Righteous Ones') and stated that they had the power to intercede with God and possessed super-human faculties. Hundreds of Hasidic communities, centred around local Kzaddiqim, grew up in Lithuania, Hungary, Russia and Palestine. Many great leaders emerged, including Jacob Isaac (d. 1815) of Lublin, Poland,

who had Messianic hopes and was a clairvoyant. The Hasidim suffered a tremendous blow in World War II when many of their fellows died in the HOLOCAUST. Thriving communities, however, exist today in the USA, Israel and London.

Haskala (Heb., enlightenment). Movement dating from 18th-century Germany whose members argued that Jews should attempt to put aside the narrower restraints of Jewish culture and adopt that of the countries in which they were living.

hatamotos (Jap., under the flag). In Japan, name given to the 80,000 retainers of the SHÔGUN, who first appeared under the Shôgun Iyemitsu in the early 17th century. Those with extensive lands furnished the Shogun with a military contingent in time of war; those with lesser estates paid him dues in money. They formed a created nobility, in contrast to the hereditary nobility of the DAIMYOS.

hatti sherif (Arab.). A FIRMAN or decree of the SUBLIME PORTE of the OTTOMAN empire, personally signed by the Sultan.

haute bourgeoisie (Fr.). Upper middle and professional classes.

havildar (Hind.). A non-commissioned native officer in the Indian armies of the British RAJ.

hawks. Name given to those Americans who wished to continue, intensify or escalate the Vietnam War (1965–1973), believing this to be the quickest and most effective way of ending it. The term became current in 1964 and is thought to have originated inside the State Department. Early 'hawks' were George Wallace and Richard Nixon, though Nixon actually headed the administration presiding over the peace negotiations which ended the war. Those advocating the opposite policy, negotiation or reduction of US involvement in Vietnam, were known as 'doves'. The terms are now generally applied to politicians taking, respectively, aggressive and moderate stances on foreign policy issues.

Heads of the Proposals. Proposals prepared by Cromwell, Ireton and other senior officers in the parliamentary army in 1647 as the basis of compromise with Charles I at the end of the English civil war. They obliged the king to meet parliament once every two years; and provided for biennial elections, a measure of electoral reform, including removal of the more notorious 'pocket boroughs' (*see* ROTTEN BOROUGHS), representation of counties in fixed relation to tax paid and a 'council of state' to control the army for ten years. Under a scheme of 'composition' royalists would be gradually readmitted to political power. The EPISCOPACY would remain but there would be complete religious tolerance. Common law was to be reformed and excise and tithe duties abolished. The 'Heads' were moderate in nature but Charles refused to reply to them, preferring instead to enter the ENGAGEMENT with the Scots.

hearth money. In England, tax of 2*s* on every hearth, first levied in 1663. It was similar to chimney money which existed as early as the Norman Conquest. It proved very unpopular and was abolished in 1689.

Heemraden (Dutch). Court first established in Stellenbosch, Cape Colony, in 1682, comprising four local burghers whose duty was to determine minor disputes in the local community. Similar courts were later established in other townships. The Heemraden were abolished in 1828 by the Charter of Justice.

Hegemony. Leadership; in politics, the predominance of one unit over other units in a group, for example, of one province in a federation (such as Prussia in the Second Reich); of one person in a committee (such as Napoleon in the CONSULATE) or of one state in a confederation (France in the EEC). Antonio Gramsci (1891–1937), an Italian communist, developed a theory of political hegemony influential in the later 20th century according to which ruling classes maintain their political power by ideological control, thereby giving the appearance of consensus and lessening the need for physical coercion.

hegira (*also* hejira; Arab., departure). The flight of the Prophet Mohammed from Mecca in 622 AD, from which date the Moslem era is computed.

Henricians. Heretical followers of Henry the Monk, active in the French-speaking areas of Europe during the early 12th century. They preached penance, argued for the rejection of the sacraments and denied the doctrine of original sin.

Heptarchy (deriv. Lat., seven). In Anglo-Saxon England, the seven kingdoms of East Anglia, Mercia, Kent, Northumbria, Sussex and Wessex. In practice, they were rarely seven in number, two or more usually being grouped under one monarch. The term also applies to the period before they were unified, from the mid-6th to the early 9th century, during which the most powerful sovereign was generally styled the BRETWALDA.

heretoga (OE). Army leaders in Anglo-Saxon England.

heriot (deriv. OE *heregeatu*, military apparel). In medieval England, a fine payable to the lord of the manor on the death of a person holding land on it, consisting of the deceased's best beast or chattel.

Hermandad (Span., brotherhood; also *Santa Hermandad*, holy brotherhood). Confederation of the major cities of medieval Castile, formed as a source of mutual protection against brigands. It gradually usurped the functions of a legislative body and used force to secure obedience to its rule.

Hermit Kingdom. Korea, which had minimal contact with the West until 1882, when it signed a trade pact with the United States, followed by similar agreements with Britain, Germany, Italy and Russia.

Herrenvolk (Germ., master race). NAZI doctrine of the natural superiority of German ARYANS, expounded in order to justify the suppression and, in some cases, liquidation of non-Aryan races. *See* FINAL SOLUTION, THE; 'HOLOCAUST'.

Herut. Israeli party formed in 1948 by former activists in IRGUN ZVAI LEUMI, headed by Menachem Begin. Herut formed an electoral bloc with the Liberal Party in 1965 and advocated Jewish control over a Greater Israel on both sides of the River Jordan.

Hezbollah (Arab., Party of God). One of the major Iranian-backed militant Islamic groups active in strife-torn Lebanon in the 1980s.

hidage (ME deriv. Lat., hide). In Anglo-Saxon England, a land tax imposed on land for war purposes. Under Ethelred the Unready (978–1016) every eight HIDES were expected to furnish a man at arms, and every three hundred hides a ship.

hidalgo. A member of the lesser nobility in Spain with the title of Don and the right to a coat of arms, the numbers of whom increased in the 16th century as the treasury sold titles to raise funds.

hide (OE). In early Saxon England, the amount of land considered necessary to support a peasant household and allotted to every free householder. Acreage varied between regions from 40 in Wessex to 120 in the eastern counties. One hide equalled four VIRGATES and eight BOVATES.

Hiemuher. The Austrian FREIKORPS.

High Church. An expression – once virtually synonymous with TORY – first used in England in 1703 to describe the Church party which insisted upon the enforcement of laws against the DISSENTERS. Since the early 19th century the term has chiefly referred to the ANGLO-CATHOLIC wing of the Church of England. *See* LOW CHURCH.

High Commission, Court of. Ecclesiastical court, established after Henry VIII declared himself head of the Church of England in 1534, to investigate and punish transgressions against the Acts of SUPREMACY and later of UNIFORMITY. Its actions were often arbitrary and it was strongly opposed by PURITANS and conscientious members of the legal profession. In the early 17th century the Stuart kings used to enforce the royal prerogative in secular matters. In the 16th and 17th centuries its jurisdiction was challenged by common law courts by means of writs of prohibition to get cases transferred to superior courts. It was abolished by parliament in 1641.

high politics. An approach to politics which sees the views and attitudes of leading political personalities and their relationships as the determining factors in policy and action.

High Tory. A TORY with traditionalist values (i.e. support for Church, Empire, the established order). The term was mainly used prior to 1945.

hijacking. Colloquialism which arose in inter-war America to describe the practice of gangsters during the PROHIBITION era of stealing from each other convoys of trucks carrying illegal alcohol. The leading truck in a convoy would be stopped by someone proffering a false greeting ('Hi, Jack!'). Today the term is often used to denote the international crime of forcing aeroplanes to fly to unscheduled destinations and holding the passengers as hostages. This crime first acquired political significance in July 1968 when Palestinian terrorists forced an Israeli aeroplane to fly to Algiers. Hijacking has remained a constant threat in the 1980s.

Hinduism. India's main religion, Hinduism has no fixed scriptural canon but draws its doctrines – which tolerate a variety of belief and practice – from such ancient works as the Veda, the Brahmanas, the Upanishads and the Bhagavidgita. Although the ritual and legal aspect of Brahmanism stresses a rigid caste system, Hinduism has undergone change under the pressure of Indian social and economic development.

hinterland doctrine. Doctrine expounded by Germany in the late 19th and early 20th centuries claiming that, in the newly-occupied countries of Africa, the possession of the coastline by an imperialist power carried with it the right to colonize the backcountry. The corollary was that no other country had the right to occupy the hinterland and so block access to the interior.

hippy. Follower of a cultural movement which emerged in California, probably San Francisco, in the mid-1960s and spread rapidly to western Europe and the rest of the USA. Hippies wore long hair and outlandish dress including flowers and beads, played rock music and used drugs such as cannabis and the hallucinogen LSD. Psychedelic patterns and paintings were produced in profusion. The movement's aims were confused and ill-defined but included the pursuit of love and peace and the rejection of conventional morality and commercialism. The movement faded in the early 1970s.

Hispaniola (Lat. deriv. Span., Spanish). Name given by Columbus to the island of Haiti.

historical materialism. The Marxist interpretation of history based on DIALECTICAL MATERIALISM. History is seen as a process of class struggles. Economic conditions are the basis of life and developing techniques of production determine a society's nature. Political and ideological systems are built upon this. The movement of history is a dialectic within each economic stage which produces the class to oppose and overthrow the social and political order.

historicism. A determinist philosophy of history which sees events to be governed by discoverable laws which, as with for example Marxism, can predict the likely direction of historical movement.

Histadrut. Federation of Labour, the organizational body of the Israeli trade union movement, which also acts as a CO-OPERATIVE organization. It controls many economic enterprises and a distribution network.

Hlutdaw. The king's council of ministers in Burma prior to British annexation. In 1886 five of the ministers were retained in office by the British to act as an advisory board on native affairs; by 1889 the country was sufficiently pacified to permit the board's abolition.

Hohenstaufen. Dynasty of medieval German emperors beginning with Conrad III in 1138 which, because of its ambitions in Italy, came into conflict with the Papacy. Frederick II (died 1250) was described as an 'anti-Christ' and in alliance with France the Papacy destroyed the dynasty in 1254, the last male of the line being executed in 1268.

Hohenzollern. The Prussian ruling house which became prominent following the THIRTY YEARS WAR. By 1721 its territory extended from the Dutch to the Polish frontiers and under Frederick Wilhelm I (1713–1740) Prussia's military and administrative development made it a rival to the HABSBURGS for supremacy in Germany. After national unification in 1871 the Hohenzollerns took the title Emperor of Germany. Wilhelm II, the last Emperor, abdicated on 9 November 1918 and fled to Holland.

hoi polloi (Gk.). The masses or the common people.

hold (ON). A noble superior in status to a THEGN in 10th- and 11th-century Northumbria.

Holkar. Family name of the Mahratta rulers of Indore in central India, derived from the village of Hol. The dynasty, founded by Malhur Rao, lasted from 1728 to 1948 and accepted British protection in 1818 under the Treaty of Mandasor. In 1948 Indore was merged into the Indian state of Madhya Pradesh.

Holocaust (deriv. Gk., a whole burnt offering). Term applied to the attempted annihilation of the Jews in Europe by the NAZIS in World War II. The culmination of centuries of ANTI-SEMITISM, the attempted planned extermination carried into effect in CONCENTRATION CAMPS and by the EINSATZGRUPPEN execution squads in conquered Russia. It destroyed an east European Jewish culture 1,000 years old, and carried out the murder of some 6 million Jews, half of them from Poland. It convinced many Jews that they could no longer live in Europe, or indeed anywhere except in their own state, and was thus the major impetus to ZIONISM.

Holy Alliance. Alliance concluded in September 1815 between Russia, Austria and Prussia whose sovereigns agreed that their policies would be guided by Christian principles. In fact, the alliance was directed against the democratic and nationalist movements spawned all over Europe by the French Revolution.

Holy Places. Centre of conflicting claims between France, Russia and Turkey over the protection of the Holy Sepulchre in Jerusalem and the Church of the Nativity in Bethlehem, partially provoking the Crimean War in 1854. In 1852 Turkey recognized French claims to administer the Holy Places. Russia's attempt to secure equivalent rights for the Orthodox Church encouraged fears that she intended to extend her influence in the NEAR EAST.

Holy Roman Empire. Major European institution from the 9th century to 1806. The old imperial title of 'Roman Emperor' was revived in 800 AD when Pope Leo III conferred it on Charlemagne (742–814), King of the Franks. From the mid-10th century when the CAROLINGIAN line died out, it was borne by the kings of a succession of German dynasties. The term 'Holy Empire' was first used in 1034 to describe the territories held by Conrad II, and the use of the name 'Holy Roman Empire' (*'sacrum Romanum imperium'*) dated from 1157.

The Empire originally included Germany, Austria, Czechoslovakia, eastern France, Switzerland, the Low Countries and northern and central Italy, though the emperor continued to be German. Initially the allies of the popes, the emperors were involved in a continual struggle with the papacy for supremacy in Europe from the 11th to the 13th centuries.

In 1806 the last Holy Roman Emperor, Francis II (one of the HABSBURGS) resigned the title, adopting instead that of Emperor of Austria in response to Napoleon Bonaparte's imperial aspirations.

Holy See. The papal seat. As bishop of Rome, the pope is head of the Roman Catholic Church and the lawful successor to St Peter.

homage. Under the feudal system, the personal submission of the tenant to his lord by which the tenant was bound to serve his lord and the lord to protect his tenant. *See* FEUDALISM.

home rule. The establishment of a parliament or council in Ireland, Wales or Scotland on to which would devolve the responsibility for the country's internal affairs in contrast to 'direct rule' from London. The Irish home rule movement has played a most important role in British politics. The Home Rule Association was founded by Isaac Butt in Dublin in 1870. Under Parnell's leadership Irish Nationalist MPs induced Gladstone to introduce two home rule bills. The first, in 1886, provided for a legislative body in Dublin with control of administration, save for safeguards as to the unity of the empire. It was to have control of all taxation except customs and excise, but could not legislate on matters of defence and foreign relations. It was defeated in the Commons. The second bill, in 1892, was defeated in the Lords. In 1912, with the power of the Lords reduced by the 1911 Parliament Act, Asquith introduced a third bill but it was strongly opposed by Ulster Protestants who feared Roman Catholic domination. Civil war threatened when the bill was given a third reading in May 1914, but its proposals were shelved during World War I. After the war, Ireland was 'partitioned'. Northern Ireland received home rule in the form of the Stormont Parliament opened at Belfast in June 1921; Southern Ireland received Dominion status in December 1921, with control of foreign as well as internal affairs.

honi soit qui mal y pense *See* GARTER, ORDER OF THE.

honor. In feudal England, knights' holdings administered as a unit from one centre, the *caput honoris*, which was usually a castle. Originally applied only to the holdings of important men, by the 13th century the term also included less important and relatively modest under-tenancies. Leading under-tenants were the honorial barons who formed the honorial court.

Honved (Hung.). Originally, the name given to the national champions of Hungary in her early history; under the Austro-Hungarian empire, the Hungarian military reserve or LANDWEHR.

Hooks (*also* Kabbeljaws). In the 14th-century Netherlands, the party of the nobility.

Hooverville. Name for the shanty towns, built from corrugated iron, old boxes, etc., in which many unemployed Americans were forced to live during the DEPRESSION of the 1930s. The term is derived from the name of Herbert Hoover, president between 1928–1932 when the Depression began. He was widely blamed for failing to act positively to cure the economic ills and was heavily defeated in 1932 by Roosevelt who promised a NEW DEAL.

Horebites *See* OREBITES.

Hospitalers, Knights. The military monks of the Order of St. John of Jerusalem. Founded c1048 to help the sick, they played a prominent part in the 12th century during the CRUSADES. In 1309 they captured Rhodes, which they held until expelled by the OTTOMANS in 1522. In 1530 Emperor Charles V gave them the island of Malta which, as Knights of Malta, they held until Napoleon dislodged them in 1798. They still survive as a sovereign order with headquarters in Rome and their medieval Benedictine habit of black with an eight-pointed cross is similar to that worn today by the St. John's Ambulance Brigade. *See* TEMPLAR.

Hospodars. Name for the Princes of

Moldavia and Wallachia after 1789 when their countries came under the sway of Russia.

hôtel de ville (Fr., town hall). Seats of municipal government in France.

hot gospeller. Originally the name given to the Protestant Edward Underhill, imprisoned in 1553 for his attack on Roman Catholicism on the accession of Queen Mary. After the RESTORATION in 1660 the term was applied to Puritans. It survives today as a description of evangelists in the USA.

hot line. A direct link by telephone and teletype between the WHITE HOUSE in Washington and the KREMLIN in Moscow, intended to serve as an instant channel of communication and negotiation in times of international crisis. Similar links also exist between London and Moscow and Paris and Moscow, the 'GREEN LINE'.

Houghers. Irish agrarian society founded in 1711, which took its name from the practice of disabling the cattle of their enemies by houghing (ham-stringing) them.

housecarles. Force of specialized fighting men introduced into England by Cnut shortly after 1016. They were a standing force until 1051, acting as a loyal and disciplined bodyguard for the king. Each housecarle had the status of a THEGN. There were about 3,000 and after 1051 most of them were granted lands on which they settled, while remaining available for military service and garrison duties. As a class, they disappeared soon after the Norman Conquest.

House of Commons. Lower chamber of the British parliament, consisting of 650 members, each elected to represent a constituency for a maximum period of five years. Election is by universal adult suffrage. The Commons originates legislation – either by public acts, normally introduced by the government but occasionally by individual MPs, or by private acts which confer special powers on certain bodies such as local authorities. They also scrutinize government activity either by questions put directly to ministers or via a large and complex system of committees. Today the Prime Minister is normally a member of the House of Commons.

House of Keys *See* TYNWALD.

House of Lords. Upper chamber of the British parliament whose members are not elected. In 1988 it consisted of about 1200 peers – including 790 hereditary peers; 371 life peers; 9 law lords and 26 archbishops and bishops. The Lords can initiate some legislation of a non-partisan nature and examines in detail bills originating in the Commons. However, the Lords cannot veto a bill sent up from the lower house, nor can it delay the bill indefinitely or force the Commons to accept amendments. In addition, the chamber acts as the final court of appeal in the land, but only the law lords take part in its legal proceedings.

House of Representatives *See* CONGRESS.

Høyre. The Conservative Party in modern Norway.

hue and cry (A Fr.). In feudal England, outcry calling for the pursuit of a suspected criminal resisting arrest. All neighbours were obliged to join the pursuit as far as the bounds of the manor, carrying arms as specified by the Assize of Arms (1181) and Statute of Winchester (1285). Failure to attend the hue and cry and calling it out without good reason were both made punishable offences in 1275.

Huguenots. French Protestants of the 16th and 17th centuries. On 24 August 1572 thousands were killed in the massacre of St. Bartholomew. In 1598 Henry IV, their former leader, who had become a Catholic, granted them religious toleration by the Edict of Nantes. When this was revoked by Louis XIV in 1685, thousands left France illegally for exile in England, Holland, America and Germany.

Huk. In the Philippines, the Hukbalahap (abbrev. of Hukbo nang Bayan Laban sa Hapon, 'People's Army against Japan'). Founded in March 1942 by Luis M Taruc and Castro Alejandrino, initially they consisted of communist-led peasants who fought their landlords in the provinces of Luzon Island, scene of much agrarian unrest in the 1930s. Attempts by its leaders failed to make the organization a united front of all classes against Japanese occupation and it came under the tutelage of, and received aid from, Chinese communists. Although disarmed by the Americans after the liberation of the Philippines, the Huk continued to challenge the landlords and the government. Taruc was elected to Congress in 1946 but was denied his seat on a charge of fraudulent election. In March 1948 the Huk and the Pambansang Kaisahang Masaka (National Union of Farmers) from which it recruited much support were declared illegal. The ban was revoked, but Taruc reorganized the Huk as the Hukbong Magpapalaya nang Bayan (People's Liberation Army). Weakened in October 1950 when most of the politburo of the

Communist Party of the Philippines were arrested, in June 1957 the Huk and the CPP were declared illegal under an anti-subversion law. In 1969–70 a number of its leaders were killed or imprisoned. Both the CPP and the Huk were reorganised yet again, the Huk being renamed Bagong Hukbo nang Bayan (New People's Army). Despite the fall of the corrupt Marcos regime and the advent of Aquino in 1986, the Huks remain a potent source of instability.

Human Leopards. African secret society which for about 20 years practised cannibalism in Sierra Leone and was responsible for the murder of several hundred people; it was discovered and suppressed in 1896 and its leaders hanged.

Humble Petition and Advice. Proposal presented to Oliver Cromwell by the second parliament of the PRO-TECTORATE on 25 May 1657, favouring a monarchy rather than a republic and expressing reaction against the MAJOR GENERALS. It gave Cromwell the right to nominate his successor as Lord Protector although he refused the title of king offered in the first clause of the petition. His income was substantially increased and he was given the power to nominate an upper chamber of parliament, the 'Other House', of 40 to 70 members. The Petition was the direct result of a decision by the COUNCIL OF STATE to exclude known republicans and it curbed the Council's powers.

humiliati (Lat., humble ones). In medieval northern Italy, loosely organized religious congregations who led a penitential life based on manual labour and preaching. After Pope Alexander III had refused laymen amongst them the right to preach they fell into heresy, but in 1201 Pope Innocent III gave regulations to those prepared to return to the Church.

hundred. In England, an ancient subdivision of a SHIRE, being the territory occupied by a hundred families, or which could provide a hundred soldiers or which equalled a hundred HIDES. It was the basis of military and administrative organization, having its own court until its abolition by the County Court Act of 1867.

Hundred Days. Period between 20 March 1815, when Napoleon Bonaparte entered Paris after escaping from Elba, and 28 June 1815 when he left Paris for the last time after his abdication. During this time the battle of Waterloo was fought, on 18 June 1815.

Hundred Flowers. Government-sponsored movement in communist China in 1956–7, which took its name from Mao Tse-tung's encouraging words, 'Let a hundred flowers bloom and a hundred schools of criticism compete.'

The aim was to attract intellectual and constructive criticism of the achievements of MAOISM but the flood of criticism which in fact arose resulted in a sharp backlash by the government.

Hundred Years' War. The virtually continuous conflict between France and England from 1338 to 1453. It had several causes, mainly concerned with the limits of English territorial possessions in France and the degree of English sovereignty in those possessions. Major factors were the claims of Edward III (1312–77) through his mother Isabel, to the French throne; French support of Scotland in her wars with England; and French opposition to England's commercial ties with Flanders.

Philip VI of France initiated hostilities by taking Gascony from Edward who replied by invading north France and aiding Flemish rebels. He renewed his claim to Philip's throne. The English won victories at sea at Sluys in 1340 and on land at Crécy in 1346; they captured Calais in 1347. A truce was then negotiated which lasted seven years. In 1355 English raids resumed in Languedoc, Normandy and north France and the French were heavily defeated at Poitiers in 1356.

Under the 1360 Treaty of Brétigny, Edward gained Calais, Ponthieu and lands in Gascony; in return he gave up his claim to the French throne. The French continued to aid rebels against Edward, the Black Prince (1330–76) in Aquitaine and defeated the English navy at La Rochelle in 1372. A French invasion fleet was in turn defeated off Margate in 1387. By the Peace of Paris in 1396, Richard II (1367–1400) was betrothed to Isabel, daughter of the French king and confirmed in his ownership of Calais and lands in Aquitaine.

In 1415 Henry V (1387–1422), taking advantage of recent civil war in France, claimed the French throne. He landed in Normandy, took Honfleur and then decisively defeated the French at Agincourt. By 1419, England possessed all of Normandy and Henry was made heir to the French throne by the Treaty of Troyes in 1420. He was also betrothed to Catherine of Valois, daughter of Charles VI of France. But Charles VII and Joan of Arc (1412–31) reversed the fortunes of the French by capturing Orleans in 1429. By 1450 Normandy was back in French hands; Bordeaux fell in 1453. England finally lost Calais to the French in 1558.

hunger marches. A series of demonstrations in Britain in the 1930s against massive unemployment. Heavy industries such as shipbuilding in Scotland were particularly badly hit and to draw attention to the scale of the problem, a group of Glasgow communists and socialists organised a 'hunger march' to London in October 1922. It was followed in January 1929 by a yet larger march. In October 1932, with unemployment at 2,750,000, the National Unemployed Workers' Movement staged the largest of all hunger marches, with 3,000 people converging on London from the depressed regions of Glasgow, South Wales and the north of England. After a demonstration in Hyde Park a petition of one million signatures was presented to parliament. Perhaps the most famous hunger march was the Jarrow Crusade of October 1936 when 200 workers from the Jarrow shipyards marched to London.

Hunger Winter *See* TURNIP WINTER.

hung parliament. Parliament in which no one party has an overall majority, i.e. seats in excess of the total held by all the other parties combined. In such situations, a coalition government may be formed, involving a combination of parties who together have an overall majority. Alternatively, the largest party may be asked by the monarch to form a government the survival of which will then depend on no combinations of other parties being made to defeat major items of legislation. The latter is a difficult course to maintain and usually results eventually in the resignation of the government.

Hungry Thirties. The 1930s as experienced by many in the distressed areas of Scotland, South Wales and the North of England, where the Depression and the decline of local industries caused mass unemployment and poverty, the bitterness of which was accentuated by the MEANS TEST and the National Government's reluctance to create work. *See* AILING GIANTS, DEVIL'S DECADE.

Hunkers. Section of the New York Democrats between 1844 and 1848 which was extremely conservative and pro-slavery. After 1848 they were known as 'Hardshell Democrats'.

Huns. Term of abuse for Germans during both world wars, which stems from the alleged atrocities committed by German troops in neutral Belgium in World War I, by comparison with the savage Asiatic horde led by Attila the Hun which swept across Europe in the mid-5th century. It is not known who was first responsible for coining the term although a poem by Rudyard Kipling refers to 'the Hun at the gate'.

Hussites. Followers of John Hus, rector of Prague University and a pupil of John Wyclif, who was excommunicated by Pope Alexander V in 1412. He continued disseminating his doctrine and was summoned to the Council of Constance. Having been assured of safe conduct by the Emperor Sigismund of Hungary, he attended but was imprisoned and burned as a heretic in 1415. Sigismund argued that he had no obligation to keep faith with heretics; his action was prompted by the contempt Hus held for all forms of authority. In 1416 Hus's principal disciple, Jerome of Prague, was also executed. Led by John of Zisca, the Hussites became a formidable body in Moravia and Bohemia, where they took up arms against the Church and the emperor. In 1424 John of Zisca died and the movement splintered. However the Hussites remained in insurrection until 1436 when their revolt was ended by the Treaty of Iglau.

hustings (OE deriv. ON *husthing*, house of assembly). In England, word generally used to denote open-air meetings held in connection with parliamentary elections. Originally, hustings usually had some legal functions, later extended in the City of London to the court of hustings, presided over by the mayor and sheriff, which recorded wills and deeds. Similar courts existed at Winchester and Boston. Such legal functions were abolished by the 1872 Ballot Act.

I

Iconoclasts (deriv. Gk., breaker of images). Name originally given to the followers of Leo III, emperor of the eastern Roman Empire, who forbade the worship of images in 726. The interdiction met great opposition and led to the Iconoclast War. The same name was given in 1560–61 to militant HUGUENOTS in France who destroyed the religious statues adorning churches and monasteries wherever they could. During the English Civil War the parliamentarians were also accused of iconoclasm.

Ike. Nickname of Gen. Dwight David Eisenhower (1890–1969), 34th President of the USA (1953–1961).

Illuminati (Lat., enlightened ones). Members of a secret society founded in 1776 by Adam Weishaupt, a Bavarian professor of canon law at Ingolstadt. He hoped to combat superstition and ignorance by establishing an association for rational enlightenment and the regeneration of the world. Under conditions of secrecy the Illuminati, whose members included Goethe and Schiller, sought to penetrate and control lodges of FREEMASONS for subversive purposes. They spread over Austria, Hungary and Italy but were condemned by the papacy and dissol-ved by the Bavarian government in 1785. The same term was also applied to a sect of Spanish heretics in the 16th century (*see* ALUM-BRADOS).

ILO. International Labour Organization, established in 1919, which acted originally as an independent body in association with the LEAGUE OF NATIONS. Its aim was to achieve social stability by improving working conditions, wage rates and health care and by protecting employment levels. The UN recognized its role and it later became a specialist UN agency. Since 1950 it has done much to protect migrant workers and in 1960 won the Nobel Peace Prize. In 1977 the USA withdrew from the ILO, after accusing it of supporting left-wing political groups.

The ILO represents employers, workers and governments. An annual conference decides policy and each member state sends two delegates to it, one representing employers, one employees. Nine governments have permanent seats because of the level of their industrial production (Canada, China, France, India, Italy, Japan, Britain, the USSR and West Germany). The other 38 places are filled by representatives elected by the conference.

Imam (Arab., leader, deriv. *amma*, to precede). Moslem title, meaning one who serves as an example; with several levels of meaning. The first Imam to lead Moslems in the ritual of prayer was the prophet Muhammed. After his death the CALIPH or his delegates, the governors of provinces, led the ritual. But the title also applied to the mosque officials who guide the faithful in prayer and may be accorded to Moslem scholars of distinction.

IMF. International Monetary Fund, established by the BRETTON WOODS conference in 1944. An agency of the UN, it has an independent international organization and its aim is to help expansion of international trade – and thus employment and production – by maintaining stable exchange rates. Members are committed to making their currencies convertible into other currencies and gold at fixed rates; they also undertake not to apply EXCHANGE CONTROLS or import restrictions without the Fund's permission. On joining each member country pays a deposit or 'quota' to the Fund, partly in gold and partly in its own currency, its size is fixed in relation to its share of world trade. It then has the right to certain automatic drawing facilities. The Fund makes foreign exchange resources available to members with BALANCE OF PAYMENTS difficulties and gives advice on problems of fiscal, monetary and credit policy. It will, if necessary, make substantial loans and standby credits, but requires evidence that the borrower is taking sufficient action to correct balance of payments disequilibrium.

The IMF has a Board of Governors on which each member government is represented. It meets once a year and most of its power is delegated to the Board of Executive Directors, who are responsible for the Fund's general operation. The members paying the five largest quotas nominate directors, and there must be at least seven other directors nominated by the other members.

immigration laws. Laws to restrict or prevent entirely the immigration of persons for reasons other than political asylum. In Britain, any citizen of the British Empire or COMMONWEALTH could enter until 1962, but in that year the Commonwealth Immigration Act was passed specifying that only Commonwealth immigrants with a job or 'special skill' of value to Britain would be admitted. The flight of Asians from Kenya in 1968 led to a further tightening of control, since many had British citizenship. In 1971 a single system was introduced, applicable equally to aliens and Commonwealth citizens. In recent years successive attempts have been made to restrict immigration further, usually by refusing entry to relatives of persons in Britain who at present live on the Indian sub-continent. Such actions have been criticized as racialist.

In Australia the trade unions have sought since 1888 to secure legislation restricting immigration, believing that a large influx of labour will force down wages. In July 1902 an Immigration Restriction Act was passed imposing a language test on potential immigrants who had to speak a European language. In 1905 this was modified to a 'prescribed language'. In 1925 the governor-general was given the power to prohibit entry of any nationality or class of aliens on racial or economic grounds. Rarely used, the Act was a reserve power designed to allay union fears of cheap labour from southern Europe.

In the USA the earliest attempts to restrict immigration came in 1882 when Chinese immigration was re-

---

duced. In 1900 and 1908 steps were taken to restrict Japanese immigration. In 1917 a literacy test was imposed on all immigrants and in 1921 a quota was applied. A limit of three per cent of the population, determined by the 1910 census, was placed on immigration by any national group, with an absolute upper limit of 357,000. The Johnson-Reed Act of 1924 severely reduced the numbers that could be admitted to only two per cent of the 1890 census, drastically reducing immigration from eastern Europe and Italy. Restrictions were relaxed in 1948 to allow DISPLACED PERSONS to enter. In 1952 the McCurran-Walter Act was passed, regularizing the procedure and relaxing the quota system; as a result, more Asian immigrants were admitted. Mounting criticism that the quota system discriminated on racial grounds resulted in an Act of 1965 removing the national-origins quota system from 1968 onwards.

impeachment (ME, deriv. Lat., to catch). In England, special arraignment, usually before parliament or some other high tribunal, of a person charged with offences against the state. Customarily, impeachment was made in the Commons and trial occurred in the Lords. The first impeachment was that of Lord Latimer in 1376; others were those of Francis Bacon, the Lord High Chancellor in 1621, the Earl of Strafford in 1641, Archbishop Laud in 1645 and Warren Hastings in 1788. Lord Melville was the last person to be impeached in 1805. In the USA, impeachment is initiated by the House of Representatives and tried by the Senate. The most famous American impeachment was that of President Andrew Johnson for dismissing his Secretary of War in May 1868.

imperialism (deriv. Lat. *imperium*, power). Acquisition and administration of an empire, often as a part of general commercial and industrial expansion. From the 15th century onwards, Spain, Portugal, Holland, France and Britain began building overseas empires. Modern imperialism, however, probably dates from the 1880s and the scramble for colonies in under-developed Africa. MARXISM-LENINISM ascribes the survival of CAPITALISM and World War I to this late surge of European imperialism. Italy, Germany and Japan failed to acquire empires in the 19th century due to their late national unification or industrialization; they attempted to do so in the 20th century by war. The USSR has been described as an imperialist power because it has absorbed the formerly independent countries of Estonia, Latvia and Lithuania and has sought to dominate neighbouring states, not only WARSAW PACT countries but also Afghanistan and China. US involvement in South-East Asia and Latin America has resulted in the USA also being termed an imperialist power. *See also* NEW IMPERIALISM.

impositions. Additions to the authorized customs duties, levied without the consent of parliament by James I. Singled out in the 1610 Petition of Grievances, they were confirmed by statute in 1641, but were not revived at the Restoration.

impressment. Forced seizure for military service, common in many countries before the establishment of CONSCRIPTION. In Britain, PRESS-GANGS forcibly recruited many men to serve in the navy, particularly during the Napoleonic Wars, but the practice was abandoned about the mid-19th century.

imprest. *See* PREST.

impropriations. Tithes and patronage rights re-allocated by the Crown to lay rectors or impropriators in the 16th century, following the dissolution of the monasteries in the reign of Henry VIII. A consequence was that TITHES tended to become simply rent tributes to absentee landlords, while the impropriators usually passed on only a small fraction of the revenue to the actual incumbents, for whose maintenance it was originally intended. It became increasingly difficult for the church to provide adequate stipends for the upkeep of the clergy before QUEEN ANNE'S BOUNTY, particularly since the gentry frustrated attempts in the 16th and 17th centuries to remedy the situation.

Inca (Peruv., lord). The rulers and, attributively, the populace of the ancient South American Indian civilization of Peru. Originally herders in the highlands, the Incas' qualities of military and social organization led to the expansion of their territory between the 12th and 16th centuries to much of modern Peru, Ecuador, Chile, Bolivia and parts of Argentina. The Inca empire was a rigid hierarchy; its detailed regulations governing the life of the masses led to ruthless suppression of dissident groups. The Inca himself was believed to be a child of the sun. Civil war over the succession in 1532 weakened the Incas and within a year the Spanish, led by Pizarro and de Almagro, had seized control of their empire.

inconfidéncia (Braz. Port.). Movement of political unrest: a conspiracy in colonial Brazil demonstrating the dissatisfaction of local inhabitants with Portugese imperial administration. The most famous of many was in 1789 in Minas Gerais which was connected with republicanism and concerned with the question of slavery.

Independents. Originally the BARROWISTS and BROWNISTS of Elizabeth I's reign; later, with the English Civil War, any of a multiplication of separatist religious movements, the main ones being BAPTISTS and CONGREGATIONALISTS. They maintained that each congregation should be autonomous and free to choose its own minister and form of worship, thus rejecting both EPISCOPACY and PRESBYTERIANISM. Cromwell, while curtailing their political activities, tolerated them; with the aid of the army, of which they comprised an important element, they became one of the most influential groups in the state. The term was also applied loosely to certain political groups in the LONG PARLIAMENT, particularly in the RUMP. Their policies are well summarized in the HEADS OF THE PROPOSALS.

Index expurgatorius (Lat., index of expurgations; also *index librorum prohibitorum*, index of prohibited books). List of books which the Roman Catholic Church forbids its members to read on grounds of immorality or heresy. The first papal Index was commissioned by Pope Paul IV in 1559 but was largely ignored by the Council of Trent (1545–63). Pope Pius IV commissioned a new list in 1564. Originally part of the counter-reformation, the Index attempted to halt the diffusion of heretical opinions; it is still in existence. Its severity varied from country to country.

Indianismo. Intellectual movement in South America for the revival of Indian culture. It holds that, in countries with a predominantly Indian population, the Indians form an element separate from the ruling Europeans and urges their return to a dominant social, political and economic position. In Mexico, Indianismo found its most striking expression under the administration of Lázaro Cárdenas (1934–40) when great efforts were made to develop the country along lines consistent with its Indian heritage.

Indian Mutiny. Rising by Hindu and Muslim troops beginning with the killing of British officers in Meerut on 9 May 1857, ostensibly because the issue of cartridges coated with animal fat offended religious sensibilities. Massacres occurred on both sides, rebel troops captured Delhi and Lucknow, and order was not restored until autumn 1858. The government of India was then transferred from the EAST INDIA COMPANY to the Crown.

Indian National Congress. Political party formed in December 1885 as an educational association to train Indians in the art of government. Initially it had the approval of the British VICEROYS but went into violent opposition when Curzon (1859–1925) decided to partition Bengal in 1905. Largely responsible for the change in attitude was the extremist Hindu Congress leader, Bul Gangadhar Tilak.

He was succeeded in 1915 by the moderate Mohandas Karamchand Gandhi (1869–1948), whose policy of non-violent civil disobedience characterized the Congress Party in the 1920s and 1930s. In 1935, the India Act gave India's eleven provincial assemblies full responsibility for their internal government; in the 1937 elections Congress took power in six of them. It withheld support for the viceregal authorities in connection with entry into World War II on the grounds that Indian opinion had been ignored. By 1942 Gandhi had decided that only independence could solve India's national grievances. Between August 1942 and 1945 Congress leaders were interned by the British; they were released to negotiate the terms of independence.

In 1947 Jawaharlal Nehru (1889–1964), who had been president of the party since 1929, became India's first prime minister. After Gandhi's assassination in January 1948, India pursued a course of industrialization at home and 'non-alignment' in foreign affairs. The Congress Party became an umbrella for nationalists of all political complexions except those of the extreme left or right.

On 2 June 1964, following Nehru's death, Lal Bahadur Shastri (1904–66) became prime minister; under him Congress retained its wide appeal. On 11 January 1966 he died suddenly of a heart attack and was succeeded by Mrs Indira Gandhi (Nehru's daughter, 1917–84) who defeated Morarji Desai to become leader of the party and prime minister.

Mrs Gandhi's modern views brought her into conflict with the 'old guard' Hindu members of the party and in November 1969 most of them left to form a separate movement under the leadership of Desai. In 1971 Congress won a landslide election victory and began preparing plans for socialist reforms. On the 26 June 1975 Mrs Gandhi declared a state of emergency; by the end of the month 675 political opponents had been arrested. In July opposition organizations were banned and she assumed dictatorial powers. On 12 July 1975 the Allahabad High Court found her guilty of corruption and debarred her from holding office for six years but she appealed against the decision and won. Opposition grew in response to repression and in the elections of March 1977 Congress lost to the Janata coalition led by Desai.

In January 1978 Mrs Gandhi formed a new Indian National Congress (Congress – I) committed more closely to her personal leadership and clearly disassociated from ex-Congress elements in Desai's government. In February 1978 the new Congress party won sweeping victories in state elections and in November Mrs Gandhi won a by-election and was returned to parliament. The following month she was found guilty of violating parliamentary privileges, was imprisoned and lost her seat. In July 1979, Desai resigned, unable to control the coalition. Elections were held in January 1980 and Congress – I won a two-thirds majority. In the 1980s, Congress has survived the assassination of Mrs Gandhi by Sikh militants in 1984. She was succeeded by her son Rajiv (*b.* 1944).

Indo-China. French south-east Asian territories in Annam, Cambodia, Cochin-China, Laos and Tonking colonized from the 1860s and held until the Geneva Agreements of 20 July 1954 that recognized the independence of Cambodia, Laos and Vietnam.

indulgences (deriv. Lat., allow time for). In the Roman Catholic Church, the remission granted by an ecclesiastical authority of the temporal punishment still due to a repentant sinner. Indiscriminate and corrupt sale of indulgences by Tetzel and other papal agents in the 16th century was one of the grievances against the Catholic Church which fuelled the REFORMATION.

industrial revolution. Phrase used by some historians to denote the radical change between about 1730 and 1850 which transformed Britain from an agricultural to a predominantly industrial nation. The process began with the mechanization of the textile industry; major developments in mining, transport and industrial organization quickly followed. Supporting the whole revolution were Britain's extensive mineral resources, particularly coal and iron ore. The use of steam engines as a source of power led to a concentration of industry around coalfields; huge industrial cities, such as Birmingham, Manchester and Newcastle, grew up. Their demand for labour drew the agricultural population into the cities. Huge advances in the application of scientific principles led to the building of canals, bridges, ships and railways.

Industrial Workers of the World. *See* IWW.

infangentheof (OE, thief seized within). In Anglo-Saxon England, a lord's right to try a thief captured in possession of stolen goods on the lord's land. The less common utfangentheof (thief seized outside) allowed the lord to try a thief wherever he could be found. In the 12th century the Angevin kings (Henry II, Richard I and John) insisted that royal officers be present at such trials. The lord's privilege of jurisdiction thus declined in importance from this time onwards.

infanta. Title given to a royal princess in Spain or Portugal.

infante. Title of the legitimate male issue of a reigning monarch, except the heir to the throne.

initiative. An instruction to the legislature directly from the people to proceed with a measure. For example, in Switzerland any 50,000 citizens may use this system to propose a total or partial reform of the constitution. The device usually supplements the REFERENDUM.

injunction. In England, a prohibitive writ by which a party is commanded not to do, or to cease from doing, an act that does not amount to a crime. Ecclesiastical injunctions, requiring the observance of church law and customs, were common during the REFORMATION. They declined in importance after 1571 when the canons of the CONVOCATION began to replace them. Today, injunctions are issued by courts to stop particular activities, e.g. of trades unions or newspapers.

INLA. Irish National Liberation Army, a terrorist group dedicated to securing the expulsion of the British from Northern Ireland.

inquilino (Span.). In Chile, a tenant farmer or a labourer on a large semi-feudal estate.

Inquisition. Ecclesiastical court of the Roman Catholic Church made into a very formidable weapon for stamping out heresy by Pope Innocent III in the 13th century. It was established in various Catholic countries in Europe but obtained its most extensive power and organization in Spain under the rule of Ferdinand V of Aragon (1452–1516) and his wife Isabella of Castile (1451–1504). The Grand Inquisitor Torquemada exercised his duties with terrible cruelty and harshness (*see* AUTO DA FE). Not until the 18th century did the Inquisition's authority and influence start to decline; its jurisdiction then became restricted to the suppression of heretical literature.

Instrument of Government. Constitution, probably drafted by Maj. Gen. John Lambert and a council of army officers, proclaimed on 16 December 1653. It established the PROTECTORATE and gave Cromwell the position of Lord Protector. He thereby assumed full executive powers, although a Council of State nominally shared them. It also provided for a parliament of 460 MPs from reformed constituencies and for elections every three years; £200,000 p.a. was set aside for the Lord Protector in order to finance the government and the army.

Integralistas (Braz. Port.). Supporters of a FASCIST and a nationalist party in Brazil, founded by Plinio Salgado, whose sympathies with the German NAZI party caused it to be banned by President Getulio Vargas in 1937.

intelligentsia. Originally, in mid-19th century Russia, the minority of people educated in Europe who held radical opinions and were alienated from Tsarist autocracy. The group was characterized by its members' rejection of conventional careers in state service, common interest in literature and fascination with philosophical and social problems. Under Nicholas I they were usually nobles with a highly developed social conscience, but at the time Bobrykin coined the term in the 1860s, they tended to be students of diverse social origins who often espoused the cause of the POPULISTS and later Marxism. The term is now taken to refer to the cultured or educated classes in general.

intendants. In France, the chief agents of government under Louis XVI (1774–93) responsible for the social and economic administration of the territorial departments up to

1789. Their authority was considerable in the PAYS D'ETATS, but their actions were moderated by permanent officials and commissions of local estates.

intendencias (Span.). Administrative units, modelled on those of ANCIEN RÉGIME France, into which the 18th-century Bourbon reforms divided Spain's South American colonies. They succeeded in eliminating corruption at local level and increasing revenue, but were responsible for much discontent and resentment amongst the CREOLE petty bureaucracy.

interdict (deriv. Lat., forbid by decree). A decree of the Roman Catholic Church to withhold services and comforts from an individual or community. Its main function was to put pressure on offenders against canon law or on secular powers with whom the papacy was in dispute. In 1208 Pope Innocent III issued an interdict against King John and the realm of England under which all church sacraments were withheld except baptism and extreme unction. The dead, for example, could be buried only in unconsecrated ground. *See* EXCOMMUNICATION.

International. An international working men's association founded by Karl Marx in 1864. Known as the First International, it was dissolved in 1876 having been weakened by internal disputes between MARXISTS and ANARCHISTS. In 1889 the Second International was formed in Paris and was effective until the outbreak of war in 1914. This was reformed in 1923 as the Labour and Socialist International which functioned as a loose association of social democratic parties, and was revived in 1951 as the Socialist International to which more than 40 social democratic

parties affiliated. The Third International or COMINTERN, was established in March 1919 and dissolved May 1943. *See also* FOURTH INTERNATIONAL.

International Brigades. Communist and left-wing volunteers from many countries who fought on the Republican side against Gen. Franco and his right-wing insurgents in the Spanish civil war (1936–9).

International Co-operation Administration. Semi-autonomous body operating within the US State Department from July 1955. Its function was to co-ordinate and oversee US foreign aid programmes whether economic, military or technical. In this role it replaced the FOREIGN OPERATIONS ADMINISTRATION but was itself superseded by the AGENCY FOR INTERNATIONAL DEVELOPMENT.

Internationale (Fr.). The 'anthem' of international SOCIALISM and COMMUNISM.

International Labour Organization. *See* ILO.

International Monetary Fund. *See* IMF.

internment. Detention without trial. In Britain and the USA during the world wars, internment took place of enemy 'aliens' – residents who had been born in, or were descended from people born in, states with which their countries were at war. In Britain internment was sanctioned first by the 1914 Aliens Restriction Act and later by the Aliens Registration Acts passed in the inter-war period. On 9 August 1971 internment was introduced in Northern Ireland to cut down terrorist offences, but in fact it increased unrest and was later suspended.

interregnum (Lat., between reigns). Period between reigns without a monarch or other legitimate ruler. In England it is usually taken to denote the period of the COMMONWEALTH and PROTECTORATE, i.e. between the execution of Charles I on 30 January 1649 and the RESTORATION of Charles II on 5 May 1660. A shorter interregnum occurred between the flight of James II in December 1688 and the accession of William III and Mary on 23 February 1689.

Intransigentes (Span., intrasigents). Extreme revolutionary party in the south of Spain in 1873.

Invincibles. An Irish secret society, based in the USA, notorious for the murders, in May 1882, of the Chief Secretary for Ireland Lord Frederick Cavendish, and the Under-Secretary, T. H. Burke while they were walking in Phoenix Park in Dublin. Those immediately involved in the crime were brought to trial, but the leaders of the society, including Tynan, the 'Number 1', were never relinquished to British justice.

IRA. The Irish Republican Army was organized from the remnants of the Irish Republican Brotherhood which staged the EASTER RISING of 1916. It became the military wing of SINN FEIN which opposed dominion status after the creation of the Irish Free State in 1922. Defeated in the Irish Civil War, the IRA lost further influence when its chief supporter, Eamon de Valera, became leader of the Irish state. The IRA was eventually outlawed by both Dublin and Ulster governments because of its opposition to the Allies in World War II.

The organization re-emerged in 1969 to protect Catholics from Protestant extremists, but split in 1971 into two factions, the Official IRA and the more violent and influential PROVISIONAL IRA.

Irgun Zvai Leumi (National Military Society). Jewish terrorist group active in Palestine between 1946 and 1948; the chief of operations was Gideon Paglin. Their most notorious action was the blowing up of the King David Hotel in Jerusalem on 22 July 1946, destroying completely the wing housing the British administration with the loss of 91 lives. More than 200 acts of terrorism against both British and Arabs were claimed by the organization.

Irish Question. The problem of the relationship between England and Ireland from the 12th century onwards, exacerbated by Protestant immigration into Ulster in the 17th century. Attempts by Liberal governments to grant HOME RULE were thwarted in 1886, 1892 and 1914. The apparent solution of the 1921 Treaty of London which created an independent 26-county Republic in the south, with Britain retaining the SIX COUNTIES in the north, failed as militant Republicanism revived in 1969. *See* PROVISIONAL IRA.

Iron Chancellor. Otto von Bismarck (1815–1898), Prussian Chief Minister after 1862, Imperial German Chancellor after 1871, the force behind national unity in a period of rapid industrialization and growing German dominance in Europe. Bismarck was noted for the rigour and realism of his domestic and foreign policies and his contempt for the niceties of political negotiation.

ironclad. Class of warship built by all the major powers between 1859 and the 1890s, characterized by armour-plating covering the wooden frames and large guns. Eventually they were replaced by ships made completely of iron and their name gave way to 'battleships' in the 1890s.

The 1860s and 1870s saw the pinnacle of the ironclads' career despite the comic nature of the first battle that took place between them in Hampton Roads, USA, in March 1862 during the American civil war: the Northern ship *Monitor* fought the Southern *Virginia* (formerly *Merrimack*) for almost a day but neither ship had guns capable of piercing the armour of the other.

Iron Cross. High award for valour, with several classes, in the German army prior to 1945.

Iron Curtain. Phrase first used in February 1945 by Joseph Goebbels (1897–1945) the NAZI Minister of Enlightenment and Propaganda. However, it was repetition of the phrase in a speech by Winston Churchill at Fulton, Missouri on 5 March 1946 that first brought it to public attention and made it a term in general use. It denotes the border between Soviet-dominated eastern Europe and the West and, more specifically, the restraints placed on ideology and movement by communist régimes in Bulgaria, Czechoslovakia, Hungary, Poland, Romania and Albania.

Iron Duke. Arthur Wellesley, Duke of Wellington (1769–1852). Victorious against France in the Peninsula War in 1814 and at Waterloo in 1815. Unpopular as Prime Minister (1828–30) because of his opposition to parliamentary reform, he was forced to protect the windows of his London home with iron shutters, though his nickname was more connected with his personal manner.

Iron Lady. Margaret Thatcher (born 1925), British Prime Minister from 1979. The title was bestowed on Thatcher by the Soviet Army newspaper *Red Star* on 23 January 1976 because of her uncompromising stance on defence and international relations.

Ironsides. Name applied both to Oliver Cromwell and, by extension, to his regiment of horse during the English civil war.

Irredentists. Italian political party founded c1878 with the aim of incorporating into Italy certain neighbouring regions (*see* ITALIA IRREDENTA). The term is sometimes applied generally to any individual or group advocating the restoration to a country of territory it formerly owned.

Irvingites. Name given to members of the Catholic Apostolic Church founded in 1832 by a Scottish minister, Edward Irving (1792–1834) and the MP Henry Drummond (1786–1860). The sect's main tenet was the imminence of Christ's second coming. Initially it attempted to organize itself on the lines of the early church but later it adopted increasingly Catholic practices. By the end of the 19th century it had little influence.

Islam (Arab., he resigned himself to God). One of the great world religions, founded by the prophet Mohammed (570–632); its adherents are known variously as Moslems, Muslims and Mohammedans. Mohammed, who claimed to be a successor of Moses, recognized the Old Testament as an inspiration and accepted Christ as a prophet although denying his divinity. Among his achievements were the abolition of idolatry; the uniting of warring tribes into one community; and the initiation of a conquest which spread throughout the Middle East, India, Indonesia, north Africa, south Italy and into Spain.

Islam is a religion lived in daily life which carries five duties: once in his life each Moslem must, with absolute conviction, proclaim that there is no God but Allah, and Mohammed is his prophet; he must pray five times daily – on rising, at noon, in mid-afternoon, after sunset and before retiring; he must give alms generously; he must keep the fast of Ramadan, the holy month, by neither drinking nor indulging in worldly pleasures between sunrise and sunset; he must once in his life, if possible, make the pilgrimage to MECCA. In addition, drinking alcohol, gambling and eating pork are forbidden; circumcision is practised. Marriage is only with the bride's consent; polygamy is permitted; sexual relations outside marriage are frowned upon; and divorce may be initiated by husband or wife. The absence of racial prejudice in Islam has helped it to spread.

The late 1970s saw a reassertion of Islam, probably sparked off by the new-found wealth and confidence of the oil-producing Arab states. The royal family of Saudi Arabia, the major oil-exporting state, have been the principal backers of the Islamic revival; they are members of the 'puritanical' Wahabbi sect.

Islamic law was enforced with great severity in Saudi Arabia, with public beheadings and amputations for offenders. However, on the first day of the Muslim year 1400 (1979), a band of Muslim dissidents seized the Great Mosque in Mecca in protest at Saudi Arabian policies. It took two weeks to suppress them and the government were clearly alarmed at the spread of Islamic militancy.

In Iran in January 1979 an Islamic revolution, headed by the Ayatollah Khomeini, ousted the Shah. Power passed to the Shi'ite Moslem clergy on the Revolutionary Council. In March 1979 Iran was declared an Islamic Republic and Islamic law is now strictly enforced.

In Pakistan, Gen. Mohammed Zia ul-Haq's military government which seized power on 6 July 1977 also insisted on strict observances of Islamic law. One underlying factor of the resurgence of Islam is national rejection of Western influence and of régimes sympathetic to the Western democracies.

Islamic revolution. *See* ISLAM.

isolationism. Policy involving minimal participation in international affairs, particularly in military alliances. It was pursued by the USA until the early 20th century, in part reflecting the hostility of German and Irish communities in the mid-West towards Britain, her Empire and allies. Isolationism stopped the USA from joining the LEAGUE OF NATIONS and secured the electoral success of Pres. Harding (1865–1923) in the 1920 election.

Throughout the 1920s and 1930s isolationist sentiment remained strong and resulted in a number of Neutrality Acts between 1935 and 1939, prohibiting loans and shipment of arms or munitions to belligerents in a civil or international war. But since 1945 the USA has been forced to adopt a role of leadership in the West although conservative Republicans continued to pursue a form of isolationism in the early 1960s, advocating withdrawal into a 'fortress America', heavily defended and with no foreign obligations, along with withdrawal from the UN. Following the Vietnam War (1965–1973), America again felt a mild form of isolationism with a reluctance to enter into new overseas military commitments which persists today.

Italia irredenta (Ital., Italy unredeemed). The territories of Trentino, Istria and the South Tyrol. Italy's acquisition of them by the treaty of St. Germain is sometimes regarded as marking the completion of the RISORGIMENTO.

IWW. Industrial Workers of the World, an American labour movement formed in Chicago in 1905 and dedicated to the overthrow of CAPITALISM. Its members were nicknamed the 'Wobblies' or the 'Bummery'. From the start it was torn between SYNDICALISM and more conventional political strategies. A conference in Detroit in 1909 supported Eugene V. Debs (1855–1926) in his decision to run for president, but other sections of the movement indulged in sabotage and sought to foment strikes. Such actions by those who rejected political methods resulted in prosecutions and the alienation of potential support, allowing the government to label the IWW as 'red fanatics'. Between 1912 and 1915, when its influence was strongest, the IWW had 100,000 members, but from 1917 it rapidly declined. Its name lives on in left-wing songs and folklore and in the tendency of labour in the USA to favour large unions of skilled and unskilled workers as opposed to small craft unions.

J

J'accuse (Fr., I accuse). Title of Emile Zola's letter of January 1898 to *L'Aurore* in which he demanded that the DREYFUS CASE be re-examined. *See* ANTI-SEMITISM.

Jacobean (Lat. Jacobus, James). The period covered by the reign of James I, 1603–25.

Jacobins. French revolutionary party formed in 1789 which used to meet at the former Jacobin monastery in Paris. Associated with Robespierre, it became the most radical of the revolutionary groups and the controlling force of the Revolution. Jacobins dominated the MONTAGNARDS and the Committees of Public Safety and General Security which governed France dictatorially until the coup of 9 THERMIDOR (27 July 1794).

Jacobites. (1) Adherents of the Stuart cause after the abdication of James II of England in 1688. First James himself fanned the flame of rebellion in Scotland and Ireland; then his son James Francis Edward (the OLD PRETENDER) challenged the HANOVERIANS. In 1715 the Scottish Earl of Mar led a Jacobite rebellion but it collapsed early in 1716. In 1745 Charles Edward Stuart, the Young Pretender, grandson of James II, landed in Scotland at the head of the Jacobite forces; they were defeated in 1746 by the Duke of Cumberland at Culloden. Scottish Jacobitism was then ruthlessly suppressed.

(2) Name applied to a monophysite heretical sect in 6th century Syria, called after their leader Jacobus Baradaeus.

Jacquerie (Fr.). Peasant rising in France in 1358, called after 'Jacques Bonhomme', the familiar medieval nickname for a peasant. The peasants murdered indiscriminately all who refused to join them and burnt some 200 châteaux; their suppression was followed by equally cruel reprisals.

Jamahiriaya. Libyan term generally translated as 'the state of the masses' but literally 'the state of the massdom'. Under Muammar Qaddafi, Libya officially became the Socialist People's Libyan Arab Jamahiriaya in March 1977.

Janata. Alliance of opposition groups in India, formed in 1977 to contest the elections against Mrs Gandhi's Indian Congress Party. It won the election and Morarji Desai became Prime Minister but in July 1979 he found himself unable to control the coalition government and resigned. Various members of Janata then tried unsuccessfully to form a stable government and in January 1980 fresh elections were held in which Janata was heavily defeated by the Congress Party.

Janissaries (deriv. Turk. *jeniceri*, new troops). Élite band of OTTOMAN foot soldiers who acted as the Sultan's bodyguard, first recruited under Bayezed I in the 14th century from Christian children taken from the conquered countries of Serbia and Albania. They were brought up as Moslems and were not allowed to marry. They gained great power in the empire but were massacred in 1826 by the Sultan Mahmud II.

Jansenists. Members of a Roman Catholic sect in 17th-century France, whose doctrines were based on the *Augustinus* of Cornelius Jansen, Bishop of Ypres, published posthumously in 1638. They were strongly opposed to the doctrinal and ethical teachings of the JESUITS and counted Arnauld, Pascal and Racine among their adherents. In 1653 the papal Bull *Cum occasione* declared five of the main Jansenist propositions regarding grace and the freedom of choice to be heretical; the condemnation was repeated in 1705 with the Bull *Unigenitus Dei filius* which was specifically aimed at the teachings of Pasquie Quesnel. In 1730 this Bull was promulgated as law in France, which finally crushed the Jansenist influence. But it survived in Holland and later spread to Italy, where it was condemned in 1786 by the Synod of Pistoia.

jarl (ON, man of noble birth). In early medieval Norway and Denmark, a non-hereditary title conferred by the king upon a chief who had distinguished himself as a war leader.

Jesuits. Members of the Roman Catholic teaching order, the Society of Jesus, founded in Paris by Ignatius Loyola in 1540 as a spearheading force in the counter-reformation. Its strict organization made it very powerful and at various times it has played an important part in politics. A long and rigorous course of study is prescribed before an applicant is admitted into the privileges of full membership.

jeunesse dorée (Fr., gilded youth). Young men of Paris who, after the fall of Robespierre in 1794 (*see* JACOBINS), attempted to bring about the counter-revolution.

Jeunesse Patriotes (Fr., patriot youth). One of several right-wing leagues which sprang up in inter-war France following the 1924 electoral victory of the *cartel de gauches*, an alliance of left-wing parties. Formed by Pierre Taittinger in October 1924, it was consciously modelled on Italian FASCISM and proved particularly attractive to university students. With other fascist groups it was active in the riots of 6 February 1934 and other disturbances of the 1930s.

Jewel in the Crown. India following the proclamation of Queen Victoria as Empress of India on 1 January 1877. So called because it was the most valuable of Britain's colonial possessions.

Jewish Agency. Body established in Palestine in 1929 by the British under a MANDATE from the LEAGUE OF NATIONS. Half of its members came from Jews in Palestine, the other half from Jews outside Palestine under the direction of the World Zionist Organization. The Agency was responsible for promoting the immigration of Jews to Palestine, organizing their settlement and administering their affairs. From 1948 it acted as the government of the new state of Israel. Members living outside Israel continued to promote investment in and immigration to the new state.

Today it acts as a world organization with headquarters in New York and Jerusalem. The Israeli state has given it extra-territorial rights and charged it with settling immigrants, conducting relations with international Jewry, and organizing land development.

jihad (*also* jehad; Arab). Holy war of Moslems against non-believers in ISLAM. *See also* BARBARY.

Jim Crow laws. Colloquial term describing the laws providing for segregation in the USA.

jingoes. Party in England in favour of the Russo-Turkish war of 1877–78. The term was derived from a music-hall song by 'The Great Macdermott', the chorus of which began, 'We don't want to fight, but by jingo if we do, we've got the ships, we've got the men, we've got the money too ...' In the last decade of the 19th century the term jingoism came to be applied to any aggressive expression of nationalism or imperialism.

joyeuse entrée. In a 1354 charter Duke John III of Brabant conceded his subjects' right to be consulted on taxation and war in return for a guarantee that his daughter Jeanne and her husband Wenceslas of Luxemburg would succeed him. Their confirmation of this on their arrival in Brussels was the 'joyeuse entrée'.

Judenhetze. (Germ., Jew-hunt). Anti-Jewish campaign which started in Berlin in 1880. *See* ANTI-SEMITISM.

July Conspiracy. Attempted COUP D'ETAT against Adolf Hitler and the NAZI régime, also called the 'Hitler bomb plot'. On 20 July 1944, Col. von Stauffenberg placed a bomb under Hitler's conference table in his East Prussian headquarters in Rastenberg. It exploded and Stauffenberg, outside the building, erroneously concluded that Hitler was dead. But he had survived with minor injuries, although officers standing next to him were killed. Stauffenberg flew to Berlin where Field Marshal von Witzleben and Gen. von Bech set afoot a move to proclaim a provisional government under Dr. Carl Guerdeler, former mayor of Leipzig. Co-conspirators seized power in Paris but their action came to nothing following the failure in Berlin. Many of the conspirators had been involved in an earlier plot when a bomb placed in Hitler's aeroplane in March 1943 failed to explode. Fifteen of the alleged conspirators committed suicide and 150 others were executed – they included high-ranking army staff, trade unionists, diplomats and politicians.

July Monarchy. Louis Philippe's régime in France, ushered in by the July 1830 revolution which ousted Charles X, and terminated by the February 1848 revolution which forced Louis' abdication. *See* CITIZEN KING.

June Days. Socialist-led Parisian working-class insurrection, 23-25 June 1848, following the February Revolution which had overthrown the monarchy and instituted the SECOND REPUBLIC. Ferociously repressed, the events undermined the position of moderate middle-class democrats and strengthened the forces of reaction represented by Louis Napoleon.

Junkers (deriv. Germ., young lords). Members of the landlord ruling class in Prussia, in some ways possessing the characteristics of a military caste. In German politics they formed the party of reaction and defence of the landed interest and supported Bismarck prior to the Franco-Prussian War of 1870–71.

junta (Span., deriv. Lat., to join). In Spain, an assembly of persons, legally summoned or self-constituted, which exercises administrative or legislative functions. One of the most famous was that of 1808 which represented those parts of Spain not under the rule of Joseph Bonaparte. The term has now come to imply collective government, usually of a nation, by a small group of individuals working in concert.

Junto (deriv. Span. *junta*). In England, the heads of the WHIG party and the leading members of the ministry formed in 1696: Somers, Russell, Halifax and Wharton.

jurandes. Committees of French trade gilds, appointed to supervise the operations of gild members, particularly the granting of apprenticeships and the concomitant payment of fees. The regulations were usually exceedingly severe.

jurats (deriv. Lat. *jurati*, sworn men). In 13th-century England, members of BOROUGH councils which consisted of 12 to 24 men sworn to uphold the liberties of the borough. In the 14th century many boroughs formed a second larger 'common council' and jurats came to be called ALDERMEN, although in some boroughs alderman signified a distinct office and in Southampton, Portsmouth and the CINQUE PORTS jurats survived as an alternative to them. In the Channel Islands they were magistrates, elected for life by local magnates and the king's ministers, who heard suits in the king's courts and formed the nucleus of the later legislative assemblies of the islands. In 13th-century Bordeaux, jurats acted with the mayor and held wide judicial powers: a body of 50, holding office for a year, elected the mayor, chose their own successors and helped to appoint councillors. Today the name may refer not only to an officer in Jersey but also to a short statement at the end of an AFFIDAVIT stating when, where and before whom it was sworn.

justice of the peace (JP). Subordinate magistrate appointed by the LORD CHANCELLOR to keep the peace within a given jurisdiction and to enquire of felonies and misdemeanours. He has a statutory jurisdiction to decide summarily many cases, to adjudicate on claims of a civil nature in some cases and to commit more serious ones to a higher court. Conservators of the 'peace' first appeared in the 13th century; in 1361 they were given judicial powers in boroughs and counties and the name now in use.

Justicia (Span.). In medieval Aragon, a court of 21 judges, 16 nominated by the city and 5 appointed by the king, presided over by the *justicia* or Chief Justice. Designed to protect subjects from royal and private injustice, it was the final interpreter of the law and could itself initiate prosecutions. From the late 15th century the office of Chief Justice became a hereditary privilege of the Lanuza family. The court's challenge to royal authority and the association of the Chief Justice Juan de Lanuza with the rebel Pérez in 1591 led Philip II to make the office dependent on royal pleasure and to annex the right of appointing all the judges.

justiciar. In 11th–13th century England, the viceroy of the Norman and ANGEVIN kings who governed while the monarch was overseas, holding a position below that of the king but above the departments of government. Holders of the office were skilled administrators dependent on royal patronage. The office lapsed in 1234, was revived in 1258 in the Provisions of Oxford, but abolished after the justiciar Hugh le Despenser sided with Simon de Montfort at the battle of Evesham (1265) (*see* BARONS' WARS). Local justiciars, men of standing whose loyalty to the crown was beyond doubt, were also appointed to hear cases referred to them by the king, thus strengthening central control of justice and increasing the number of judges. Local justiciars were replaced by justices in EYRE and by central courts.

K

kabbeljaws. *See* HOOKS.

Kabouters (Dut. 'Gnomes'). Advocates of an 'alternative society' in Holland in the 1960s and 1970s who dressed as garden gnomes. They attempted to spread a sense of HIPPY consciousness through street events, sought the creation of a libertarian 'Orange Free State' and won 5 of the 45 Amsterdam City Council seats in June 1970 before collapsing in disillusion. *See* PROVOS.

Kadets (Russ., Konstitutsionnye Demokraty, 'Constitutional Democrats'). Post-1905 Revolution party representing views of the liberal professional and academic classes. Prominent in the DUMA, the Kadets were increasingly critical of Tsarism. Favouring a democratic republic after the February 1917 Revolution, the party was declared an 'enemy of the people' by the Bolsheviks in January 1918 and outlawed.

kaimakam (Turk., one standing in another's place). In the admininstrative system of the OTTOMAN empire, a lieutenant-governor or deputy governor.

kainga (Maori). An unfortified open village.

Kaiser (Germ., Caesar). Title of the German emperor, assumed by the kings of Prussia following German unification in December 1870. William of Prussia was the first Kaiser.

kamikaze (Jap., divine wind). Japanese suicide-planes in World War II which, laden with bombs, were flown directly into Allied warships; attributively, the pilots of such planes. The name derives from a legendary occasion in the 13th century when the fleet of Kublai Khan was destroyed by a typhoon while preparing for the invasion of Japan. The first kamikaze attacks were made in November 1944 on US warships in Leyte Gulf; they became severe in January 1945 after the Americans landed on Luzon in the Philippines. Heavy attacks were made on the Allied armada off Okinawa in April and May 1945, seriously damaging the British aircraft-carriers *Indefatigable, Formidable* and *Victorious*.

KANU. Kenya African National Union, a political party led by Jomo Kenyatta (1897–1978) from June 1947. As President of KANU, Kenyatta denounced the MAU MAU but was imprisoned by the British colonial authorities between August 1952 and April 1953 in the mistaken belief that he was responsible for their atrocities. On 1 June 1963 he became the first Prime Minister of a self-governing Kenya and President of the Republic of Kenya in December 1964. His party's strength lay in the Kikuyu, the most numerous of Kenya's 13 tribes. Under Kenyatta, parties representative of other tribes, such as the Luo-based Kenya People's Union, were outlawed.

karl (ON). A holder of ODAL or freehold land.

Karmathians. Members of a Moslem sect which first appeared in 890 who took their name from Karmath, a disciple of Babek. Their leading tenets were the indifference of all human actions and the non-existence of private property. At one time the sect was in control of MECCA, but after what was said to have been a hundred battles, they were exterminated by the more orthodox believers of ISLAM.

Karos. *See* SAMURAI.

kasbah (Arab., citadel). Palace or citadel in the Arab towns of northern Africa.

Kellogg–Briand Pact. Officially the General Pact for the Renunciation of War, which originated with the French Foreign Minister, Aristide Briand, in April 1927. He proposed to US Secretary of State, Frank B. Kellogg (1856–1937), that France and the USA set an example by formally renouncing war and expressing an intention of seeking settlement of disputes by peaceful means. Wishing to widen support, Kellogg called a nine-power conference in Paris and on 27 August 1928, Belgium, Britain, Czechoslovakia, France, Germany, Italy, Japan, Poland and the USA signed the pact. Fifty-six other governments including

Germany and Russia later adhered to it. However, it made no provision for restraining aggressors and the intensification of international tension in the 1930s rendered it ineffective.

Kemalism. The modernizing and secularizing nationalism of Kemal Ataturk (1881–1938), President of Turkey 1923–38, who abolished the Sultanate in 1922, and the Caliphate – the religious authority – in 1924. He imposed Western dress and customs, banned polygamy, encouraged industrialization, changed from the Arabic to the Latin script, and in 1934 ordered the adoption of surnames, his own – Ataturk – meaning Father of the Turks.

Keren Hayesod. A Zionist Organization fund set up in 1920 to raise money internationally for the development of a Jewish national home in Palestine.

kerns. *See* GALLOGLASSES.

Keynsianism. An approach to economic affairs deriving from Keynes's *General Theory* (1936). It emphasizes the effectiveness of state intervention with regard to demand management and economic growth, together with the adoption of a fiscal rather than a monetary stance towards economic policy. *See* MONETARISM.

keynote speech. Speech at a party CONVENTION in the USA setting out the programme in which the party or candidate will campaign, allocating priority to certain points in it, and setting the tone for later speakers and the campaign itself.

KGB (Russ., Komitet Gosudarstvennoe Bezopasnosti, 'Committee of State Security'). Title of the Soviet secret police since March 1954. Responsible for espionage, counter-espionage, internal surveillance, training and funding of terrorist organizations, administration and security of Russian work camps and psychiatric hospitals used to confine DISSIDENTS.

khaki (Urdu, dust-coloured). The brownish-yellow cloth adopted for uniforms in the British army during the BOER War (1899–1902) and used in both world wars. It gave its name to the 'Khaki' Election of 1900 when a Conservative government was returned to power on a wave of patriotic and jingoistic fervour generated by the Boer War. *See* JINGOES.

Khalistan. The name used by SIKHS for the independent homeland which their activists seek.

Khalsa (deriv. Arab., pure, sincere, free). In India, the Sikh Commonwealth in the Punjab, the 'brotherhood of the pure'; also a land revenue collected directly by government officials.

Khedive (deriv. Pers. *khadir*, lord). Title granted in 1867 by the OTTOMAN sultan Abdulaziz to Ismail, hereditary pasha of Egypt. It was adopted by his successors Tawfig and 'Abbas Hilmi II but replaced by the title of sultan when Egypt became a British protectorate in 1914.

Khmer Rouge. The Cambodian (now Kampuchean) communist movement, which took its name from the country's former name of the Khmer Republic. In March 1970 Prince Sihanouk (b. 1922), the reigning Cambodian monarch, was overthrown in a militarist revolt led by Marshal Lon Nol. The USA, believing that Sihanouk's neutralist policy favoured communist North Vietnam, supported Lon Nol who proclaimed the Khmer Republic (1970–76). From exile in Peking, Sihanouk gave support to the communist Khmer Rouge who by 1974 had taken control of the countryside. In April 1975 they captured the capital city of Phnom Penh and secured final victory. A Marxist revolution then commenced with Sihanouk returning as head of state in September 1975 and Penn Nouth becoming Prime Minister. Foreigners were expelled and the whole population of Phnom Penh was forced into work on the land to increase food production and to complete their political re-education.

At the beginning of April 1976 Sihanouk's uneasy alliance with Penn Nouth ended when the latter resigned and was replaced by the communist Khieu Samphan. The government fell and was replaced by a cabinet led by Pol Pot. In early 1976 the population of the entire country was forced to follow the capital city's example and return to the countryside so that the economy could be reconstructed along communist lines. Reports began to reach the West of political killings on a scale tantamount to genocide.

From September 1977 onwards, border clashes escalated with the traditional enemy, Vietnam. In late 1978 the Vietnamese launched a full-scale invasion and by 8 January 1979 had captured Phnom Penh where they established in government the Cambodian Liberation Front for National Renewal. The forces of the deposed Pol Pot continued guerrilla warfare against the Vietnamese in the jungle and mountains.

In December 1979 Khieu Samphan replaced Pol Pot as leader of the Khmer Rouge while Pol Pot remained head of the guerrilla army, thought to have been 30,000 strong and to have controlled one-fifth of the country. In 1980, the Heng Samrin government extended its control over most of the country and forced the Khmer Rouge into a small area in west Kampuchea.

Despite the brutal reputation of the Khmer Rouge and the relative stability of Cambodia under Vietnamese control, in the late 1980s many members of the international community were pressing for the return of a Khmer Rouge government.

khozain (Russ.). Head of a household in the Russian MIR. Until the emancipation of serfs in 1861 it was usual for a family to own all property in common; members who migrated to the towns sent a percentage of their wages back to the common fund, which was administered by the khozain.

kibbutz (Heb., gathering). An Israeli collective farm. The place and function of the kibbutzim has played a large part in independent Israel.

Kindergarten. Name derisively applied by Sir William Marriott to the corpus of young Oxford graduates who assisted Alfred Milner, High Commissioner of South Africa and Governor of the Cape Colony, in his work of reconstruction in South Africa (1902–1905) following the BOER war. They included Geoffrey Robinson, Philip Kerr, R.H. Brand and John Buchan; L.S. Amery was a close associate. They returned to Britain in 1910 to found the journal *Round Table* in which they argued the case for 'imperial federation'; a federal empire with a parliament of representatives from each colony and dominion.

King's/Queen's Speech. In Britain, the Speech with which the reigning monarch opens each session of parliament, also known as the Speech from the Throne. It is written, not by the monarch, but by the government of the day, outlining their legislative programme for the coming session. A debate follows, lasting several days, in which the government's policies are discussed.

kitchen cabinet. Political term, originating in the USA, to denote a group of unofficial advisers as opposed to a formal office-holding cabinet. It was first used of advisers to Pres. Andrew Jackson who between 1829 and 1831 were held to have more influence than the official cabinet; they included Amos Kendall, Duff Green and Francis Preston Blair.

KKK. Ku Klux Klan, a secret society formed in the southern states of the USA shortly after the civil war ended in 1865. It was both a means by which whites could resist the 'reconstruction' of the south and a final attempt to reinstate the hegemony of the white plantation owners. For poor whites the Klan, together with the KNIGHTS OF THE WHITE CAMELIA, was a way of denying political rights to blacks.

The Klan was founded as a social club in Polaski, Tennessee in 1866, but was reorganized on political lines in Nashville in 1867. A hierarchical system was devised to rule over the 'Invisible Empire of the South', presided over by a 'grand wizard' and below him 'grand titans', 'grand cyclopses' and 'grand dragons'. White hoods and robes were donned partly to hide the identity of members involved in violence against blacks, including whippings, shootings and hangings.

Escalation of such violence led the grand wizard to order the society to disband in 1869, but local branches refused to do so. The Force Act and the 'Ku Klux Klan' Act of 1871 were passed to combat their activities, and allowed the president to suspend HABEAS CORPUS, use military force and impose heavy penalties on Klan members. As a result the Klan was effectively suppressed in the 1870s and 1880s. However, in 1915 the organization was revived at Atlanta, Georgia, and attained great power in the 1920s. It remains a racist, anti-semitic, anti-Catholic and anti-communist organization. Its resurgence in the 1960s following the CIVIL RIGHTS legislation led Pres. Johnson to denounce it publicly in March 1965.

Knesset. Israeli legislature, consisting of a single chamber of 120 members elected for 4 years. The franchise is universal and the electoral method is one of proportional representation.

knight (deriv. OE *cniht*). In medieval England, the mounted warrior, equivalent to *chevalier* in France. The mounted warrior was introduced to England by the Normans in 1066; Anglo-Saxons and Danes had ridden to battle but fought on foot. A man was 'dubbed' a knight when he was invested with a set of arms by his lord or father. He received a FEE, usually land, in return for which he was obliged to fulfil certain duties towards his lord. These included garrison duty; a fixed term of military service on campaign; payment of various feudal duties; and the provision of counsel and aid.

In the 11th and 12th centuries the knight was little more than a professional soldier but from the late 12th century onwards his status rose as he was called on to participate in local central government. By the 15th century his military role was declining as tactics developed away from massed cavalry charges and warfare became more specialized.

Knights, particularly the wealthier ones, continued to play an important role in politics until the 19th century. The wealth, prestige and tradition accumulated by families in the Middle Ages meant that in their later guise of country gentlemen knights were the mainstay of local government and county administration and a powerful body in the House of Commons. Knighthood now signifies a social honour accorded to a person of rank below that of baronet.

knighthood, orders of. In Britain, the main orders of the GARTER, the Bath, the Thistle, and St Patrick; and the other orders including those of St Michael and St George, the Royal Victorian Order, and the Most Excellent Order of the British Empire.

Military orders or fraternities of KNIGHTS date from the CRUSADES of the 12th century, when the HOSPITALERS and the TEMPLARS were founded. Under this impetus arose the chivalric values of gallantry, courtesy, honour, bravery and dignity which coloured the ideology of European knighthood. They provided the model for royal orders of knighthood, of which many were established by European monarchs in the 14th and 15th centuries. Membership of them was granted as an honour and as a reward for service and loyalty. From the 17th century onwards orders were received as a sign of merit.

Knights Hospitalers. *See* HOSPITALERS, KNIGHTS.

Knights of the Golden Circle. Society founded in the southern states of the USA in 1859 to argue the case for annexation of Mexico, held to be desirable as a means of increasing the size of the slave-owning territories and thus countering the growing strength of the industrial northern states. Many COPPERHEADS joined it, particularly in Ohio, Indiana and Illinois. Its most notable spokesman was Clement L. Vallandigham of Ohio. In 1863 it merged with the Order of American Knights and became more openly anti-war. In 1864 it changed its name to 'Sons of Liberty' and a number of its members were tried for treason in Indianapolis. Their conviction proved a boon to REPUBLICAN propaganda in that year's elections, but the death sentences imposed were suspended in 1866 and the convicts released.

Knights of the White Camelia. US organization, similar to the KKK but less flamboyant, founded at Franklin, Louisiana, in May 1867. It established national headquarters in New Orleans the following year and held its conventions there. Members were called 'brothers' and 'knights', and their leaders 'commanders'. The society was suppressed in the 1870s but in 1935 George Edward Deatherage and fellow-descendants of original members met in West Virginia and revived it. The main plank of the new organization of the 1930s was its ANTI-SEMITISM.

Knights Templars. *See* TEMPLAR.

Know-nothings. Political party formed *c*1855, based on the eastern seaboard and southern states of the USA. Officially titled the 'American Party', it supported slavery and was particularly opposed to Roman Catholic immigration. One of its main tenets was the need to keep the government in the hands of 'genuine' Americans; to this end it proposed a 21-year residence qualification for naturalization. The party was short-lived and barely survived the 1856 elections. The name derives from its

members' standard answer to inquisitive questions.

kolkhoz (abbrev. Russ. *kolektivnoye khozyaistro*, collective economy). Collective farm in the USSR. In 1930, to aid the 1928–33 FIVE YEAR PLAN, all individual farms and small-holdings were combined into the kolkhoz system. Land is state property and leased back to them: they farm it jointly, using government-run machines and factory centres. In the 1950s there were 250,000 collective farmers (*kolkhozniki*). Members may own a house and a plot of land individually, and keep a few cattle for personal use. *See also* SOVKHOZ.

Komeito. The 'Clean Government Party' founded in Japan in 1964, initially as the political wing of the Buddhist lay movement. Komeito favoured democratic socialism and attempted to form a centre-left coalition in opposition to the ruling Liberal-Democratic Party.

Komsomol (abbrev, Russ., *Kommunisticheski Soyuz Molodezki*, Communist Union of Youth). Youth organization of the Communist Party of the USSR.

Koran (Arab., recitation). The sacred book of ISLAM, held to have been revealed orally to the prophet Mohammed by the angel Gabriel over a period of 20 years, first at Mecca and then at Medina. It is divided into 114 suras or chapters, written in classical Arabic and must be memorized by Moslems.

Koreagate. Scandal exposed in 1977 in which several US Congressmen were shown to have accepted bribes from South Korean agents in return for supporting continued large-scale economic and military aid to the politically repressive South Korean régime of Pres. Park. At the time Pres. Carter of the USA was committed to a reduction of aid to the regime, which he publicly criticized. The derivation of the term is by analogy with the more sensational WATERGATE scandal.

Kossuthists. Hungarian nationalists, followers of Lajos Kossuth (1802–94), a political reformer and head of the movement for Hungarian independence from Austria. Imprisoned for subversion in 1837, he was released in 1840 and commenced agitation for Hungary's economic independence. He was elected head of the national DIET in Pozsony (modern Bratislava) and became a virtual dictator. In 1848–49 he led an abortive revolution and was elected 'Governor' of Hungary in 1849. With the suppression of the revolution, he fled to Turkey and then to London. He attempted to prevent the reconciliation of Austria and Hungary, but in 1867 the DUAL MONARCHY of Austria-Hungary was formed and, realizing his cause was lost, he never returned. However, as a symbol of nationalism and opposition to Austrian influence, his name remained an inspiration for advocates of Hungarian independence for more than a century.

kotsetla. In feudal times, a free peasant or CEORL who was obliged to labour one day a week for his lord and extra days during the harvest. In return, he farmed a small part of the common land.

Kraft durch Freude (Germ., strength through joy). Recreational organization founded by the DEUTSCHE ARBEITERFRONT in November 1933 to perform the social functions of the German trade unions which the NAZI party had suppressed, e.g. pro-

viding cut-price theatre tickets, running adult educational institutes, etc. By 1939, 40 million Germans had taken advantage of its subsidized tourism. It also helped to finance German rearmament by means of the Volkswagen savings swindle, a fraud by which people paid in instalments in advance for new cars which never materialized.

Kremlin (Russ., citadel). The citadel within a Russian city which afforded protection and served as an administrative and religious centre. That of Moscow, now the headquarters of the USSR government, contains within 15th-century walls an imperial palace and the cathedral where the Tsars were crowned. The term is often used to denote the USSR government; experts in Russian affairs, particularly politics, are called Kremlinologists.

Kristall Nacht (Germ., crystal night). 9 November 1938, when the NAZIS were organized to destroy Jewish property, littering the streets with glass. A massive amount of damage was done, many thousands of Jews imprisoned and hundreds brutally attacked. *See also* ANTI-SEMITISM.

Kshatriya. (Sansk., rule). The second, military, caste among Hindus, bound to a life which includes certain standards of chivalry. It is not strictly a caste but consists of several true castes among which the Rajputs are predominant.

Ku Klux Klan. *See* KKK.

kulak (Russ., tight-fisted person). Originally, Russian peasants enabled by the 1906 agrarian reforms to become proprietors of medium-sized farms. They vigorously opposed agricultural collectivization under Stalin who, in response, ordered the entire kulak class to be liquidated as part of his first five-year plan (1928-1932). Large numbers were deported to Siberia or executed in their villages; in August 1942 Stalin confessed to Churchill that the numbers killed amounted to some ten million people.

Kulturkampf (Germ., culture struggle). Conflict of beliefs between Bismarck and the Roman Catholic Church between 1871 and 1887. Bismarck, alarmed at decrees of the Vatican which implied that the church and not the state had prior claim on the citizen's obedience (*see* ULTRA-MONTANISM), and at the creation of an anti-Prussian Catholic Centre Party, passed the FALK LAWS in May 1873 subjecting the church to state regimentation. However, negotiations with Pope Leo XIII led to the restoration of Catholic rights by 1887.

Kuomintang (KMT) Chinese Nationalist party, founded in 1891 by Sun Yat Sen, which participated in the first Chinese revolution of 1911, led the second the following year, and by 1930 dominated southern China. On the death of Sun Yat Sen in 1925 Chiang Kai-shek became leader. From 1928 it was the effective government of China and conducted her defence against Japan from 1937 to 1945. The KMT government departed from Sun Yat Sen's original principles of democratic republicanism along Western lines and degenerated into a reactionary and corrupt military oligarchy. The régime collapsed in 1949 and was replaced by the Communist Party, leaving Chiang and his followers to rule Formosa (Taiwan) with American aid.

kurucz (Hung., wearers of the cross). Crusaders, title given to the followers of Dōzsa, Tököli and Rákóczy, leaders of various Hungarian uprisings against Austrian rule.

L

laager (S. Afr.). Boer encampment defended by a circle of wagons.

Labancz (Hung., foot people). Name given by the Hungarian followers of Tököli and Rákóczy (*see* KURUCZ) to their opponents.

labour aristocracy. *See* ARISTOCRACY OF LABOUR.

lagting. *See* STORTING.

laissez-faire (Fr., let do). Doctrine, derived from the classical economists Smith, Ricardo and Malthus and from the tradition of Bentham and the philosophical radicals, that the government should not interfere in economic affairs but leave the economy to itself where it would operate 'naturally' at peak efficiency and maximize social welfare. The belief, particularly advocated in England by the middle-class businessmen of the MANCHESTER SCHOOL, was a central tenet of mid-19th century Liberalism (*see* UTILITARIANISM).

lama (Tibet.). In Tibet, a Buddhist priest or monk. The chief priest and ruler is the DALAI LAMA.

Lancastrians. (1) The kings of the English House of Lancaster, descended from John of Gaunt (Duke of Lancaster), who reigned from 1399 to 1461 and who included Henry IV, Henry V and Henry VI.

(2) Supporters of Henry VI in the Wars of the Roses (1455–85) against the YORKISTS.

Landamman. (Germ.). Chief magistrate in the Forest CANTONS of Switzerland (*see* LANDSGEMEINDE).

landdrost (S. Afr., land bailiff). In Dutch South Africa, a local magistrate with responsibility for superintending the farms and out-stations of the Dutch East India Company; he also acted as president of the HEEMRADEN. The first one was appointed at Stellenbosch in 1685. The office was abolished in British areas of South Africa in 1832 but in the independent Dutch states it survived into the 20th century.

Länder (Germ.). Name given to the member states of Germany under the constitution of 1919, with the exception of the states of the WEIMAR republic which preferred to be termed Freistaaten (free states) to demonstrate their constitutional position. The name has remained for the states of the post-1945 Federal Republic of Germany.

Landesknecht. Mercenary infantry first raised by Emperor Maximilian in Germany in 1492, employed by France, Italy and England in the 16th century.

Landfriede (Germ., land peace). In medieval Germany, a local confederation pledged to preserve the peace, formed to end brigandage and private wars. A number of such associations sprang up and in 1235 Emperor Frederick II proclaimed a national Landfriede throughout Germany. During the 14th and 15th centuries regional Landfriedes were of great importance, particularly the Swabian League (1376) and the Rhenish League (1381) in south-west Germany.

land fyrd (OE). In Anglo-Saxon England, local militia in which all free men were obliged to serve in the shire which they inhabited.

Landrate (Germ.). Local government officials, recruited from the ranks of the nobility, who were responsible for taxation and military administration in Prussia, Brandenburg, Magdeburg and Pomerania at the turn of the 17th and 18th centuries. They were established in Russia in 1713 by Peter I where they proved a check on the power of the provincial governors.

Landrecht (Germ.). Also known as the Code Frédéric, the codification of Prussian law published under the auspices of Frederick the Great in 1751.

landrica (OE). In Anglo-Saxon England, wealthy landowners who acted as the king's representative within his own locality and had jurisdiction over the smaller freeholders.

Landsgemeinde (Germ.). Ancient popular assembly in the forest CANTONS of Switzerland which elected the chief magistrate (the *Landamman*), exercised judicial functions and had the power to levy taxes.

Land Stände (Germ.). In medieval Germany, provincial assemblies – comprising representatives of the nobility, clergy, towns and, occasionally, the peasantry – which were convened by the German princes for the purpose of securing extraordinary taxation. Some of them developed considerable powers but declined in the modern period as the power of the princes grew.

Landsturm (Germ.). Final military reserve of Germany and Austria before World War I which could be mobilized only in emergencies.

Landtag. Legislative body in the Länder (states) of West Germany and Austria.

Landwehr (Germ.). Prussian territorial reserve or militia founded in 1813 to counteract the manpower shortage in the standing army. All males between 17 and 40 years of age were liable for service.

Lanterne, la (Fr.). Group of revolutionary extremists, followers of Robespierre, among the MONTAGNARDS. Denunciation of them by Danton and Camille Desmoulins resulted in the execution of the DANTONISTS in April 1794.

lastage (ME deriv. OE *hlœst*, load). Duty levied on exports assessed on the measure of the 'last' (in the case of wool, for example, this was 10 sacks). It originated in Anglo-Saxon times but gradually decreased in importance from the late 13th century with the development of national customs duties.

Lateran treaties. Agreements reached on 11 February 1929 between Mussolini and Pope Pius XI (pontiff 1922–29), under which the sovereignty of the Vatican City State was recognized and a substantial indemnity paid to it in respect of papal possessions confiscated during Italian unification in 1870. A CON-CORDAT was established between the church and the FASCIST government of Italy.

latifundium (Lat.). A large ranch type of farm worked by slaves in ancient Rome. Today, the term is used to describe similar large estates, worked by underpaid and semi-servile labour, which are still common in South America and parts of Spain and Italy. They are, in effect, asylums for capital – under-utilized and only marginally profitable.

latitudinarian. In 17th and 18th-century England, a member of that section of the Church of England favouring breadth of thought in relig-ious belief and practice. In the 17th century they stood roughly mid-way between the extreme PURITANS and the advocates of EPISCOPACY; later their criticism of both ritual and episcopacy promoted laxity of wor-ship and opportunism. In the 18th century there was a danger of the Church becoming simply an adjunct of government, when latitudinarians were given preferment by successive WHIG administrations as a means of weakening the 'High Church' and hence the TORY party. In the 19th century the influence of latitudina-rianism was challenged by both EVANGELISM and the PUSEYITES.

Latter Day Saints *See* MORMONS.

Laudian. Supporter of the policies of William Laud (Archbishop of Can-terbury 1633–45) in the 17th-century Church of England. Laudians were influenced by the ARMINIANS, and strove to enforce discipline and uni-formity of worship on the basis of the prayer book. They also emphasized the essential catholicism of the Angli-can church and the desirability of ritual and the use of vestments. Sup-porters of the STUART claims to the supremacy of the Crown, they recruited royal aid in their attempts to anglicanize the Scottish church in the 1630s (*see* BISHOPS' WARS). In their efforts to supress the PURITANS they made full use of the law and prerogative courts, while the Puri-tans charged them with seeking to eliminate PROTESTANTISM from the Church. Laud was executed by ATTAINDER in 1645. The restoration of the Church of England in the 1660s in some ways represented the triumph of Laudianism in liturgical and doctrinal terms though the social policy advocated by Laud himself was abandoned.

Laureanistas. Right-wing Catholic conservatives, led by Laureano Gómez, who sought to spiritualize Colombia in the 1930s through the Catholic faith, giving the clergy the task of administering social services and paternalistic government pro-grammes. In the countryside the masses were to be freed of the Liberal CAUDILLISMO by the estab-lishment of local collective and co-operative associations run by the clergy. Rural society was to be recon-structed on a corporative basis and parliamentary democracy was to be discarded.

lawman. In Anglo-Saxon England, a man with specialized knowledge of the law. In the DANELAW 12 lawmen directed the proceedings in the local courts, which apportioned the GELD payments due from the community, administered the raising of the FYRD and received and enforced royal commands.

lay impropriator. In 16th-century England and later, a layman in receipt of TITHES, i.e. ecclesiastical revenues. Lay impropriators originated partly from the grants of land made by abbeys and other church communities to powerful laymen in return for their protection, but mainly from the IMPROPRIATIONS made at the dissolution of the monasteries by Henry VIII.

League of Nations. International organization established in 1919 to preserve international peace through the settlement of disputes by arbitration. The need for such an organization had been argued by a number of statesmen including Pres. Wilson of the USA (1856–1924), Field Marshal Smuts (1870–1950) and Viscount Cecil of Chelwood (1864–1958). Its formation was the last of Wilson's FOURTEEN POINTS.

The League's constitution, a covenant of 26 articles, was adopted at the 1919 Paris Peace Conference and incorporated in the peace treaties ending World War I. It bound members to respect each other's independence and territorial integrity and to preserve them against aggression. Disputes were to be referred to the League for arbitration, and only if a settlement had not been reached peacefully after nine months were the nations to resort to force. SANCTIONS were to be applied against nations guilty of AGGRESSION in breach of the covenant.

The League's headquarters were in Geneva and the first secretary general (1919–1932) was a Briton, Sir Eric Drummond, Earl of Perth. A League Council of 15 members (including three permanent members – Britain, the USSR and France) met three times a year and the full assembly met annually: decisions had to be unanimous.

The League's history was not a happy one. The US CONGRESS refused to ratify the Treaty of Versailles and the USA never became a member, a point exploited by Hitler when the USA and the League criticized him. The League had some administrative success with the MANDATES, Upper Silesia and the free city of Danzig, and some diplomatic success in settling disputes arising in South America and the Balkans in the 1920s. It was also able to finance the reconstruction of the economic infrastructures of the Danubian states and to press for improved conditions of work through the ILO.

But the League's fatal flaw was the absence of an international armed force by which wayward members could be coerced. Sanctions alone were not effective and their half-hearted application against Italy following her invasion of Abyssinia (1935–36) totally discredited the League. It also proved unable to stop the aggression of two other members: Japan towards China from 1931, and the USSR's invasion of Finland in 1939. Three of its founder-members left after criticism: Brazil in 1926, Japan in 1933 and Italy in 1937. Germany was a member only between 1926 and 1933 and the USSR between 1934 and 1946. By the late 1930s the major powers were ignoring the League which was obviously incapable of coping with the deepening international crisis. Throughout World War II the League continued to fulfil its non-political functions and transferred its remaining responsibilities to the new UNITED NATIONS in April 1946.

Lebensraum (Germ., living space). Slogan adopted by German nationalists and the NAZIS, especially between 1933 and 1945. The term was used with reference to Germany's alleged over-population, her need to acquire more territory in order to produce her own food, and her claim to the right to bring certain neighbouring zones, particularly in east Europe, within her sphere of influence. *See also* DRANG NACH OSTEN.

leet. A unit of local government in Anglo-Saxon East Anglia. The HUNDRED was divided into groups of villages or leets for the purposes of collecting revenue.

legations. Name given to the provinces of Bologna, Ferrara and Romagna, over which the papacy claimed rights, but which were surrendered to France in 1797 by the Treaty of Tolentino.

legatus a latere (Lat., legate from the side of the pope). In the Roman Catholic Church, a Cardinal legate with plenipotentiary powers e.g. Thomas Wolsey under Henry VIII.

Legion d'Honneur (Fr., legion of honour). French order of knighthood, instituted in 1802 by Napoleon. Though military in form it is open to civilians.

legitimists. Supporters of the claims to the throne of the Bourbon branch of the French royal family between 1814 and 1883. When the Comte de Chambord died without issue in 1883 most legitimists transferred their allegiance to the Orleans branch, although a small section, the BLANCS D'ESPAGNE, preferred to support the claims of the Spanish Bourbons.

lend-lease. Act passed by the US CONGRESS on 11 March 1941 which allowed Pres. Roosevelt to lend or lease equipment to countries 'whose defence the President deems vital to the defence of the United States'. In this way, arms and other material could be supplied to Britain, although the USA had not yet entered World War II. Aid was sent to the USSR and China as well as to Britain which received about £5,049 million of materials between March 1941 and the termination of lend-lease in August 1945.

Leonists. *See* LYONISTS.

Lepenism. Ideology of the French National Front, led in the 1980s by Jean-Marie Le Pen, a former paratroop officer, which advocates extreme nationalism, reduced taxation and the repatriation of Arab immigrants, who are blamed for unemployment and crime. Le Pen gained 14% of the vote in the first round of the April 1988 Presidential election, but his anti-semitism increasingly alienated many potential supporters, the party's vote declining in the May 1988 general elections and falling to 5% in the September 1988 departmental elections.

lépero (Mexican). A vagabond, a disorderly element, one of the rabble.

lettre de cachet (Fr.). In prerevolutionary France, a warrant of arrest issued by the king or his ministers by which persons incurring the Court's disfavour might be imprisoned indefinitely without trial.

lettre de marque (Fr.). Commission granted to a private individual by a belligerent nation, authorizing him to arm ships and seize merchant vessels flying the enemy's flag. Lettres de marque originated in the 14th century and lasted in Britain up to 1870 when British subjects were debarred from receiving them.

Levant (deriv. Fr. *lever*, to rise, i.e. the east where the sun rises). General name for the countries on the coast of the eastern Mediterranean, ties with which were first established by western Europe during the CRUSADES. The term also denoted Anatolia (Asia Minor) and was used as a synonym for the Near East as a whole. In the 16th and 17th centuries the Far East was referred to as the 'High Levant'. In 1918 the name Levant States was given to the MANDATES received by France, present-day Syria and the Lebanon.

levée en masse (Fr.). In France, an enactment by the Committee of Public Safety in August 1793 requiring compulsory enlistment for military service. Applying to all males between 18 and 25, it introduced the principle of total mobilization of the population for national defence.

Levellers. Radical democratic group existing during the English Civil War and under the COMMONWEALTH. Stressing the birthright of freeborn Englishmen, they advocated extension of the suffrage, republicanism, abolition of the House of Lords and religious toleration. A heterogeneous party, they were led by, among others, John Lilburne. From 1647 to 1649 they were a dominant element in the NEW MODEL ARMY; they combined demands for redress of professional grievances with agitation for political and social reforms and produced many of the ADJUTATORS. They had no great love of Cromwell and considered the COMMONWEALTH to be as bad as the Stuart monarchy. They led a mutiny in November 1647 following inconclusive debates in the army council on their programme for reform, *Agreement of the People*. They were responsible for more serious mutinies in May 1649, notably at Burford.

Their influence declined in the early 1650s when Lilburne became a QUAKER and other leaders fell away. There was some revival in 1659 and their colour, sea-green, was worn by some of Monmouth's rebels in 1685. The 'true levellers' were the DIGGERS, led by Gerrard Winstanley.

Liberal Unionist. Party formed by seceding Liberals who opposed Gladstone's 1886 Irish HOME RULE Bill. Ninety-three Liberals voted against: forty-six were Radical Unionists following Joseph Chamberlain, and the remainder WHIGS and moderate Liberal Unionists led by the Marquess of Hartington. Both groups founded organizations to fight the 1886 general election: Chamberlain set up the National Radical Union and Hartington the Liberal Unionist Association. In 1889 Chamberlain restyled his organization the National Liberal Union and the two groups virtually amalgamated. In 1891 Hartington went to the House of Lords when he became the 8th Duke of Devonshire; Chamberlain was elected leader in the Commons. When the Liberal Unionist leaders took office in a Conservative government in 1895 the two parties virtually fused; they maintained separate organizations and funds until 1912 when they merged as the Conservative and Unionist Party.

liberation theology. The belief and practice of some Central and South American Roman Catholic priests who attempt to combine Marxist social and economic analysis with Christian theology and argue that the Church should have a 'bias to the poor'.

liberties. In medieval England, areas free from royal jurisdiction, usually by virtue of royal grant. Holders of liberties varied from lords of the manor who held certain judicial pleas to the quasi-royal holders of PALATI-NATES. They existed in Anglo-Saxon England and multiplied in the late 11th century, being granted both as an honour and also, in cases such as the palatinate of Durham which defended the Scottish border, as a necessity. But as kings sought to strengthen central government, liberties (always a potential source of dispute and an obstacle to efficient administration) were revoked. Edward I sought to curtail the powers of the lords on the Welsh MARCHES, who claimed their liberties by right of conquest and not as grants from the English kings. The Tudors abolished liberties of SANCTUARY and Charles II attacked BOROUGH liberties.

Libertins (Fr.). (1) In Switzerland, those who opposed the extreme stringency of CALVINISM in Geneva in 1541. They were repressed by the CONSISTORIUM.

(2) In France, a sect of free-thinkers and hedonists c1730.

liberum veto (Lat.). In Poland, the nobility's right of dissent or veto in the national assembly. The basis of an obstructive technique which was often detrimental to national interests, it was abolished by the constitution of 1791.

Lib-Lab. In 19th-century England a term applied to those representatives of labour, usually trade unionists, who were returned to parliament as Liberal MPs before the foundation of the Independent Labour Party. In the 1870s and 1880s opposition to them grew among the representatives of labour, partly because the Liberal party organization grew more rigid and local associations, dominated by the middle-classes, became reluctant to adopt working-class candidates.

Furthermore, many of the working class were disillusioned by the attitude of Gladstone and other Liberal leaders during the 1880s and 1890s to questions of social reform such as the 8-hour day. In 1893, the Independent Labour Party was founded and, following changes in trade union law, the unions largely agreed to the formation of a Labour Representation Committee in 1900, which became the Labour Party in 1906. Although closely allied to the Liberals in its early years, the Labour Party's aim was to act as an independent force representing the working classes. But it was not until 1909 that the bulk of the remaining Lib-Lab MPs, the nominees of the miners' unions, joined the Labour Party. The miners' reluctance to renounce 'Lib-Labism' stemmed from their power, through the number of votes they commanded, to force candidates of their choice on the Liberals in mining areas.

liege homage. Under FEUDALISM the duty of a tenant to his main, or liege, lord. The liege lord had a prior claim on his vassal's loyalty and feudal obligations in any dispute with another landlord; he was usually the landlord of the vassal's largest estate or the one held longest. Liege homage was first introduced in 11th-century France and may have originated in Normandy. By the 13th century, the aspect of military service that it carried was of little significance and its main purpose was to indicate which of several landlords had prior claim to the pecuniary profits due from overlordship of a tenant. The concept became meaningless when tenants started to pay liege homage to several lords. Further, as the monarchy asserted itself in the countries of feudal Europe, the king began to lay claim to every man's liege homage and to specify such claims in all feudal contracts.

Ligurian Republic. Republic, with Genoa as its capital, established by Napoleon in 1797; in 1802 it was made a French *departement*.

likin (Chin., a measure of money). System of inland duties levied on waterways and trade routes in China prior to the 1902 Anglo-Chinese Convention. The duties, farmed out to the MANDARINS who derived large incomes from them, proved a great hindrance to trade.

Likud. Alliance of various right-wing Israeli parties which, under the leadership of Menachem Begin, won the general election of 17 May 1977, displacing MAPAI and the Israeli Labour Party from government for the first time in Israel's history. Likud has continued to enjoy electoral success, as for example in the general election of 1988.

Lima Declaration. Declaration by the Pan-American Conference which met in the Peruvian capital in December 1938, stating that any threat to the peace, security or territory of any American republic would be a matter of concern to all republics. It was a successful attempt by Pres. Roosevelt to rally opinion on the American continent against totalitarianism in Europe, although some South American signatories openly sympathized with FASCISM rather than the liberal democracy of the USA.

limoger (Fr.). Word denoting the process by which inefficient French officers in World War I were relieved of battlefield command, but not of rank, by being transferred to army headquarters in the quiet area around Limoges. A substantial number of officers suffered this treatment during 1914 and 1915.

Link, The. A pro-Nazi group formed in July 1937 to further Anglo-German friendship by Admiral Sir Barry Domvile, a former Director of Naval Intelligence. Funded by big business and with a widespread branch organization throughout Britain, it had little political influence. The Link was outlawed in 1940 and Domvile was interned.

Liqoqo. The parliament of Swaziland.

lit de justice (Fr., bed of justice). In pre-revolutionary France, a sitting of the STATES-GENERAL with the king in attendance to enforce by edict an ordinance or law to which they had previously denied their consent. The mechanism was usually used only after parliamentary refusal to accept a bill, although extensive use was made of it in the 18th century.

The ceremony involved was rigidly adhered to. The king rested on cushions (the bed) surrounded by peers, crown officials and representatives of the states-general, their position being hierarchically defined. The decree was then read, opinions heard, and the measure declared law.

literati (Lat.). Refers to those persons in pre-republican China who had passed public examinations in literature, thereby qualifying for official positions in the state. The term is now used loosely to refer to any body of learned people or men of letters.

Lithsmen (OE). In 11th-century London, a guild of merchants and shipowners.

Little Boy. Name given to the atomic bomb dropped on Hiroshima on 6

August 1945. *See also* MANHATTAN PROJECT.

Little Englander. In the 1890s and early 20th century, one who opposed expansion of the British Empire and the establishment of a federal system of imperial rule, based on close economic and commercial ties with the colonies, arguing that Britain should rather address herself to social reform and to the industrial development of the domestic sector.

Little Entente. Pejorative term, first used in the Hungarian newspaper *Pesti Hirlap* on 21 February 1920, for the series of alliances between Yugoslavia and Czechoslovakia (1920), Czechoslovakia and Romania (1921), and Yugoslavia and Romania (1921), which were consolidated by the Treaty of Belgrade in May 1929. Their aim was to provide for mutual assistance in preventing Austria or Hungary from asserting claims to territory lost in World War I. The alliances were undermined by Yugoslavian co-operation with Germany in 1935–38 and collapsed when France and Britain abandoned support of Czechoslovakia at Munich in 1938.

livery and maintenance. In medieval England, pay given by a lord to his retainers (livery), and illegal support of another person, by word or deed, in a law suit (maintenance). Since pay included clothes and robes in the lord's colours, livery came to denote the uniform of a lord's military retainers and domestic servants. In late feudal times, livery and maintenance became closely linked. By the late 13th century, lords had begun to extend support and protection to larger numbers of retainers; since lords were expected to support their own tenants and servants in court, the practice of maintenance also grew. Judges, witnesses and jurors were frequently bribed or threatened and court sessions disrupted by violence in cases where retainers were involved. Liveried retainers were prominent as both receivers and agents of maintenance. Legislation was introduced to curtail the related problems of maintenance and the disorder caused by liveries' retainers in 1390 by a statute which sought to limit the numbers of short-term retainers and to restrict the ranks of society who might be retainers or have them, and who might give or receive livery. Long-term retainers, the core of the lord's retinues in the national army, were not affected. But it was not until the Star Chamber Court Act of 1487 that such legislation became strictly enforced. In 1503 an act was passed forbidding retaining or the gift of liveries to anyone outside a lord's particular household. However, the problems of livery and maintenance were only really solved when it became increasingly expensive to support retainers and when the state acquired a monopoly of armed force.

livery companies. Craft or trade associations of the City of London, which developed on lines similar to the older guilds. From the 13th century they exercised increasingly strong control over apprenticeships, trade monopolies and other aspects of commercial life. Their name comes from the distinctive livery worn in medieval times to signify membership (*see* LIVERY AND MAINTENANCE). With their increasing wealth, they promoted charitable and educational schemes, founding St Paul's and the Merchant Taylor's schools. With the City corporation they were responsible for the foundation of the City and Guilds of London Institute in 1878. There are now 84 livery companies: 72 'minor companies' and 'The Great Twelve'.

Lobby, the. The American Israel Public Affairs Lobby which allegedly influences US foreign policy in Israel's interest by organizing campaigns against politicians who question American support for Israel.

lobby correspondent. Reporter or journalist from a political newspaper, so named from the 'lobby' of the legislative building where elected representatives may be approached for comments and information.

lobbying. Process of asserting influence on members of legislative assemblies to secure support for, or opposition to, proposed legislation. The term originated in the USA where approaches to legislators are made outside the legislative chamber in the lobbies or other parts of the building. Lobbying may be carried out by individuals with political, economic or cultural interests or by organizations. Certain sectional interests can exert undue influence under the system; in the USA, federal and state legislatures have attempted, but with little success, to introduce measures to stop improper influence.

localismo. In South America, strong regional or local loyalty, a trait shared by both Spanish and native elements which creates an obstacle to political unity.

lockout. In industry, the opposite of a strike, occurring when an employer tries to impose conditions on workers by refusing to allow them into the factory, thereby denying them the opportunity to earn wages until they accept his proposals. Lockouts were common in the early years of the INDUSTRIAL REVOLUTION (mid-18th century) and were still frequent in the mining industry during the early 20th century, prior to nationalization. In the 1870s farmers imposed lockouts on their labourers in response to the campaign led by Joseph Arch to organize farmworkers and raise their wages.

Locofocos. Radical section of the American Democratic Party in 1835. The name arose from an occasion when an opponent turned off the gas at one of their meetings. Candles were produced and were lit by matches with the trade name 'Locofoco'.

loet (OE). In Anglo-Saxon England, labourers dependent on the feudal lord whose land they worked. Their status was higher than that of THEOWS.

log-rolling. American term for the process by which legislators bargain for each other's support for their measures.

Lollard (deriv. Dutch *lollaerd*, mumbler). Member of a group of religious reformers and followers of John Wycliffe (*c*1320–84). They were reviled and persecuted during the reign of Richard II (1377–99) and again under Henry IV (1399–1414) who had a friend, the Lollard leader Sir John Oldcastle, burnt at the stake. *See* WYCLIFFITE.

Lombards. Members of the Lombard League, formed in the 12th and 13th centuries to defeat the attempts of the Holy Roman Emperor (*see* HOLY ROMAN EMPIRE) to reduce the liberties enjoyed by the Lombard communes of northern Italy. The League was founded on 1 December 1167 with a membership of 16 cities, including Venice, Padua, Brescia, Milan and Mantua; four others joined later. The alliance was originally to last 20 years, with 'rectores', representatives from each member city, appointed to administer the League's affairs. With papal support it achieved a number of military victories over Frederick II (1194–1250), and its life was renewed in 1198 and 1208. In 1226 the Emperor again asserted himself in northern Italy and the League was re-formed for a period of 25 years, including Milan, Bologna, Vicenza, Brescia, Padua, Mantua and Tremiso; later Lodi, Piacenza and Verona joined. It continued to provide effective opposition to Frederick and was an important force in Italian politics. It dissolved in the years after Frederick's death.

Lomé Conventions. Agreement reached in Lomé, capital of Togo on 28 February 1975 between the EEC and 46 developing states, under which the EEC promised aid and investment capital to the states and gave them access to the EEC market. A further convention was signed in 1979.

Lone Star State. Texas, one of the largest of the United States, which rose against Mexican rule in 1835, and entered the Union in 1845; so-called because of the single white star on the state flag.

Long March. In China, the migration of some 100,000 communists during their war with the KUOMINTANG in the 1930s. A communist SOVIET founded in 1931 in the Kiangsi province was successfully blockaded by the Kuomintang; in 1934 the communist leader Mao Tse-tung decided to establish instead a communist region in Yenan in north-west China, where the mountains would offer protection. In October 1934, under the leadership of Mao, Chu Teh and Lin Piao, the 8,000 mile march from Kiangsi began. The marchers, covering between 40 and 70 miles a day, finally reached Shensi on 20 October

1935: only 30,000 of the original 100,000 survived. In Yenan a strong position was established, enabling the communists to challenge Chiang Kai-shek and, between 1937 and 1945, to engage the Japanese invaders.

Long Parliament. Parliament which met on 3 November 1640 and sat, with intermissions, until 16 March 1660. Summoned following the BISHOPS' WARS, it immediately impeached the Earl of Strafford and Archbishop Laud for their part in them (other ministers fled the country). It passed an Act of ATTAINDER to secure Strafford's execution in May 1641; a Triennial Act to ensure that parliament met frequently and an Act to prevent the king from dissolving parliament without its consent. TUNNAGE AND POUNDAGE and SHIP MONEY were abolished; the courts of STAR CHAMBER and HIGH COMMISSION were dissolved.

In December 1641 it presented Charles I with the GRAND REMONSTRANCE and he, in January 1642, sought unsuccessfully to arrest the FIVE MEMBERS. In February 1642 he had to consent to the exclusion of bishops from the House of Lords, and to a bill raising troops to suppress the Irish rebellion. On June 1642 he rejected the NINETEEN PROPOSITIONS and in August 1642 civil war broke out.

Parliament was divided on the question of abolition of the EPISCOPACY and for a time the PRESBYTERIANS were dominant. They clashed with INDEPENDENTS in the NEW MODEL ARMY and when Charles I escaped from Parliament's grasp on 11 November 1647 they entered into negotiations with him. The army, convinced that neither Charles nor the Presbyterians could be trusted, expelled such members on 6 December 1648 (*see* PRIDE'S PURGE). The RUMP which was left established the COMMONWEALTH and was expelled by Cromwell in April 1653. Parliament did not meet again until 1659 when the PROTEC-TORATE fell. General Monck restored its full membership and it then dissolved itself to make way for the CONVENTION PARLIAMENT.

Lord Chamberlain of the Household. Office devolved from that of CHAM-BERLAIN.

Lord Chancellor. Highest judicial functionary in Britain, and the prolo-cutor or 'Speaker' of the House of Lords. The Chancellor is a privy councillor and cabinet minister by virtue of office and usually a peer of the realm; Roman Catholics are excluded from holding the office. The early lord chancellors were usually ecclesiastics and custodians of the GREAT SEAL. Their judicial role evolved as they were charged with administering equity in CHANCERY. The office enjoyed its greatest politi-cal power when held by Cardinal Thomas Wolsey (1475–1530). *See* CHANCELLOR.

Lord Great Chamberlain. Hereditary office created in 1133 and conferred on Aubrey de Vere (d.1141). *See* CHAMBERLAIN.

Lord Lieutenant. (1) One of the prin-cipal honorary officers in the counties of Britain. Henry VIII (1491–1547) first appointed crown lieutenants for specific regions in times of military emergency, a practice continued by Lord Protector Somerset (1506–1552) in dealing with the Cornish revolt of 1549. Their function was to muster the local MILITIA for protec-tion of the county. Under Elizabeth I (1533–1603) the number, powers and prestige of the lord lieutenants were greatly increased and they received other local government functions such as those of ecclesiastical or grain commissioner or commissioner for public loans. They lost their military responsibilities in the army reforms of 1870 and 1871.

The Lord Lieutenant is assisted in his duties by JUSTICES OF THE PEACE and magistrates are still appointed on his recommendation. He remains the principal representative of the Crown in the counties, though centralization of government has reduced his powers drastically over the last two centuries.

(2) Formerly the VICEROY of the Crown in Ireland.

Lord Paramount. In feudal England, the head of the feudal system, i.e. the sovereign.

Lords Appellant. Five peers who impeached the Archbishop of York, the Duke of Ireland and other favourites of King Richard II for high treason in 1387. They were Richard Fitzalan, Earl of Arundel (1346–97), Thomas of Woodstock, Duke of Gloucester (1355–97); Thomas de Beauchamp, Earl of Warwick (d.1401); Henry Bolingbroke, Earl of Derby, later Henry IV (1367–1413) and Thomas Mowbray, Earl of Nottingham (1386–1405). In 1388 they convened the 'Merciless' or 'Wonderful' parliament which consis-ted mainly of the Duke of Glou-cester's supporters, and which spent most of its 122-day session removing Gloucester's enemies from power.

Lords Ordainers. Commission appointed by Edward II on 16 March 1310 with powers until Michaelmas 1311 to reform the royal household and the machinery of government. Consisting of the Archbishop of Can-terbury, six bishops, eight earls and five barons, it was set up in response to protests by a powerful section of the BARONAGE mainly about Edward's extravagance and his loss of Scotland. The commission produced certain ordinances in 1311, but Edward took the earliest opportunity to evade them; only after a brief period of civil strife did he agree to abide by them.

Lords Spiritual. Bishops who sit in the House of Lords, i.e. the Archbishops of Canterbury and York, the Bishops of London, Durham and Winchester and 21 other Anglican bishops.

Lords Temporal. Peers of the realm who sit in the House of Lords consisting mainly of royal and other dukes, lords who are peers of the UK and hereditary peeresses. All the Scottish peers are also lords temporal (an electoral system of selecting Scottish peers to attend the Lords was abolished in 1963) as are the nine lords of appeal (who are life peers) and the life peers and peeresses created under the 1958 Life Peerages Act.

lost deposit. In British politics, phrase indicating that a candidate in a general election has failed to win 5 per cent of the votes cast in the constituency and has therefore forfeited the £500 lodged as a condition of standing for election and as a sign of serious intent. It was widely felt that the previous deposit was too low and encouraged sensation-seekers with no serious political interest to stand for election.

Los von Rom (Germ., away from Rome). Movement started c1899 in the German areas of Austria-Hungary by the Austrian Pan-German Deputies, whose aim was to detach their followers from the Roman Catholic Church so that, in the event of the Austro-Hungarian

empire breaking up, the German states of Austria would be more acceptable as members of the German empire.

Louisiana Purchase. The territory bought by the USA from France in 1803 for $15 million. The area involved – most of which Spain had ceded to France in 1800 – was enormous, stretching from Canada to the Gulf of Mexico and from the Mississippi River to the Rocky Mountains; by the Purchase the United States doubled its size.

Low Church. The LATITUDINARIAN wing of the Church of England, close to Protestant nonconformity, which in the 17th and 18th centuries attached less importance than the HIGH CHURCH to the sacraments and the priesthood. The term was revived in the mid-19th century to refer to EVANGELISM within the Church of England.

Low Countries. Collective name commonly given to the Netherlands, Belgium and Luxembourg. *See also* BENELUX.

Loyalist. (1) American colonists who supported Britain in the American War of Independence.
(2) A member of the majority Protestant community in Northern Ireland who wishes to retain the link with Britain.
(3) A supporter of the Republican Government in the Spanish Civil War, 1936–39.

Luddites. In early 19th-century England, a group of factory labourers and peasants who from 1811 deliberately destroyed spinning and farm machinery believing that such devices would destroy their livelihood. They derived their name from one Ned Ludd. The Luddite riots were severely repressed by the government, seventeen men being executed in 1813. The term is sometimes applied today to opponents of industrial and technological change.

Luftwaffe (Germ.). German air force, used during World War II as the chief instrument of the BLITZKRIEG.

lumpenproletariat (Germ.). Term coined by Karl Marx to describe the uneducated common people.

Lyonists. In late 12th-century Europe, moderate WALDENSIANS who took their name from the movement's original centre, Lyons. After splitting from the Waldensians and, in 1205, from the POOR LOMBARDS, they survived for some time in France and its neighbouring areas.

M

McCarthyism. Name given to the wave of anti-communist hysteria in the USA during the COLD WAR of the 1940s and 1950s, derived from the name of Senator Joseph McCarthy (1909–1957) who rose to prominence by making unfounded attacks on the integrity of government employees. In February 1950 he claimed to know of 205 communists in the US State Department, a number he changed first to 57 and then to 81. Many liberals were accused of communist sympathies during this period and often lost their careers and livelihood as a result. In 1954 the Senate censured McCarthy for bringing it into disrepute.

Machajskism. The theory of Jan Machaski (1867–1932), imprisoned in Siberia from 1892–1903 for political activity, that socialism was the ideology of a new class seeking power, the INTELLIGENTSIA, rather than the working class. Using the workers to overthrow capitalism, the intelligentsia would become a ruling class by virtue of its superior knowledge. Marxism would become a state religion holding out an increasingly distant prospect of communist utopia.

machine politics. Control over decision-making in a party or other organization by a group which maintains dominance through its own sometimes covert internal discipline.

Machtpolitik (Germ.). Power politics, particularly negotiations under an implied threat of force.

Machtübernahme (Germ.). Takeover of political power by violent means.

McMillanites. CAMERONIANS after 1689, who took their name from their minister McMillan.

MAD. 'Mutually Assured Destruction', the idea governing the BALANCE OF TERROR theory of international relations, which is that no country will start a nuclear war because of the massive damage which will be inflicted upon it when the nation subjected to its aggression retaliates in kind.

Mafia (Ital.). Criminal society with a hierarchical structure which first emerged in 13th-century Sicily. It was successful in imposing a rule of terror on its enemies and rough justice on its friends, surviving because Sicily was usually governed by foreign powers who alienated the local populace. A code of silence (*omerta*) was strictly imposed on members. After unification in 1861,

Italy tried to root the society out, but it was too deeply ingrained in Sicilian society. In the 1920s, the FASCISTS came close to crushing it.

In the late 19th and early 20th century, Sicilian immigrants transported the organization to the USA. During the prohibition era, the Mafia established itself as the dominant force in organized crime in the USA. By the 1970s the Mafia had made large inroads into legitimate business. However, in the 1980s the Mafia enjoyed enormous profits from the drugs network.

Maginot Line. Series of French fortifications stretching from Longwy (near Luxembourg) to the Swiss border, along the eastern frontier of France. It was built between 1929 and 1934 and named after the French War Minister, André Maginot (1877–1932). Due to Belgian objections the fortifications did not extend along the Franco-Belgian border: it would either have had to cross Belgium along her western border with Germany, or extend on French soil along Belgium's eastern border, implying that France would not defend Belgian territory if her neutrality was violated. As Belgium refused the former and France was reluctant to imply the latter, the line ended short. Senior French officers consoled themselves with the misguided belief that German armour could not penetrate the Ardennes forest.

In May 1940 the German BLITZKRIEG quickly turned the line by a thrust through Belgium, bypassing Sedan. The network of forts was irrelevant to the course of World War II and most of the line was completely intact when France surrendered to Germany on 22 June 1940.

Magna Carta (Lat., great charter). The charter sealed by King John at Runnymede on 15 June 1215 at the insistence of his barons. Not a radical document, it laid down what the barons took to be the recognized and fundamental principles for the government of the realm, and bound both king and barons to maintain them. Its main provisions were that no man should be punished without trial before his peers, that ancient liberties generally should be preserved, and that no demands, other than those recognized, should be made by an overlord of his vassal without the sanction of the MAGNUM CONCILIUM. In the 17th century Magna Carta became the symbol of English liberties and fundamental laws and has remained so in the popular mind ever since.

Magnum Concilium (Lat., great council). In post-Conquest England, the council which replaced the Anglo-Saxon WITAN and was the forerunner of modern parliament. It was comprised mainly of the king's great vassals who, with the king, initiated taxation and exercised legislative functions. Its composition and the mode of its convention was prescribed in MAGNA CARTA.

Magyar. Native name for Hungarians. Magyars first came from western Siberia in the 5th century and roamed through the Khazar Turkish empire. In the early 9th century they crossed the river Don and settled in Hungary. The Austrians in the 18th and 19th centuries considered them to be social inferiors. Despite attempts by the HABSBURGS to Germanize them, their national consciousness remained alive. In 1867 Hungary received autonomy by the AUSGLEICH and in 1918 was given independence.

maharajah (Hind., great king). An Indian prince.

maharanee (Hind.). The wife of a MAHARAJAH.

Mahatma (deriv. Sansk. great soul). Title accorded to Indian national leader Mohandas Karamchand Gandhi (1869–1948) by his Hindu followers. His asceticism and self-purifying fasts, together with his simple dress, elevated him to the level of a saint in the eyes of the Hindu masses.

Mahdi (deriv. Arab., *mahdi al*, one who is rightly guided). To SHI'ITE Moslems, the term signifying the IMAM who has gone into concealment, but who will return, almost as a messiah, to restore justice and truth to the earth. Several pretenders have claimed the title, the most famous being Mohammed Ahmed, 'the mad Mahdi' (1840–85), who led a rising against Egyptian rule in the eastern Sudan, capturing Khartoum in 1881.

Maillotins (Fr.). Group of insurgents who rose in Paris in 1382 against a tax on the sale of provisions and merchandise. Their name was derived from the heavy iron maces with which the majority armed themselves.

mainprise (ME). In medieval England, an early form of the modern system of bail. Persons arrested were not imprisoned if they could find others to pledge that they would appear in court. Those standing surety, known as mainpernors, were liable to forfeiture if the defendant did not appear.

maintainers. In medieval England, retainers in the service of the great feudal lords who expected protection in return for service. The abuses which arose from the system, known as LIVERY AND MAINTENANCE, led to the establishment of the STAR CHAMBER COURT.

maintenance. *See* LIVERY AND MAINTENANCE.

maires du palais (Fr.). Prime ministers and *de facto* rulers of the ROIS FAINÉANS. The last was Charles Martel, the founder of the CAROLINGIAN dynasty.

mairie (Fr.). Administrative office of a French municipality.

Maison du Roi (Fr.). Military household of the 10th-century Louis IV of France, consisting of 12,000 men, and divided into the Mousquetaires du Roi and the Gardes du Corps.

Majlis. Iranian National Consultative Assembly, the chief legislative body in Iran under the Shahs. In 1961 the last Shah, Mohammed, dissolved the assembly, which was full of landowners, after it had refused to pass his land reforms and took executive and legislative powers into his own hands.

Majlis shura an-nuwah (Arab., assembly of delegates). Egyptian assembly instituted 22 October 1866 by decree of the KHEDIVE Ismail. Its 75 members were predominantly from the landowning class and their term of office was three years; they could only discuss taxation, education and agriculture and had no legislative power. However, from 1875 onwards the Majlis became more vocal in its criticism of the government, insisting on an end to foreign intervention in Egyptian affairs and demanding ministerial powers and control of finance. The Khedive prorogued the assembly and ordered it to dissolve on 19 March 1879, but it refused to disperse and continued to meet in secret. In June

1879 the Khedive was deposed by the OTTOMAN sultan and in 1880 the assembly was dispersed under the 'law of liquidation' although it met again once, briefly, in 1881.

Major Generals. Officers appointed to command the twelve military districts into which Cromwell divided England in 1655. Their duties were to command the MILITIA, suppress any royalist uprising, supervise the collection of the 10% tax levied on royalist sympathizers (*see* DECIMATION) and to undertake, in association with commissioners, a number of local government functions. In 1657 the scheme was abandoned, parliament refusing to vote money for the militia and Cromwell failing to come to its support.

Makhnovschtchina. Uprising in the Ukraine between 1917 and 1921 led by Nestor Makhno, an anarchist peasant, whose Insurgent Army fought against both the WHITES and the Reds, distributed land, organized peasants' and workers' councils on libertarian principles, and which was defeated by the RED ARMY in August 1921.

Malcontents. Catholic nobles in the Netherlands, opposed to William of Orange after 1578, who desired the supremacy of the 'Catholic religion. They placed themselves under the leadership of the French Duke of Alençon; their ranks included Montigny, Hèze and Lalaing. Originally anti-Spanish, their dislike of Calvinism caused them to return to allegiance to Spain.

maletolt (A Fr., deriv Lat. *mala tolta*, bad tax). In medieval England, a general term for an unpopular tax, especially the customs duties on wool introduced towards the end of the 13th century.

Malignants. Name given by the parliamentarians to those who had fought for Charles I in the English civil war. The term was current during the latter part of the war and under the COMMONWEALTH.

Malthusianism. Theory expounded by the Rev. Thomas Malthus (1766–1834) in his work *An Essay on Population* (1798), holding that, since human population would always adjust to an increase in the means of subsistence, food would always be scarce in relation to population – food increasing in arithmetical progression and population in geometrical progression. The only restraints on this process were 'moral restraint' (chastity), 'vice' (birth control) and 'misery' (starvation). His theories had widespread influence in the 19th century.

Malvinas. The Argentinian name for the Falkland Islands (pop. 2,000) in the South Atlantic, possession of which is disputed between Britain and the Argentine. The islands were occupied by Argentine forces on 2 April 1982 and recaptured by Britain on 14 June.

mamelucos (Braz. Port.). In Brazil, usually the offspring of an Indian and a white; occasionally and more loosely, the offspring of any mixed blood, e.g. Negro-Indian, Negro-white.

Mameluk (*also* mamluk, mameluke; Arab., slave). In 13th-century Egypt, one of the bodyguard of Turkish and Circassian slaves in service to the SULTAN. They attained such influence that in 1250 they were able to appoint one of their own number to the throne. Mameluk sultans reigned until 1570 when the Turks annexed Egypt. For a time they resumed government after Napoleon's conquest of Egypt, but in 1811 were decoyed into the citadel of Cairo and massacred by order of the Egyptian governor, Mehemet Ali. *See also* HALEUCA.

Managerial Revolution, The. Process described by New York University lecturer James Burnham in his book of that name, published in 1941. According to Burnham, control of the means of production was passing from their owners, the capitalists, to business and government admini-strators. The governing class of the future would possess technical or administrative skills rather than wealth, athough their position would ensure that they reaped the greatest benefits of the fruits of production.

Manchester School. Political and economic school of thought which originated in the meetings of the Manchester Chamber of Commerce (founded 1820). Their leaders included Cobden and Bright and their attitudes dominated the Liberal Party in the mid-19th century. Many adherents of their philosophy of free trade, free competition and freedom of contract were businessmen, rather than economic theorists or politicians. They advocated an individualistic policy, were usually isolationist regarding foreign affairs and tended towards pacifism. *See also* LAISSEZ-FAIRE.

Manchukuo. Chinese province of Manchuria, so named by the Japanese when they seized it in 1931 and installed a puppet regime led by the last Chinese Manchu emperor, Henry Pu Yi (1906–67). With Soviet aid, the Japanese were ousted by the Chinese communists in 1945.

Manchus. Nomadic tribe who originally inhabited northern Manchuria. In the 17th century they invaded and conquered China, establishing an imperial dynasty which lasted from 1644 to the revolution of 1911.

mandamus (Lat., we command). In English law, term used especially of the writ from a high court ordering a lower court to carry out a certain matter.

mandarin (deriv. Sansk. *mantrin*, counsellor). (1) In China, a powerful official, civil or military, under the regime of the MANCHUS. Also, the name for a member of an élite.
(2) The major language of northern China.

mandate, electoral. Commission conferred by the electorate on the winning party at an election to act as their representative. Much argument abounds as to whether a 'mandate' really exists and if so, its extent. Naturally the victors in an election argue that the electorate has implicitly approved all their policies. Oppositions normally claim that only those items explicitly stated in an electoral manifesto can receive a mandate.

mandates. Former colonies of Germany and the OTTOMAN Empire, excluding Turkish areas, for which the LEAGUE OF NATIONS assumed responsibility in -1919–1920. The League gave certain of the ex-Allies a 'mandate' to administer the colonies and to make annual reports on conditions in them: these mandatories were Britain, South Africa, Australia, New Zealand, France, Belgium and Japan.
There were three classes of mandate: 'A', those which would be administered for a short time only, as they prepared for full independence, for example Iraq, Palestine and Transjordan under British mandate, Lebanon and Syria under French;

'B', those to be administered indefinitely as separate territories because of the backward state of the peoples, for example all 'German Africa' except South-West Africa; 'C', those also to be indefinitely administered but which, because of their small size and contiguity to the mandatory state could be treated as part of the mandatory's territory, for example South West Africa, New Guinea and Samoa. Any complex problems arising from the administrations were to be referred to the Permanent Commission of the League.

In 1946 the Trusteeship Council of the UNITED NATIONS assumed the Commission's responsibilities. South Africa refused to recognize the UN's rights and, since the League had ceased to exist, claimed the right itself to continue the administration of South-West Africa or Namibia (*see* SWAPO).

Manhattan Project. Code name for the project of developing an atomic bomb, begun at Oak Ridge, Tennessee, in August 1942. A large community of US, British, Canadian, Jewish and other refugee scientists worked on it. An experimental bomb was exploded in the desert of New Mexico on 17 June 1945. On 6 August 1945 US aircraft dropped a bomb on the Japanese city of Hiroshima which killed 78,000 people and wounded 90,000 more: a second bomb was dropped on Nagasaki three days later. On 14 August 1945 the Japanese government surrendered to the Allied forces.

Manichaeism. Asiatic religion founded by Mani, a Persian born in 216 AD in Babylonia, who obtained the permission of his ruler Shapur I to found a religion which would have the same impact on Babylonia as Christianity had on the West. It was a development of ZOROASTRIANISM, influenced also by Buddhism and Gnosticism. With 12 disciples Mani represented himself as a paraclete or comforter, equivalent to the Holy Spirit in Christianity. The rapid expansion of Manichaeism in Persia antagonized the Zoroastrian priests, who resented Mani's reforms of their religion and regarded him as a dangerous heretic; in 276 he was crucified.

Manichaeist beliefs were extremely complicated, but their underlying tenet was one of dualism, i.e. that there is an eternal struggle between God as the spiritual or light and matter as darkness. The religion spread to India and China, where it flourished until the 11th century. In the West its influence was felt in Spain and North Africa where it had an effect on the Christian bishop of Alexandria and Carthage. St. Augustine of Hippo (354–430 AD) was for a time a believer. Manichaeism was eventually suppressed as a heresy in the West during the 4th and 5th centuries, but its name continued to be used in connection with dualist heresies, such as that of the ALBIGENSIANS.

Manoa. Capital city of the legendary land of El Dorado, said to be situated somewhere east of the Andes, where gold was reputed to be so plentiful that it was used to build the city's roofs and gates. In 1539 Gonzalo Pizarro led a Spanish expedition in search of the fabled city, which was followed by numerous other expeditions by the English and Spanish. All proved unsuccessful.

manumission (deriv. Lat., sending forth from one's control). In medieval England the official freeing of a VILLEIN from bondage, performed in the county court. In theory a villein had no private funds but might occa-

218 Maoism

sionally purchase his freedom through a third party or be given it for his services.

Maoism. System of communism adopted in China under Mao Tsetung (1893–1976). MARXISM guided the Chinese Communist Party between 1921 and October 1949 (when the People's Republic was proclaimed); but from 1949 onwards Mao sought to interpret it to fit Chinese conditions. He had achieved a communist revolution in a peasant, not a capitalist, economy and as early as 1926 had maintained that the peasantry was an ally of the proletariat, not an enemy left over from earlier modes of economic production. A rural revolution, in which the feudal classes would be overthrown, could therefore occur, making it possible to by-pass the capitalist stage if proletariat and peasantry acted together.

Maoism therefore envisages a more flexible system than Marxist-Leninism in which self-reliance, suited to the peasantry, is more important than state authority. The concept of revolutionary momentum, as expressed in the CULTURAL REVOLUTION, counts for more than the state machine. Continual struggle is necessary if the revolution is to endure: there can be no question of establishing a socialist state and then waiting for it to wither. Rather, pressure must be applied to ensure that both state and party adhere to the broad wishes of the masses. A final strand of Maoism, partly resulting from China's territorial conflicts with the USSR, is its denial that the USSR is the leader of the world revolution.

Mapai. *Miphlegeth Poalei Israel* or Israeli Workers' Party, founded in Palestine in 1930 and usually called the Labour Party. Its dominant figure

between 1930 and 1965 was David Ben-Gurion (1886–1973). A moderate left-wing party, it had a place in every coalition government from the foundation of Israel in 1948 up to the general election of 17 May 1977. In January 1968 the Mapai combined with two democratic socialist splinter parties, the *Rafi* and the *A'hdut Avodu*, to form the Israeli Labour Party. The leader was Levi Eshkol (1895–1969) who was succeeded by Golda Meir (1898–1978). In April 1974 she resigned and was replaced by Gen. Rabin. In 1977 Shimon Peres took over the leadership. After losing to the LIKUD in the elections of 1977 and 1981, Mapai and Likud formed an uneasy coalition government of national unity from 1984 to 1988.

Mapam. United Workers' Party, an Israeli socialist party far to the left of MAPAI and the Israeli Labour Party; it draws much of its support from the kibbutzim (*see* KIBBUTZ).

Maquis (Fr. deriv. Ital. *macchia*, thicket). The dense scrub of Mediterranean France and Corsica. Providing excellent cover for outlaws and bandits, it gave its name to the Corsican resistance movement which liberated the island in 1943, and to resistance groups in France during World War II. The number and membership of such groups increased greatly in 1943 and 1944; in Brittany they were particularly effective in hampering German movements prior to the Allied invasion of Normandy on 6 June 1944.

Maquisard (Fr.). Member of the MAQUIS.

marabout (deriv. Arab. *muràbit*). A Moslem hermit or monk.

march (O Fr.). Boundary or frontier.

such as those between England and Wales or England and Scotland. In medieval Britain, these were notoriously restless areas constantly susceptible to cross-border raids.

Mare Nostrum (Lat., our sea). Italian name for the Mediterranean.

margrave (deriv. Germ. *Graf*, count, + march). Ruler of one of the large military districts established by the CAROLINGIANS on the frontiers of their territories. Their number was later greatly extended by the Holy Roman Emperors and in Germany the title became hereditary.

mark (OE), In early medieval England, an economic unit commonly used in the DANELAW, representing 128 silver pennies or 10*s*. 8*d*. Its use later spread over the whole country, and its value rose to 13*s*. 4*d*.

mark system. In very early German history, form of communistic land tenure, which was possibly introduced to England by the Saxon invaders. Traces of it may be found in the common lands.

Maronite. Member of the Maronite church, an Orthodox Christian church in union with the HOLY SEE. The Pope is head of the church but immediately below him is the Patriarch of Antioch and all the East, in residence at Bkirki near Beirut. The Maronite Church is one of the largest practising the eastern rite but in communion with the Roman Catholic Church. It was founded by a Syrian hermit, St. Maron, in the late 4th century but owes its survival to St. John Maron, Patriarch of Antioch, 685–707, who in 684 had defeated the Byzantine army and made the Maronites independent. There are 400,0000 Maronites in Lebanon, Syria, Israel and Egypt, and about

half a million more scattered through the Americas and southern Europe, descendants of those forced to migrate to avoid OTTOMAN persecution in the 19th century.

Maroons (deriv. Span. *cimarron*, wild slave). Jamaican fugitives, freed from slavery by the Spanish in 1655 to harass the English who had seized the island. They took refuge in the mountains, engaging in guerrilla warfare, and the English were unable to dislodge them. In 1738 they were granted semi-autonomy and territorial rights. They helped the British governor against Jamaican rebels during the 1865 Morant Bay rebellion. Today they are still a recognized communal society in Jamaica.

marquis (*also* Marquess; ME). Originally a European title denoting the commander of a MARCH; by the late 14th century, a style of nobility.

Marseillaise (Fr.). Marching song of the army of the Rhine composed by Rouget de Lisle in 1792, and popularized in Paris by the FÉDÉRÉS from Marseilles. After the Franco-Prussian War of 1870 it became the French national anthem.

marshal. Senior officer of the medieval royal household, whose peacetime duties were to regulate the household and its travelling arrangements, collect receipts and keep tallies in the EXCHEQUER. In time of war he was to maintain discipline and record all services performed.

Marshall Plan. Programme to aid European recovery after World War II which stemmed from a proposal by US Secretary of State Gen. George Catlett Marshall (1880–1959) in a speech at Harvard on 5 June 1947. He thought the USA should help 'assist in the return of normal economic health in the world without which there can be no political stability and no assured peace. Our policy is directed not against any country or doctrine but against hunger, poverty, desperation and chaos . . .' The British Foreign Minister Ernest Bevin (1881–1951) and his French counterpart Bidault warmly welcomed the proposal but Molotov (1890–1986), the Soviet foreign minister, rejected it.

In April 1948 the Organization for European Economic Co-operation was established representing Austria, Belgium, Britain, Denmark, France, Greece, Iceland, Ireland, Italy, Luxembourg, the Netherlands, Norway, Portugal, Sweden, Switzerland, Turkey, the USA and Canada, to encourage economic expansion and administer aid. The USA set up the ECONOMIC CO-OPERATIVE ADMINISTRATION for the same purpose. Some $17,000 million was provided by the USA, the bulk of it between 1948 and 1952, an act of generosity which was the crucial factor in Europe's speedy economic recovery after the war.

marshalsea (ME). In medieval England, the royal household's transport office supervized by the MARSHAL; also the title of a court which enforced discipline in the Household, presided over by the marshal together with the Steward of the Household. The marshalsea court later came to hear criminal and some civil cases as it travelled around the country with the Household. In 1612 it was reconstituted as the Court of the Verge to hear cases within a 12-mile radius of royal residences. In 1630 it was renamed the Palace Court and survived until 1849.

Marxism. Communist philosophy embracing the social, economic and political bases of life and containing also ideological, moral and religious conceptions. Its roots are deeply embedded in the work of Karl Marx (1818–83) and Friedrich Engels (1820–95) and, though Marx never stated it in a systematic form, it is closely connected with the theory of DIALECTICAL MATERIALISM. At the same time, exponents of Marxism have felt free to interpret it to suit their immediate circumstances, the most significant interpretations being MARXISM-LENINISM and MAOISM.

Marx gave a scientific basis to socialist and communist aspirations and his theory is linked to a conception of inexorable historic forces following discernible laws. Previously, the advocates of socialism and communism had tended to rely on pious aspirations bearing little weight against the arguments of the classical ECONOMISTS. Though Marx himself in the *Communist Manifesto* (1848) displays a disciplined mind but no scientific system, it is clear that he had specific aims (*see* COMMUNISM). With the publication of *Das Capital* (1867–94) his world view became clearer: he believed that history is the unfolding of thesis, antithesis and synthesis, a process showing forth economic modes of production and, with them, classes which would be in conflict until the final triumph of the proletariat and the achievement of communism.

Each age reflects economic conditions and associated classes; thus medieval Europe, based on an agricultural economy, produced a feudal nobility and laws and philosophies suited to FEUDALISM. At the same time it spawned the conditions which allowed a mercantile BOURGEOISIE to emerge, putting down the roots of mercantilism and commerce. In its turn, capitalism developed but, riddled with contradictions, will give way eventually to communism.

Class structure, values and lifestyles in each age are conditioned by the economic mode of production. Social behaviour is therefore explicable as class behaviour, determined by the way classes relate to conflicting economic interests. The state, the super-structure of the underlying economic system, is controlled by the dominant economic class and is used as a weapon in class warfare.

When Marx wrote, capitalism was the predominant system of economic production and he spoke highly of its achievements which marked a milestone on the road to communism. He disparaged social reform because it merely delayed the inevitable historical process. Under the rule of the proletariat, economic conditions will no longer give rise to conflict so both state and classes will disappear.

As well as providing an ideology for communist revolutions, Marxism has given to social studies a new vision of behaviour and to political science and history a clearer conception of the relationship between political and economic events. But one irony of Marx's work is that the revolutions of most significance occurred not in the developed capitalist countries but in the agricultural nations of Russia and China.

Marxism-Leninism. The interpretation of Marxist theory by Lenin (1870–1924) who was eager to explain why capitalism had not collapsed as Marx prophesied. Following the works of the English FABIAN J.A. Hobson and the AUSTRO-MARXIST Hilferding, he concluded that the concentration of capital inherent in the capitalist system resulted in economic monopolies of trusts and cartels. These, in alliance with the banks, exerted an influence on political parties and opinion that controlled the state. Capitalism turns to imperialism in its

search for new materials and new opportunities for investment and the competing rush for colonies results in war between various states, for example World War I.

At home capitalism becomes increasingly parasitic and luxury industries replace true productive industries. One product of imperialism is that colonial profits can be used to pay skilled workers more, thus 'bribing' the 'labour aristocracy'. This 'aristocracy' of skilled workers then seeks to control the labour movement and lead it towards social reform rather than revolution, therefore delaying the collapse of capitalism. It was in the rest of the working class, the lower sections, that Lenin sought the raw material of revolution (*Imperialism as the highest stage of capitalism*, 1915).

The Party must be the spearhead of revolution, since the economic split in the working class means that it is unlikely to rise above a primitive trade unionism (*What is to be done?*, 1902). This is a radically different view from that of Marx, who held that revolution would occur spontaneously as capitalism collapsed.

By 1917 Lenin's strategies had placed him at the head of the Russian Revolution. When the revolutionary élite, the Bolshevik party, had control of the state, what should they do with it? Lenin stressed two references by Marx to the 'dictatorship of the proletariat' (*State and Revolution*, 1918).

The socialist state was to embody this dictatorship, and destroy capitalism in the interests of the proletariat. This 'lower phase' of socialism will lead to the 'higher phase' of communism, in which class distinctions will disappear and the state itself will wither.

Lenin's explanation for such a revolution beginning in Russia, an economically backward country, rather than in the more highly developed capitalist West, was that Russia represented a weak link in the chain of international capitalism – Marx's revolution would be world-wide. The USSR thus leads the international revolutionary socialist movement, seeks to undermine capitalism in Europe, and supports the battle of colonial peoples for emancipation.

The importance of Marxism-Leninism lies therefore in its explanation of the failure of capitalism to collapse internally as Marx predicted; its analysis of international relations in terms of imperalist interests; its guide to the organization of the revolution and the role of the socialist state, and its support for the struggle of 'colonies'. The majority of the world's revolutionary socialist parties adhere to Lenin's theories in some degree.

Mascates (Port., pedlars). (1) Term used in Brazil to refer to the civil war in Pernambuco (1710–11) which resulted from the discontent of the sugar planters of Olinda when city status was denied to the nearby port of Recife, which was occupied mainly by Portuguese-born merchants.

(2) Also used in Brazil to denote the Turcos or Arab-speaking immigrants who settled in the country in the late-19th century as itinerant pedlars. They invested their profits in shops and eventually produced a large number of industrialists and some of the richest families in Brazil. The term generally bears a 'rags to riches' implication.

Mason-Dixon Line. *See* DIXIE.

Masons. *See* FREEMASONS.

master race. Race believed by its members to be inherently superior to all others, expressed, for example, in the NAZI ideal of the HERRENVOLK.

Mau Mau. Secret anti-European terrorist movement founded among the Kikuyu tribe of Kenya between 1948 and 1952. It indulged in ancient tribal customs and sought by murder and arson to expel white colonists from traditional Kikuyu lands. Violence began on 20 October 1952; the Kenyan authorities reacted by arresting Jomo Kenyatta on the charge of managing the movement and declared a state of emergency. A massacre by the Mau Mau at Lari in March 1953, in which 80 people, mainly Africans, were killed, provoked a feeling of revulsion even amongst the Kikuyu. By late 1954 the authorities had virtually extinguished the movement by the use of troops and aircraft. 11,000 Kikuyu Mau Mau were killed, many by Africans, while around 2,000 people were killed by the Mau Mau. The state of emergency was lifted in November 1959. Kenyatta completed his sentence in April 1959 but remained confined in a remote area until 22 August 1961.

May Events. Student educational protests on 2 May 1968 led to violent and increasingly politicized riots in Paris, reaching a peak on 10–11 May and encouraging ten million workers to mount a general strike which, as it continued into June, threatened the survival of the FIFTH REPUBLIC. The Events ended with the granting of reforms to workers and students and though President de Gaulle went on to win an ensuing election his position was weakened.

mayor. In England and Wales, the chairman of the council of a BOROUGH. The title Lord Mayor is given to the mayor of the City of London and certain other major cities.

mayorazgo. In Spain and her American colonies, a legal device by which a landed estate was entailed, making succession subject to primogeniture and limited to the eldest son or next of kin. The system helped perpetuate a landed aristocracy, since holders of such land were automatically elevated to the status of nobility. *See* ENTAIL.

means test. Survey of an individual's income and possessions. In 1931 the British government made a household means test compulsory for persons claiming certain types of unemployment relief from the state. All forms of income, including pensions and contributions from sons and daughters, were taken into account and the amount of relief granted reduced accordingly. The test was carried out by the local Public Assistance Committee, successors to the old POOR LAW guardians. It was very unpopular, many people believing that weekly unemployment insurance contributions should have ensured that benefit was paid as a right.

In the integrated system of the welfare state created after World War II means test was rejected in the case of basic benefits such as sickness and unemployment, which were to be paid for as of right from national insurance contributions. It continues to be applied, however, in the case of supplementary benefit.

Mecca. Birthplace of the prophet Mohammed (570–632). He was forced to flee Mecca in 622 by idol worshippers, but returned in 630. His descendants, the HASHEMITES, were hereditary amirs of Mecca. *See also* ISLAM.

Meiji Restoration. The revival of Imperial government in Japan on 3 January 1868, led by the younger SAMURAI to forward Japan's military and technological development through economic, political and social modernization.

Mein Kampf (Germ., 'My Struggle'). Title of book written by Adolf Hitler (1889–1945) while serving a prison sentence following the abortive Munich PUTSCH of 1923; he was helped in the work by his deputy Rudolf Hess (1894–1987). The book encapsulates his thoughts on Germany's role in world affairs, LEBENSRAUM and COMMUNISM and reflects his ANTI-SEMITISM and dislike of DEMOCRACY.

Menshevik (Russ., member of the minority). Moderate faction of the Russian Social Democratic Party after the party split in 1903. Opposed to the BOLSHEVIKS, they were formally suppressed from 1922 onwards.

MEP. British abbreviation for a Member of the European Parliament.

mercantilism. Commercial policy pursued by England, Holland and other European nations in the 16th and 17th centuries, as nations expanded the commercial sectors of their economies and a shift of emphasis towards trade and away from domestic agriculture occurred. The policy was aimed at securing an inflow of precious metals and raw materials in return for an outflow of finished goods. It went hand-in-hand with aggressive nationalism and the search for overseas colonies: colonies were to supply raw materials to the mother country and buy her finished goods. Exports to other countries by both the colonies and mother country were actively discouraged by measures such as the Navigation Acts. The first challenge to the policy came in 1722 when Walpole (1676–

1745) abolished a large number of export duties and, more particularly, tariffs on the import of new materials and semi-finished goods. The final demise of the system came in the 19th century with the triumph of FREE TRADE.

Merchants Adventurers. Trading company incorporated in 1407 which came to supplant the HANSEATIC LEAGUE. It was based first in Bruges, then moved to Antwerp in 1446, Calais in 1493, Antwerp again in 1496, Hamburg in 1567 and back to Holland in the 1580s. By 1550 it had control of more than three-quarters of English foreign trade. Its monopoly status provoked great criticism and in 1689 its charter was withdrawn.

merchet (A Fr.). In medieval England, payment due from a VILLEIN to his lord when the villein sold a beast, gave his daughter in marriage or sent his son outside the manor to school. In Scotland a freewoman paid a due to her lord on marriage; in Wales a similar payment, *amobys*, was exacted.

Merovingians. Name given to the dynasty founded by Clovis which ruled France from *c*500 to 750 AD. The last of the line was Childeric.

mesne (ME). In feudal England, the name given to an intermediate tenant who held land from the king in return for service and sub-granted it to a third party for rent. If the mesne lord failed in service, the king could reclaim the land from the sub-tenant, whose only course was to bring an action against the mesne lord to compel him to fulfil his obligation. Such actions, regulated by the Statute of Westminster in 1285, could prove very difficult especially if the chain of tenure was long, since all tenants to the land had to be traced and informed.

mestizo (Span., mixed). Latin American of mixed Spanish and Indian parentage who occupied a legally equal, but in fact subordinate position in colonial society. Today mestizos predominate in many Latin American countries and are often socially and economically disadvantaged.

métayage (Fr. deriv. Lat., half). In pre-revolutionary France, a form of land tenure whereby the landlord provided his tenant (the *métayer*) with farming implements and stock and the produce, after payment of taxes, was divided between them.

Methodism. English religious movement founded in 1738 by John Wesley (1703–91) with the aim of spreading scriptural holiness. Wesley was greatly influenced by the MORAVIANS whom he had encountered in North America. He organized the movement (described as 'People called Methodists') into 'societies', united into 'circuits' under ministers. The circuits in turn were united into 'districts' and all brought together into a single body by a conference of ministers which has met annually since 1744. Local lay preachers were also employed and moved from circuit to circuit each year. Chapel services were designed to supplement, rather than conflict, with the Church of England, of which Wesley always considered himself a member. Methodists were to attend church in the morning and chapel in the evening; they met regularly at class-meetings and at the end of every quarter, if their attendance had been regular, they received a ticket entitling them to come to monthly sacramental services. If a member's attendance was inadequate his or her name was removed from the list. Wesley started Sunday Schools, composed many hymns and revived the Agapae or 'love feasts' of the early church in meetings designed to increased the society's sense of brotherhood. Copying the open-air meetings of the Calvinist preacher, George Whitefield, he found that his sermons caused religious ecstasies amongst the congregation. Similar groans, tears and fainting-fits were produced by other Methodist preachers, including lay speakers, leading the Church of England to claim that its services would be 'without enthusiasm' of the type manifested by Methodism.

From 1784 onwards, Wesley personally consecrated clergy to go as missionaries to America; the movement finally broke with the Church of England in 1795. Differences arose within the movement regarding the status of the laity and the relationship of the movement to the Church of England. In 1797 the Methodist New Connection emerged giving the laity equal representation with ministers, and in 1810 a more important schism occurred with the formation of the Primitive Methodists who gave the laity even more power and reintroduced camp-meeting style services. In 1811 there was a split between the Calvinists, who accepted the doctrine of predestination, and the ARMINIANS, who did not. In 1815 the Bible Christians ('Bryanites') were formed and a further schism, ostensibly over the foundation of a theological college, led to actions in the law courts. The movement remained divided until 1932 when a conference at the Albert Hall, London, led to the unification of the Wesleyan Methodists, the Primitive Methodists and the United Methodists in the Methodist Church.

MI5. Division 5 of the British Directorate of Military Intelligence, established in 1916 to take over counter-espionage work from the former MO5 (Military Operations Directorate) which was established in 1904. Since 1916 MI5 has been active in counter-espionage both within and outside Britain. It is, however, well known for its failures, particularly its failure to stop the defection to the USSR of two communist spies, Guy Burgess and Donald MacLean in May 1951, both of whom had worked for a number of years in MI5 and MI6. MI5 then investigated Harold (Kim) Philby, another employee who was known to be close to the defectors. They failed to establish that Philby was also a spy and he defected on 23 January 1963. They were, however, successful in identifying a fourth man, Anthony Blunt, but granted him immunity from prosecution in return for information.

MI6. British Secret Intelligence Service (SIS) responsible for intelligence work in foreign countries.

MIC. Military–Industrial Complex, a phrase first employed by Pres. Eisenhower in 1960 when he warned of the excessive political power over economic and foreign policy which might accrue to the armed forces and armaments manufacturers as a result of their growing mutual dependence. As military expenditure escalates, so more of the economy is directed towards meeting military requirements; the companies involved then press for greater military expenditure which the military seeks to justify, and so on.

Middle Ages. A term coined by the 17th-century German historian Christoph Keller to describe the period 400–1500 AD, between the decline and fall of the western

Roman Empire and the fall of Constantinople to the Turks. It was a period characterized by monasticism, the CRUSADES, Gothic art, feudalism and Islamic supremacy in learning, ending with the decline of Christendom and the opening of the RENAISSANCE.

Middle East. A geographical region first delineated in 1902 to describe the area around the Persian Gulf. Now generally agreed to reach from Turkey in the north to Aden in the south, and from Central Asia westwards to Morocco. *See* NEAR EAST.

Migrant labour. Generally, any body of transient or non-national labourers working in a foreign country, for example Turks and other 'guest-workers' employed in Germany. However, the term is usually specifically applied to the black labour force in South Africa who are housed in large-scale barracks or hostels by their employers, separated from their families who remain in the BANTUSTANS.

Mikado (Jap., exalted door). European name for the hereditary sovereign of Japan in the early days of Western intercourse with that country. The Mikado was always recognized as the *de jure* head of state, but from the time of the Shôgun Iyeyasu in the early 17th century his functions as a temporal ruler were usurped by the SHÔGUNS. After the 1868 revolution the Mikado was restored to his rightful position as emperor of Japan, but the title fell into disuse and the emperor came to be known as the Tenno. *See also* SUBLIME PORTE.

militarism. A broad term applied to many and various ideologies and societies. In essence, militarism may be said to exist where there is an exaggerated regard for the moral values, activities and requirements of the armed forces; it often also denotes the control of political power by members of the military. Societies generally accepted to be militaristic include Prussia in the 19th and early 20th centuries, Japan until its defeat in World War II, and NAZI Germany. Militarism is also often ascribed to post-World War II industrializing nations such as Pinochet's Chile or communist Vietnam, and to industrialized countries with a powerful Military–Industrial Complex (*see* MIC).

militia (Lat.). In England, a military force which was a development of the LAND FYRD and originally controlled by the SHERIFF, but in Tudor times by the LORD LIEUTENANT. During the early 17th century counties were given quotas to fill and troops for the militia were generally found by IMPRESSMENT; it was a defensive force and service was only in the locality. Charles I and Parliament competed for its control as civil war approached in 1642, and it was reorganized in 1662–3 with responsibility for supplying arms and men being placed on property owners. Individuals called for service could provide substitutes, but service could from then on be anywhere in the kingdom. It remained poorly trained; an Act of 1852 changed it virtually to a volunteer force. It was abolished in 1907 by the Territorial and Reserve Forces Act.

millenarianism. The belief that the MILLENIUM will begin in the 6001st year after the Creation, computed by Archbishop Ussher (1581–1650) as having taken place in 4004 BC. Associated with the notion of the second coming of Christ and similar eschatological beliefs, it was unduly regarded during the English Civil

War and INTERREGNUM (1642–60). The term is now used in the wider connotation.

Millenary Petition. Puritan appeal to James I in 1603 for changes in the liturgy and form of worship, including discontinuance of the ring in marriage and the sign of the cross in baptism, a request for stricter sabbath observance and a greater emphasis on preaching. The authors of the petition claimed that it bore the signatures of 1,000 Puritan ministers, hence the name. James promised to consider the matter at the 1604 Hampton Court Conference, but by then he had allied himself with the Anglican bishops and told the Puritans that if they did not conform he would 'harry them out of the land'.

millenium. A period of a thousand years, used particularly to refer to the period during which Christ will return and reign in person on earth (Rev. 20: 1–5).

Milnerism. The name applied to the ideas and followers of Alfred Milner. *See* KINDERGARTEN.

Ming. The last native Chinese imperial dynasty which ruled from 1368 to 1644 in a period marked by order, stability and cultural development.

Minuteman. (1) One of a group of colonial militiamen in America, existing before and during the War of Independence (1776–1784). They were founded in Boston in 1774 and were most active in Massachusetts. During the war they fought against the British. Their name derives from the claim that they could be ready for military service with one minute's notice.
(2) In World War I, a volunteer speaker who gave public addresses urging the audience to purchase US government 'liberty bonds', issued to finance the war effort.
(3) US nuclear missile-bearing warhead.
(4) Member of an extreme right-wing society, formed in the USA in the early 1960s to organize resistance to a feared communist invasion. Its several hundred members lived mostly in California and Illinois. In 1965 the attorney-general declared the organization to be subversive.

mir (Russ.). In pre-revolutionary Russia, a peasant community with land held and tilled in common. Land was divided into plots which were allotted to each family according to size; families farmed the plots and paid a fixed sum to the mir, keeping the remainder of the profits. The mir was responsible to the government for the payment of the community's taxes, usually in the form of a poll-tax on all adult males. Its affairs were controlled by the SELSKI STAROSTA (village elder) who was elected by the heads of families. The origin of the system is unknown but after 1724 it took on a redistributive role, periodically reallocating land to meet the families' needs and conditions on the basis of an egalitarian but economically inefficient system of strip farming. The system became a subject of intellectual debate c1848 and was misleadingly held by Western observers to be democratic. After the emancipation of the serfs in 1861 the mir was retained for fiscal and administrative reasons but its compulsory basis was abolished by the agricultural reforms of Stolypin in 1906–11.

mise (O Fr.). In medieval England, a term with a number of meanings. It denoted a tax or tallage, costs and expenses; the issue of a writ of right and occasionally the writ of right itself; the payment made to each new Earl of Chester by his tenants to retain their special privileges; and the final settlement of accounts or the conclusion of a dispute, e.g. the Mise of Amiens.

Misls. *See* SIKH.

mission civilisatrice (Fr., civilising mission). The self-appointed duty of European nations to bring civilization to their subject colonial peoples. *See* WHITE MAN'S BURDEN.

Missouri Compromise. Proviso attached to a bill passed by the US Congress in 1820 according to which slavery would be barred from any territory formed north of latitude 36° 31' from the LOUISIANA PURCHASE except Missouri. The Compromise was ambiguously worded and postponed rather than settled constitutional questions and the issue of slavery.

mita. In the Spanish Andean colonies, a system of forced labour by which Indian communities had to contribute a fixed number of labourers aged between 15 and 50 for periods of work on government projects such as mining. Conditions were appalling and many Indians perished, particularly in the Peruvian silver mines.

Mitteleuropa (Germ.). Concept of a supra-national state in central Europe, one of whose earliest supporters was the Austrian minister, Schwarzenberg, in 1848. The project of German domination of southeastern Europe and the Balkans was later rejected by Bismarck but in October 1915 it received renewed interest after the publication of Friedrich Naumann's best-selling book *Mitteleuropa*.

Mizrachi (deriv. Hebrew *Merkaz Ruhani*, spiritual centre). A religious movement within ZIONISM founded in 1902 and leading in 1922 to the formation of the influential Mizrahi Worker Party which supported the Socialist Mapai Party in the KNESSET. In 1956 Mizrachi provided the basis for a new National Religious Party.

MNR (Movimiento Nacionalista Revolucionario, National Revolutionary Movement). A Bolivian populist, national socialist and anti-semitic alliance of militant tin miners and peasants under middle-class leadership formed in 1942. The MNR supported a military coup which promised reform in 1943 and its leader Victor Paz Estenssoro was President 1952–56 and 1960–64 when he nationalized the mines and divided the larger estates.

Mobutism. From Sese Seko Mobutu, born 1930, a general who became President of Zaire (the former Belgian Congo) in November 1965. Ruling through the People's Revolutionary Movement, Mobutism stresses national unity and Africanization rather than socialism.

Model Unionism. Mid-19th century craft unions – notably the Amalgamated Society of Engineers (formed 1851) and the Amalgamated Society of Carpenters & Joiners (1861) – which set a pattern for future labour organization with London headquarters, centralized finance and full-time national officials.

moderados. In 19th-century Mexico, moderate republicans who favoured constitutional government and opposed both the anti-clericalism of the liberals and authoritarianism of the conservative church party. They comprised the upper and professional classes of the CREOLES and dominated Mexican politics c1832–60. Their influence ended after the civil war of 1858–60 between liberals and conservatives.

modus vivendi (Lat., mode of living). Term used to denote an agreement between the papacy and a government on relations between the Roman Catholic Church and the state. It is a substitute for a CONCORDAT where that more concrete agreement cannot be attained. The term is also used to describe temporary or unofficial political agreements which secure the peaceful coexistence of states or political parties.

Mogul. A Moslem dynasty founded by Babur (reigned 1526–30) which ruled much of India from the 16th century to the mid-18th century and which attempted to unite Moslems and Hindus in one state.

Molinists. In 17th-century Europe, followers of the Spanish JESUIT Luis de Molina (1535–1600), a principal antagonist of the JANSENISTS.

monetarism. An economic school influential in the 1970s and 1980s which argues that the money supply is the main factor in economic activity. Monetarists believe that the only way government can promote economic stability and growth is by monetary rather than fiscal measures; government should control the rate of growth of money supply, tying its expansion to the potential growth in gross domestic product. See KEYNESIANISM.

Monroe Doctrine. Doctrine stated by US President James Monroe (1758–1831) in 1823: 'The American continents, by the free and independent conditions which they have assumed and maintained, are henceforth not to be considered as subjects for future colonization by any European powers'. Fears of renewed French and Spanish attempts at colonization in Latin America prompted Monroe's statement, and with a few exceptions the European powers have respected the doctrine. At the same time, however, Monroe's assertion has been used to justify US imperial ventures in Central and South America in the 19th and 20th centuries.

Montagnards (Fr., members of the mountain). Members of an extremist political party in the French Revolutionary Legislative Assembly and National Convention comprising CORDELIERS and JACOBINS, they derived their name from sitting on the highest point of the left side of the Legislative Assembly. They developed the idea of the expediency of the Revolutionary War and came to an end with the fall of Robespierre on 9 THERMIDOR.

monteneros (Span.). Irregular cavalry bands of GAUCHOS during the years following Argentinian independence in 1816. They were prone to banditry but were often hired by the local caudillos (see CAUDILLISMO) who ruled over the interior, and acted as a military check on the attempts of Buenos Aires to dominate the country.

Montfortians. Supporters of Simon de Montfort, Earl of Leicester from 1258 to 1265. Originally concerned to define and reform the system of royal government, they were popular amongst the English BARONAGE and left Henry III with little support. Their efforts resulted in the 1258 Provisions of Oxford which functioned for 18 months before divisions amongst the baronage allowed Henry to recover strength. In May 1261 he received dispensation from the papacy from his oath to uphold the Provisions and dismissed from office the more determined reformers. De Montfort, who had gone abroad in 1261, returned in 1263 and began rallying the baronage. Civil war broke out in 1264, De Montfort being supported by the earls of Gloucester and Derby, a number of bishops, and many knights, gentry and citizens of London and the CINQUE PORTS. The king had the support of the northern barons and the barons of the Welsh MARCHES. After the defection of Gloucester, de Montfort was defeated and killed at Evesham in 1265, but the war continued until 1267 when the DISINHERITED barons submitted. *See* BARONS' WAR.

Montt-Varistas. In mid-19th century Chile, the extreme reactionary wing of the Pelucones, who took their name from President Montt and his Secretary of State, Varas.

Moonlighters. In Ireland, agrarian secret society, similar in constitution and methods to the WHITEBOYS, and guilty of many outrages in 1881.

moot (deriv. OE *gemot*, assembly or meeting). In medieval England, assemblies found in all organized communities which dealt with a variety of topics – legal and administrative, lay and ecclesiastical. The smaller the community the less the power of its moot and the smaller its area of competence.

Moral Majority. A right-wing pressure group influential in American politics in the 1980s which takes a Christian fundamentalist position on such issues as family life, homosexual rights and pornography.

Moravians. Members of the Moravian Church, a revival of the 'Bohemian Brethren' (*see* UNITAS FRATRUM) in 1722. As a Protestant sect it was persecuted by Emperor Ferdinand II and barely survived. But in the 18th century it was re-established by Count Zinzendorf in Saxony and built the town of Herrnhut ('God's protection') which became the centre from which Moravian missionaries spread their doctrine all over the world. Their central tenet (which strongly influenced John Wesley, the founder of METHODISM) was that goodness of behaviour, piety and orthodoxy are of no avail without faith, the 'sufficient sovereign saving grace' that comes as a direct illumination from God.

Morgenthau Plan. Proposal made by US Secretary of the Treasury Henry Morgenthau (1891–1967) at the Quebec conference between Roosevelt and Churchill on 13–16 September 1944. Roosevelt and Churchill accepted his suggestion that Germany should be 'pastoralized' – i.e. that all industry be removed from the country – but both the US State Department and the British Foreign Office considered the idea absurd, seeing no point in subsidizing a rural Germany after the war. The NAZIS made much of the proposal in their attempts to encourage resistance to the Allied armies.

Mormons. American religious sect founded in 1830 by Joseph Smith (1805–44) after a vision of two heavenly messengers who forbade him to join an existing church but told him to become the prophet of a new one. He also claimed to have been told of two hidden gold plates which he uncovered in 1827 and translated with the aid of the 'angels' from 'reformed Egyptian' into English. The resulting *Book of Mormon* was published in 1830 and a small church founded in New York State. The *Book* identified the American Indians as the ten lost tribes of Israel and alleged that Christ had appeared in America after his ascension.

The sect encountered hostility from the local community for styling themselves the 'Chosen People' and participating in politics as Smith directed. In 1844 Smith was murdered and became a martyr for his church. He was succeeded as leader by Brigham Young who led the sect across a thousand miles of desert to Salt Lake, Utah in July 1847. By 1851 30,000 Mormons had arrived and Salt Lake City was built as their headquarters. In 1852 the Reorganized Church of Jesus Christ of Latter-day Saints, with its headquarters at Independence, Missouri, became a separate and distinct body though it holds similar beliefs.

The Mormons have two orders of priests or leaders: the Melchizedeks, or high order, who attend to the spiritual affairs of the church and include the apostles or ruling elders and the high priest; the Aaronic priesthood, or lower order, who attend to temporal affairs. Polygamy, sanctioned by Brigham Young, was renounced in 1890. The Mormons are believers in MILLENARIANISM, abstain from alcohol, coffee, tea and tobacco and lay stress on community welfare and the importance of revelation through visions.

mortmain (OFr. deriv. Lat., dead hand). In medieval England, lands held by the church which were not liable to the feudal dues, such as RELIEFS and ESCHEATS, that were obigatory on land held in FRANKALMOIN. It became common practice for laymen to give land to the church and then receive it back as tenants, in order to avoid their feudal obligations. The Statute of Mortmain introduced in 1279, forbade the gift of land to the church without the prior consent of the crown.

mortuary (ME deriv. Lat.). A gift from the estate of a deceased man at the time of his death to the parish clergy. The practice developed from the SOUL SCOT; the gift was originally the second-best beast, and later the second-best possession. Eventually cash sums were paid instead which opened the way to abuse and was a source of anti-clerical feeling in late medieval England. In 1529 Parliament set a limit to the size of mortuary fees. They continued to be collected up to the 18th century.

moshav. Israeli settlement run on CO-OPERATIVE lines.

Mossbacks. In late 19th century and early 20th century USA, name given to an old-fashioned section of the Democratic Party, most numerous in the state of Ohio. The name is derived from the popular term for the snapping turtle, recognizable by the growth of a species of aquatic moss on its shell.

most favoured nation. Clause found in many trade treaties, by which each signatory to the treaty is pledged to grant to the others any tariff reduction or trading preference it might in future offer to a third party, thus preventing preferential treatment of any particular country. Such clauses have always proved useful in reducing obstacles to international trade, thereby allowing increases in world production and employment.

moujik (Russ.). In pre-revolutionary Russia, a peasant.

Mountain (Fr., *Le Montagne*). Collective name for the MONTAGNARDS (so called because they sat on the topmost benches of the French

Assembly), extreme democrats who wielded a controlling majority on the Committee of Public Safety which effectively ruled France in 1793–94. Many were executed in the THERMIDORIEN reaction of 1794–95.

MPLA. People's Movement for the Liberation of Angola, a socialist liberation movement which fought with UNITA and the FNLA between 1961 and 1975 to secure Angolan independence from Portuguese rule. Following independence on 10 November 1975, the MPLA fought a civil war with UNITA and the FNLA for control. With Soviet arms and the assistance of Cuban troops, the MPLA were in control of most of the country by February 1976 and their 'People's Republic' was then recognized as the true government of Angola. Civil war has, however, continued with UNITA throughout the 1980s.

muezzin (Arab.). Crier who calls the Moslem faithful to prayer at the prescribed times.

mufti (Arab., one who gives a *fetwa*). Jurists trained in Islamic law who gave authoritative decisions (*fetwa*) on legal problems, distinct from a judge and usually with private rather than official status. In the MAMELUK sultanate of Egypt and Syria a mufti was appointed as representative of each of the four schools of Islam while under the OTTOMAN empire the Mufti of Istanbul had the status of Sheikh al-Islam. *See also* GRAND MUFTI.

Muggletonians. Members of an English religious sect founded *c*1651 by two journeymen tailors, Lodowick Muggleton and John Reeve. Unlike most sects of the period they had no political interests but were purely religious. They rejected the doctrine of the Trinity; asserted that God had a human body; maintained that the Father, not the Son, died on the cross and that he left Elijah in control. Muggleton and Reeve believed that they represented Aaron and Moses (Rev. 11: 3–6).

mugwumps (deriv. Amer. Ind. *mugguomp*, great chief). Term coined by Charles Anderson Dana of the *New York Sun* to describe members of the Republican Party who deserted James G. Blaine and chose to support the Democrat Cleveland in the Presidential election of 1884, attracted by his advocacy of civil service reform. The term is now used to denote independent members of a political party, or those who temporarily change party allegiance in a particular campaign.

Muldergate. South African political scandal in 1978, taking its name from Connie Mulder, Minister of Information, by analogy with WATERGATE. It culminated in the resignation in June 1979 of Vorster from the Presidency.

mullah (deriv. Arab. *mawlā*). Moslem specially learned in theology or law.

multilateralists. Those in favour of a policy requiring two or more states to undertake the same action on any problem, commonly used in international politics with reference to nuclear disarmament. In this sphere it has two separate meanings: (1) Supporters of the Multilateral Nuclear Force (MLF) suggested by the USA which would consist of an initial force of 25 surface vessels with Polaris missiles manned by mixed crews from the NATO countries. The proposal was designed to prevent France pursuing an independent programme of nuclear development and

to allow NATO members to participate in control of a European nuclear
deterrent under an overriding US
veto. France rejected the idea outright but West Germany signed an
agreement in June 1964 to establish
the MLF within a year. Britain
sought to modify the proposal by
suggesting an Atlantic Nuclear Force
(ANF) whereby her existing air and
submarine forces would be integrated with the new MLF, in order to
save money.

(2) Those who favour a policy of
nuclear disarmament requiring the
USSR to begin reducing its armaments at the same time and at the
same pace as the West. Critics of the
policy claim that many of its supporters have no real desire to disarm and
use the difficulty of negotiations as an
excuse to forestall positive action on
reducing the level of nuclear
weapons in their own country. *See*
UNILATERALISTS.

murage (ME). In medieval England,
tax levied on the burgesses for the
upkeep of the town walls.

Muscovy (Fr. deriv. Russ. *Moskvā*,
Moscow). Russia.

Mustafiz (Arab.). Militia or second
military reserve of the OTTOMAN
Turkish army.

Mutualists. In France, secret organization amongst the weavers of
Lyons, comprising the *chefs d'ateliers*
or middlemen, who ordered a strike
of workmen in April 1834. The strike
developed into a rising which was
quickly suppressed; the leaders were
prosecuted under the French
Association Laws.

Mutual Security Agency. Agency
established by the US Mutual Security Act of 1951 for the purpose of
supplying friendly nations with military, technical and economic aid.
Having the overall aim of furthering
world peace, the agency's powers
were wider than those of the ECON-
OMIC CO-OPERATIVE ADMINISTRA-
TION which it replaced. In 1953 it was
superseded by the Foreign Operations Administration.

My Lai. Vietnamese village, synonymous with low morale and over-
reaction by US forces fighting in the
Vietnam War (1965–73). In November 1969 investigations commenced
in the USA into reports that on 16
March 1968 US troops massacred all
the inhabitants of the village. On 29
March 1971 Lieut. William Calley
was convicted of the murder of at
least 109 Vietnamese and sentenced
to life imprisonment (a sentence
later substantially reduced). His
immediate superior, Capt. Ernest
Medina, was acquitted. It was
revealed at the trial that the action
formed part of a punitive operation
against areas suspected of aiding the
VIET CONG. Grave doubts were
raised in the USA about the role its
armed forces were playing in
Vietnam.

N

NAACP. National Association for the Advancement of Colored Peoples, founded in the USA in 1909 to press for CIVIL RIGHTS for blacks. At one time its membership was 400,000. More moderate than CORE, it was eclipsed by the more radical BLACK POWER movement.

nabob (deriv. Urdu *nawwāb*, deputy). Name given to employees of the EAST INDIA COMPANY who returned to England after making their fortunes in India. Their ostentatious wealth, acquired during the years after Clive took Bengal (1757), was derived from revenue corruption, presents, bribes, contracts, private trade and speculation. On returning to England many bought large estates and secured seats in parliament; once there they prevented reform of the Indian government. Their opulence was eventually reduced by the stricter discipline imposed on EAST INDIA COMPANY officials by the Governor-General Cornwallis (1786–1793); by the influence of EVANGELISM in India after 1785; by rising standards of public duty and by the Company's successive retrenchments.

Narodniks. Members of a secret Russian movement in 1873–1874 and 1876. Its first supporters were university students who attempted to convert the rural population to socialism. The movement was savagely repressed by the Tsarist government in 1877.

Nassau Agreement. Agreement reached on 18 December 1962 between Pres. Kennedy (1917–63) of the USA and the British Prime Minister Harold Macmillan (1894–1986) after negotiations in Nassau in the Bahamas. The USA agreed to provide Polaris missiles for use on Royal Navy submarines operating under NATO command, which was seen as strengthening Anglo-American co-operation. It was criticized by Pres. de Gaulle (1890–1970) of France, who took it as evidence that Britain's policies were not oriented to Europe; a month later he vetoed Britain's application to join the EEC.

nationalism. Belief that states should be organized on the basis of nationality, usually reflecting group sentiment derived from common characteristics such as language and culture, and a tendency to stress differences between national units. Modern nationalism took root in the 18th and 19th centuries and was greatly influenced by the French Revolution of 1789, the conquests of

Napoleon I (1769–1821) and nationalist revolutionary movements of the early 19th century. It was the antithesis of the concept of a universal empire, a remnant of the earlier Roman Empire, which was prevalent in the Middle Ages and reflected both in the Holy Roman Empire and the Catholic Church. Nationalism was also a challenge to the vestiges of feudalism, directing loyalty towards the national state and away from the feudal lord. There was a sense of egalitarianism in the nationalist movement, its determinants being not rank or position but common factors, especially language. In France and the USA, therefore, it was closely allied to democracy.

The two world wars created a great upsurge in nationalism, reinforced by the post-war settlements of 1918–19, stressing rights of 'national self-determination' and the anti-colonialism that followed World War II. In the anti-colonialist movements nationalism has often been connected with COMMUNISM. The concept defies easy definition and takes diverse forms. Rather than being categorized by objective tests it grows more from a subjective belief by people of common heritage that they belong to a nation. This belief is often known simply as 'national feeling', with the term nationalism being reserved for its more strident and exaggerated expression. In some cases, modern nationalism has a right-wing or even fascist slant.

nationalization. Taking into state ownership an industry, with or without payment of compensation to previous owners. The 1945–51 Labour Governments nationalized the Bank of England, coal, cables and wireless, transport, electricity, iron and steel.

National Minority Movement. Launched by the British Communist Party in 1924 in the mining, engineering and rail unions to encourage greater militancy, the NMM claimed by 1926 to have the support of a quarter of the total union membership, but it was weakened by the failure of the General Strike and faded into insignificance.

Nationalverein (Germ., national association). Association founded by Baron Benisgen of Hanover in 1859 with the declared aim of substituting the German constitution of 1848, under the hegemony of Prussia, for the Confederation. Austria was to be completely excluded.

NATO. North Atlantic Treaty Organization, established by the North Atlantic Treaty of 4 April 1949. Those signing were the members of the Brussels Treaty Organization (Belgium, France, Luxembourg, the Netherlands, and Britain) and the USA, Canada, Italy, Norway, Denmark, Iceland and Portugal. The first treaty by which the USA had undertaken commitments towards Europe in peace time, it was the product of western European concern about the territorial ambitions of the USSR; a disappointment at the failure of the UN Security Council to function effectively in the face of Russia's veto; and an immediate response to the BLOCKADE of Berlin.

Signatories are pledged to take such action as they deem necessary to assist a fellow signatory suffering from AGGRESSION and 'to safeguard the freedom, common heritage and civilization of their peoples founded on the principles of democracy, individual liberty and the rule of law.' There is, however, no obligation for signatories to fight if their allies are attacked. On 18 February 1952

Greece and Turkey joined NATO, followed by West Germany on 9 May 1955.

Tension continues between the aims of Europe and the EEC and those of the USA, the latter being particularly desirous of establishing an 'Atlantic Community' and committing the European members to a definite stance against Soviet aggression. French suspicion of the USA's aims led France to leave NATO in March 1966 at which the North Atlantic Council's headquarters, its Military Committee and International Secretariat were moved from Fontainebleau to Brussels.

On 17 August 1964 Greek military forces were withdrawn from NATO due to tension with Turkey over Cyprus (*see* ENOSIS) but Greece re-entered in October 1980. In the 1980s, opposition to the siting of US Cruise missiles in Europe, particularly in the Netherlands and Britain, has led many American politicians to question the will of European nations to support NATO. It has been suggested that NATO might collapse if western Europe does not take a more active part in its own defence.

naturalia. In the Frankish kingdoms, contributions in kind exacted for the support of the royal household.

Naxalites. Members of marxist guerrilla groups active in West Bengal in the 1970s.

Nazi. A member of the National-sozialistische Deutsche Arbeiter Partei (German National Socialist Workers' Party). The title was adopted by the former German Workers' Party at Munich in October 1920. The party's philosophy was similar to the romantic right-wing authoritarianism of Italian FASCISM but after Hitler became leader he imposed his anti-semitic, racialist doctrines of ARYAN superiority and demands for revision of the Versailles Treaty upon the party. Fascist ritualism was retained. The Nazi party expanded rapidly between 1930–32 due to the mass unemployment of the depression and on 30 January 1933 Hitler became Chancellor. In February 1932 party membership stood at two million. Nazi government policies such as GLEICHSCHALTUNG helped raise membership to six million by 1945. In that year the party disintegrated and it was outlawed by the constitution of the German Federal Republic.

Near East. The geographical area covered by the OTTOMAN Empire and its former south-eastern European possessions, a term which came into use in the 1890s.

neck-verse. In medieval times, verse of the Psalms (usually from Psalm 51) which criminals claiming BENEFIT OF CLERGY were required to read to establish proof of their clerkship, by which they would secure trial by the ecclesiastical rather than the secular authorities, thereby saving their necks.

Negus (Amharic, king). Title of the kings of Abyssinia or Ethiopia. The last emperor of Ethiopia, Haile Selassie, was deposed by a military COUP D'ETAT on 12 September 1974.

Neri and Bianchi (Ital., blacks and whites). (1) The two factions of the GUELPH party in Florence *c*1300.

(2) In late 19th- and early 20th century Italy factions which supported, respectively, the temporal claims of the Vatican and the House of Savoy.

New Deal. Name applied to the social and economic programme of Pres. Franklin D. Roosevelt's first and second administrations (1932–40), egarded as being primarily inspired by the BRAINS TRUST. Aimed at alleviating the worst effects of the DEPRESSION, the first New Deal programme (1933–35) involved devaluation of the dollar by 40 per cent, expansion of business credit through an Economy Act, an Emergency Banking Relief Act and a Federal Emergency Relief Administration.

Various public works projects were initiated to create employment, including the Civilian Conservation Corps (1933–41) which created two million jobs in reforestation work; the Civil Works Administration (four million jobs on public works); and the Tennessee Valley Authority (TVA), an independent public body responsible for serving parts of seven states with hydro-electric power. The executive was given the power to regulate industrial competition by the National Industrial Recovery Act.

The second New Deal (1935–46) was designed to increase the social security of the industrial population and the small farmers. The National Labour Relations Act of 1935 codified and strengthened the rights of workers to form trade unions, while a Social Security Act introduced a scheme of social insurance. A Works Progress Administration was also formed to co-ordinate the work of the ALPHABET AGENCIES.

The New Deal has been seen as a form of 'creeping socialism' and certain measures, including the National Labour Relations Act, were in part declared to be unconstitutional by the Supreme Court. But there was no systematic national plan in a truly socialist sense, merely an extension of the states' responsibilities. The New Deal did not eradicate unemployment in the USA, but it did reduce the workless from 17 to 10 million. After Roosevelt's death, his vice-president Henry A. Wallace accused the Democratic Party of abandoning the New Deal; he formed a Progressive Party to champion it. But in the 1948 election, Pres. Truman as leader of the Democrats, convinced the electorate that his FAIR DEAL was directly evolved from the New Deal.

New Economic Policy (NEP). Change of approach in Russian economic policy introduced at the 10th Party Congress in March 1921 by Lenin. Disturbances and riots amongst the peasantry, caused by food shortages, made it necessary to modify the application of communist doctrine by permitting a degree of private commerce and freedom of internal trading activity. State banks were also re-established. The net result was increased efficiency in production and distribution of food of which the peasants were the main beneficiaries. However, many Communist Party members considered the policy to be at variance with strict MARXISM and at the 15th Party Congress in January 1929 it was abandoned in favour of Stalin's programme for collectivization of agriculture according to FIVE-YEAR PLANS.

New Imperialism. The second phase of European imperial expansion at the end of the 19th century, particularly in the 'scramble for Africa', marked by increasing British uneasiness at the growth of its German rival.

new industries. Capital-intensive industries – aircraft and automobile production, chemicals, electrical engineering and generation, food processing and consumer goods – developed in Britain between the wars, usually sited in the South and Midlands rather than the traditional industrial regions. *See* AILING GIANTS.

New Liberalism. The progressive social reformism of Liberal Governments after 1908 which differed from traditional Liberalism by its belief in state intervention and spending. David Lloyd George (1863–1945) and Winston Churchill (1874–1965) were its leading figures.

New Model Army. The name given to the reformed Parliamentary army. The New Model Army was established by parliamentary ordinance in February 1645 and the armies of Waller and Essex were reorganized into a single force of 22,000 men. Thomas Fairfax was appointed head of the army and Oliver Cromwell was made Lieutenant General. The morale of INDEPENDENTS and the discipline of the troops was considerably improved, partly by better pay.

'New Order'. Expression denoting Hitler's concept of a Europe integrated under centralized political and economic control. NAZI propaganda was directed towards convincing the world that such a system would benefit all of Europe rather than merely provide the economic resources desired by Germany.

New Puritanism. A radical and often authoritarian rejection of the PERMISSIVE SOCIETY of the 1960s which emerged in the 1980s, encouraged by the spread of Aids. *See* MORAL MAJORITY.

New Style. The Gregorian calendar, which replaced the Julian calendar or OLD STYLE. It was introduced by Italy in 1582 but not adopted in Britain until the 1752 Calendar Act, by which date Britain was 11 days behind the rest of Europe. Russia, however, did not introduce it until 1918.

New Unionism. A dramatic upsurge in unionization among the unskilled in 1889–92, with a socialist-led London dock strike in the summer of 1889 at its centre. In 1890 the new unions – 'new' because unlike their predecessors they levied low dues and depended for success on aggressive tactics – were 320,000 strong, but by 1896 this had fallen to 80,000.

New World. Term used for the Americas once it was realised in Europe that Columbus had discovered a previously unknown continent in 1492 and not a passage to the East. It fell out of general use in the late 17th century.

Night of the Long Knives. Night of 29–30 June 1934 when the SS, on Hitler's orders, murdered Capt. Ernst Röhm and some 150 other SA leaders. Some were killed at the Stadelheim Prison in Munich, others at the Cadet school at Lichterfelde near Berlin. Non-Nazis were also murdered, including the ex-Chancellor Gen. Kurt von Schleicher and his close friend Gen. Kurt von Bredow. The aim of the slaughter was to crush the political power of the SA: in a speech on 13 July 1934 Hitler announced that 61 persons, part of an alleged conspiracy, had been shot; a further 13 had died resisting arrest, and 3 had committed suicide. It has been claimed since, however, that more than 1,000 were killed. Hitler first described the episode as 'the Night of the Long Knives' at a speech in Berlin on 13 July 1934.

Nihilist (deriv. Lat., nothing). Member of a Russian revolutionary society which issued a manifesto after the assassination of Tsar Alexander II in 1881. Its object was the amelioration of the condition of the peasantry and the reform of Russian government. Since attempts to achieve a new political system peacefully had been repressed, violence was endorsed as a means to attain their objectives. Term first used in 1862 by Turgenev in his novel *Fathers and Children*.

Nikkei Dow. The name for the index of the Tokyo Stock Market. Named after the DOW JONES.

'Nine, the'. Members of the EEC between 1973 (when Britain, Eire and Denmark joined) and 1982 when Greece became the tenth member. There are now 12 members.

Nineteen Propositions. Series of parliamentary demands presented to Charles I on 1 June 1642. Civil War was by this time almost inevitable, though Charles's rejection of the demands marked the final breakdown in negotiations between Parliament and the Crown. The propositions called for strict enforcement of anti-Catholic measures; reform of the church on more Protestant lines; parliamentary control of the militia, and the appointment of Crown ministers approved by parliament.

1922 Committee. Tory backbench MPs as a group, named after a meeting held in the Carlton Club on 19 October 1922 at which Conservative backbenchers forced their reluctant leaders to withdraw from the Lloyd George Coalition government, ensuring its immediate collapse.

Nippon. An alternative term for Japan and the Japanese.

nisi prius (Lat., unless previously). In medieval England, a judicial writ commanding the SHERIFF of a county to bring the men empanelled as jurors in civil action to the court at Westminster on a certain day, unless the justices in EYRE should come into the county first. The system, developed after the 1285 Statute of Westminster, later included specially commissioned justices who were appointed to go into the counties, thus forming the basis of the modern system of circuit judges.

nithing (OE). In Anglo-Saxon England, a man without honour. Public pronouncement by a formal assembly that a man was a nithing placed him completely outside the social pale. The concept was introduced to England by King Cnut (1017–35) and was last used in 1088 by William II against people trying to avoid LAND FYRD.

nizam (Arab., order). Regular army infantry of the OTTOMAN empire; also, title of an Indian ruler.

Noces Vetmeilles (Fr., the blood red wedding). Marriage between the Protestant Henry of Navarre and the Catholic Marguerite de Valois in May 1572, which was followed three months later by the massacre of thousands of HUGUENOTS on the eve of the feast of St. Bartholomew.

Noche Triste (Span., sad night). The night of 20 June 1520, when the Spaniards, led by Cortes, suffered very heavy losses in an attack by Mexican Indians.

Non-compounders. The name given in 1692 to a Roman Catholic section among the JACOBITES which offered unquestioning loyalty to James II, influential in the exile court at St. Germains, where James had fled after his defeat at the Battle of the Boyne in July 1690.

Nonconformist. Member of those Christian bodies which do not conform to the doctrines of the Church of England. Until the 1662 Act of Uniformity they were usually termed 'puritans' or 'dissenters' and were often persecuted. The oldest bodies of nonconformists are the BAPTISTS, INDEPENDENTS and (in England) the PRESBYTERIANS. In Scotland the Presbyterians are the official Church of Scotland and hence it is the Anglicans who are 'nonconformists' in Scotland. The METHODISTS date from 1738 but refused to consider themselves nonconformists until some time later.

non-interventionist. Foreign policy of not interfering in war or disputes. Britain and France pursued such a policy with regard to the Spanish civil war (1936–9); NAZI Germany and FASCIST Italy and the USSR claimed to follow suit, but in fact intervened on a large scale.

Non-jurors. The High Church clergymen, three to four hundred in number, who refused to swear the oaths of allegiance and supremacy on the accession to the English throne of William III and Mary in 1689.

non-resistance. Doctrine, also known as the 'doctrine of Passive Obedience', which held it to be a deadly sin to oppose the will of the King. The roots of the doctrine lay in theories of DIVINE RIGHT OF KINGS and it was much preached by the Anglican clergy during the reign of Charles I (1625–1649).

Noraid (acronym for the Northern Aid Committee). An organization which channels funds from sympathizers in the United States of the PROVISIONAL IRA.

Norsemen. *See* VIKINGS.

North Atlantic Treaty Organisation *See* NATO.

Northeast Passage. Sea route between the Atlantic and Pacific oceans, navigable through Siberian waters. The Muscovy Company, founded in England in 1555 to trade with Russia, was responsible for most of the earlier attempts to find the route. One of its members, the Genoese Sebastian Cabot (1474–1557), had tried to find the Passage in 1548 while in the service of the English Crown; Sir Hugh Willoughby and Richard Chancellor (d.1556) made a similar attempt in 1553. After 1555 the Company sponsored most voyages. Henry Hudson (d.1611) sought the Passage on two voyages (1607 and 1608) but it was a Swede, Nils Nordenskjöld, who first navigated it in 1878–79.

North-West Frontier. Border area of Afghanistan and India in the northwest of the Punjab, inhabited by warlike Pathan tribes who were mostly followers of ISLAM. The Khyber Pass dominated the frontier and was of great strategic importance to the defence of India. Britain annexed the region in 1849 and made it a separate Indian province in 1901. It has been part of Pakistan since 1947.

Northwest Passage. Sea route from the North Atlantic to the Pacific Ocean, much sought in the 16th century as a short way from Europe to the east and its 'riches'. In 1497 the Genoese explorer John Cabot (1425–1500) sailed in the service of Henry VII of England to find it. Instead he discovered Newfoundland and Nova Scotia and believed them to be part of Asia. His son Sebastian (1474–1557) reached the Hudson Bay in 1509 on a similar quest. In 1576 the English explorer Sir Martin Frobisher (1535–1594) reached Labrador and Baffin Land (Frobisher Bay) and in 1609–10 Henry Hudson (d. 1611) penetrated deep up the Hudson

River in search of it. In 1847 Sir John Franklin (1786–1847) and the crew of the two ships *Erebus* and *Terror* perished on an expedition to find the Passage. Roald Amundsen (1872–1928), a Norwegian, was the first to navigate the Passage in the fishing smack *Gjoa*: it took him from 1903 to 1906. The Canadian coastguard vessel *St. Roch* made the first navigation of it in a single season.

notary (deriv. Lat., clerk). In medieval times a clerk licensed to draw up documents in the form required by civil and canon law. In Europe there were papal notaries and imperial notaries, the latter being eventually licensed by national authorities. In England, because of the prominence of common law, there were fewer notaries and these were licensed by bishops on papal authority. Their numbers increased with the growth of international trade and the development of the civil law Court of Admiralty. Today, notaries who attest deeds or writings to make them authentic are generally solicitors.

November criminals. Term of abuse commonly used in Germany between 1918 and 1945 to describe those persons who had negotiated the country's surrender in 1918 and the subsequent Treaty of Versailles. They were made scapegoats for the economic and military collapse of Germany in 1918.

Noyades (Fr., drownings). Name given to the JACOBIN massacre of French royalists who had moved from their stronghold in La Vendée to Nantes in 1793. They were crowded on to boats which were towed to the middle of the river and sunk.

Nuevas Ordenanzas (Span., new laws). Code of laws promulgated at Madrid in 1543 designed to ameliorate the condition of the Indians in the Spanish colonies.

Nullifiers. Upholders, mainly in the southern states, of STATES RIGHTS in the USA in the 19th century. The term originated with South Carolina's declaration in 1832 that an Act of Congress imposing duties on textile fabrics was unconstitutional, and its claim that states had the right to nullify federal laws.

'Number 10'. 10 Downing Street, off Whitehall, London; the official residence of the British Prime Minister in London. The residence of the CHANCELLOR OF THE EXCHEQUER is at 11 Downing Street.

nuncio (Ital. deriv. Lat. *nuntius*, messenger). Title given to papal envoys in foreign capitals.

Nuremberg Rallies. Mass rallies of hundreds of thousands of people staged by the NAZIS at their Party Congresses in Nuremberg between 1933 and 1938. These rallies made great use of oratory and other propaganda devices to appeal to observers and participants.

O

Oakboys. Agrarian society in Ulster in 1763, whose purpose was to protest against the action of the Grand Juries who had decided to build roads which the rural population held to be solely in the interests of great landowners.

OAS. (1) *Organisation de l'Armée Secrète*, a French terrorist organization which posed a serious threat to the Fifth Republic in 1961–62. Most of its members were ex-Algerian colonists aggrieved at Pres. Charles de Gaulle because his desire to end the Algerian War (1954–62) led to Algerian independence. Under the leadership of Gen. Salan, the OAS were responsible for several attempts on de Gaulle's life including the machine-gunning of his car in March 1962. The imprisonment or flight of their leaders removed the threat of the OAS by early 1963.

(2) Organization of American States, founded at the Bogota Conference of American States (March–April 1948) to promote the joint welfare of countries on the American continent by peaceful settlement of disputes and economic development. Latin American states have been critical of US dominance of the organization, but supported the USA in the CUBAN MISSILE CRISIS. The headquarters are in Washington, DC.

OAU. Organization of African Unity, established at a 'pan-African' conference held at Addis Ababa, Ethiopia, in May 1963, 'to promote the unity and solidarity of the African and Malagasy States' and 'to eradicate all forms of colonialism from Africa'. Heads of the 48 member states were to meet each year, with a council of ministers meeting every six months. The Organization succeeded in settling the Algeria-Morocco border dispute but had no success in the Nigeria-Biafra dispute (1967–70), the Ethiopia-Somalia conflict or the Angolan civil war. The prestige of the Organization was at its highest in the early 1960s when its leadership included Gen. Nasser (1918–70) of Egypt, Pres. Nkrumah (1909–72) of Ghana and Haile Selassie (1892–1975), Emperor of Ethiopia. Since that time its significance has greatly declined and only seven heads of state attended the 1976 Mauritius conference. It has set up specialized commissions to deal with problems of interest to developing African states, such as health, education, finance and social affairs.

Oberstuhlherr (Germ.). Chief of the medieval Westphalian VEHM-GERICHTE who acted as representative of the emperor. The post was usually held by the Archbishop of Cologne.

242

October Revolution. Seizure of power in Russia by the BOLSHEVIKS led by Lenin (1870–1924) on 6–7 November 1917 (October in the Julian calendar). Their chance came after the failure of the FEBRUARY REVOLUTION to end the war and food shortages. A successful coup was led in the capital, St. Petersburg, from Bolshevik headquarters in the Smolny Institute against the Kerensky government in the Winter Palace on the night of 6 November. The next day an All-Russian Congress of Soviets authorized the Bolsheviks to establish a Council of the People's Commissars which was to assume executive power. On a promise of 'Peace, Land, Bread' the Bolsheviks were able to take power in other cities. Workers were given control of the factories, private trade was abolished and property belonging to the Church and to 'counter-revolutionaries' was confiscated by the state. By the end of December 1917 the counter-revolutionary armies (the 'Whites') had mobilized and a civil war commenced that lasted for three years. Russia's capital was moved to Moscow on 12 December 1918 and a Soviet Constitution promulgated in July 1918.

Octobrists. Faction of the Russian liberal constitutional movement which split following publication of the 1905 October Manifesto. They comprised the right-wing of the movement and were prepared to co-operate with the government in the Duma. Their support was drawn from the right-wing of the ZEMSTVO movement and the business classes. The other faction were known as the KADETS.

octroi (Fr.). In pre-revolutionary France, a tax levied on articles brought into towns; also the name of the customs-station at which the tax was collected.

odal (*also* udal; Norw.). Form of land tenure originating among the Norse under which property in land was absolute. Land allotted to a warrior at the time of conquest was held by him and his descendants for three generations, after which it became odal. In Orkney, udallers held land on such tenure until recent times.

odelsting. *See* STORTING.

OGPU. The Soviet security police agency, originally founded in 1922 as the GPU or State Political Administration and retitled Unified State Political Administration after the formation of the USSR in 1923. Its function was to suppress counter-revolutionary elements. In the 1920s it was used by the Communist Party leadership to uncover political dissidents and after 1928 to enforce the collectivization of agriculture. From 1930 onwards it monopolized police activities in the USSR until in 1934 it was absorbed by the NKVD.

Ohio Gang. *See* TEAPOT DOME SCANDAL.

oidores (Span., they who hear). Judges who sat in the AUDIENCIAS, the highest courts of appeal, in Spain's South American colonies. A highly trained group, with political as well as legal power, their lifestyle was subject to strict legal guidelines in order to ensure impartiality. The Spanish crown relied heavily on them and they were the most consistently loyal and effective branch of Spain's colonial bureaucracy. Originally usually PENINSULARES, by the 18th century most were CREOLES.

Oireachtas (Ir., national parliament). Parliament of the Republic of Ireland, consisting of the President, the DÁIL EIREANN and SENAAD EIREANN. The term is, however, generally used to refer to the two Houses alone without the President.

Okhrana. Russian secret police at the time of the TSAR.

Okies. Migrants to California between 1933 and 1935 from Oklahoma, Kansas, Colorado and Texas, whose homes had been reduced to a vast dust bowl by wind and drought.

Old Catholics. Dissident Catholics in Austria, Germany, Holland and Switzerland who broke with Rome in the 18th and 19th centuries, rejected the 1870 Doctrine of PAPAL INFALLIBILITY and united in the 1889 Declaration of Utrecht.

'Old Contemptibles'. Nickname adopted by members of the British Expeditionary Force (BEF) sent to France in August 1914 at the start of World War I. The force consisted of six infantry and one cavalry division, superbly trained but, by European standards, extremely small. It was thus described by the Germans as 'a contemptible little army'. Its value as a fighting force was shown in the Mons area and at the Battle of the Marne (August–September 1914), which led to German abandonment of the SCHLIEFFEN PLAN.

Old Hunkers. Name given to the conservative wing of the Democratic party in New York between 1824 and 1848.

Old Pretender. James Edward Stuart (1688–1766), son of James II of England. *See* JACOBITES.

Old Style. The Julian calendar, introduced by Julius Caesar (101–44 BC). With its leap year it placed the average length of a year at 365¼ days. This was in fact 11 minutes too long,

the earth's orbit being 365 days, 5 hours, 48 minutes and 46 seconds of mean solar time. The cumulative error which resulted was rectified by the NEW STYLE whereby century years do not count as leap years if they cannot be divided by 400. Italy abandoned the Old Style in 1582 and Britain in 1752; Russia continued to use it until 1918.

Old World. World known to Europeans prior to the discovery of America in 1492, including Europe, the Middle East and the coast of North Africa. Marco Polo (1256–1323) and others had been to the Far East but little was known of the fabulous CATHAY.

oligarchy (deriv. Gk. *oligos*, few + *archeis*, rule). Rule of a few, implying the rule of a small, self-interested and unrepresentative élite. Because of these connotations, the term is rarely used in political analysis, some more neutral word being preferred.

ombudsman (Sw., representative). An officer, charged with the specific task of investigating complaints against central administration, introduced to the Swedish constitution in 1809. The idea was adopted by Finland in 1919, Denmark in 1954, Norway in 1962 and Britain in 1965. Appointed by Parliament after each general election, the ombudsman then has security of office until the next election. He has the power to call for persons and relevant documents relating to a complaint and if he finds the complaint justified it is his duty to inform the parties to the case and to publicize his findings. Although he does not have the power to reverse a decision by the administration, nor to award damages, public opinion and the press are able to ensure that a government department takes notice of his recommendations.

In Britain the ombudsman's official title is Parliamentary Commissioner for Administration (PCA). He is appointed by the Crown, yet is a servant of Parliament. He differs from the Scandinavian ombudsman in that he acts only at the request of an MP; in other respects his powers closely approximate to those of the Scandinavian model. Investigations of the behaviour of local authorities and public corporations is beyond his remit.

Omladina. Nationalist, pan-Slavic secret society, which was based in Serbia and influential in the late 19th century. Its philosophy was also republican with an IRREDENTIST element. It helped push Serbia and Montenegro into declaring war on Turkey in 1876 and raised money to fight the Turks. In the 1890s it was responsible for sporadic outbursts of unrest directed against Austria, particularly riots in Bohemia in 1891.

Oncenio. Period between 1919 and 1930 when Peru was ruled by the dictator Augusto B. Leguiá, marked by paternalistic government, a massive programme of educational reform, nationalist indoctrination and economic provision for the social advancement of the middle class. The régime was authoritarian and many were punished for opposing it. The Leguiá government was toppled in 1930 by a military COUP D' ÉTAT.

ope (Maori). A large war party or army.

OPEC. Organization of Petroleum Exporting Countries, constituted in January 1961 following discussions the previous year between delegates from Iran, Iraq, Kuwait, Qatar, Saudi Arabia and Venezuela at Caracas. Their aim was to stabilize the price of crude oil and to co-ordinate oil export policies. They agreed to force oil companies to 'maintain their prices steady and free from all unnecessary fluctuations which affect the economic development of both producing and consuming countries.' This would be achieved by regulating production to maintain prices and by members refusing to supply companies imposing sanctions on other members. Indonesia, Abu Dhabi, Libya and Nigeria soon joined while from 1967 Egypt, Syria and Algeria became associate members. The organization maintained a secretariat in Vienna, while twice a year delegates met in conference.

Initially OPEC had little effect despite continued reaffirmation of purpose, as at the July 1965 Tripoli Conference, when it was agreed that 'unrestricted competitive use of excess producing capacity' would be checked. However, rising demands for oil in the late 1960s, and restrictions on the output of certain Middle Eastern pipelines, gradually increased OPEC's power over the Western oil companies. By the early 1970s the Arab states produced two-thirds of western European oil requirements. In May 1970 Libya's decision to decrease output to raise prices forced 24 oil companies to negotiate with OPEC with the result that in February 1971 a uniform price increase was agreed after a conference in Tehran. By late 1973, OPEC was strong enough to force a four-fold increase in oil prices.

Between October 1973 and March 1974 the Arab members, acting as the Organization of Arab Petroleum Exporting Countries (OAPEC), placed an embargo on oil exports to the USA and some of its Western allies in retaliation for US and Western aid to Israel in the October 1973 Middle Eastern war. The action was strongly criticized by non-Arab OPEC members.

Price increases continued to be uniform, though in 1977 Saudi Arabia had to use its power as the major producer to force smaller price rises on the other members. Saudi Arabia was perhaps the first member to realize that high oil prices were forcing the Western economies into recession and that the consequent fall in demand for energy, together with oil finds in Mexico and the North Sea, would undermine OPEC's position.

These fears were correct. By the turn of the decade it was clear that oil was being overproduced. The poorer members of OPEC, particularly Nigeria, who have to export oil in quantity to finance loan repayments to the West and to prop up a failing domestic economy, began offering discounts in order to sell their crude oil. Nigeria offered particularly large discounts in August 1981. In January 1983 OPEC members met to try and agree a restriction of output in order to maintain a rapidly falling oil price. However, the insistence of Saudi Arabia and other Gulf exporters that African states charge a higher premium proved unreasonable given the weak oil market and Nigeria's need for foreign exchange. The conference quickly broke up with no agreement being reached. Sheikh Yemani, the Saudi oil minister, declared that OPEC no longer existed, and that the possibility of a free-for-all scramble to sell crude oil might develop. Attempts were quickly made by Venezuela to arrange informal meetings in Caracas for further attempts at price stabilization.

Open Door Policy. Policy proposed by US Secretary of State John Hay in September 1899 for the economic development of China, which would preserve its independence and political unity. The policy – defined in the 1900 Anglo-German agreement as the free access, under equal conditions, of all nations to the ports, rivers and littorals of China – was in contrast to that of 'spheres of influence' and was in principle accepted by Japan and the major European powers. In effect, it was destroyed by the revival of Chinese nationalism and by encroachment from Japan, despite a formal reaffirmation of it at the Washington Conference of 1921–22. Today the term refers generally to any commercial policy based on trade with all nations or individuals on equal terms without giving any particular country preference or a monopoly.

Opium War. Fought between 1839–42 over the Chinese authorities' confiscation and burning of opium imported into China by British traders. Britain asserted that this was a declaration of war. The 1842 Treaty of Nanking gave Hong Kong and extensive trade concessions to Britain, and opened the 'Treaty Ports' of Amoy, Canton, Fuchow, Nagoo and Shanghai to European commerce.

optimates (deriv. Lat., aristocratic). Historically, members of the patrician order in ancient Rome; generally used to refer to the aristocracy.

Opus Dei. A Roman Catholic organization dedicated to the progress of faith and reform in its members' professional spheres. Founded in 1928 by a Spanish priest, Josemaria Escriyá de Baláguer (1902–75), it has 72,000 lay and over 1,000 clerical members.

ora (OE). In Anglo-Saxon England, a monetary unit, but not a coin, much used in the DANELAW. It was equal in value to 16 silver pennies.

Orange Book. *We Can Conquer Unemployment*, published by Lloyd George (1863–1945) and the Liberal

Party in 1929; it took its popular name from the colour of its cover. It went much further than the YELLOW BOOK in its recommendations, proposing a massive programme of government expenditure and public works, including extensive road and house construction. The schemes were eventually to be self-financing and it was claimed that the initial cost of starting them would be balanced by savings in the payment of unemployment benefit as employment increased.

Orangemen. Members of the Orange Order, an Irish society formed in Ulster in 1795 to uphold Protestantism, whose name is taken from William III, Prince of Orange, who defeated James II at the Battle of the Boyne in 1690. The society, an influential and bitterly anti-Catholic body, largely maintains the Unionist Party of Northern Ireland which ruled from 1921 to 1972. Although it chiefly flourishes in Ulster, the Order has branches in many English-speaking countries, particularly in mainland Britain in cities associated with Ulster such as Glasgow and Liverpool.

Oratorians. A secular order of Catholic priests founded by Philip Neri in 1556 to undertake moral and religious teaching work. Cardinal Newman introduced the order to Britain in 1847.

Ordainers, Lords. *See* LORDS ORDAINERS.

ordeal. Form of trial, Norse in origin, practised in Anglo-Saxon and early Norman England. It took various forms, all based on an appeal to God's judgement. Freemen were required to carry a hot iron, innocence being proved if no scars were present after three days; the unfree were thrown into water and were held to be guilty if

they sank; the clergy had to swallow a 'cursed morsel', e.g. food containing a feather, and were considered guilty if they choked. All ordeals were supervised by the clergy. The Normans introduced trial by battle as an alternative, the accused being found innocent if victorious in an exchange of arms with a crown nominee (*see* APPROVERS). The Fourth Lateran Council in 1215 forbade the clergy to undergo the ordeal and in England justices in EYRE were advised to find alternative systems of determining innocence or guilt.

Order in Council. Order made by the sovereign 'by and with the advice' of the PRIVY COUNCIL, normally signed by the Clerk of the Privy Council. Thus, in exercise of the powers of the royal prerogative, the sovereign may issue decrees such as proclamations relating to coinage. However, the sovereign may not issue orders which alter common or statute law unless in the exercise of a statutory power. A government may receive statutory powers to issue detailed regulations or orders, thus enabling complicated matters to be dealt with without undue waste of parliamentary time. In the 19th century much use was made of such orders to avoid the necessity of facing parliamentary discussion of controversial issues; one example was the introduction of various army reforms between 1868 and 1871.

ordonnances (Fr.). Laws enacted by French kings from Philip IV in 1287 to the overthrow of the monarchy in 1789, beginning with 'In the name of the King' and ending 'Such is our pleasure'.

Orebites (*also* Horebites). Sect of radical HUSSITES from Hrade Králové (Königgrätz) in eastern Bohemia. They founded a community and formed a military force comparable to that of the TABORITES. Their name is derived from their town, renamed after the scriptural Mount Horeb.

Organisation de l'Armée Secrète. *See* OAS (1).

Organization of African Unity. *See* OAU.

Organization of American States. *See* OAS (2).

Organization of Petroleum Exporting Countries. *See* OPEC.

oriflamme (Fr.). Crimson flag attached to a gilded lance; the ancient standard of France.

Orleanists. French Royalist party which supported the claim of the Orleans branch of the royal family to the French throne, as opposed to that of the Bourbons. When the last of the French Bourbons died in 1883, the majority of the LEGITIMISTS transferred their allegiance to the Orleanist cause.

Ormée (Fr., deriv. *orme*, elm). Insurrectionary government established at Bordeaux in 1652 and known during the civil wars also as the Fronde. The name is derived from a large elm tree near the Fort du Ha where leaders of the movement held their meetings.

ORPA. *Organisacion Revolucionario del Pueblo en Armus*, a left-wing guerrilla group founded in 1979, active in north and west Guatemala and Guatemala City. With the EGP and FAR it is dedicated to the overthrow of the military government of Gen. Lucas Garcia and the establishment of a democracy.

Ossewa-Brandwag (Afrikaans, Oxwagon Sentinel). A para-military organization founded in South Africa in 1938 dedicated to creating a Christian, nationalist republic. Antisemitic and pro-Nazi at the outbreak of World War II, it merged with the National Party in 1948.

Ostpolitik (Germ., eastern policy). Policy of the German Federal Republic, developed by Kurt Kiesinger as an attempt to normalize relations with communist countries other than the USSR. The policy, which included recognition of the German Democratic Republic, led to the conclusion of peace treaties with the USSR and Poland in 1972, and to border agreements relating to traffic and communications between East and West Berlin.

Ostrogoths. Eastern branch of the Goths who maintained a monarchy in Italy from 493 to 555. *See also* VISIGOTHS.

Otokodaté (Jap.). In old Japan, a friendly association amongst the CHÔNIN, whose purpose was to provide mutual assistance against oppression and to benefit its members by providing aid to those in need through misfortune. Entry was subject to strict character requirements.

Ottoman (deriv. Turk. *Osman*). Dynasty, founded by Osman, which ruled the Turkish empire until the abolition of the sultanate in 1922. The name was given first to the Turkish state which was formed c1300 and later to the Ottoman empire. The expansion of the Ottoman state, based on the morale of JIHAD and the administrative skills acquired by ISLAM, reached a peak in the late 16th and early 17th centuries, when the empire stretched north-westwards from Asia Minor to the Danube. In the 18th century it could not keep pace with the development of Europe. In decline throughout the 19th century, it finally collapsed under the impact of nationalism from within, and its defeat in World War I.

outlawry. A punishment common in Anglo-Saxon England by which a transgressor was placed outside the law, losing all of his rights and forfeiting his property. Possibly it originated as a punishment for crimes for which WERE-GILD could not atone, or in cases where the guilty party could not afford it. The system of outlawry gradually became more refined and developed into a final sanction against an accused person who, after four summonses to a shire court, still refused to appear and answer the charge. Once outlawed he could, in some areas, be killed on sight; only the king could reverse the act. Under the Normans the system declined as lesser criminal penalties were devised.

Outremer (Fr., overseas). (1) Term used with particular reference to the French colonial empire existing between the 17th and 20th centuries.

(2) Crusader kingdoms established in the Middle East at the end of the 11th century, including the principality of Antioch (1098–1263); the counties of Edessa (1098–1144) and Tripoli (1109–1289); the kingdom of Cyprus (1191–1489, then a Venetian colony until 1571) and the kingdom of Jerusalem (1100–1187) and then the kingdom of Acre until 1291. These states were run on the lines of European FEUDALISM, though the European population of them was always in the minority. It was only successive CRUSADES and the establishment of military orders such as the TEMPLARS and HOSPITALLERS which enabled them to exist for 200 years amidst hostile Moslem states and a subject Moslem population. Internal power struggles amongst the ruling families, treachery and disregard for the native populations, both Moslem and Christian, helped weaken them. As interest in the Holy Land declined in Europe it became impossible to attract sufficient Europeans to Outremer to enable it to survive. One by one, the states collapsed under Moslem pressure.

over-full employment. State described by Lord Beveridge (1879–1963) in his *Full Employment in a Free Society*. A rate of three per cent unemployment constituted an optimum 'full employment' in Britain so that a rate of less than three per cent would represent 'over-full employment', with attendant inflationary pressures to the economy.

Overlord. Code name for the Normandy landings of 1944 by the Allied armies. The name was first used in August 1943 at the conference of Roosevelt and Churchill in Quebec, by which time Gen. Sir Frederick Morgan and his staff had been planning the invasion of Europe for over eight months. Their plan was revised between January and June 1944 following the appointment of Montgomery as head of 21st Army Group and thus commander in the field for the invasion. Gen. Eisenhower was Supreme Allied Commander with overall control.

The logistics of the landings were staggering. On D-DAY 4,000 ships left Britain for the coast of Normandy. More than a million and a half American troops had already been transported to Britain for the landings. German coastal installations were smashed by air attacks or local sabotage. Mine sweepers preceded the waves of landing craft. Behind the fleet, complete prefabricated harbours ('Mulberries') were towed across the channel. By 12 June 326,000 men were established in a bridgehead 50 miles wide. By 2 July a million allied troops were in France. On 15 August another US army landed in the south of France and by the end of 1944 most of France and Belgium had been liberated.

OVRA. Secret police established in FASCIST Italy in 1927.

Owenite. (1) The followers of Robert Owen (1771–1858), industrialist and social reformer whose model industrial community at New Lanark, Scotland, was an inspiration to the co-operative movement. (2) A supporter of Dr. David Owen, British Labour Foreign Secretary 1977–79, founder member of the Social Democratic Party in March 1981 and its leader from June 1983. When the SDP voted to amalgamate with the Liberal Party in 1988 Dr. Owen and his supporters refused to follow and retained allegiance to a continuing SDP.

Oxford Movement. *See* PUSEYITES.

oyer and terminer (AFr.). In England, a special commission to hear and determine specific, and later all, pleas of the Crown, dating from the 13th century. It arose as a supplement to the EYRE, was given to judges and to SERJEANTS, and has developed in modern times into the largest commission given to judges on circuit.

P

pacifist. One who believes in the necessity and possibility of preventing war, and who refuses to perform military service. Since World War I most democratic states have recognized a right – rigorously tested by tribunal – to CONSCIENTIOUS OBJECTION on religious grounds.

Pact of Steel. Military alliance concluded between NAZI Germany and FASCIST Italy in 1939.

Pahlevi. Iranian dynasty founded by Reza Khan in 1925, continued by his son Mohammed Reza Shah and was overthrown by revolution in 1979.

pakeha (Maori, foreigner or stranger). Term for a European.

Paladins. Elite band of Frankish knights in the service of Charlemagne whose most famous member was Roland. In 778 many of the Paladins including Roland were killed at the Battle of Roncesvalles where Charlemagne was defeated by the Moors.

palatinate. Under the feudal system, area where a feudal lord, though tenant of a king, exercised quasi-regal jurisdiction; usually established for military reasons. In England palatinates, or Counties Palatine, were usually earldoms encompassing counties. They were established after the Norman Conquest in Kent, Shropshire, Durham and Cheshire; those of Kent and Shropshire were later abolished after rebellions. The largest English palatinate was Lancaster, established in 1351, which acted as a kingdom within the realm of England. In Europe, the most famous was the Palatinate of the Rhine (Rhenish Palatinate).

palatines. Commanders of military forces raised in the palatinates of Poland.

Pale, the (OFr., deriv. Lat., boundary). That portion of Ireland subdued and settled by the English during the 1170s in the reign of Henry II. By the 14th century the area under English law and royal government consisted of Meath, Trim, Louth, Dublin, Kildare, Kilkenny, Waterford, Wexford and Tipperary. However, the original area of English rule gradually shrank under Irish encroachment, and was only re-established by Henry VIII's reconquest of Ireland in the 16th century.

Palestine Liberation Organization. *See* PLO.

palikar (Gk.). Albanian or Greek soldier in the service of the sultan of Turkey.

pallium (Lat.). Robe of office sent by the pope to high dignitaries of the Catholic Church, signifying that they have received authorization.

Palmach. Élite striking force of the HAGANAH, founded by Yitzhak Sadeh and imbued with his Marxist principles.

Panamino (Ital., 'little Panama'). Italian bank scandal of 1893. The allusion was to the Panama Canal scandal of 1892 in which the Panama Canal Company went bankrupt. It was found that large sums of shareholders' money were not properly accounted for and that three million francs had been spent bribing French deputies and senators to ensure the passage of the Panama Lottery Bill in 1888.

Pancasila ('Five Principles'). State ideology formulated by Achmed Sukarno (1901–70), Indonesia's first president, which became part of the constitution in 1945. The principles were: one god, legal justice, national unity, consultative democracy, and social justice.

Pandours. A force of Hottentots and half-castes raised by the Dutch EAST INDIA COMPANY at the Cape in 1793.

Pan-Germanism. In German, *All deutschtum*, an imperialist movement aimed at uniting all German-speakers in a common empire. It was fostered in the first decade of the 20th century by the *Alldeutscher Verband* (Pan-Germany Association) headed by a lawyer named Heinrich Class. Its programme included the conquest of territories in eastern Europe, colonial expansion overseas and naval rearmament. Class was also anti-semitic and in 1913 told the movement that 'the Jewish race is the source of all dangers'. He also expounded racial theories and prophesied that a FÜHRER would arise to unite the German race in its opposition to the Jews.

Pan-Germanism was particularly strong in the German-speaking areas of the Austrian empire; it is probable that while in Vienna in his youth Hitler absorbed its beliefs. After the NAZIS took power in Germany he sent a telegram of recognition to Class. The movement worshipped Bismarck despite the fact that he had favoured the preservation of Austria and a 'Little German' solution to the problem of German unity. Some Pan-Germanists even regarded the Low Countries as German, their Dutch and Belgian inhabitants being termed Lower Germans. They differed from the *Gross-deutsche* (Greater Germans), who also sought unification of German speaking peoples but were liberal, did not subscribe to extreme racial theories and did not seek an aggressive expansion of territory.

pannage. In medieval England, manorial rent paid by villeins for the right to pasture pigs in woodland.

panzer (German armour). Term used to refer to an individual tank or armoured vehicle, or to denote an armoured division.

Papal Infallibility. Doctrine of the Roman Catholic Church proclaimed in July 1870 by the Vatican Council summoned by Pope Pius IX, claiming that the Pope, when speaking in his official capacity on questions of morals or faith, is protected by God from any possibility of error. It has been suggested that the new dogma was intended to counter the Church's loss of temporal power in the 19th century by increasing the pope's authority. Many people, including the German priest and historian

Döllinger, were excommunicated for refusing to accept it.

Its basis is that the Bible does not contain answers to every question of morals and faith and that a sure and final court of appeal is provided by the Church as Christ's temporal teaching authority. After studying a problem carefully and receiving all possible help from the Church, the answer given by a pope to the question at issue must be correct and not open to doubt. No superhuman intelligence is attributed to the pope nor is it suggested that God gives him an answer to every conceivable question. The pope may, of course, be wrong in a personal capacity and his sphere of infallibility is strictly limited.

Only when speaking officially (*ex cathedra*) as supreme leader of the Church and definer of doctrine does his decision have to be accepted by all Catholics; furthermore, pronouncements are only infallible if specifically so defined. The vast majority of statements on matters of ethics and doctrine, such as the 1968 encyclical on birth control (*Humanae Vitae*), do not involve infallibility. In July 1973 the Sacred Congregation for the Doctrine of the Faith published a strong reaffirmation of the doctrine of infallibility.

parage. Medieval system of land tenure, found in England's French dominions, by which the eldest son inherited a FIEF as the sole lord. He in turn granted lands to his brothers but because they did not do HOMAGE for it, the FIEF was not by SUBIN-FEUDINATION. True parage was rare in England, where PRIMOGENITURE had been accepted from early times.

Pariah (Tamil). Member of the lowest caste in India.

Paris Commune. *See* COMMUNARD.

Parlement (Fr.). Judicial body which replaced the *Cours Plénières* or Baronial Courts of the early French kings, organized by Louis IX. In 1302, in the reign of Philip the Fair, it was established in Paris and became known as the Parlement de Paris. It was composed of two prelates, two nobles, thirteen clerics and thirteen laymen. Later, similar bodies, also known as Parlements, were organized in the leading provincial centres.

Parnellites. Followers of Charles Stuart Parnell, leader of the Irish Nationalists from 1880 to 1890. At the General Election of 1880, 61 Irish HOME RULE candidates were elected, many with Parnell's backing; Parnell himself was chosen as chairman of the parliamentary party by 23 votes to the 18 of his rival W. Shaw. Shaw's followers refused to serve under Parnell but did not form a new party. During the 1880–85 Parliament Parnell's supporters proved to be the only effective Home Rule party; their strength rose to 40. In 1885 they won 86 seats; in 1886 85 seats. In 1890 Parnell's leadership was called into question when he was cited as co-respondent in the O'Shea divorce case. The scandal caused the party to split; 45 Nationalists demanded his resignation while 26 continued to support him. His death the following year did not reunite the party; in the 1892 election only nine Parnellites were returned under Redmond, compared with 71 'anti-Parnellites', under Justin McCarthy. In 1900 the two wings of the party were reunited under the leadership of Redmond.

Parsees. *See* ZOROASTRIANISM.

partisans. Term originating with the Russians who raided French supply lines on Napoleon's 1812 Moscow campaign; now used generally to refer to armed bands offering resistance behind enemy lines. In World War II it took on a specifically left-wing connotation when Stalin urged partisan activities in German-occupied Russian territory in 1941–42. At the same time communist-led partisan bands were formed in Albania, Slovakia and Greece. In Yugoslavia the communists led by Tito styled themselves 'partisans' in July 1941, thereby distinguishing themselves from the non-communist 'CHETNIKS'. In November 1942 at the Bihac Assembly the small partisan groups were organized into 'the National Army of Liberation and Partisan Detachments of Yugoslavia'. Although largely isolated in self-sufficient units, the Yugoslav partisans succeeded in collaborating with the RED ARMY and in resisting major offensives by the occupying forces.

pasquinades. Political lampoons. The term is derived from the name of an Italian tailor, Pasquino, who issued a series of satires on the authorities in late 15th-century Rome.

Passagians. Small sect of Christian heretics, centred in Lombardy, condemned by Pope Lucius II in 1184. They followed a literal observance of Old Testament precepts, including circumcision.

Pass Laws. Legislation requiring black South Africans to carry pass-books at all times, severely restricting their freedom of movement and providing a source of great discontent.

Pastoureaux. Spontaneous rising of a group of peasants and shepherds in north-east France in 1251, with the primary object of rescuing King Louis IX, captured on crusade in Egypt, and the subsidiary aims of reforming Church abuse and liberat-

ing the Holy Land. Led by a Hungarian styling himself 'the Master of Hungary', their campaign soon degenerated into local pillaging and excesses against priests and scholars and was soon suppressed.

patarene (Ital.). Heretics, particularly Cathars. The term became current after the third Lateran Council of 1179.

Pataria (Ital.). Name given to an 11th-century reform movement in Milan, possibly derived from the Milan rag-market. The movement aimed to reform abuses in the Church and had Papal support.

Pathet Lao. Communist movement in Laos. Between 1954 and 1973 Laos suffered from civil war between royalist, pro-American army officers and the Pathet Lao led by ex-Prince Souphanourong (b. 1902). By February 1973 the Pathet Lao controlled most of the country. A ceasefire was signed and in September a joint royalist and communist government took office. However, the communist victory in Vietnam in 1975 resulted in a complete Pathet Lao takeover and on 2 December 1975 the monarchy was abolished and the People's Democratic Republic of Laos established.

Patrimonium Petri (Lat., 'Patrimony of St. Peter'). A medieval expression for the estates held by the Church in Rome.

patrimony (deriv. Lat., father). Inherited estate. A legal endowment of a church or other religious body is ecclesiastical patrimony.

Patriotic Front. *See* ZANU; ZAPU.

Patriot Parliament. Irish Parliament, largely Roman Catholic, summoned by James II in 1689, which claimed the exclusive right to legislate on Irish affairs, abolished civil disabilities on religious grounds, and proposed to confiscate property belonging to over 2,000 Protestants, threatening the position of English Protestants in Ireland. Military defeat prevented James's efforts.

Patriots. Group of WHIGS, led by Pulteney, who strongly opposed Walpole's Excise Bill in 1733. They were supported by the Young Whig Party led by William Pitt and by a small remnant of the TORY party headed by Bolingbroke, but were unsuccessful and retired from Parliament.

patronato real (Span., royal patronage). Right granted to Spanish and Portuguese kings by the Papacy to appoint candidates to ecclesiastical benefits in South America, placing the Latin American Church effectively under Crown control.

Patroon. The title given from 1629 to members of the Dutch West India Company in New Netherlands, Dutch North America, who established colonies of 50 adults on land provided by the Company. This attempt to extend Dutch influence was largely unsuccessful.

pavage. In England, a levy raised from the 12th century onwards, mostly in towns, for the maintenance and repair of roads. The burden of road repairs later fell to urban and rural district councils and the county councils.

Pax Britannica. Phrase invented by Joseph Chamberlain in 1893, by analogy with PAX ROMANA, referring to the peace established within the British Empire by British rule.

Pax Romana. Peace enforced within the boundaries of the Roman Empire by Roman rule.

pays d'elections. In 14th-century France, provinces in which tax was collected, supervised by royal officials known as *élus*, first appointed in 1355 and increased in 1386. At the end of the 16th century, *élus* were superseded by INTENDANTS who, with their greater powers, exercised untrammelled control over the *pays d'élections* until the revolution.

pays d'états. French provinces, annexed to the Crown on a semi-contractual basis, which in theory kept a measure of fiscal and general autonomy. Many of the estates of the *pays d'états* had disappeared by the 17th century and in the 18th century only the more recently annexed provinces such as Brittany, Languedoc, Corsica and Burgundy retained effective estates and fiscal privileges.

Peacock Throne. Throne of the Shahs of Iran (Persia until 1925). Shahs of the Qajar dynasty ruled from the late 18th century until 1925, when Col. Reza Khan (1878–1944) seized power in a COUP D'ÉTAT and was elected Shah. He reigned as Reza Shah Pahlavi, until he abdicated in favour of his son Mohammed on 16 September 1941. Mohammed was deposed and forced into exile on 16 January 1979; two months later Iran was proclaimed an Islamic Republic by popular vote.

Pearl Harbor. Major US naval base on Hawaii which was attacked by Japanese aircraft on 7 December 1941. The Japanese aeroplanes were transported on aircraft-carriers forming part of a larger fleet which had left the Kurile Islands on 25 November. The fleet had moved clandestinely towards Hawaii so that the airstrike would take the Americans unaware. There was no official declaration of war preceding the attack and it is generally regarded as a disgraceful episode in military and international history. It has recently been suggested that US intelligence sources may have known in advance of the attack by having broken Japanese diplomatic codes, but certainly as the attack took place diplomatic negotiations between the two powers were continuing in Washington.

In less than two hours 5 US battleships, 14 smaller vessels and 120 aircraft were destroyed; and 2,000 US seamen and 400 civilians killed. The Japanese lost only 29 of their 353 aeroplanes. But US aircraft-carriers (later to prove invaluable in the battle of the Pacific) were not in port when the attack occurred, and three damaged battleships were repaired. The following day, Congress declared war on Japan; this led Japan's allies Germany and Italy to declare war on the USA on 11 December. The attack failed in its main objective which was to give Japan decisive superiority at sea and the initial advantage gained by the Japanese proved to be transitory.

Peasants' Revolt. Name given to a series of uprisings in Britain in 1381 by artisans and peasants. The most serious were in Kent, Essex and East Anglia and were a manifestation of the unrest caused by POLL TAXES, the STATUTE OF LABOURERS and various other economic and social ills. The rising in East Anglia was crushed by the Bishop of Norwich, but those in Kent and Essex were not so easily put down. In Kent, rebels led by Wat Tyler seized Rochester Castle. They then joined the men of Essex and entered the City of London on 13 June 1381, destroying various properties including that of John of Gaunt, Duke of Lancaster (1340–99). The fourth son of Edward III and virtual ruler of England between 1371 and 1399, John's policies were widely blamed for the troubles.

The next day, King Richard II met the Essex bands at Mile End and agreed on a general pardon, the abolition of villeinage (*see* VILLEIN) and various commercial and economic reforms. Meanwhile the Kentish men had seized the Tower of London and killed Simon Sudbury, Chancellor and Archbishop of Canterbury, and the Treasurer, Sir Robert Hales. On 15 June Richard and William Walworth, Mayor of London, met the Kentish rebels at Smithfield. Walworth slew Wat Tyler and in response to Richard's overtures the rebels dispersed. By September the government had recovered control of the country and the promises made by Richard during the crisis were never fulfilled.

pecsovics. Name given by the Magyars to those suspected of sympathizing with Austria after the Hungarian rising of 1848.

Peelites. Conservatives who supported Sir Robert Peel in his repeal of the Corn Laws in 1846, many of whom voted out of loyalty to Peel rather than belief in FREE TRADE. Administrators and business men, they included almost all the ex-Conservative Cabinet Ministers and party officials. In the 1847 election 89 Peelites were elected to Parliament, where they constituted a body of moderate centre opinion. After Peel's death in 1850 they joined the coalition formed by the Peelite Prime Minister, Lord Aberdeen, in 1852.

Peep-o'-Day Boys. Bands of Ulster Protestant peasants formed in 1782, active in ejecting Catholic tenants from their farms and searching Catholic houses at daybreak for arms. After the Battle of the Diamond (21 September 1795) most of them joined the new Orange Society (*see* ORANGEMEN).

Pelucones. *See* PIPIOLOS.

Peninsulares (Span.). In Spain's American colonies, Spaniards born in Spain, as opposed to CREOLES.

Pentagon. US Department of Defense building in Virginia on the outskirts of Washington, DC., so named because it has five sides.

peonage. Latin-American labour system under which money or goods were advanced to the *peon* (peasant), binding him by debt to his employer. The system originated in the colonial era and was most common in Mexico until its abolition after the 1910 revolution.

People's Budget. Introduced in 1909 by Liberal Chancellor of the Exchequer Lloyd George, the budget proposed a redistributive super-tax and land value duties. Its rejection by the Lords provoked a clash between the Commons and peers over their respective rights, leading to a General Election and to the 1911 Parliament Act which reduced the power of the Lords to delay legislation.

People's Charter. Document published in 1838 which gave its name to CHARTISM. Largely drafted by William Lovett (1800–77), a founder in 1836 of the London Working Men's Association, it made six demands: annual parliaments; universal male suffrage; equal electoral districts; voting by ballot; payment of MPs; and an end to the property qualification for MPs.

perestroika (Russ., 'restructuring'). The attempted radical reform in the management of the Soviet economy which began with the emergence of Mikhail Gorbachev as Communist Party Secretary in March 1985 (President from September 1988). By extending self-management in industry, weakening agricultural COLLECTIVIZATION, encouraging market forces, and partially democratizing the Party machine, the reformers hoped to end Soviet economic stagnation. *See* GLASNOST.

Periwig Period. The period of stagnation and decline in the Netherlands in the 18th century following the great period of Dutch expansion in the 'golden age' of the previous two centuries.

permissive society. A loosening of the reigns of cultural, political and moral authority in Britain during the 1960s marked legislatively by the Labour Government's encouragement of reform in the areas of abortion, divorce, homosexuality and the ending of theatre censorship.

Peronismo. Political, economic and social programme, pursued by the Argentinian dictator Juan Domingo Peron between 1946 and 1955 (also called justicialismo). Midway between communism and capitalism and in some ways analogous to FASCISM, it involved a five-year economic plan; government control of the press, education and labour; nationalization of banks, railways and telecommunications; the fostering of mixed public and private enterprises and the end of British influence on the Argentinian economy. Political opposition was strictly limited. Argentinian claims to the Falkland Islands and the Antarctic were pressed and at one time an anti-USA stance was adopted.

personality cult. Political phenomenon whereby a leader, usually the head of state, is elevated above his colleagues to a position where he is seen as responsible for all the nation's or party's achievements but for none of its failures. Such elevation is achieved by a massive propaganda exercise including posters and statues of the leader, the naming of towns after him, etc. Joseph Stalin (1879–1953) set the pattern as Soviet leader but others have followed, for example Adolf Hitler in Germany and Mao Tse-Tung in China. Such cults appear to flourish only in totalitarian régimes.

Peshwa (Pers., chief). Minister under the Mahratta princes of India, in effect the true ruler of the state. The seven Peshwas who succeeded each other may be said to have formed a dynasty, which ended with the 1802 Treaty of Bassein.

Peterloo Massacre. On 16 August 1816 a crowd of 70,000 rallied at St. Peter's Fields, Manchester, in support of parliamentary reform. When an attempt to arrest Henry 'Orator' Hunt, a noted radical leader, failed, magistrates ordered in the Yeomanry who charged, killing 11 and injuring 400. 'Peterloo' was an ironic reference to the military triumph at Waterloo a year before.

Peter's Pence. In England, a tribute to the pope paid first by Offa in the 8th century; that paid by Ethelwulf in the 9th century was to provide funds for the support of a Saxon College at Rome. A tribute also paid to Rome in the time of King Alfred (871–899) later came to be regarded by the pope as a right and was standardized as HEARTH MONEY of £200 a year from the whole country. Peter's Pence was abolished by parliament in 1534.

petit bourgeoisie (Fr.). Lower middle classes.

Petitioners. Signatories of petitions to Charles II in 1679 urging him to summon parliament after he had prorogued the new parliament for twelve months preventing it from undertaking any business. Loyalists in their turn forwarded addresses to the king, abhorring such petitions (*see* ABHORRERS).

Petition of Right. Declaration of the 'rights and liberties of the subject', presented to Charles I by parliament in 1628. Largely drafted by the lawyer and MP Sir Edward Coke (1552–1634), it expressed parliament's opinion on the extent of the royal PREROGATIVE. Its four clauses laid down: (1) 'that no man hereafter be compelled to make or yield any gift, loan, benevolence, tax or such like charge, without common consent by Act of Parliament'; (2) that no free man be held in prison without the cause being shown; (3) that soldiers should not be forcibly billeted on people; and (4) that commissions for proceeding by martial law ought to be abolished. It was hoped that the demands would safeguard property from arbitrary taxation and people from arbitrary arrest and prevent the army from being used to dispense with parliament. Presented not as a parliamentary bill but as a petition seeking confirmation of ancient liberties, it in fact gave a new interpretation of liberties. The Commons forced Charles to accept it with a reply normally used for assent to a private bill. The Commons also defeated a move by Charles and the Lords to insert a clause saying that the Petition intended 'to leave entire the sovereign power' or 'royal prerogative'.

Petrobusians. Followers of Peter of

Bruis, a French village priest from the Embrun region who preached in south west France between c1120 and 1140, who rejected all external forms of worship.

Petroleuses (Fr.). Group of women COMMUNARDS who burned public buildings in Paris with petroleum in the last hours of the Paris Commune. They were shot on sight by government troops.

Pfahl-Bürger (Germ., burgesses of the palisades). Those who sought refuge from the strictures of feudal barons by living outside city walls, but within the line of palisades which allowed them certain rights and privileges.

Pffafenbrief (Germ., priests' charter). Ordinance issued in 1370 by the Federal States of Switzerland, declaring that clerics were subject to state authority and could claim no special privileges in relation to secular rule.

Philadelphia Charter. Declaration issued by the ILO in May 1944 at Philadelphia, USA, expressing the right of all people to freedom, dignity, economic security, material well-being, spiritual development and equal opportunity.

Philosophes (Fr.). Name given to leading thinkers in pre-revolutionary France, including Montesquieu, Voltaire, Rousseau, Condorcet and Diderot. Mainstream thought of the Philosophes emphasized the power of human reason, leading to criticism of irrational privilege and abuses. Hence the 1789 Revolution was held by conservatives to be influenced by the writings of the Philosophes.

Phoney War. Phase of World War II between the invasion of Poland by Germany on 1 September 1939 and the German occupation of Denmark and invasion of Norway in April 1940. The American usage was adopted by the British to describe the period of relative inactivity in western Europe: after the rapid fall of Poland little appeared to happen and, indeed, in October and November 1939 Hitler made peace overtures to Britain and France for propaganda purposes. The French dubbed the period *la drôle de guerre* and the British also called it the 'Bore War', 'funny war' or, as Churchill termed it in his work *The Second World War*, the 'Twilight War'.

Physiocrats. Adherents of an 18th-century French school of economics known at the time as *Les Economistes* but later renamed by DuPont de Nemours, one of their number. Other members were Turgot, Quesnay and Mirabeau. They held the common 18th-century view of the bounty of nature and the goodness of man in his natural state. They believed that the government ought therefore to conform to nature and, provided people did not interfere with each other's liberty or combine amongst themselves, leave citizens alone. Madmen, criminals and monopolists were to be eliminated but otherwise LAISSEZ-FAIRE should prevail. From this followed a doctrine of FREE TRADE between nations on the grounds of justice and economy, in the belief that competition would force men to economize the cost of their labour to the general advantage. Adam Smith was influenced by the physiocrats and greatly developed their teaching.

Piagnoni (Ital., the weepers). Name given to the followers of Savonarola, the guiding spirit of the Florentine Republic, established during a temporary eclipse of the power of the Medicis in 1493.

Pickelhaube (Germ.). Spiked helmet worn by German troops during World War I.

pied noir (Fr., black foot). Term for a European settler in Algeria, so called from the black shoes worn by the European settlers.

pikarts. Medieval term of abuse for heretics.

Pilgrim Fathers. The 101 English PURITANS and other CONGREGATIONALISTS who, after living for some years in exile in Holland, sailed for America in the *Mayflower* on 6 September 1620. They landed at Plymouth, Massachussets, on 4 December, where they founded a settlement. They are regarded as the pioneers of American colonization, although a small colony had been founded in Virginia 13 years earlier.

Pindaris (Hind.) Indian mounted mercenaries and freebooters, originally formed in the 17th century by the last Mohammedan dynasty of the Deccan who gave them licence to plunder. In the early 19th century they were employed by the Mahratta Confederacy and after its dissolution continued to carry out predatory raids until they were dispersed in 1818.

Pipiolos (Span., novices). In Chile, a derisive nickname given to the Liberals who contested power with the Pelucones in the early years of independence.

placemen. In England, members of the House of Commons holding places or offices of profit under the Crown. Crown patronage grew quickly after the RESTORATION of 1660 and was used by governments as a means of securing support amongst members of parliament. Offices were given in the expectation that their holders would then support the government. From the accession of William III in 1689 continuous attempts were made by opposition groups to limit the influence of such patronage. Amongst those whose offices fell under the term 'placemen' were ministers, civil servants, household and court officers, members of the army and navy, legal officers of the Crown, government pensioners and contractors. By a series of Place Acts between 1782 and 1870 placemen were gradually excluded from sitting in the Commons.

Plaid Cymru (Welsh, Party of Wales). Welsh political movement founded in 1925 and originally known as Plaid Genedlaethol Cymru (Welsh Nationalist Party). It hopes to separate Wales from the UK and by so doing to preserve the Welsh language, culture and economy. It first put forward candidates in a general election in 1929; its best performance was in the 1970 election when it won 175,000 votes. The first Plaid Cymru MP was Gwynfor Evans, elected in the 1966 Carmarthen by-election.

The party has returned MPs in five elections, including three in 1987. Their lack of success has at times led extremist members of the party to become involved in bomb incidents and arson. The nearest Plaid Cymru have come to seeing their wishes fulfilled was perhaps in March 1979 when the Welsh people were asked to vote in a REFERENDUM on the question of Welsh devolution. But the vote was overwhelmingly against it.

Plain, The. Independent and moderate members of the French Convention, led by Danton who acted as the chief intermediary between it and the Paris Commune, who conspired with the Right to overthrow Robespierre.

Plantagenets (deriv. OFr. *plante genêt*, sprig of broom). The kings of England between 1154 and 1485, including members of the houses of Lancaster and York; the name is thought to derive from the broom worn in the cap of the founder of the dynasty, Geoffrey of Anjou (1113–51). Correctly they are styled ANGEVINS.

plebiscite (deriv. Lat., ordinance of the people). System of government by which questions are submitted to a direct national vote instead of being determined by parliamentary representatives.

PLO. Palestine Liberation Organization, formed in Jordan in May 1964 to reconcile the disparate political groupings of the Palestinians, and dominated by the Syrian Al Fatah group led by Yasir Arafat. The PLO have mounted numerous guerrilla raids into Israel and Israeli-held territory; some of its members have been responsible for terrorist actions such as hijacking and murder. In September 1970 King Hussein of Jordan sought to restrict its activities, resulting in civil war in Jordan and the formation of BLACK SEPTEMBER. The PLO guerrillas were forced to move their bases to Syria and the Lebanon.

In October 1974 representatives of Arab states meeting at Rabat recognized the PLO as having responsibility for all Palestinians in national and international affairs; on 22 March 1976 the UN admitted PLO representatives to a debate on conditions on the WEST BANK. Israel does not recognize the PLO as the legitimate leaders of the Palestinians and refuses to negotiate with them.

Holding the PLO responsible for attacks on north Israel from the Lebanon, the Israeli army entered the Lebanon and in July 1982 forced the dispersal of PLO guerrillas in Beirut to various Arab states, leading to a rapprochement between the PLO and Jordan. US Pres. Reagan, in seeking a solution to the Palestinian problem, suggested that Jordan negotiate with Israel on behalf of the PLO. It looked for a time as if Arafat could persuade his followers to accept this, but the more radical elements in the PLO eventually vetoed the idea and by mid-1983 a serious revolt against Arafat's leadership had taken place. However, the popular Arab uprising in the occupied West Bank in 1988 has brought Arafat and the PLO to the fore again.

pluralism. The simultaneous holding of more than one ecclesiastical office or benefice which continued despite a papal bull of 1317 and strenuous efforts to prevent it at the 16th-century Council of Trent. Pluralism was forbidden in England by successive Acts of Parliament in 1529, 1838, 1850 and 1885.

Pocket Borough. *See* ROTTEN BOROUGH.

pocket veto. Constitutional procedure in the USA, whereby legislation at the end of a session which the President has not passed is dropped. The President's VETO – by which he returns a bill to Congress, with his objections, within 10 days of receiving it – can normally be overridden by a two-thirds majority in both Houses of CONGRESS. In the case of a controversial bill which the President dislikes but does not wish actually to veto, by not returning it to Congress within the allotted time, it will become law, but without his signature. The pocket veto occurs if Congress adjourns within the 10 days, before the President has passed or returned the bill.

podestà (Ital.). In 13th-century Italian cities, the chief magistrate, elected annually by the citizens to perform judicial functions and, in some cities, executive duties, such as controlling the military forces.

pogrom (Russ., destruction). Term used to denote anti-Jewish violence, first used to describe attacks on the Jews authorized by the Tsarist authorities in 1881. Pogroms in eastern Europe forced many Jews to emigrate to Britain and the USA in the late 19th and early 20th centuries. In 1938 Hitler ordered a general pogrom in Germany which led to the destruction of all synagogues and nearly all Jewish shops, homes and hospitals.

Poitevins. Subjects of the English kings in their capacity as Dukes of Aquitaine and Counts of Poitou. In the late 12th and early 13th centuries a number entered Crown service in England and the term has come to be applied particularly to a group of councillors and ministers appointed by Henry III. Most of them were in fact English but their leaders – Peter de Rivaux and his uncle Peter des Roches, the Bishop of Winchester – were Poitevins. They remained Henry's principal advisers from 1232 to 1234 when the rebellion of English barons against their influence led by Richard Marshall, Earl of Pembroke, forced Henry to dismiss them.

police state. Dictatorship or totalitarian state in which opposition to the régime is suppressed and dissenters imprisoned by the police on purely political grounds.

Politburo. Senior communist party executive committee in communist states.

political levy. Money paid by British trade unions to finance the Labour Party, dating from 1900 when the Labour Representation Committee was sponsored by the trade unions for the purpose of reversing anti-union legislation. The amount each union gives is calculated on the basis of its membership. Conservatives have always been critical of the levy, arguing that it forces unionists to finance the Labour Party even if they do not support it; they have always been keen to substitute CONTRACTING IN for CONTRACTING OUT.

Politiques (Fr.). French Catholic party, led by the Montmorency family and formed after the St. Bartholomew's Day massacre of Parisian HUGUENOTS in 1572, which wished to put an end to such religious persecution.

poll tax (ME *poll*, head). In medieval England, a personal tax, collected by special officers, assessed on all men and women on a fixed or sliding scale. It was first levied in 1222 to finance a crusade, but became a regular tax in the 14th century. It caused great discontent and helped to provoke the peasant rising under Wat Tyler in 1381. It was last imposed in Britain in 1698; although a similar system of taxation is to be introduced in the late 1980s.

In France a poll tax was first levied by Louis XIV in 1695 and was revived from 1701 until the revolution. It bore most heavily on the middle classes and the peasantry. Peter the Great introduced poll taxes to Russia in 1724 and they lasted until the mid-19th century.

polycentrism. The attempt by the Italian Communist Party in 1956 under Palmiro Togliatti to distance itself from the Soviet Union following the revelations of Stalinist excesses and the invasion of Hungary. Polycentrism advocated national Communist Parties' independence from Moscow. *See* EURO-COMMUNISM.

pontage. In feudal times a tax imposed on all freemen for the maintenance and repair of bridges.

Pontifex Maximus (Lat., chief priest). In ancient Rome, the official head of Roman religion; after the rise of Christianity the title, abbreviated to Pontiff, was adopted by the popes.

Pontiff. *See* PONTIFEX MAXIMUS.

pontificalia (Lat.). Ecclesiastical term for the vestments of a pope or bishop.

Poor Laws. Laws governing provision of relief for the poor in Britain. In 1536 an act was passed to grant relief for 'impotent poor', though 'sturdy beggars' were to be compelled to work. The cost of relief was to be met from voluntary subscribers and the parish was to administer it. 'Parish registers' of the poor were introduced in 1552–53 and in 1563 and 1597 JUSTICES OF THE PEACE were empowered to raise funds by compulsion. This was extended in the 1601 Poor Law Act which imposed a rate for poor relief on property owners. In 1662 an Act of Settlement was passed allowing overseers to send back to their parish of birth any persons not from the parish, owning no land and being unemployed.

The problems of discouraging people who had work from applying for relief was the next concern of the authorities. The 1723 Workhouse Test Act required the poor in receipt of relief to enter a WORKHOUSE, though a 1782 Act forced the parish to find work or 'outdoor relief' for able-bodied poor. The SPEEN-HAMLAND SYSTEM resulted in the

1834 Poor Law Amendment Act which was characterized by the withdrawal of outdoor relief and the forcing of all paupers into workhouses in which conditions were unpleasant by design. Six hundred 'unions' of parishes were created which were to consist of boards of 'guardians', elected by local rate-payers, charged with administering the local poor relief. In 1905 a Royal Commission on the Poor Laws was appointed. Reporting in 1909, it did not wholly accept the reforms proposed by its member, the FABIAN Beatrice Webb (1858–1943), but attitudes had clearly changed. The Poor Laws were gradually replaced by a series of new institutions, including old age pensions, national unemployment and health insurance and a decision that after World War II an integrated system of social security should exist.

Poor Lombards. A wing of the medieval WALDENSIANS, initially based in northern Italy, who were influenced by radical and anti-Church opinions and followed the trend of the region by forming congregations supported by manual labour. They split from the LYONISTS in 1205 and were active missionaries, particularly in the German-speaking areas of Europe.

Popish Plot. So-called Jesuit plot, 'exposed' in August 1678 by Titus Oates and Israel Tonge, to assassinate Charles II of England, install his Catholic brother James on the throne and massacre Protestants. French forces were also to invade Ireland. This nonsense resulted in a frenzy of anti-Catholicism, and even the more responsible elements were alarmed to learn of the unexplained death in October 1678 of Sir Edmund Berry Godfrey, the magistrate who had first heard Oates's dispositions. On 31 October the House of Commons resolved 'that there has been and still is a damnable and hellish plot, contrived and carried on by popish recusants for the assassinating and murdering the King, and for subverting the government and rooting out and destroying the Protestant religion'.

A number of suspects were executed and tension mounted further when it was discovered that Edward Coleman, secretary to the Duchess of York, was corresponding with the Jesuit La Chaise, adviser to Louis XIV of France. Finally, it was revealed that the King was obtaining subsidies from France and a movement grew to exclude James from the succession to the throne and replace him by Charles's natural son, the Duke of Monmouth. Charles responded by dissolving the CAVA-LIER PARLIAMENT and declaring Monmouth illegitimate. James Duke of York went voluntarily into temporary exile in the Spanish Netherlands.

Popular Front. Name given by communists to the collaboration of communists, socialists and liberal democrats against FASCISM and NAZISM between 1935 and 1939. Their platform involved defence of capitalistic democracy coupled with social reform and opposition to the extreme right with the question of true SOCIALISM being put aside. The communists had initially rejected the policy as opportunist but with the failure of revolutionary communism to defeat the Nazis in Germany and the Fascists in Italy, together with the increasing threat to the USSR from Germany, Stalin (1879–1953) conceded the need for alliance with the western democracies.

From June 1936 to October 1938 a Popular Front held power in France with Leon Blum (1872–1950) becoming France's first socialist Prime Minister. Despite opposition from

the French senate, Fascist groups were suppressed and social reforms introduced. However, the Front broke after left-wing discontent with the approach of the radical Daladier (1884–1970) at the meeting with Hitler and Chamberlain (British Prime Minister 1937–1940) at Munich in September 1938. In Britain Sir Stafford Cripps, a leading member of the Labour Party, led a campaign for a popular front and was expelled from the Labour Party in January 1939 in consequence. In Spain Popular Front governments held power from February 1936 until March 1939 when Franco finally won the Spanish Civil War (*see* CAUDILLO). In Chile a Popular Front government led by Pres. Aguirre was established in 1938. It survived until 1947 when there appeared a strong anti-communist movement which succeeded in introducing a number of major social reforms. The impetus for Popular Fronts in Europe diminished after the signing of the Nazi-Soviet non-aggression pact on 23 August 1939.

Populists. Name given to the People's Party of the United States, founded in Cincinnati in 1891. Their programme, drawn up by Ignatius Donnelly, proposed the abolition of national banks, free coinage of silver, laws against alien land-owners, graduated income-tax and national control of the railways. A certain distrust of big business and of the banks remains a significant element in American politics, particularly in the agrarian mid-west.

Possibilists. The opponents of the GUESDIST wing of the French Socialist Party in the late 19th and early 20th century who argued that the interests of the working class would be best served by collective bargaining, strikes and electoral support for progressive candidates regardless of their party affiliation.

Post Nati (Lat., those born after). Name given to the Scottish subjects of James VI who were born after his accession as James I to the English throne in 1603. They were adjudged in the Calvin Case (1606–7) to be natural-born subjects of the king of England. Prior ,to this, James's attempt to secure the union of England and Scotland (1604–6) had failed since Parliament refused to agree to the naturalization of his Scottish subjects as English, except on the basis of a common parliament and law for both countries.

Potato Famine. In 1845 and 1846 three-quarters of the Irish potato crop, the staple diet of the population of four million, was destroyed by blight. The disaster was compounded by a European corn harvest failure and British maladministration, causing a million deaths from starvation and the enforced migration of a further million people.

potwallopers (*also* Potwallers; pot + *wallop*, boil). Voters in certain English boroughs, subdivisions of the SCOT AND LOT BOROUGHS, where the FRANCHISE depended upon the proof that a voter provided his own food, was master of a hearth at which to cook it and controlled the doorway of his dwelling. This franchise evolved from the practice in medieval boroughs of occasionally eating in public to establish that one was a freeman and not a serf.

Poujadist. A follower of Pierre Poujade, a bookseller from central-southern France, who formed a right-wing political movement violently active in France between 1954 and 1958. The Union de Défence des Commerçants et Artisans (more commonly known as Poujadism) was anti-socialist, anti-intellectual and anti-European. It recruited its membership mainly from shop-keepers and the petit-bourgeoisie, a class which was suffering the consequences of rapid inflation. Poujadists won 52 seats in the National Assembly at the 1956 election, but the return of de Gaulle to active politics and the foundation of the Fifth Republic led to their rapid decline. *See* LEPENISM.

poundage. *See* TUNNAGE AND POUNDAGE.

Powellite. Wing of the British Conservative Party which supported Enoch Powell (b. 1912) in the late 1960s. Associated with anti-immigration, anti-EEC policies.

Praemunire, Statute of. English statute passed in 1392 confirming the earlier Statute of Provisors which declared the English realm to be free of all earthly subjection. The procurement of BULLS or other Papal instruments was made punishable by OUTLAWRY and FORFEITURE.

Praesidium (Lat., defence). Term now used to refer to the executive committee of the Supreme Soviet of the USSR.

Pragmatic Army. An army organized in the Netherlands by Britain in the 1740–48 War of the Austrian Succession, with contingents from Austria, Britain, Holland, Hanover and Hesse and which, commanded by George II, marched up the Rhine and defeated the French at Dettingen on 27 June 1643.

Pragmatic Sanction. Law announced by Emperor Charles VI on 19 April 1713 to ensure that the Habsburg succession would pass to his daughter Maria Theresa, his male heir having died. Though acknowledged by most European powers by 1738, Frederick II of Prussia's rejection of the agreement on Charles' death in 1740 brought about the War of the Austrian Succession.

Praguerie. Revolt against Charles VII of France in 1439 by the Dukes of Bourbon and Alençon and others provoked by the Ordonnance of Orleans which imposed a tax on their lands for military purposes. The Dauphin Louis joined them but they were defeated in 1440. Civil war again erupted in 1441 but the revolt was finally suppressed within the year.

Prague Spring. A period of 'socialism with a human face' following the appointment of Alexander Dubcek as Czechoslovak Communist Party First Secretary on 5 January 1968 and the adoption of a reform programme on 5 April. Without questioning the Party's central authority, it promised economic, intellectual and a degree of political liberalization. Terminated by the Warsaw Pact invasion on 20/21 August 1968. *See* BREZHNEV DOCTRINE.

Prairial (Fr.). Law forced through the French Convention of Robespierre on 10 June 1794, which allowed the Tribunal to dispense with the hearing of defence evidence. Trials were thus reduced to a simple decision of acquittal or death which led to an intensification of the Terror. Robespierre's opponents in the Convention deposed him before he had a chance to bring them to trial.

precariae. In medieval England, grants of Church land to laymen, generally only for the life of the grantee, but occasionally renewed to his successor. They were often extorted from the Church by force.

predestination. Doctrine of CALVINISM and other Protestant faiths which holds that God has destined some souls to salvation and others to damnation and that nothing individual people can do will change their allotted destinies.

Preobajensky (Russ.). Regiment of royal bodyguards formed by Peter I of Russia and named after his childhood home on the Yauza river near Moscow. During the 18th century, the regiment was active in palace coups which led to the succession first of the Tsarina Anna in 1730, then of Elizabeth in 1741 and finally of Catherine II in 1762. In 1917 it supported the provisional liberal government deposed by the BOLSHEVIKS.

Prerogative. The rights and privileges of the sovereign over and above other persons, held by virtue of the crown and independent of statute and the courts. It was widely used by the Tudor monarchs when its powers were still undefined. In the early 17th century its extent became subject to dispute due to the use made of it by the Stuarts and the development of parliament. It was criticized by the LONG PARLIAMENT and by common lawyers, and the crown was forced to accept its limitation by statute. The Bill of Rights (1689) further limited the prerogative and during the 19th century the monarch's rights to choose ministers and to interfere in government policy were gradually eroded. The residue of discretionary powers surviving in the prerogative is now exercised by the government in the name of the crown.

Presbyterianism (deriv. Gk., elder). A system of Church government by presbyters who are all of equal rank.

Its doctrinal standards, generally accepted by Scottish, English and Americans as a thorough and logical statement of CALVINISM, are contained in the 1647 Westminster Confession of Faith.

In Britain, the leading Presbyterian church is the Church of Scotland. At the REFORMATION the Scots demanded a fundamental change of doctrine, discipline and worship. The leading Scottish Protestant John Knox had worked with Calvin in Geneva, and Calvinism was to be the system introduced into Scotland. The Reformed Kirk was based on the *Scots Confession*, drawn up and signed by Knox, the *Book of Discipline* and the *Book of Common Order*, the so-called 'Knox's Liturgy', an English translation of the liturgy used by Calvinists in Geneva. However, Laud's attempts in the 1630s to force a prayer book on the Scottish Church led to the abandonment of these liturgies in favour of 'free prayer'.

Under James I and Charles I the EPISCOPACY was re-established but was abolished by the 1638 Glasgow Assembly. Cromwell abolished General Assemblies and at the restoration Charles II re-established the Episcopacy. Those COVENANTERS who opposed Episcopacy were persecuted until in 1690 William III reinstituted Presbyterianism.

Presbyterianism lay uncompromising stress on the word of God, revealed in the Old and New Testaments, as the supreme rule of faith and life, and emphasized the value of a highly trained ministry. The Church of Scotland provides for democratic representation through a hierarchy of courts. Ministers are elected by their congregations. A local kirk session comprises the minister and lay Church elders, also elected, who assist the ministers. Above the kirk session is the court of the presbytery which has jurisdiction over a specified area. The court of synod rules over a large number of presbyteries and finally the General Assembly is presided over by the Moderator: it acts as the supreme court of the Church with both judicial and legislative powers. In 1972 the Presbyterian and CONGREGATIONALIST Churches in England merged to form the United Reformed Church.

presidios (Span.). Frontier blockhouses of Latin America, extensively used by the Spaniards in the colonial period. Staffed by small bodies of soldiers, they were usually run in conjunction with a Church mission, the idea being both to pacify and convert the natives of northern Mexico and the south-west of North America.

press-gang. Body of sailors or soldiers employed to force men into the armed services by IMPRESSMENT. Press-gangs were frequently used in England particularly during the Napoleonic Wars of the early 19th century, but fell out of use after *c*1850.

prest (*also* imprest). In medieval England, a loan, usually from the king to private individuals, to an army serving away from home or to royal officers for daily expenses.

prétendant (Fr.). Claimant to the throne of France. Under the law of June 1886, not rescinded until June 1950, the *prétendants* were banished from France.

pretender. Claimant to a throne that is already occupied. In England the most famous were James Stuart, the Old Pretender (1688–1766) son of James II; and Charles Stuart, the Young Pretender (1673–1760), grandson of James II (*see* JACOBITES).

Pride's Purge. Expulsion of about 140 MPs from the LONG PARLIAMENT on 6 December 1648, when Col. Thomas Pride (d. 1658) and a number of soldiers entered the House of Commons on the orders of the army council to arrest or expel dissident members who had been negotiating with Charles I at a time when the army had decided it could no longer trust him. The remnant of Parliament after the Purge was the RUMP, which voted that the king be tried. Pride was one of the judges who signed Charles's death warrant.

primaries. Primary elections, an institution of US politics designed as a safeguard against corruption. To prevent a 'BOSS' or someone with vested interests from securing the nomination of a particular candidate, a movement began in the early 20th century to allow people a free choice of candidates. Primaries are not an election to office, but a means of selecting a candidate to stand in the election – i.e. the election of party candidates by party members. They may be either 'closed', with only members of a particular party being allowed to vote for its candidates, or 'open', in which the right to vote is not restricted to party adherents. They may also be 'direct', with candidates being chosen for office, or 'indirect', in which delegates are chosen to attend CONVENTIONS which will in turn nominate candidates.

Primitive Methodists. *See* METHODISTS.

Primrose League. Conservative Party organization founded in 1883 by the FOURTH PARTY as part of their attempt to democratize the party by broadening its base of support and reforming its organization. The name was chosen because the primrose was the favourite flower of the great Conservative leader, Benjamin Disraeli (1804–1881).

prisage. (1) In England, the right of the Crown to purchase a portion of goods shipped into the country, often at less than the commercial price. An example was the Crown's right to take two tuns of wine from every ship importing twenty tuns or more into England. Edward I (1271–1307) extended ancient prisages and commuted some of them to cash payments. The goods and sums collected by special officers at the ports were used to defray military expenses. Prisage was abolished in 1811.

(2) Also, the Crown's share of merchandize taken at sea as a lawful prize of war.

privatization. Selling of nationalized industries and other parts of the public sector to private businesses and individuals.

Privy Council. In 16th- and 17th-century England the governing council, presided over by the monarch, which developed from the king's council, a larger body, in the 1530s. Its register dates from 1540 and it received its own seal in 1556. Consisting of the major officers of state and the royal household, it met according to the sovereign's will to discuss both great matters of policy and the minutiae of administration. From the 18th century onwards, its functions have been assumed by the cabinet; today its duties are purely formal. Membership is given to persons who have attained high office and the Lord President is always a member of the cabinet.

Privy Seal. Seal employed from the 11th century in the CHANCERY and EXCHEQUER to issue royal instructions to Crown officials. Its use increased as that of the GREAT SEAL became formalized. The Privy Seal is used in matters of small importance which do not receive the Great Seal, and also on warrants for use of the Great Seal. The Privy Seal Office was abolished in 1884 though the post of Lord Privy Seal, which has no particular duties, continues to exist and is of cabinet rank.

proclamations. In England, notices publicly given by the monarch to the subjects, originally having an authority similar to that of medieval ordinances. Under the Tudors, proclamations were extensively used to supplement statutes and correct legislative and administrative omissions. They dealt with a large and miscellaneous range of subjects including trade, religion and ENCLOSURES, and were issued under the royal PREROGATIVE.

As Parliament developed, opposition arose under James I to the use and apparent abuse of proclamations and the Commons petitioned against them in 1610. The courts decided that no new offence could be created by proclamations and that they could not overrule common law. The abolition in 1641 of the STAR CHAMBER COURT, which had enforced proclamations, greatly reduced their use. Today they are employed only to summon and dissolve parliament or as described in the 1714 Riot Act and 1920 Emergency Powers Act.

proctor. One who manages another person's affairs or represents them in a canon or civil law court. In medieval times, the powers of a proctor were limited to the terms of his letter of proxy. Crown agents on foreign missions or those negotiating truces and treaties were necessarily appointed proctors. Today, the term is applied to one who acts as the representative of a principal in the courts and also to someone chosen to repre-

sent a cathedral or collegiate church or the clergy of the diocese in the Lower House of Convocation of the Church of England. It may also refer to an executive officer of a university.

prohibition. Interdict by authority; the forbidding of an action by law. The term most commonly denotes the outlawing of the manufacture, sale and distribution of liquor in the USA between January 1920 and December 1933. As early as the 1830s temperance societies had pressed state legislatures to prohibit alcohol. National agitation was commenced in 1895 by the Anti-Saloon League and by 1920 the liquor trade was restricted in 19 states. In World War I German-born citizens were believed to control the drink trade, so consumption of alcoholic liquor was deemed unpatriotic.

The 18th Amendment to the Constitution instigating prohibition was put to Congress in December 1917 and ratified in 1920. The law, widely ignored in the 1920s, greatly increased the price of drink: large profits gave a permanent boost to organized criminals who commenced 'bootlegging' – distilling, brewing, distributing and selling drink on a massive scale. In 1928 the DEMOCRATS promised repeal of the 18th Amendment if elected. When they came to power in 1932, the 18th Amendment was repealed by the 21st, ratified on 5 December 1933. Under the 21st Amendment, states retained the right to make their own laws on drink and Federal prohibition was repealed.

proletariat (deriv. Lat. *proles*, offspring). Originally, that class in Ancient Rome who served the state only by providing children. The term is nowadays used to refer to those who derive a living solely by the sale of their labour.

pronunciamento (Span., pronounce-ment). In Spain, and more particu-larly Latin America, usually a revolt or call to arms against the government, generally taking the form of a manifesto listing the fail-ures of the existing régime and pro-posals to put them right.

proportional representation. System of voting designed to ensure that the legislature accurately reflects the strength of support for the various parties among the electorate. Minority parties receive a fair number of seats in the legislature so that a vote for a small party is not a 'wasted' vote. Proportional represen-tation may take several forms.

prorogation. Prerogative power of the Crown to put off a sitting of parliament, thereby effectively ending the session; the date of the next meeting is announced at the time. Unfinished parliamentary busi-ness must be restarted *ab initio* (from the beginning), meaning that bills introduced but not passed are lost. In this respect it differs from an adjournment which is separately effected by each House (sometimes at the instigation of the Crown), and after which interrupted business is continued from where it was left off.

Protectorate. (1) The period of the INTERREGNUM, from 16 December 1653 to 25 May 1659, when England was governed by a Protector. Follow-ing the expulsion of the RUMP and the failure of the BAREBONES PARLIAMENT to act effectively and in compliance with the desires of the army leaders, Parliament's powers were transferred to Oliver Cromwell (1599–1658). The INSTRUMENT OF GOVERNMENT was drafted and Cromwell appointed Lord Protector. The system was never able to pro-duce a balance of power between Cromwell, Parliament and the army: Cromwell could not establish a work-ing relationship with his first Parlia-ment (1654–55) and accordingly dissolved it. In March 1655 Col. John Penruddock (1619–55) headed a roy-alist rebellion in Hampshire which, though quickly crushed, led Crom-well to institute a direct army rule via the MAJOR GENERALS. THE HUMBLE PETITION AND ADVICE offered by his second Parliament sub-stantially increased the powers of the Protector. Thus, when his opponents tried to undermine the Protectorate, Cromwell was able to dissolve Parlia-ment. He died in September 1658 and his son Richard succeeded him. A new Parliament met in January 1659 and recognized Richard, but in April Parliament sought to assert greater control over the army, and the response of the generals was to force the Protector to dissolve it. Power was thus clearly in the hands of the army and after it restored the remnant of the Rump in May 1659 Richard resigned office.

(2) Territory under the protection, power and jurisdiction of another state, which does not, however, have full sovereignty over it. The only common feature of the many types of protectorate is an obligation of obedience in return for protection and a reluctance on the part of the protecting state to allow the protec-torate independent relationships with other states. Former British protec-torates, now independent, include Aden (now Southern Yemen), Uganda, Bechuanaland (now Bots-wana) and Zanzibar. Their inha-bitants were not British citizens and the states themselves were treated as foreign territories.

Protestant Ascendancy. The religious and political dominance of the Pro-testant minority in Ireland from the 17th to the 19th centuries.

Protestantism. Collective term applied to that part of Western Christianity which denies the authority of the pope and emphasizes Christians' responsibility to God rather than to the Church and its sacraments. The term was first applied to the supporters of Martin Luther (1483–1546) who were critical of the intolerance of reform that was displayed by the Roman Catholic Church at the second Diet of Speyer (1529), which reversed the decision of the first Diet of Speyer (1526) that reform was needed. Most Protestant churches severed their links with the Catholic Church at the time of the REFORMATION.

protest vote. A vote intended to express disapproval of a candidate or administration, usually given to a party with little possibility of winning office. In Britain it often takes the form of a vote for parties other than Tory or Labour, in the US for a third party presidential candidate.

Provisional IRA. Wing of the IRA primarily concerned with expelling British troops and government from Northern Ireland. The IRA was inactive in Northern Ireland until 1968–69, when civil rights demonstrations by Catholics there provoked violent reprisals by Protestant extremists and the police authorities in the province proved unwilling to protect Catholic areas. Catholics in the north were forced to seek arms in the Republic. The arrival of British troops in the province in April 1969 encouraged the IRA to renew its traditional struggle for a united Ireland and on 18 August 1969 the IRA chief of staff announced a resumption of activities.

Between January and March 1971 it became clear that a split had arisen between the official IRA based largely in the Republic and the more radical 'Provisional' IRA in the north, probably dating back to the initial failure of the IRA to act effectively in 1968–69. Support for the Provisionals, or 'provos', dates from their attempts to secure guns and to provide protection at that time. In May 1972 they refused to accept a ceasefire declared by the official leaders and the two wings were for a time at war with each other. Since the early 1970s it is the Provisional IRA which has continued urban guerrilla warfare in Northern Ireland and which has been responsible for murders and bombings on the mainland of Britain. *See also* IRA.

provisor. Originally, one who was appointed to an ecclesiastical living by the pope before the existing incumbent was dead; later, any right of patronage usurped by the pope. In 1351 the English Crown passed the Statute of Provisors, directed against the papal claim to appoint men to BENEFICES, which enacted that the king and the lords were to appoint to benefices of their own and their ancestors' creation. Papal BULLS were thereby made illegal and Crown patronage increased.

Provos (Dutch slang, 'Provocateurs'). Dutch youth movement seeking social reform which became prominent when its members threw smoke bombs and fought police at the March 1966 wedding of Crown Princess Beatrix to a German alleged to have SS connections. Though they soon faded as a specific movement their support for minority groups attracted support, made Amsterdam a HIPPY centre, and led to the emergence of the KABOUTERS.

Provost. Official in Scotland holding a position roughly equivalent to that of MAYOR in England and Wales. The title Lord Provost is given to the provosts of Aberdeen, Edinburgh, Glasgow, Dundee and Perth. The heads of certain Scottish colleges are also styled provost.

Prudhommes (Fr., good men and true). In 12th-century France, leading citizens elected to act as an advisory body to the provost of the town or to the representative of the king or trade tribunals, made up of masters and workers, appointed to decide trade disputes. They were revived by Napoleon I (1769–1821) and re-established during the Third Republic (1870–1940).

Puppet Emperor. Pu Yi, the last Chinese Emperor, who was deposed as a boy in 1911 and brought up in Japan, was made President by the Japanese of their puppet state MAN-CHUKUO in March 1934 and given the title Emperor with the name Kang Teh. When the Chinese communists took power Pu Yi was 're-educated' and ended his days as a gardener in Peking.

puppet government. Nominally independent government which is in reality controlled by some greater (and usually external) power, e.g. MANCHUKUO.

purge. Imprisonment or murder of political opponents within a party or country. The most notorious purges were in the USSR under Joseph Stalin (1879–1953). Between 1934 and 1938 an incalculable number of people, including potential rivals to Stalin, communist party members, Russian citizens and non-Russian minorities, were executed or sent to labour camps. It is thought that up to seven million arrests were made by the secret police and that some three million people died.

Puritans. Extreme PROTESTANTS of the 16th and 17th centuries, including PRESBYTERIANS and INDEPENDENTS. The Puritans emphasized individualism in religion, had a strict code of morality, a high sense of public duty and were opposed to certain forms of art and amusement. They came into dispute with ARMINIANS over ritual and later over the EPISCOPACY. Elizabethan prosecutions drove many of them to Holland and despite a show of strength in the MILLENARY PETITION, many emigrated to America during the reigns of the first two Stuarts. Charles I and the LAUDIANS pushed them into violent opposition and they were a dominant political force in the struggle between parliament and the crown. Following the RESTORATION, the Act of Uniformity (1662) ejected Puritan ministers from their livings. Those who conformed came to be known as the Low Church party in the Church of England; those who did not became DISSENTERS or NONCONFORMISTS.

puros (Span.). Advocates of radical social change in Mexico, active from the time of the first republic (1823) to c1855. They challenged the position of the landed CREOLE families and criticized the wealth of the Roman Catholic Church. Most were MESTIZOS.

purpresture. In medieval England, an illegal encroachment on Crown property, such as building on the king's land. Theoretically, the property of the person responsible for the encroachment was subject to FORFEITURE but, in practice, the land was left with the encroacher, who paid rent on it to the SHERIFF.

purveyance. In medieval times, the right of the itinerant royal household to make compulsory purchases or to purvey supplies. The system was open to abuse and even when payment was made it could cause hardship. In wartime the whole country was subjected to purveyance by itinerant royal purveyors, officers appointed to procure supplies who were far from ready to pay for them. Merchants could be forbidden to export goods and were forced to sell supplies to the crown. Complaints against purveyance were common in the late 13th century and continued into the Tudor period despite the introduction of numerous statutes to regulate it. Today, purveyance still exists in the form of compulsory purchase orders on houses and lands for development.

Puseyite. Follower of Dr. Edward Pusey (1800–82), one of the leaders of the OXFORD MOVEMENT, so called because its leaders were members of Oxford University. Its adherents sought to reassert the authority of the Anglican Church to counter the spread of 'liberal theology' in the 19th century. One motive force was the fear that the 1832 Reform Act would take power out of the hands of the TORIES and Churchmen and place it in those of Liberals and DISSENTERS.

The movement dated from July 1833 when John Keble preached a sermon criticizing a bill for the suppression of 10 Irish bishops. Between 1833 and 1841 Keble, Newman and Hurrell Froude issued a series of pamphlets, *Tracts for the Times*, stating their position. (From the title, adherents also became styled TRACTARIANS.)

The movement saw the Church of England as threatened by secular power. Emphasis was laid on it as a divine institution and on ritual and the continuity of the Catholic faith. In Tract 90 Newman showed that the 39 Articles could be made to square with Roman doctrine. In October 1845 Newman, followed by many of his supporters, was received into the Roman Catholic Church, while Pusey and Keble persisted in their efforts to secure recognition of Catholic liturgy and doctrine in the Anglican Church by emphasizing ministry, worship, ceremonial and religious community life.

putsch (Germ., revolt). Conspiracy to overthrow the régime, the most notorious being the Kapp Putsch of March 1920, an abortive right-wing coup by a journalist, Wolfgang Kapp, with the backing of General von Lüttwitz and the sympathy of Ludendorff. Berlin was seized but the putsch failed, partly because the officer corps did not support it and also because it faced the opposition of workers and the security police.

Q

qadi. One of a number of judges trained in Shari'a, the sacred law of ISLAM, who played an important part in local government business in the OTTOMAN empire. Their duties included deciding cases, acting as guardians of minors and orphans and appointing deputies.

Quadrilateral. The four fortified towns of Legnara, Mantua, Peschiera and Verona in northern Italy, which formed the strong point of the Austrian defence of Venetia in 1848 and 1859 during the struggle for Italian unification.

Quai d'Orsay. Parisian embankment where the French Foreign Office is situated: hence, by analogy, the Foreign Office itself.

Quakers. Society of Friends, a religious body founded in 17th-century England by George Fox whose central tenet is that each believer communicates with God and is directly guided by him in the ways of truth. Quakers do not have ordained ministers, prepared sermons or ritual; much reliance is put on the Holy Spirit moving members of the congregation to speak. Speaking in tongues and physical 'shaking' in religious ecstasies earned the movement its nickname.

To escape persecution, many Quakers emigrated to Pennsylvania which William Penn had founded in 1682. From there missionaries were sent all over the world. Quakers championed the movement for the abolition of slavery and helped in prison and educational reform. Today they often provide help to refugees and victims of natural disasters and are ardent pacifists.

quarterage. In early 18th-century England, an extraordinary tax levied on Catholics who established businesses in Ireland.

Quebec Libre (Fr., free Quebec). Slogan of the Canadian separatist movement, Parti Quebecois, founded in the mid-1960s by René Levesque. Pres. de Gaulle of France first used the phrase on 24 July 1967 when he exclaimed, 'Vive le Quebec libre!' from the balcony of the Montreal town hall. Four-fifths of the population of the province is French-speaking and its electorate have always aspired to independence from the former British colony; for many years, the province supported Canadian Liberals who responded by supporting French culture and language.

The Parti Quebecois won 25 per cent of the vote in the 1970 elections and its popularity continued to increase until it was seriously thought that the province might attempt to secede from Canada. It became clear that the separatist movement also had a militant wing when members of the Front de la Liberation du Quebec kidnapped a British trade commissioner, forcing the Canadian government to invoke the War Emergency Act. For a time it appeared that militancy had weakened the movement but in 1976 Levesque was elected Premier of Quebec: he announced that a referendum would be held before 1981 on the question of independence. In August 1977 a law was passed making French the only official language in the province; in November 1977 the French government treated him as a head of state. However, a referendum held on 20 May 1980 to decide whether the province should negotiate a looser form of political association with the rest of Canada proved a blow to the Parti Quebecois and checked its drive towards independence. 84 per cent of the population of Quebec voted; almost 60 per cent were against secession.

Queen Anne's Bounty. Fund established in 1704 by Queen Anne for the augmentation of the maintenance of poor clergy from her revenues from first fruits and tithes. In the 19th century parliamentary grants and private donations supplemented the fund, which was administered by ecclesiastical commissioners. On 1 April 1948 they and the Bounty became embodied in the Church Commissioners for England.

Queremistas. Supporters of Getúlio Vargas in the 1945 Brazilian presidential election who was dictator 1937–45 and 1951–54, when he committed suicide. Their name derives from their slogan '*queremos getúilo*' ('We want Getuilo').

quietist. Exponent of quietism, a doctrine of extreme asceticism and contemplative devotion embodied in the works of Miguel Molinos, a 17th-century Spanish priest condemned by the papacy.

quilimbos (Braz. Port.). In colonial Brazil, settlements of runaway slaves located far from centres of population; *cumbes* or *palenques* in Spanish colonies.

quinto (Span., fifth). Royalties derived by the Crown of Spain from the mines in her American colonies; they totalled about one-fifth of the yield.

Quisling. Name originating in England during World War II to describe a collaborator, FIFTH-COLUMNIST or traitor, derived from Vidkun Quisling (1887–1945), leader of the Norwegian Nasjonal Samling (National Unity) movement founded in 1933 in imitation of the German NAZI party. In December 1939 Quisling met Hitler and discussed a possible COUP D'ÉTAT in Oslo; in April 1940 he revealed details of Norwegian defences to the Germans. He became head of a PUPPET GOVERNMENT after the German invasion of April 1940 and was executed for treason in October 1945.

quo warranto (Lat., by what warrant). In medieval England, commissions from King Edward I to enquire how estates and judicial rights had passed from the Crown to private corporations and individuals and to ascertain which were the royal manors.

R

Rachmanism. Synonym for ruthlessly exploitative landlordism, deriving from Peter Rachman (1919–62) who arrived in Britain penniless in 1946 but who by 1955 owned a slum property empire in London's Notting Hill area. He violently evicted statutory controlled tenants paying low rents, replacing them with immigrants willing to pay high rents.

raison d'état (Fr., reason of state). Belief that the greater interest of the state can justify violation of the normal moral code and even of the law.

Raj (Hind. sovereignty). Term most commonly used to refer to British rule in India (1858–1947).

ralliement (Fr.). In France, policy initiated in an encyclical of Pope Leo XIII in 1892, which attempted to end the estrangement of Catholics from the Republic. However, most Catholics and monarchists remained hostile to the Republic; the monarchist right-wing proved to have a considerable nuisance value in French politics.

Ralliés (Fr.). Catholics and conservatives in France who renounced reactionary principles and declared their adhesion to the Republic in the 1890s. Their leader was Cardinal Lavigerie, Archbishop of Algiers.

Ramadan. *See* ISLAM.

ranee (Hind.). Wife of a RAJAH.

Ranters. (1) In Commonwealth England, fanatical sect of pantheists and 'antinomians', who did not believe that Christians were bound to keep the law of God.
(2) Primitive METHODISTS, so called because of their noisy preaching.

Rapacki Plan. Plan proposed by Polish Foreign Minister, Adam Rapacki (1909–70), in the UN General Assembly on 2 October 1957 and developed and presented to diplomatic representatives in Warsaw on 2 February 1958. It recommended that there should be no manufacturing or stationing of nuclear weapons in Poland, Czechoslovakia, East or West Germany. Joint teams of observers from NATO and WARSAW PACT states would ensure that it was kept. A zone free of nuclear weapons would thus be created; it was Rapacki's hope that similar zones could be established elsewhere. He also wanted similar steps to be employed to reduce conventional forces. The USSR approved the plan but the

USA and Britain rejected it, partly because it favoured the USSR which had larger numbers of conventional forces, and partly because the USSR wished it to be preceded by direct talks on the future of East and West Germany, a course unacceptable to the latter country.

rape (OE *rap*, rope). In the Saxon kingdom of Sussex, a unit of local government. It later fell between the SHIRE and the HUNDRED for purposes of administration and taxation and most of its functions were gradually absorbed by the hundred. Under Norman rule each rape became a CASTLERY.

rapparees. Irish brigands who waged guerrilla warfare against Protestant settlers in Ireland *c*1711.

rapprochement (Fr.). Re-establishment of friendly relations between states following a period of hostility.

Raskol. Great religious schism in the 17th-century Russian church, which arose because of attempts by the Patriarch Nikon to introduce innovations in ritual for the purpose of correcting errors that had arisen from careless copying of the liturgies and other religious books. Dissenters were excommunicated and thousands fled the country.

Rastafarianism. Movement originating in the West Indies which takes its name from *Ras* (a term of respect in Africa) Tafari Makonnen (1892–1975) crowned Emperor of Ethiopia with the title Haile Selassie in 1930. Haile Selassie has a mystical role in the cult as has Ethiopia itself: as the one part of Africa that was never colonized, it is seen as the spiritual home of the black man. Life in the West Indies or in Britain is seen as time in Babylon by analogy with the sufferings of the Israelites as slaves in exile.

ratecapping. Legislation to reduce local authority spending introduced by the Conservatives in 1984 which empowered the Government to prevent councils making up reductions in central grants by increasing rates. In 1985-86 18 councils were ratecapped for exceeding spending targets.

Reaganomics. A largely cynical term applying to the economic policies of the Reagan administrations in the 1980s.

Realpolitik (Germ., politics of realism). Term coined in 1859 by the liberal journalist and historian, Rochau, to describe Bismarck's policy. Bismarck believed that a naked struggle for power and a ruthless pursuit of self-interest were the only realistic options for a great state.

Rebecca Riots. South Wales protests in 1843 against turnpike gates in which rioters dressed in women's clothes, the leader and his followers being known as 'Rebecca and his daughters', an allusion to Genesis XXIV : 60. Troops and London police imposed order and the riots ended with a government pledge to enquire into the Turnpike Laws.

recall. Political process similar to RESELECTION, except that the local party can demand a representative to appear before it and explain his actions whenever it chooses, that is, during the lifetime of a parliament and not only at the end of his term of office.

recognizance. Deed, recogizing a debt or obligation made before a court of record, binding a party to undertake a particular act (such as appear in court or keep the peace) or pay a debt within a certain time and giving the creditor power to call on the aid of the Crown in the case of default. In mercantile law, such a deed was called a statute and the documents recorded at local registries.

reconcentrados. Inhabitants of rural areas of Cuba laid waste by Gen. Weyler during the 1895–99 insurrection. Weyler ordered these people to be 'concentrated' in camps where thousands died of disease and famine due to government negligence.

recorder. Originally, a city or borough officer appointed to keep the records of the courts of Quarter Sessions; later, the city's chief legal officer and sole judge. Today recorders, who must be barristers of not less than five years standing, are appointed by the Crown and are debarred from sitting in the House of Commons.

Recruiters. Name applied by royalists to members of the LONG PARLIAMENT who were elected to the House of Commons to fill the places of those 'disabled' from sitting because they had joined the king's army.

recusants (deriv. Lat., refuse). Those who refused to attend the services of the Church of England, most commonly Roman Catholics. Recusants were first fined under the Acts of Uniformity of 1552 and 1559. Elizabeth I fined both Catholics and recusant Protestants.

Red Amsterdam. An Amsterdam demonstration against Dutch Nazis on 4 July 1934 (which followed violent protests against unemployment benefit reductions) erupted into five days of riots in which six demonstra-tors were killed by police gunfire and in which a pirate radio station proclaimed the birth of 'Red Amsterdam' under a 'Red Front'.

Red Army. (1) Army of the USSR, taken from the red flag of socialist revolution. The original communist army in Russia was hastily assembled and organized by Trotsky (1879–1940) as Commissar for War to fight off the counter-revolutionary ('White') armies assembled in December 1917 to crush the OCTOBER REVOLUTION. Until 1946 the army's official name was 'the Red Army of Workers and Peasants'; it was changed to 'the Soviet Army' but is still generally referred to as the Red Army. The name was also given to groups involved in communist uprisings in Hungary in 1919, Germany in 1921 and China in 1927–44.

(2) (Rote Armee Faktion). *See* BAADER-MEINHOF GROUP.

Red Baron. Manfred von Richthofen (1892–1918), German air ace who between 1915 and 1918 shot down 80 Allied aircraft, a figure unequalled on either side. He flew a distinctive blood red Fokker and was killed over the Somme valley on 21 April 1918.

Red Brigades. Left-wing urban terrorist organizations active in Italy since the early 1970s. On 16 March 1978 Red Brigades kidnapped Aldo Moro (five times prime minister), killing five of his bodyguards, apparently hoping to provoke an over-reaction and further weaken Italian democracy. Signor Moro's corpse was found in Rome on 1 May.

Political murders by the Red Brigades and right-wing groups have steadily increased in the 1980s.

Red China. The People's Republic of China, proclaimed in Peking on 1 October 1949 after the communist victory over KUOMINTANG forces in the civil war.

Red Guards. Young members of the People's Liberation Army of China, authorized to travel the country helping to further the revolution. They came to prominence during the CULTURAL REVOLUTION for which their fanatical enthusiasm was notorious, with attacks on REVISIONISM, 'bourgeois decay' and Western diplomats. With the end of the Cultural Revolution attempts were made to bring them to order but by then they had firmly supplanted the Communist Youth League. It is probable that their remaining influence has been felt in outbreaks of 'Shanghai' radicalism (*see* GANG OF FOUR).

Redif. The military reserve of Turkey in the OTTOMAN empire.

redshanks. *See* GALLOGLASSES.

Red-shirts. Followers of Garibaldi during the RISORGIMENTO.

'Red Terror'. Imprisonment or execution of opponents of the BOLSHEVIK government established by the OCTOBER REVOLUTION.

reducciones (Span.). Mission villages in Spanish colonial South America where natives were concentrated or 'reduced' to receive religious instruction and training. The most famous were organized in Paraguay by the JESUITS. In Portuguese colonies they were called *reduçoẽs*.

reeve (deriv. OE *geréfa*). In medieval England, the local representative of a lord. Numerous types of reeve existed from the SHERIFF to the manorial reeve, often a VILLEIN, elected to help organize the day-to-day running of local affairs.

referendum (deriv. Lat., refer). Reference of a specific political question to the electorate for a direct decision by popular vote. In some countries, e.g. Australia, the constitution can only be altered by a referendum. In Britain a referendum was held in 1975 on withdrawal from the European Economic Community and in Scotland and Wales in 1979 on proposals for devolution. *See* INITIATIVE.

Reformation. Great religious reform movement of the 16th century which led to the establishment of PROTESTANTISM. In the 14th and 15th centuries John Wycliffe and John Hus had acted as forerunners; when Luther (1483–1546) in Germany and Zwingli in Switzerland took up the case for the reform of Catholicism, adherents became numerous. Abuses such as the sale of INDULGENCES by papal agents had incensed many and Luther's denunciation of such acts in 1517 found a receptive climate of opinion.

Amidst much controversy, the reformers evolved new doctrines based on principles which produced a variety of strands of Protestantism. They claimed justification (salvation) by faith and the direct use by the faithful of the scriptures. They rejected the Catholic doctrine of TRANSUBSTANTIATION, the adoration of the Virgin and the saints, and the supremacy of the pope. Luther was excommunicated, but the principles of the Reformation spread, converting large parts of Germany, Switzerland, the Low Countries, England and Scotland. *See also* CALVINISM.

Reformverein (Germ.). Association founded in 1862 with the aim of promoting the unification of Germany under the leadership of Austria.

Refuseniks. Soviet citizens, predominantly Jews, who seek to emigrate from the Soviet Union but are denied exit visas by the government.

régale (Fr.). Right claimed by French kings to present to BENEFICES that fell vacant when the bishop's see of the same diocese was also vacant and to collect the revenues of vacant sees. The papacy disputed the claim and a conflict arose between Louis XIV and Pope Innocent XI in 1681.

Regency. The period from 1811–20 during which the Prince of Wales (later George IV) acted as Prince Regent. Marked by a distinctive classically-influenced style in architecture and furniture.

regicides. In general usage a regicide is the killer of a king, but in England the term refers particularly to those 49 persons who sentenced to death and signed the instrument for the execution of King Charles I in 1649, plus the two anonymous executioners. After the RESTORATION, 29 of this number were put on trial in October 1660; 10 were sentenced to death.

regidors (Span.). Unsalaried councillors who sat on the *cabildo* in Spanish American colonial towns to deal with municipal administration. Originally they were elected by the town's property owners and held office for one year; later the Crown began to grant or sell the office for life, often giving a particular family hereditary rights to it. Regidores were at first drawn from the upper classes of the community though as the *cabildo* declined in importance more CREOLES came to be appointed. The term originated in Castile.

regium donum (Lat., gift of the

king). Annual grant from the English Crown, introduced by Charles II, for the maintenance of PRESBYTERIAN ministers in Ulster. James II allowed it to lapse, but it was revived by William III. It was finally abolished at the time of the DISESTABLISHMENT of the Irish Church in 1869.

Regulators. Members of associations formed in 18th-century North Carolina to regulate such affairs as law enforcement, civil disputes and the keeping of the peace. The associations were formed by the herdsmen and farmers of the western part of the colony who had difficulty attending the law courts in Charleston. After conflicts with the authorities in 1770–71, members of the associations emigrated westwards to colonize Tennessee.

Reich (Germ., empire). Designation of the Holy Roman Empire, used for traditional purposes following the creation of a unified German state in 1870. The first Reich was the medieval Holy Roman Empire; the second was formed by Bismarck in 1871 after the defeat of France by Prussia; and the 'Third Reich' was the period of government by Hitler between January 1933 and April 1945.

Reichsbanner. An unarmed force established in May 1924 to mobilize citizens loyal to the Weimar Republic. Its full name was Reichsbanner Schwarz-Rot-Gold (the Republic's colours) and its leaders, and the bulk of its 100,000 members, were Social Democrats. It was outlawed by Hitler on his assumption of power in 1933.

Reichskammergericht (Germ.). Standing high court of justice of the old German empire, reorganized from the Imperial Council in 1495 by Maximilian I. The emperor nominated the president who was assisted by eight nobles and eight doctors of law approved by the REICHSTAG; expenses were provided for by a general tax, the 'common penny'. It adopted principles of Roman Law and, unlike the Aulic Council which accompanied the emperor wherever he went, it sat permanently in one place, first Frankfurt and then Speyer. In the mid-16th century Ferdinand I increased the membership to 24 but by the end of the century it was overwhelmed with legislation and proved a slow and clumsy tribunal.

Reichsrath (Germ.). The old Austrian parliament, comprising two houses, the upper composed of princes of the blood, nobles, archbishops, bishops and life-members nominated by the emperor, and the lower consisting of elected members.

Reichstag (Germ.). The old German parliament in Berlin. The showpiece of the Imperial Constitution of 1871, it was elected by universal suffrage and represented Bismarck's concessions to democratic sentiment. In the 1890s, during the reign of William II, it became the focal point of German politics. The destruction of its building by an arsonist in February 1933 was exploited by the NAZIS for propaganda purposes and used as an excuse to tighten their control over Germany.

relief. In England, the tribute paid to a feudal lord by the heir on succession to a FIEF. The lord determined the sum paid and some kings, e.g. John, set a very high sum. MAGNA CARTA laid down regulations for the amount of reliefs after which they ceased to be a subject of dispute. Reliefs were abolished along with feudal tenures in 1661.

remembrancer. One of two EXCHEQUER clerks, known as the King's and the Lord Treasurer's remembrancers. The Lord Treasurer's remembrancer was allocated the duties of collecting fixed revenues and debts due to the Crown by the 1323 Cowick Ordinances. His importance declined with that of the Crown's ancient revenues. The office was abolished in 1833 and its duties reassigned.

To the King's remembrancer the Cowick Ordinances assigned duties pertaining to casual Crown revenues and their documentations, e.g. taking bonds for debts, making out processes for breach of such bonds and initiating proceedings against defaulters. In 1877 the office was transferred to the Supreme Court; since the 1925 Judicature Act the Senior Master of the Supreme Court has performed these duties.

Remonstrants. (1) In the Netherlands, name given to those ARMINIANS who, in 1610, presented a remonstrance to the States-General against the charges of heresy made against them. The document contained the *Five Articles of Arminianism*.

(2) In Scotland, name given to those COVENANTERS who, after the defeat of Dunbar in 1650, remonstrated to the Committee of Estates against the alliance of Argyle and others with the royalists. They refused to acknowledge Charles II until he proved himself true to the Covenant. The remonstrance was in turn condemned by a resolution of the Estates, which caused opponents of the remonstrants to be nicknamed 'resolutioners'

Renaissance (Fr., rebirth). Term first used by Vasari in 1550 to denote the revival of art and literature which began in 14th-century Italy. It became widely current only in 1860 when the Swiss historian Jacob Burchardt published *The Civilization of the Renaissance in Italy*. Today the term is used to refer not only to the revival in art, but to a total change in outlook which influenced science, economics and philosophy as well.

The Renaissance originated in the rise of a new merchant class which developed individualist attitudes towards economic affairs and led to individualism and humanism. Merchants became patrons of the arts, leading to new judgements of art that were not dependent on the Church, which had previously provided the only patronage. Medieval art sought to instruct and elevate man; Renaissance art sought to delight him. Out of such freedom came the rise of modern science and technology.

The Renaissance derived a corpus of philosophical, scientific, medical and mathematical knowledge from Arab scholars that had itself been taken from ancient Greek culture. The Arabs, however, had shown little interest in Greek art and literature: for this, Byzantine culture was studied, Greek scholars having fled to Italy after the fall of Constantinople. Translated and widely distributed by means of the newly-invented printing press, their manuscripts allowed a fuller understanding of the Greek spirit. From the works of Latin writers, insights into the humanism and scepticism of the Roman culture were also derived.

In the period *c*1400–1500, termed the Early Renaissance, the painters Massaccio, Uccello, Piero della Francesca, Botticelli and Bellini interested themselves in the problems of anatomy, composition, perspective and the representation of space; they laid the foundations of painting for all subsequent periods, including the present. In the High Renaissance, *c*1500 to the sack of Rome in 1527, a pure, balanced, classical harmony was reached and some artists achieved complete mastery of techniques learned earlier. This brief period produced the earlier works of Michelangelo, most of Leonardo's and all the Roman works of Raphael. In time, France, Spain, Germany, northern Europe and England were all affected.

RENAMO. The name of the anti-Government, South-African backed guerrillas attempting the oust the Marxist government of Mozambique in the 1980s.

Rentenmark. New currency introduced into Germany in 1923 by Chancellor Gustav Stresemann (1878–1929). It was necessary to help stablize the economy after the French had occupied the Ruhr following the German failure to pay REPARATIONS.

reparations. Payments imposed on powers defeated in war to make good the costs of the victors, once known as war indemnities. The most important were those imposed on Germany in 1919–20. The victorious allies did not lay down a definite sum in the Paris Peace Treaty, but in April 1921 reparations were fixed at £6,600 million plus interest (132,000 million gold marks) and £50 million was paid almost immediately. However, hyper-inflation forced Germany to withhold payments in 1922 and in retaliation French and Belgian troops occupied the Ruhr. The DAWES PLAN, providing for annual payments of 2,000 million gold marks, was introduced in 1924. The payments were reduced under the 1929 YOUNG PLAN, which gave Germany until 1988 to complete payment.

In 1931 the international financial collapse (*see* DEPRESSION) made it impossible for Germany to pay and in spring 1932 it was decided at a conference in Lausanne to cancel all further reparations. By this time Germany had paid just over one-eighth of the sum originally demanded, but had received more than this in foreign loans. The extraction of enormous sums from defeated nations was criticized by leading economists, including J.M. Keynes (1883–1946) who pointed out that the difficulties caused to Germany would dislocate the entire pattern of international trade. Reparations, greatly resented in Germany, proved a useful subject for NAZI propaganda.

repartimiento. (1) In 16th-century colonial Latin America, a labour system on the Caribbean islands similar to the later one of concessions, itself akin to the mainland's ENCOMIENDA.

(2) In colonial Mexico, a system of forced labour similar to the Peruvian MITA in which natives were divided into districts and government depots established to provide them with necessaries. Outrageous extortion ensued, with officials forcing commodities on the natives which they did not want. Difficult to administer, the system could only recruit unskilled labour on a rotational basis, and was further hindered by the great decline in the native population in the 16th century. In the 17th century its operation was limited first to food production, urgent public works and mining, but as food production and mining came to rely heavily on PEONAGE, repartimiento was further restricted in 1632 to public works and mining and then solely to public works. In the late 18th century serious unrest, caused partly by the system, contributed to its abolition.

Repealers. Followers of Daniel O'Connell who agitated from 1825 onwards for repeal of the Union of Ireland and Britain.

republic. State not ruled by a monarch, for example the USA. The head of state is usually a president who may or may not play a political role or be democratically elected.

Republicans. Members of one of the two major US political parties. The Republican Party was founded in 1854 by an alliance of National Republicans (ex-DEMOCRATS who favoured high tariffs) and northern Democrats, both groups opposed slavery. The first Republican president was Abraham Lincoln, who took office in 1861. With short intervals (1885–89, 1893–97, 1897–1901) the Republicans held the presidency until 1912. In the 19th century it was the party of high tariffs, US expansionism and a strong federal government. Its power lay in an alliance of the industrial east which wanted tariffs and the agricultural west where it granted free land to the farmers.

In the 1920s the party believed in ISOLATIONISM but today it favours a vigorous foreign policy. Republicans are generally held to be more right-wing than Democrats, though some are more progressive than many members of the Democratic Party.

requeté (Span., recruit). Name given particularly to a recruit to the CARLIST cause in Spain; also applied to a member of the Carlist regiments who supported Gen. Franco during the Spanish Civil War.

rescate (Span., ransom). Purchase of Indian slaves from other Indians in the Latin American colonies. In the Spanish colonies it ended with the outlawing of slavery in 1542, but it continued in Brazil until the mid-18th century. The equivalent Portuguese term is *rezgate*.

reselection. Political process whereby the representative of a constituency must answer to his constituents or to his local political party at the end of each term of office. If his conduct has not been satisfactory, some other person may be chosen as candidate in the ensuing election. The process prevents a candidate from being selected for life or until retirement and makes him more dependent on the wishes of his local party organization. *See also* RECALL.

residencia (Span.). Review of an official's conduct at the end of his term in Spain's American colonies, designed to ensure high standards of efficiency and to enforce Crown control.

Resistance, the. Popular name for the opposition to German occupying forces in World War II, particularly in France. In January 1942 the 'Free French' movement began to co-ordinate resistance groups and in May 1943 the National Council of Resistance met in Paris. In September 1943 resistance forces liberated Corsica (*see* MAQUIS). Resistance agents in France provided intelligence prior to the Allied landings in Normandy in June 1944, and hampered German troop movements by destroying railways and bridges.

Resolutioners. *See* REMONSTRANTS.

responsible government. The granting by the colonial government of the management of domestic affairs to an elected government chosen by settler groups. First granted to New Zealand and Canada in the mid-19th century, Britain retained control over constitutional affairs, foreign relations and international trade.

Restoration. The restoration of the English monarchy, secured in 1660 by the accession of Charles II to the throne. It was the result of Gen. George Monck's obtaining the self-dissolution of the RUMP of the LONG PARLIAMENT and its consent to the election of the CONVENTION PARLIAMENT which met in April, accepted Charles's Declaration of Breda and recalled him in May. The Restoration settlement had a number of facets. The Act of Indemnity and Oblivion provided for Crown revenues and a land settlement; DIVINE RIGHT was deprived of its absolutist powers and the PREROGATIVE was limited by acts passed between 1640 and 1642. Prerogative courts and arbitrary taxation were not reinstituted. The religious settlement involved the restoration of the Anglican Church, the Clarendon Code against those who rejected the 1662 Prayer Book, the success of the EPISCOPACY and the downfall of PRESBYTERIANISM. Between 1661 and 1663 the militia was reconstituted, but parliament would not countenance more than the nucleus of a standing army. Following the Restoration, the propertied classes increased their power by gaining control of parliament and of local administration.

revanche (Fr., revenge). Term used particularly to refer to the desire of the French to win back Alsace-Lorraine, ceded to Germany in 1870; restored by the Treaty of Versailles in 1919; lost again to the THIRD REICH in 1940 but liberated in 1945.

revanchism. Policy based on vengeance.

revisionism. Term applied by orthodox MARXISTS to attempts to reassess the basic tenets of revolutionary socialism. The term originated in

Germany during the 1890s and 1900s where the chief exponents of revisionism were Edouard Bernstein and Karl Kautsky. Revisionism has always been treated as heresy in the USSR, but with the advent of Gorbachev to power this situation has changed.

ribbonism. Agrarian movement in the south and west of Ireland c1869, whose main purpose was to agitate for security of tenure. Its methods, initially innocuous, soon degenerated into terrorism.

Riding (deriv. ON, a third part). Unit of local government in the DANELAW. The old kingdom of Lindsey in Lincolnshire was divided into north, south and west ridings; Yorkshire into east, west and north ridings.

Right deviationism. A faction in the Soviet Communist Party in 1927–28 led by Bukharin, Rykov and Tomsky which, while accepting Stalin's proposals for industrialization, urged a gradual approach and rejected too forceful a move against the KULAKS and the NEW ECONOMIC POLICY. Effectively removed from influence in 1929, the three leading spokesmen were later killed in Stalin's PURGES.

Rigsdag. The old Danish parliament consisting of two houses: the Landsthing, made up partly of elected, partly of ex-officio members; and the Folkething, elected on universal suffrage. Since 1953 there has been only one chamber, the Folkething, whose members are elected every four years.

Rising Sun. The emblem of the Japanese flag, hence, by association, Japan or Japanese policies.

Risorgimento (Ital., resurrection). Name given to the movement for Italian unification in the 19th century whose intellectual origins lie in the immediate post-Napoleonic period. The expression was first used by Cavour in 1847. The movement culminated in the proclamation of the Kingdom of Italy in March 1861, followed by the acquisition of Venetia in 1866 and of Rome in 1870.

rissaldar (Hind.). Native commander of an Indian cavalry regiment.

robot (Czech., forced labour). (1) System of forced labour, similar to the CORVÉE, which operated in Bosnia and Herzegovina when they were under Turkish rule. It was abolished by the Austrians in 1892.
(2) A mechanical person, from a play by a Czech playwright Karel Capěk (1923).

Rocardism. The attempt by the French Socialist Prime Minister Michel Rocard to create a progressive consensus after the May 1988 general election by sharing power with centre parties. Non-socialist ministers were allocated half the government posts, but although the policy was encouraged by President Mitterrand it appeared to divide Socialist supporters.

Rohosz. In old Poland, a self-constituted assembly of nobles which took the lead in calling the nobility to arms if it became necessary to force the king to accede to their demands.

Roi Soleil (Fr., sun king). Sobriquet of Louis XIV of France.

rois fainéans (Fr., idle kings). Name applied to the later MEROVINGIAN kings of France who took little part in government and left almost all public affairs to the MAIRE DE PALAIS.

Romanism. An expression, often used pejoratively, for the Roman Catholic church.

Romanov. The family of German or Prussian-Lithuanian origins which ruled Russia from 1613 to 1917. Tsar Nicholas II, who abdicated on 13 March 1917, was the last of the dynasty to rule and was executed with his family at Ekaterinburg on 16/17 July 1918.

Rome-scot. Another name for PETER'S PENCE.

rônin (Jap., wave man). A Japanese SAMURAI who had ceased to owe allegiance to a feudal lord. In the 16th century there were very many of them: some became hired swashbucklers, others fell in the social scale and entered a trade. A socially disruptive force, they were a threat to the government and in 1651 were responsible for an abortive rebellion.

Rosicrucians. Mystical society, supposedly founded by Christian Rosenkreuz in the 15th century, which attempted to find a theoretical link between the ancient Egyptian religions and Roman Catholicism, drawing ritual and philosophy from both. It barely survived the death of its founder but has since been revived by various rival factions of which the best known is the Rosicrucian Order founded by the American H. Spencer Lewis. The Order preaches the Brotherhood of Man, the reincarnation of the soul and the immense latent potential of the human mind. It advertises extensively and is deeply involved in business activities.

rotos (Span., broken ones). In Chile, the landless, rural poor; also more loosely, the poorer classes in general.

rotten borough. In England, borough constituencies which, though seriously depopulated, continued to send Members of Parliament to Westminster until the 1832 Reform Act. The term comes from Chatham's description of borough representation as the 'rotten part of the Constitution'. Such boroughs were often controlled, through bribery or local influence, by powerful patrons who could virtually choose the MP to be elected. The worst examples were Old Sarum, Dunwich, Galton, Rye and Winchelsea. The almost synonymous term 'pocket borough' described the constituencies in the gift or 'pocket' of such patrons.

roturiers. In feudal France, purchasers of land from feudal lords, whose descendants became ennobled after they had possessed the land for three generations. The custom of ennoblement by possession of land was abolished by Philip the Fair (1285–1314) and thereafter roturiers remained a class distinct from the nobility.

Roundhead. Term of derision given during the English Civil War by ROYALISTS, who usually wore ringlets, to PURITANS and members of the parliamentary party who wore their hair cut short.

Royalists. Those who supported Charles I during the English Civil War (1642–49); also known as CAVALIERS.

Ruckversicherung (Germ.). Secret treaty between Russia and Germany, securing the contracting parties mutually against invasion by Austria. It was signed in 1887 after the Austro-German alliance and remained in force until 1890. Its existence was revealed by the *Hamburger*

Nachrichten (which was under the control of Bismarck) and was not denied by the German government.

rugged individualism. Policy of the US REPUBLICAN party in the 1920s, stressing that the strong would compete and survive and that everyone else should look after themselves as best they could. Associated with a LAISSEZ-FAIRE attitude, it meant that the government intended to interfere very little in US business.

Rump. Members of the LONG PARLIAMENT not expelled in PRIDE'S PURGE, who voted to try Charles I and who declared the COMMONWEALTH. They fell into two groups: men of principle devoted to religious toleration or to a republic, and a corrupt element. The two were united only in resisting a dissolution of parliament. The army, tired of the Rump's inefficiency and corruption, wanted a more representative parliament to vote regular taxes for its upkeep. Accordingly, on 20 November 1653, Cromwell's troops ejected it and the BAREBONES PARLIAMENT took its place. The expulsion, termed the 'interruption', divided soldiers and civilians in the republican ranks. On 5 May 1659, following the fall of the PROTECTORATE, the army recalled the Rump in an attempt to secure political stability. The Rump tried to assert control over the generals and was expelled in October 1659 before a final recall in December. Gen. Monck (1608–70) forced it to readmit the members excluded by Pride. The reconstituted parliament dissolved itself on 16 March 1660 to make way for the CONVENTION.

runes (deriv. ON, secret lore). Characters of an early Germanic alphabet found cut into buildings and implements of stone or wood in many parts of northern Europe. The runic alphabet originally had 24 letters and scholars believe that some of the characters are derived from Greek and Latin.

Russification. To make Russian in culture, language, customs, etc. Both under the TSAR and communist rule, attempts have been at Russifying the national minorities of the Russian empire and the USSR to prevent regionalism and a break-up of the state.

ruytergeld (Du.). In feudal Holland, a tax paid in lieu of military service, similar to SCUTAGE.

Ryotwari (Urdu). System of land tax collection in India under the British RAJ, in which peasants were treated as the proprietors of their land and paid taxes directly to the government. It contrasted with the ZEMINDARI system, which developed from one used under the Mogul emperors, under which a *Zemindar* was responsible for collecting a district's taxes.

S

SA (Germ., abbrev. *Sturmabteilung*, storm-troopers). Paramilitary unit which supported Hitler in his rise to power, founded in 1920–21. The distinctive 'brownshirt' uniform which gave them their nickname dates from August 1921, when a 'Gymnastic and Sports Division' was set up within the NAZI party to organize youth. Many of the recently disbanded FREIKORPS joined and on 5 October 1921 the movement adopted the name Sturmabteilung. Under its first leader, Klintzsch, the SA fought a number of pitched battles with socialists and communists and by autumn 1923 it numbered 15,000. Members were paid out of party funds and increased with unemployment in the late 1920s and early 1930s. In September 1930 the Berlin SA mutinied to protest over pay and express discontent with the party leadership. Hitler restored authority and made himself supreme SA leader, appointing Ernst Röhm as Chief of Staff SA in January 1931.

By 1933 the SA numbered 400,000 and proved increasingly difficult to control once Hitler had become Chancellor on 30 January 1933. Its members had always been strong exponents of socialism and were eager for a true shift of wealth and power in German society: they expected a 'second revolution' with Hitler in power. Röhm saw the SA primarily as a military force, thus incurring suspicion from the regular army. Hitler, eager to gain the support of the army, ordered the NIGHT OF THE LONG KNIVES in June 1934 to break the power of the SA. After this the SS became the most powerful body in the Nazi Party.

sac and soc (OE). In medieval England, words used in charters that granted freedom from the jurisdiction of the HUNDRED, usually connected with a grant of land. From this arose the private jurisdiction of feudal lords over their own estates and the townships that grew up on them. Such grants were common before the Norman conquest; although the two words are first found together in 956, the concept of private jurisdiction predates this by some time.

sachem (Amer. Ind.). (1) Supreme chief of an American Indian tribe.

(2) A member of the governing council of the League of the Iroquois.

Sadat Initiative. Declaration by Pres. Sadat (1919–81) of Egypt of his willingness to explain the Arab position on the Middle East before the Israeli KNESSET, brought on by Egypt's mounting economic crisis resulting

resulting from her high level of defence expenditure. The Israeli Prime Minister Menachem Begin (b. 1913) accepted the offer and Sadat visited Israel on 19-21 November 1977. The two leaders agreed to pursue contacts and to find some means of representing the Palestinians at negotiations which would be acceptable to Israel: the first tacit recognition by an Arab head of state of Israel's sovereignty. Sadat's initiative was condemned by the PLO, Syria, Libya and Algeria, and his continuing quest for peace in the Middle East was the major cause of his assassination in 1981 by members of his own army. Further negotiations took place between Israeli and Egyptian representatives in Egypt, Leeds Castle, Kent, and CAMP DAVID.

saga (ON). A Norse chronicle recounting the exploits of Viking chiefs, the earliest dating from the 6th century.

St. Andrew's House. The building housing the Scottish Office in Edinburgh.

St. Simonism. Political system of the Comte de St. Simon (1760–1825), founder of French socialism. His ideal system called for the abolition of the hereditary principle and the vesting in the state of the means of production. Workers were to be rewarded individually according to their capacities rather than receive equal divisions of the fruits of production.

SALT. Strategic Arms Limitation Talks between America and the Soviet Union beginning in November 1969 and ending in May 1972 with a treaty restricting anti-ballistic missile development. A second round opened in November 1974 but proved less successful and the US withdrew from further discussions in May 1982.

samizdat (Russ.). Literature critical of the communist state, written by Russian DISSIDENTS in great secrecy, and circulated by hand from one person to another. The authorities strongly disapprove of it and strict penalties are imposed on those who are caught.

Samuelites. The 33 Liberal Party followers of Sir Herbert Samuel (1870–1953, Home Secretary 1931–32) who went into opposition against the National Government when Samuel resigned on 28 September 1932 in protest against the imposition of tariffs under the Ottawa Agreements.

samurai (Jap., attendant). Term which came to denote the warrior class of feudal Japan which emerged in the provinces in the 9th and 10th centuries. Its members usually belonged to the local aristocracy. In the Tokugawa period (1603–1867) the samurai class was subdivided hierarchically into a large number of sub-classes which become hereditary, with the SHŌGUN, the DAIMYOS and the Karos (house elders) at the top. From the 17th century onwards, the samurai class gradually became scholars rather than soldiers but they did not discard their martial code and personal loyalty to their lords. Although their special legal position as a class was abolished after 1868, the samurai retained a dominant influence in government, the police and the army.

sanbenito (Span.). Long garment of yellow cloth enforced on penitent heretics by the Spanish Inquisition.

sanctions. An economic BOYCOTT of a country by other countries. As an economic weapon, sanctions were the chief means of coercion by the League of Nations on countries that were thought not to be fulfilling their international obligations. Under Article XVI of the League's covenant sanctions were imposed on Italy in October 1935 following her invasion of Ethiopia. Embargos on oil, iron and steel were not applied, however, and the League did not disrupt the trade of Italy's non-League trading partners, so the sanctions proved ineffective. They were lifted permanently in July 1936.

Rhodesia's unilateral declaration of independence under Ian Smith in 1965 led Britain and the United Nations to impose economic sanctions which were initially expected to topple the régime within weeks. But evasion by individual companies proved difficult to eradicate and their effectiveness was questionable.

sanctuary. In England, the right claimed by the Church since Anglo-Saxon times to afford protection to criminals and others seeking refuge in churches and consecrated precincts. After 40 days the coroner would enter the sanctuary and impose an oath on the fugitive that he would abjure the realm. Some sanctuaries, however, such as those at Ripon, Durham and Beverley, provided a permanent refuge that allowed a fugitive to defy the law indefinitely. In 1486 judges ruled that sanctuary could not protect second offenders and those accused of treason. The powers of sanctuaries were further drastically curtailed in the reign of Henry VIII (1529–40). Sanctuary in criminal cases was abolished in 1623 and in civil cases by acts of 1697 and 1723.

Sandinistas. The radical Sandinista Liberation Front which conducted guerrilla warfare in Nicaragua against General Anastasio Somoza, ousting him in July 1979. Widely supported in the unions, middle classes and the Church, the Sandinistas were in a majority on the post-revolutionary Council of State, a majority confirmed in elections held in 1985.

Sanfedisti. Secret society established in Naples in the early 19th century with Papal approval, to support the Catholic Church and to oppose the CARBONARI.

sans-culottes (Fr., without breeches). Name used by Parisian militants to signify that they were manual workers, who wore trousers rather than the kneebreeches of polite society. Between 1792 and 1794 the name referred to a specific group of political activists who were attempting to put pressure on the Convention through the mobilization of local clubs and assemblies.

sansculottides. Name given in honour of the SANS-CULOTTES to the complementary days at the end of the year in the French Republican calendar. The expression was outlawed by the National Convention on the adoption of a constitution in 1795.

Saracens. Name given in the first three centuries AD to Arab tribes in Syria and adjacent territories. By Christians it was applied to Arabs in general and later to Moslems, especially those fighting in the CRUSADES in Syria, Palestine and Egypt in the 11th, 12th and 13th centuries.

SAS. Special Air Services, an élite regiment in the British army which developed out of the Long Range Desert Patrol Group formed during World War II. The regiment is unorthodox in its tactics and structure and is deliberately surrounded by secrecy. Entry into it depends on passing severe endurance tests; on joining, members must surrender all previously held commissions. In action the regiment operates in small teams, each member having some speciality.

The regiment came to public prominence in April 1980 when it successfully stormed the Iranian embassy in London, which had been taken over by 7 gunmen who took 24 people hostage. Six gunmen were killed and one captured. Members of the SAS also played an important role in recapturing the Falkland Islands from the Argentinians in 1982. The SAS have featured in many of the killings of PROVISIONAL IRA members both in Ulster and elsewhere (e.g. the killings of three IRA terrorists in Gibraltar in 1988).

satyagraha (Sansk.). The political policy of passive resistance associated with Gandhi.

Savak. Iranian secret police under the rule of the Shah, dispersed following the Islamic revolution and the expulsion of the Shah in 1979. Many of its former members were murdered by the people in revenge for crimes of torture and murder.

Saxe-Coburgs. Sovereigns who reigned in Britain from 1901 to 1917. Albert (1819–61), Prince Consort of Queen Victoria, was prince of the Duchy of Saxe-Coburg and Gotha in Germany; his family name was Wettin. Their son Edward VII (b. 1841), the first sovereign of the Saxe-Coburg dynasty, ruled between 1901 and 1910. He renounced his rights to Saxe-Coburg and Gotha which passed to his younger brother in 1893. Edward's second son George V (b. 1865) succeeded him in 1910 and reigned until 1936. However, he changed his name to Windsor in 1917

in deference to anti-German feeling generated by World War I.

SBS. Special Boat Service, the Royal Naval equivalent of the SAS. It played a large role in recapturing the Falkland Islands in 1982.

scabini. In medieval France, the twelve judicial assessors chosen by the owners of ALLODIAL LAND to accompany each count to the general assemblies summoned by the early French kings.

scalds (ON). Bards.

Schlieffen Plan. Plan designed in December 1905 by the Chief of the German General Staff, Gen. Count Alfred von Schlieffen (1833–1913). Although constantly revised over the next nine years, it formed the blueprint for the German attack in the west in August 1914 at the start of World War I.

Schoolmen. Those who, from the mid-9th century onwards, attempted to reconcile Christian beliefs with the philosophy of Aristotle and Plato. From the time of Augustine, philosophy, like science, had received little attention, but interest in Greek philosophy revived in the 9th century in an attempt to use it to justify Church teaching. Interest increased in later centuries as western Europeans came into contact with the Islamic world which had already absorbed Greek science and philosophy. Among the more famous Schoolmen are the Irish-born John Scotus Erigena (c800–c877); St. Anselm, Archbishop of Canterbury (1033–1109); Peter Abelard (1079–1142) who had a school in Paris; his contemporary, Bernard of Chartres; and St. Thomas Aquinas of Naples (1225–74).

The philosophies of the Schoolmen, closely integrated because limited by the Church, are known as 'scholasticism'. Some of their great internal arguments were those between the orthodox Realists, headed by Aquinas (who held that the world of appearance is illusory and that ideas, forms or universals are the true realities beyond matter and appearance) and the Nominalists (who held 'universals' or abstract concepts to be mere names without any corresponding realities). There were also arguments between the Ancients, comprising the Thomists who followed Aquinas and the Scotists who followed John Duns Scotus (c1265–1308), and the Terminalists, followers of William Occam, a Nominalist. In the late 15th century all became reconciled to meet the threat of the philosophy of humanism, expounded by Erasmus of Rotterdam (1466–1536).

Schrecklichkeit (Germ., frightfulness). Deliberate policy of committing atrocities to subdue a subject people.

scot and lot (ME). In later medieval England, payments by burgesses as borough and national taxation, corresponding to modern rates. Liability to pay scot and lot came to be regarded as a qualification for the burghal FRANCHISE.

scot and lot boroughs. In England, parliamentary constituencies in which the franchise depended on payment of the poor rate or the church rate, the equivalent of the earlier SCOT AND LOT. In some, the franchise depended simply on residence and on proof that the voter had not been a charge on the poor rate, thus giving the vote to a large proportion of the inhabitants. Before the Reform Act of 1832 about 60 such boroughs existed.

Scrap of Paper. German Chancellor Bethmann Hollweg's description of the 1839 Treaty of London, a five-power guarantee of Belgian neutrality which Germany violated by invasion on 4 August 1914, provoking a British declaration of war. He told the British ambassador that 'just for a scrap of paper, Great Britain is going to make war on a kindred nation which desires nothing better than to be friends with her.'

scrivener (ME, scribe). In medieval England, clerks who wrote documents for private individuals in the same way as CURSITORS wrote writs. They specialized in simple documents such as BONDS; the money they received was placed out again at interest or used to raise money on production of security to give to those in need of loans.

scrutin d'arrondisement (Fr.). In France, a single-member electoral constituency. After forming his ministry in 1881, Léon Gambetta began campaigning to replace such constituencies by *scrutins de liste*, voting on a departmental basis. In January 1882 he resigned on the rejection of his proposals but the 1885 elections were conducted on the new system.

scutage (deriv. Lat., shield; *also* escuage). In medieval England, a money payment extracted by feudal lords from their vassals in lieu of personal military service. Originating in the late 11th and early 12th centuries, from the late 12th century it was assessed at a fixed sum and enabled the king to hire mercenaries for his foreign wars and to dispense with the services of his barons. However, the sovereign's right to extract scutage was restricted by MAGNA CARTA and was difficult to collect because of complicated divisions of fees. It was last levied in 1327.

SDI. Strategic Defense Initiative announced by President Reagan in March 1983 when he revealed that research was being undertaken into the feasibility of protecting the United States from nuclear attack by destroying incoming missiles with satellites outside the atmosphere. Denying any aggressive intent, Reagan offered to share the technology with other powers.

Sea Beggars. *See* BEGGARS OF THE SEA.

sea-dogs. English privateers of the early Elizabethan period who preyed on French commercial shipping in the Channel. They sailed under LETTRES DE MARQUE granted by Condé and the French HUGUENOTS. These were withdrawn after reconciliation between the Huguenots and Catholics and the sea-dogs then joined the Dutch 'BEGGARS OF THE SEA' in attacking Spanish shipping instead.

Seamless Garment. A united Ireland, the demand and aspiration of Irish nationalists in both Northern Ireland and the Republic. At present the 'seam' is the border around the SIX COUNTIES.

SEATO. South East Asia Treaty Organization, established by the Manila Treaty on 8 September 1954 and signed by Australia, Britain, France, New Zealand, Pakistan, the Philippines, Thailand and the USA. It was an attempt to emulate NATO, providing for collective action by the signatories if one of them was attacked or weakened by internal subversion. France and Britain sought from the start to avoid any long-term commitment and both countries refused to accept that the treaty applied to Vietnam, Laos and Cambodia. On 7 November 1973 Pakistan formally withdrew and on 30 June 1974 France followed suit. In September 1975 it was agreed at a meeting in New York that the organization would gradually be closed down due to the changed conditions in the area.

Second Empire. The rule in France of Louis Napoleon (1808–73) from 2 December 1852, which effectively ended with his capture in the Franco-Prussian war on 3 September 1870. Voted in as 'Prince-President' of the SECOND REPUBLIC in December 1848, Louis Napoleon was elected Emperor by 8 million votes to 250,000 in a plebiscite.

Second Front. Following the German attack on the Soviet Union in June 1941 Stalin asked Britain to launch an invasion in Western Europe to ease the pressure on Russia. Churchill was reluctant without long preparation, despite a vigorous 'Second Front Now' campaign in Britain in 1942. The Second Front – agreed at the Quebec Conference in August 1943 – opened with the Normandy landings on 6 June 1944.

Second Republic. Proclaimed in France on 25 February 1848 on the overthrow of Louis Philippe. The 1848 JUNE DAYS weakened the Republic's moderate democrats and the representative of reaction Louis Napoleon was overwhelmingly elected 'Prince-President' in December. In 1851 he mounted a coup which led to the end of the Republic on 2 December 1852. *See* SECOND EMPIRE.

Second Reich. *See* THIRD REICH.

Sectaries. Puritan extremists in the fragmented church during the English Civil War who stressed their inner light and the hearing of divine voices, including ANTINOMIANS,

BAPTISTS, FIFTH MONARCHY MEN and RANTERS.

sede vacante (Lat.). Vacancy of a bishopric, used particularly of the papal see.

seignurie (Fr.). Estates of a French feudal lord.

seisin (ME). Feudal term denoting possession, rather than ownership, of a freehold estate in land. The concept, probably dating from Anglo-Saxon times, was later extended also to goods and chattels.

Seljuk. The dynastic house originating in Turkey which dominated the eastern Moslem Empire from the entry of its forces into Baghdad in 1055 until the death of Sanjar in 1157.

selski starosta (Russ.). In Russia, the village elder, elected head of a MIR.

Sendero Luminoso (Peruvian, 'Shining Path'). Marxist guerrilla movement founded as the Communist Party of Peru in 1970. Its title derives from a declaration by José Carlos Mariátegui, an earlier Peruvian Marxist, that 'Marxism-Leninism will open the shining path to revolution.'

Senead Éireann (Ir.). The Irish senate in the OIREACHTAS, or parliament, consisting of 60 members, 11 nominated by the TAOISEACH and 49 elected variously by the National University of Ireland; the University of Dublin; and panels of candidates representing national language and culture, literature, art, education, agriculture, labour, industry and commerce, public administration and the social services. Elections must take place within 90 days of the dissolution of the DÁIL ÉIREANN.

Senussi. Moslem religious fraternity, founded at Fez *c*1830 by Mohammed es-Senussi, which spread over northern Africa and was a powerful force for the unity of African Moslems.

separatists. Those who believe that a particular area or group should be detached from a larger whole. Examples are those in Quebec who favour severance from the rest of Canada, and those in the Basque country who favour independence from Spain.

Sepoy (Anglo-Ind., deriv. Urdu, horseman; *also* Sipahi). An Indian serving in the army of the British RAJ. From an early date, the British found sepoys superior on their own territory to troops recruited in Britain. They mutinied frequently: at Vellore in 1764 and 1806; at Barrackpur in 1824, 1844, 1850 and 1857. Most of these uprisings were due to disputes over wages, except for the 1857 mutiny which was sparked by religious causes.

Seppuku (Jap; 'self-disembowelment'). The ritual method of suicide – also known as HARI-KARI – practised by members of the SAMURAI class in feudal Japan. Officially abolished in 1873.

Septembrists. Portuguese democrats who in September 1836 demanded the abrogation of the Charter of 1826 and a return to the democratic form of government established by the Constitution of 1824. In 1852 they reached a compromise with the supporters of the Charter.

serjeant at law. In medieval England, a professional introduced to conduct legal cases because of the increasing complexity of common law. Attorneys-in-law represented their principals while narrators undertook oral proceedings; by the early 14th century narrators had become serjeants. They formed a guild with offices in St. Paul's Cathedral, London; it was called the Order of the Coif after their white caps that were fastened under the chin. Though small in number, they exercised great legal authority. The Order of the Coif was dissolved in 1877.

serjeanty. Term denoting a wide range of feudal tenures given in return for service; the holders were called serjeants. Some performed military service or paid SCUTAGE and others gave service in the king's household, such as the king's DISPENSER, his tailor and the keeper of the Fleet Prison. Some of these services were negligible and the greater serjeanties were of little importance except at great feasts. In later years lawyers drew a distinction between Grand Serjeanty and Petty Serjeanty, but both were abolished in 1922.

Shadow Cabinet. Alternative government formed by the leadership of the opposition party in Britain. A fundamental tenet of British parliamentary democracy is the right of an opposition to organize itself and to oppose the government of the day, while still remaining loyal to the Crown and the constitution. Another important principle is that the Queen's government should always be carried on. The major opposition party in parliament therefore appoints spokesmen to put forward its policy on matters covered by each department of state. Hence there are spokesmen on foreign affairs, defence, etc., who act as 'shadows' to the government's foreign secretary, minister of defence and other cabinet ministers, and arguing the alternative policy of the opposition against that of the government. Should the government fall unexpectedly, the Shadow Cabinet would be immediately able to form a true cabinet and thus continue the government of the country.

Shakers. Members of a revivalist group, the United Society of Believers in Christ's Second Appearing, which seceded from the QUAKERS in 1747. In 1758 Ann Lee, a young convert from Manchester, claimed to have had 'revelations' that she was the female Christ. 'Mother Ann' became leader of the sect and in obedience to her prophetic visions set out with nine followers to find 'Emmanuel's land' in America. She located it in New York state near Albany where the group lived communally, gaining prosperity and the reputation of good agriculturalists and craftsmen. They held that God had a dual role, the male principle becoming incarnate in Christ and the female in 'Mother Ann'. The sexes were equal and women preached as often as men. Their nickname was given to them in ridicule of their involuntary movements in moments of religious ecstasy. The movement declined after 1860.

shaman. Medicine man who used magic to cure the sick and protect the community from evil spirits. Found in all primitive societies, the shaman was a man apart who wore distinctive dress to signify his authority. Shamanism still exists in primitive cultures who practise magic through incantations, self-torture, trances and dances.

SHAPE. Supreme Headquarters, Allied Powers in Europe; the headquarters of NATO, originally at Fontainebleau, but in Brussels since 1966.

sheikh (Arab.). Chief or headman of a family, tribe or village.

sheriff (deriv. OE, shire + reeve). Title which superseded the designation of reeve in 11th-century England, and denoted a royal officer charged with administering the royal DEMESNE in a SHIRE. He was the deputy of the EALDORMAN until the latter was replaced in the 11th century by the EARL; he then became a central figure in local administration. Appointed by the Crown, he controlled the FYRD, performed legal duties and accounted to the EXCHEQUER for revenues from royal demesnes. The office was open to abuse and in the late 12th century a number of sheriffs were dismissed and some of their powers transferred to new officers who were elected by the shires. The office declined with the development of new courts and administrative techniques; today the sheriff's powers are largely of a ceremonial nature.

Shi'ites (Arab., faction). Adherents of Shi'ah, an heretical Moslem sect in Iran, who maintain that Ali, the son-in-law of the prophet Mohammed, was his true successor. They are opposed by the orthodox SUNNIS who accepted the succession of Omar.

Shin Bet. The name of the Israeli secret service.

Shintoism (Jap., way of God). A Japanese splinter version of Buddhism with a strong bias towards ancestor-worship and the divine powers of natural forces. Unusually, it has no recognized founder nor written dogma. It permeated Japanese life in a most vigorous way until the country's defeat in 1945. It was disestablished by the American occupying forces after 1,500 years and Emperor Hirohito 'abdicated' his divine powers. Recently interest in Shintoism has revived as many Japanese have become dissatisfied with the aims and methods of their highly industrialized society.

Ship money. In England, originally an occasional tax on port towns in lieu of the provision of ships for the royal navy. It was extended inland by Charles I in 1635, ostensibly to provide revenue for protection against Algerian pirates and Dutch aggression; in reality it was to provide him with revenue to build up the navy without recourse to parliament. In 1637 John Hampden brought a test case against ship money but by the narrowest of margins the judges decided in favour of its legality. It was abolished by Parliament in 1641.

shire (OE *scir*, care or charge). The main unit of local government in medieval England. It was assessed for taxation at a round number of HIDES and was the basis of the FYRD. Originally administered by the EALDORMAN, it was later run by the SHERIFF on behalf of the EARL, each a representative of the Crown. The shire court, presided over by the local bishop and earl or sheriff dealt with lay and ecclesiastical cases and with administration. The shire itself was sub-divided into HUNDREDS and WAPENTAKES. Most shires were in existence by *c*1000 and their boundaries have altered little since.

Shōgun (Jap., abbrev. of *Sci I Tai Shōgun*, barbarian-conquering great general). Japanese title, originating between the 8th and 11th centuries, given to Minamoto Yoritomo in 1192. It had been held by most heads of the government in feudal Japan and after 1192 it became hereditary. The dynasty of Tokugawa Jyeyasu, who was of Minamoto ancestry, held the office from 1603 to 1867, during which time the Shōgun usurped the functions of temporal ruler from the MIKADO. The division was restored along with imperial rule in 1868. When relationships with the west first began, the Shogun adopted the title of Tycoon (Great Prince).

Short Parliament. Parliament which sat between 13 April and 5 May 1640, summoned by Charles I, with the intention of securing funds for the BISHOPS' WARS. But parliamentary leaders such as John Pym (1583–1643), Lord Saye and Sele (1582–1662) and John Hampden (1594–1643), were already in touch with the Scots and had no intention of voting funds until the king had redressed various grievances. Charles dissolved parliament, had the leaders arrested and turned to Ireland and the CONVOCATION for aid.

show trial. Trial to which great publicity is given for propaganda purposes, held in a way that appears just but with the verdict predetermined. Show trials were numerous in the USSR during the Stalinist PURGES.

shuttle diplomacy. Mediation between conflicting parties which involves constant travel by the representative from one antagonist to the other in order to arrive at a settlement.

Sick Man of Europe. Nicholas I of Russia's description in the 1850s of the OTTOMAN Empire, which he dismissed as 'a sick man dying'. His plans for its division in the event of a sudden collapse aroused British suspicions of Russian motives, setting the scene for the Crimean War in 1854.

Siegfried Line. Originally, the defences between Lens and Rheims on the German WESTERN FRONT in September 1918; later, the defences built to emulate the MAGINOT LINE which the NAZIS believed invulnerable. Not as extensive as the Maginot Line, it was strong enough around Saarbrücken to resist French attacks at the beginning of World War II. American forces reached this German line of defence in the west on 1 February 1945; British and Canadian forces broke through it the same month, crossing the Rhine near Millingen in the northern sector where the line was weaker on 8–9 February.

signa (Lat., *signa crucis*, sign of a cross). Mark used to authenticate documents in an age of illiteracy, used in England from the 8th century and in Europe from earlier times. The names of guarantors were written at the foot of a document where they added an autograph cross. The sign was eventually replaced by a seal.

signet (deriv. Lat., sign). A single-sided seal introduced into England during the reign of Edward II (1307–27), which gave its name to the documents on which it appeared. Today, secretaries of state are vested with office on receiving their signets from the monarch.

Sikh (Hind. deriv. Sansk., disciple). Member of a sect founded by Nanak (1469–1538) with the aim of uniting Moslems and Hindus. Nanak condemned the formalism of both Hinduism and Islam and preached a gospel of universal toleration and the unity of the Godhead. The Moghul Emperor Akbar (1542–1605) accepted his ideas and allowed the Sikhs to build a centre at Amritsar (*see* GOLDEN TEMPLE), to compile their sacred writings (the Adi Granth) and to improve their organization.

In the 17th century a fanatical Moslem became emperor and under their leader Govind Singh (1666–1708) the Sikhs became warriors to protect themselves. Govind Singh instituted a number of ceremonies: admission to the fraternity was by special rite; caste distinctions were abolished; hair was worn long; and the word *singh* ('lion') was added to Sikhs' original names. The Sikhs were organized into 12 *misls* (confederacies) but internal divisions soon appeared.

With the rise of Ranjit Singh (1780–1839), a single, powerful Sikh kingdom was established. Anglo-Sikh wars followed in 1845–46 and 1848–49 and ended with Britain's annexation of the Sikh commonwealth of the Punjab. Up to the independence of India, the Sikhs proved loyal British subjects. During the 1980s, demands by Sikhs for an independent homeland (Khalistan) brought violence to the Punjab.

Silk Roads. The routes from China to the west which by the 13th century had become traditional lines of travel for traders from the Middle East and along which early western travellers, including Marco Polo, made their way to China.

Simonites. The 23 followers of Sir John Simon (1873-1954, Foreign Secretary 1931-35, Home Secretary 1935–37, Chancellor of the Exchequer 1937–40), who left the Liberals in support of protectionism to form the Liberal Nationals on 5 October 1931, going on to win 35 seats in the 1935 General Election.

simony. In medieval times, the presentation of a person to an ecclesiastical benefice in return for money, gift or other reward, named after Simon Magus who offered Peter and John money for the power of the Holy Spirit (Acts 8: 18–24). Although much condemned, simony was common. Since the Church itself controlled estates and derived profit from them, it could be argued that a lord with a right of presentation to a benefice was also entitled to a share in its profits.

Sinarquismo (Span., without anarchy). Title of a Mexican FASCIST movement founded in 1936 with the aim of basing the state on Catholic principles and eradicating anticlericalism, communism and liberalism. It desired an authoritarian form of government, was in favour of Franco and antagonistic towards the USA. By 1940 it claimed to have a million members, but in 1944 it split into two factions, a non-political body and the Popular Force Party. Today its successors have little influence.

Sindhia. Title of the old Mahratta rulers of Gwalior in India, a dynasty founded by Ranoji Sindhia in the early 18th century.

Sinn Fein (Ir., ourselves alone). Irish nationalist movement founded by Arthur Griffith in 1902, originally with the aim of securing political and economic independence from Britain by peaceful means. He was superseded by the more militant leaders Connolly, Pearse and Plunkett who organized the 1916 EASTER RISING in Dublin. The subsequent execution of those involved gave the movement its first martyrs.

In 1918 Sinn Fein won 73 parliamentary seats under the leadership of de Valera, who was himself in prison together with 35 other candidates. They refused to go to Westminster, establishing instead the DÁIL ÉIREANN in Dublin in 1919, after which time the party regarded itself as being at war with Britain. After HOME RULE in 1920, it split in 1922 between those such as Griffith who accepted the Irish Free State and those under de Valera who wished to fight on through the Irish Republican Army. The party virtually disintegrated, but from 1969 onwards recovered influence as the IRA's political wing. Its electoral successes in the 1980s have greatly troubled the British Government which has responded by forbidding the media to interview members of Sinn Fein.

Sioux. The largest of the Great Plains tribes of American Indians whose relations with the advancing whites were generally peaceful until 1854 but who – after a series of clashes including Little Big Horn in 1876 and the massacre at WOUNDED KNEE in 1890 – were forced onto reservations.

Sirdar (Hind., military leader). Term applied to the British commander-in-chief of the Egyptian army.

situationism. A left-wing 'critique of everyday life' made by the Situationist International, which was formed in 1957, collapsed in the early 1970s, and had an affinity with COUNCIL COMMUNISM. Situationism advocated a revolutionary overthrow of capitalism based not on traditional political methods but on total rejection in every sphere of what it saw as consumer society's banality. Situationist slogans were prominent in the MAY EVENTS and its rhetoric has influenced the European left.

Sitzkrieg. Ironic pun on the German term BLITZKRIEG to describe the period of military inactivity on the Western Front between September 1939 and May 1940, also known in Britain as the PHONEY WAR.

'Six, the'. Name given to the members of the EEC prior to the entry of Britain, Denmark and Ireland in 1973.

six counties. The counties of Northern Ireland: Antrim, Armagh, Down, Fermanagh, Londonderry and Tyrone. With Cavan, Donegal and Monaghan they formerly comprised the province of Ulster, but in 1921 these three were made part of the new dominion of Ireland. The six counties remain part of the United Kingdom and it has always been the ultimate aim of the IRA to secure their detachment from Britain and integration in a united Ireland.

Six Day War. 5–10 June 1967. Provoked by an Egyptian naval blockade of its shipping in the Gulf of Aqaba, Israel shattered Arab air power with bombing raids on Egypt, Iraq, Jordan and Syria on 5 June; occupied the West Bank of the Jordan and destroyed Egyptian armour in Sinai on 7 June, advancing to the Suez Canal; and took the strategic Syrian Golan Heights.

Sixth Fleet. The United States naval presence in the Mediterranean since the end of World War II.

Skinners. Bands of American marauders who made attacks on the east bank of the Hudson River during the US War of Independence (1775–8).

skippet. Box, similar to a HANAPER, which held single documents.

Skoptsi (Russ.). Schismatic religious sect in Tsarist Russia whose members practised self-mutilation, interpreting literally the scriptural injunction, 'If thine eye offend thee, pluck it out'.

Skuptschina. The National Assembly of Serbia.

Slavophiles. Small group of nationalist Russian intellectuals in the 1840s and 1850s, who rejected the belief that Russia should follow western paths of development and aimed instead at the restoration of an idealized pre-Petrine form of Russian society. Part of their ideal was that the authority of the Tsar should be personal and patriarchal.

slush fund. Money obtained from undeclared sources used by a US Congressman to maintain his office and for other administrative expenses.

Smith Square. The location in Westminster, London of Conservative Central Office and, until 1978, of Labour Party headquarters at Transport House (now moved to Walworth Road).

Sobranje. The National Assembly of Bulgaria.

socage (ME). In England, feudal land tenure free from military or knight service. Such tenures, which had varying degrees of freedoms, were held in return for a certain service or a rent which could either be large or nominal. Lands held in socage were alienable and could be divided among all heirs, although gradually primogeniture was adopted. In 1660 all feudal tenures (with a few exceptions) were turned into free and common socage. *See also* GAVELKIND.

social contract. (1) Political concept probably best expounded by the French philosopher Jean-Jacques Rousseau (1712–78) in his work *Le Contrat Social* (1762), though certain strands implicit in it had earlier been suggested by Thomas Hobbes (1588–1679) and John Locke (1632–1704). The theory argues that at an early stage of human development men tacitly agreed to surrender their personal freedom of action in return for rights which society would protect. These rights were therefore inalienable though for various reasons they were no longer fully acknowledged. ('Man is born free and everywhere he is in chains'). It was therefore quite legitimate to take action to restore in full these human rights and create a just society. Critics point out the absurdity of supposing that an actual contract was ever made anywhere and argue that 'rights' are an artificial legal device.

(2) In Britain, an agreement between the 1974-79 Labour government and the Trades Union Congress reached back in 1973 under which the unions agreed to measures designed to control inflation in return for the abolition of the Pay Board and associated statutory controls on pay, repeal of the 1971 Industrial Relations Act, and acceptance of the concept of a 'social wage'. The social wage took account of the general living standards of the population, to improve which the Labour Party promised food subsidies, price controls and increased payments towards old-age pensions. Inflation was for a time brought under control but in 1977 both sides broke the agreement, effectively ending the contract.

social credit. Concept developed by Maj. C.H. Douglas and William Aberhart that economic ills are the result of an insufficient money supply and that monetary reform increases prosperity. They postulated an 'A' + 'B' theorem in which prices equall A + B where A equal payments to individuals in wages and salaries and B equals payments by producers (for bank charges, raw materials, etc.) to other producers and represents working capital. Since working capital B cannot be consumed, only A creates purchasing power. The A payments represent national income and A + B represents prices: purchasing power, therefore, is always deficient by B and the gap is made up by repayable loans from the banks. As total prices exceed total income there is overproduction.

The social credit movement argued that banks should place the new money they create each day in the hands of consumers. Retailers would sell at a loss and that loss plus commission would be credited to their bank accounts. Prices would be arranged so that A payments could cover all goods for sale. Alternatively, a national dividend related to the overall level of economic activity could be paid to everyone, thus increasing purchasing power. The theory has been dismissed as inflationary and obsessed with circulation rather than production problems.

Social Darwinism. A school of thought which holds that the evolutionary process described in DARWINISM is equally applicable to human society, influential before World War I, arguing that only by constant moral, physical and economic development could a society maintain both its internal cohesion and its defences against competing societies. *See also* EUGENICS.

Social Fascist. Communist term of abuse towards Social Democratic and Labour Parties from 1928 to 1934, reflecting the Comintern view that moderate socialists who were rivals for working-class support were 'the left wing of Fascism'. *See* CLASS AGAINST CLASS.

socialism. Social system under which there are no economic divisions but an approximation to a classless society, with the means of production owned and controlled by the community and the productive effort directed to public not private good. The economic system of communal control requires either a democracy or the dictatorship of the proletariat.

There are many 'schools' of socialism. Modern socialism perhaps began with the writings of Babeuf during the French Revolution, which had great influence on the utopian socialists in mid-19th century France who described non-existent but perfect economic and social systems. In Britain the word came into use in 1834 in relation to the model community at New Lanark run by Robert Owen (1771–1858), which was based on CO-OPERATIVE lines. In 1848, with the advocation in France by Louis Blanc of the establishment of ATELIERS NATIONAUX, socialism emerged as a political factor in Europe. Blanc was opposed by Proudhon (1809–65), an ANARCHIST who favoured a more flexible system of co-operativism and people's banks. Also in 1848, Karl Marx published his *Communist Manifesto* (*see* COMMUNISM). In Britain, a CHRISTIAN SOCIALIST movement was founded by Charles Kingsley (1819–75) and others, but the intervention of Marx set socialism on a different road of class struggle and revolution. Russia, China, Cuba and other countries have followed this revolutionary path.

In western Europe, however, Social Democratic parties have emerged, such as the British Labour Party, which believe that socialism can be achieved without revolution. Its roots partly founded in FABIANISM, the Labour Party exemplifies the view that by education, people can be brought to realise the economic and social advantages of socialism and will vote for it. This theory is denied by communist parties which hold that it merely confuses the issue and delays revolution.

World War I and the Russian Revolution of 1917 marked the break in socialism between these two wings. Socialist parties of the school of MARXISM-LENINISM normally adopt the title communist though in the 19th century the two terms were synonymous.

Socinians. Followers of Laelius Socinus, who founded a sect in 1560 with doctrines similar to those of the later UNITARIANS. They attracted many adherents in Poland and in 1658 the Diet of Warsaw proscribed them, after which they gradually declined.

Soft-shell Democrats. Section of the New York Democratic Party between 1848 and 1854 which opposed slavery.

soke (ME). An association in the DANELAW in which rights of private jurisdiction, SAC AND SOC, were exercised. Arising from the personal commitment to a particular lord made by Danish freemen who invaded England in the 9th century, the rights were at first based on personal ties rather than on land, but later came to be dependent on land. Occupants of land that formerly belonged to members of the soke themselves fell under the jurisdiction of the lord. Soke tenants were freemen, could sell their land by their own choice and could be scattered through a number of villages, but remained under the lord's private jurisdiction. Sokes began to disappear by the late 11th century but some lasted until the 18th century.

sokemen (*also* sokmen). In the DANELAW, freemen owing suit to the lord's court or SOKE.

Solemn League and Covenant. *See* COVENANTERS.

Solidarity. Name given to Poland's National Confederation of Independent Trade Unions, formed on 8 September 1980 under the leadership of Lech Walesa and representing 10 million industrial workers. Rural Solidarity was formed later in the year representing 500,000 farmers. Solidarity grew out of the workers' reactions to rising food prices during 1980. Throughout the summer of 1980 industrial unrest worsened Poland's economic crisis.

However, the growing power and political confidence of Solidarity unnerved the authorities while the impossibility of stepping up food production angered the union. In early 1981 Gen. Jaruzelski replaced Pinkowski as prime minister and in October also replaced Stanislaw Kania as party leader. In December, amid rising tension, the army took control. Solidarity was banned and its leaders imprisoned (Walesa was later released in 1983). Despite this crackdown, Solidarity has continued throughout the 1980s both to exist and to represent the voice of the mass of the workers in Poland.

solidité (Fr.). System of taxation in 17th-century France whereby a peasant was held responsible for his neighbour's taxes even if he had paid all his own.

Solid South. Political term used in the USA to refer to the fact that the southern states have always tended to support the DEMOCRATS. A wavering in this support occurred in the late 1960s when the south hoped that the REPUBLICANS would give greater support to STATES' RIGHTS and less to implementing CIVIL RIGHTS legislation. A major attraction of the Democrats has been their willingness to provide farm subsidies.

Presidential elections in the 1980s suggest that support for the Democrats in the south is declining.

Sonderbund (Germ.). League formed in December 1845 by the seven Catholic Swiss cantons of Lucerne, Uri, Schwyz, Zug, Underwalden, Fribourg and Valais to resist attempts by radicals to strengthen the central authority of the Federal Government. The Federal Diet condemned the league as a secessionist movement and after a brief civil war in November 1847 it was dissolved.

soul scot. In Anglo-Saxon England, the custom of making a gift from the goods of a deceased to the parish priest. Later the term was used loosely to denote all bequests made for religious purposes.

soutane (Fr.). Cassock or long-buttoned coat worn by Roman Catholic ecclesiastics.

Southcottians. Followers of Joanna Southcott (1750–1814) who revealed that, although over 50, she was about to give birth to a divine human being called Siloh (Rev. 12: 1–2). After a hysterical pregnancy no child, human or divine, appeared and Miss Southcott died soon afterwards of what would appear to have been a broken heart. She left behind a number of sealed boxes which, she indicated, contained among other things the secret of the universe. They were to be opened a hundred years after her death. One of them turned up in 1927 and was publicly opened at Caxton Hall, London, but contained only a few coins, a horse pistol, a woman's nightcap and a slightly improper novel called *The Surprises of Love*. A tiny sect of Southcottians, however, still survives.

South East Asia Treaty Organization. *See* SEATO.

South Sea Bubble. Overvaluation and subsequent slump in the value of the shares of the South Sea Company in 1720. This joint-stock company was floated in 1711 with the intention of trading largely in slaves with the Spanish colonies of South America. In 1720 parliament accepted its offer to assume responsibility for much of the national debt, the result of which was a huge rise in share prices. Their rapid collapse left many bankrupt, and involved three government ministers in charges of corruption. Two mistresses of George I (1660–1727) were also implicated, but the political skill of the paymaster-general Walpole (1676–1745) averted a royal scandal. The 'Bubble Act' was passed in the same year to regulate the formation and activities of joint-stock companies.

soviet (Russ., council). Russian administrative system. Workers' soviets originated in the 'October Revolution' of 1905 and reappeared in 1917 as key organs of the revolution and later of the national administrative machinery. Prior to 1936 a hierarchical system of soviets characterized Russian government, lower soviets electing the higher indirectly, e.g. district soviets chose regional soviets which in turn chose state soviets. The system was held to guarantee the participation of the masses in the political system, which was marked by the unity of executive and legislative power and by close links between state and local authorities. Indirect elections were abolished under the 1936 Constitution and all soviets are now directly elected by the people, whatever their level.

sovkhoz (abbrev. Russ. *sovietskoye khozyaistro*, soviet farm). State farm in the USSR, state-owned and run by state employees. In the 1950s there were 4,000 sovkhozes and the AGRO-GORAD was designed to further the system. *See also* KOLKHOZ.

Spanish Main. Correctly, the mainland between the Orinoco and the Isthmus of Panama; the term is often used incorrectly to refer to the Caribbean.

Spartacists. A group of radical German socialists, active from early summer 1915, who founded the German Communist Party (KPD) in 1918. Following a week of street violence in Berlin in January 1919, their leaders were either imprisoned or murdered by members of the FREI-KORPS. The Spartacists were led by Rosa Luxemburg and Karl Liebknecht, both of whom opposed what they saw as the REVISIONIST tendencies of the German Social Democratic Party. Their name was taken from that of Spartacus, leader of a slave revolt against Rome in 73 BC.

speakeasy. Premises used for the illegal sale of liquor in the USA during the PROHIBITION era.

special relationship. A term used chiefly in Britain for the relationship between Britain and the United States which is alleged to go beyond diplomatic expediency by virtue of its underpinning by historical and sentimental links of culture and kinship.

Speenhamland System. System of poor relief introduced in 1795 by JUSTICES OF THE PEACE in Berkshire sitting as local government administrators at Speenhamland (Newbury). It was gradually adopted in most areas of England and Wales although historians are divided as to how fully it was implemented. Its broad design was that the wages of rural labourers should be supplemented from parish rates according to the size of their family and the price of wheat. The result was a fall in wage rates and the pauperization of labourers, together with an increasing strain on the rates. This form of outdoor relief was abolished with the reform of the POOR LAWS in 1834

Speronists. Followers of Ugo Speroni of Piacenza, who founded a minor sect preaching a heretical doctrine of predestination and rejecting the sacraments and doctrine of original sin. They were condemned by Pope Lucius III in 1184.

Spetznatz. The Soviet equivalent of the British Special Air Services. *See* SAS.

Sputnik. Russian space satellites. Sputnik I, the first man-made satellite, was launched on 4 October 1957 and Sputnik II containing a dog followed a month later. Sputnik III, launched in May 1958, carried a fully-equipped space laboratory.

squadrismo. The activities of Italian nationalist youths, ex-servicemen and unemployed workers who formed gangs in the early 1920s to attack socialist and Catholic premises and individuals, to break strikes and who occupied the disputed territories of Fiume and Trentino in 1922. They were absorbed into Mussolini's Fascist Militia in 1923.

SS (Germ. *Schutzstaffeln*, guards detachment). Initially a small group of 200 men, aged 18–20 and drawn from the SA, who acted as a personal bodyguard to Hitler. They wore black uniforms and were known as blackshirts. In 1928 Hitler appointed Himmler as chief of the SS and it rapidly expanded; by February 1934 it had over 20,000 members. Goering, head of the GESTAPO, gave the SS a free hand to plot the downfall of Röhm, head of the SA. On 1 April 1934 Hitler was made head of the Gestapo; since he was also Reichsführer of the SS this placed the Gestapo under SS control. In June 1934 the SS was responsible for the murders of the NIGHT OF THE LONG KNIVES and thereafter became completely independent of the SA.

In 1932 a security service, the SD (Sicherheitsdienst), had been formed by the SS to ensure the loyalty of NAZI party members. In 1934 it became an intelligence unit of the secret police, with 3,000 full-time members and 100,000 'part-time' informers. In 1935 the first concentration camps were opened and the duty of guarding them was given to the SS; in 1936 the entire German police force was placed in SS hands.

When war broke out in 1939 the SS formed its own fighting units, the WAFFEN SS. The loyalty and fanaticism of SS members made these fighting units an élite, but the atrocities committed by other units has earned the SS a notorious reputation.

Stadtholder. Office in the Low Countries introduced in the 15th century by the ruling Burgundian dukes and retained by their Habsburg successors. Stadtholders – who were initially noblemen – acquired wide powers in the UNITED PROVINCES of the Netherlands including presiding over assemblies and commanding provincial armies. The office was abolished by French revolutionary armies who occupied the territory in 1795 with Dutch support.

Stahlhelm (Germ., steel helmet). Para-military organization, active in WEIMAR Germany, founded by Franz Seldte at Magdeburg in 1918. By 1930 it had 500,000 members. The Seldte wing of the Stahlhelm were moderate nationalists on good terms with Stresemann's Deutsche Volkspartie. But by 1924 a radical element led by Theodore Duesterberg had become powerful enough to push the

Stahlhelm into violent anti-republicanism and opposition to the 1929 Young Plan. In 1931 it helped organize the 'Harzburg Front' to unite national opposition to the Weimar republic. Duesterberg ran for the presidency against Hindenburg and Hitler in 1932 but Seldte entered Hitler's cabinet in January 1933 and proved a loyal minister. Having initially approved this action, Duesterberg later changed his views and began attempting to obstruct Hitler's chancellorship. In April 1933 he was removed from his post of second Büdesführer (league leader) in the Stahlhelm. Hitler's order to Seldte to liquidate the organization was carried out by November 1935.

Stalinism. Stalin's revolution from above to build 'Socialism in One Country', forced agricultural COLLECTIVIZATION laying the basis for rapid heavy industrial development. It was carried out in an atmosphere of intense nationalism and increasingly arbitrary rule exerted through a bureaucracy and was connected with Stalin's PERSONALITY CULT and the brutal political purges of the 1930s. Latterly, but often inaccurately, a general description of the régimes in the Soviet Union and its East European satellites.

stalking horse. A candidate fielded in American elections to draw votes from a rival to enable a preferred third candidate to win or to cover the appearance of a more significant candidate.

staller (ON, place man). Title used for important officials in the English royal household after the Danish invasion of 1016; it disappeared after the Norman invasion of 1066.

Stalwarts. Section of the US Republican Party, led by Senator

Conkling of New York, which opposed President Garfield in 1881 on civil service reform. Garfield was assassinated by the Stalwart Guiteau, who gave as his reason the wish to reunite the Republican Party which he believed Garfield had split.

stannaries. Tin mines of Cornwall and Devon, technically the property of the Crown, which may only be worked under royal licence.

staple. In medieval England, name given to the country's chief products, especially wool, and also to certain towns in Europe where these commodities were alone permitted to be sold. In 1294, for example, Edward I made Dordrecht the staple for wool: all wool was exported and sold to foreign buyers there, thus facilitating the collection of customs. The wool staple was later moved to Malines (1295), Antwerp (1296), St. Omer (1314) and Bruges after 1325. In 1336 Edward III appointed 14 English towns as home staples and prohibited English ships from exporting wool: it had to be collected by foreign buyers at the home staples. In 1363 the staple moved to Calais where the export and sale of wool was vested in a monopoly established by 26 merchants known as the Company of Merchants of the Staple. With the fall of Calais in 1558 the continental staple moved to Middelburg, then to Bruges, but in 1617 the export of English wool was declared illegal and the staple permanently abolished.

Star Chamber Court. Court of law which met in the Star Chamber of Westminster Palace; it developed from the king's council and heard subjects' petitions. In existence by 1487 (possibly earlier), it was originally charged with the duty of trying offences against the Crown. Henry VII (1457–1509) made extensive use of it to restore order after the Wars of the Roses (1455–85) extending its jurisdiction into a court of first instance rather than that of appeal and encouraging plaintiffs to appear before it. Charles I (1600–49) used it to harry his opponents and it was abolished by parliament in 1641.

Stars and Stripes. The flag of the USA which consists of 13 stripes, signifying the 13 original states of the Union and 50 stars, representing the present states. When a new state accedes to the union a new star is added.

START. Strategic Arms Reduction Talks between the USSR and the USA, begun in Geneva on 30 November 1981. Following the refusal of the US Senate to ratify the agreement reached in SALT II, the USSR refused to enter further negotiations on arms control. But in July 1980 Chancellor Schmidt of West Germany visited Moscow and persuaded the USSR to modify its stance. It agreed to further bilateral talks with the USA but with the proviso that no new agreement could be made until SALT II was ratified. Shortly before the talks started Pres. Reagan made his zero-option proposal.

Star Wars. *See* SDI.

state capitalism. Lenin's description of the compromise made with financial interests in 1918 to ensure BOLSHEVIK survival, while simultaneously reinforcing central control over the economy. More recently, a pejorative description of Soviet socialism in which a privileged bureaucracy is said collectively to dominate economic life with the same relationship to the working class as employers under private capitalism.

states-general. National assembly in which the chief 'estates' of the realm were represented in separate bodies. The parliament of the Netherlands retains the name though not the form of the older assembly. It has two chambers, a first chamber of 75 members elected for six years by the provincial Diet and a second of 150 members elected for four years by universal suffrage.

The government of France up to 1789 provides a good example of the original 'states-general', consisting of the three estates of nobility, clergy and commons and first summoned in 1302 by Philip IV to gain support from the bodies represented in his quarrel with Pope Boniface VIII. It met rarely as the French monarchy became more powerful and not at all between 1614 and 1789. Louis XVI then assembled it in an attempt to quiet the growing unrest in France, but as soon as it met it declared itself a National Assembly, a decision which marked the start of the 1789 revolution.

states rights. Political doctrine in the USA that individual states retain sovereignty over their internal affairs and do not surrender it to the federal government, rejecting the clause that makes the Constitution the supreme law of the land, subject only to interpretation by the Supreme Court. The doctrine, popular in the southern states, was a major factor in opposition to the implementation of constitutional amendments on CIVIL RIGHTS.

Statute of Labourers. Act passed in England in 1351 in consequence of the labour shortage occasioned by the BLACK DEATH which had allowed labourers to demand higher pay. The statute specified that wages were not to exceed those that were standard prior to the Black Death

and that all landless men under 60 years of age had to accept work at those rates. Obviously the statute was unpopular with labourers, but it also displeased employers who were prohibited from competing for the labour they required. Bitter opposition to the statute led to the PEASANTS' REVOLT.

Steelboys. Irish secret agrarian society founded in 1772, mainly active in Down and Antrim, especially on the estates of the Marquis of Donegal, where wholesale evictions had occurred. A number of outrages took place; to ensure judicial impartiality it was necessary to try defendents in Dublin.

Stormont. The building housing the Northern Ireland Parliament until the imposition in 1972 of direct rule from London. The location of the Northern Ireland Office and, in 1973–4, of the Northern Ireland Assembly.

Stormtroopers. *See* SA.

Storting (Norw.). Parliament of Norway consisting of 150 representatives elected every four years by proportional representation. They select a quarter of their own number to form the Lagting (upper house); the other three-quarters forming the Odelsting (lower house). Questions relating to laws are discussed by each house separately; other matters are discussed by both together.

Stranniki (Russ,). Sect of religious ascetics, active in Tsarist Russia, who emerged in the reign of Catherine II. They opposed military service, refused to recognize secular authority or to pay taxes, and believed the TSAR to be the Antichrist.

Strelitzi (Russ.). Semi-professional,

semi-military body stationed c1535 by Ivan IV in Moscow and other major Russian towns to repel Tartar incursions. Following their revolt in 1697 under Peter I, they were disbanded, their power broken and many of them killed.

Stuart. The Scottish dynasty which provided England with its monarchs from 1603 to 1688 (James I, Charles I, Charles II and James II) during a period of revolutionary transition – including the beheading of Charles I and the overthrow of James II – between TUDOR personal rule and HANOVERIAN parliamentary government. *See* JACOBITES.

Stundists (Russ.). Dissenting Russian religious sect which objected to the ikon-worship of the orthodox church.

Sturm und Drang Zeit (Germ., period of storm and stress). Phrase used to describe the late 18th century when the French Revolution led many people to criticize existing institutions and Europe was convulsed in war.

subahdar (Urdu). Chief native officer in command of a company of natives (SEPOYS) in the Anglo-Indian army, roughly equivalent in rank to a captain.

subinfeudination. In feudal times, practice adopted by holders of hereditary FIEFS of making grants of land to sub-vassals on terms similar to those on which they themselves held land, thus extending the feudal system to its fullest development.

Sublime Porte. The high gate in the wall of the main governmental building in Constantinople. The name was used by extension to refer to the government of the OTTOMAN empire.

subsidy. (1)In medieval England, a grant to the Crown over and above customary revenue. The first was in the reign of Edward I and took the form of a tax on movables; under Edward III wool was taxed at the rate of an additional 40s on each sack exported above normal duties. In 1514 lands and goods were taxed ('the Tudor Subsidy') and in the reign of Charles I parliament imposed a tax levied at 4s in the pound on real property and 2s 8d in the pound on property to meet the Crown's demands for money. Aliens and Catholic RECUSANTS had to pay double the standard rate. Subsidies may still be granted to the monarch by parliament on occasions of urgency.

(2) The term is now used more generally to denote a range of payments, such as made from revenue by parliament to producers of goods for the purpose of preventing factory closures or unacceptable price rises.

Sudras (Sansk.). The fourth and servile caste among Hindus since the first millenium BC. It actually comprises a number of true castes some of which are 'clean' and whose members cause no pollution to members of higher castes, and some of which are 'unclean' and therefore subject to various degrees of discrimination.

Suffragette. A member of the Women's Suffrage Movement, which agitated for the extension of the franchise to women in Britain and was responsible for a number of criminal offences prior to 1914. Led by Mrs. Emmeline Pankhurst, her daughters Sylvia and Christabel, Mrs. Fawcett, Annie Kenney and others, many of them were imprisoned for crimes against property and subjected to the extreme discomfort and indignity of being forcibly fed during prison hunger-strikes. The role of women during World War I led to British women aged 30 and over being given the vote in 1918; in 1928 the age limit was reduced to 21, the same as for men.

In the USA, the Women's Suffrage Association was founded at Cleveland, Ohio, in November 1869; it merged with Susan Brownell Anthony's 'National Woman's Suffrage Association' in 1890. Women were given the vote in Wyoming (1889), Colorado (1893), Idaho and Utah (1896) before the 19th Amendment of the Constitution (28 August 1920) under President Wilson extended the franchise to all women nationwide.

Suffragists. Advocates of the extension of the suffrage to women. The rivals of the militant SUFFRAGETTES.

sulung (OE). In early medieval Kent, a measurement of land equal to the area which a plough-team of eight oxen could cultivate in a year – possibly 200 acres of arable land together with rights of pasture. It later served as a unit of tax assessment.

summit conference. Personal meeting between heads of government of major powers, normally in time of war or international tension, but also to discuss matters of long-term common interest. Such conferences had for many years been common practice before Winston Churchill (1874–1965) coined the phrase in February 1950 by calling for a 'parley at the summit'.

sumptuary laws. Laws which outlaw or restrict consumption of goods. The most famous 20th-century example is the Prohibition Amendment Act to the US Constitution which banned the manufacture, sale and transportation of alcoholic drink from 1919 to 1933.

Sun King. *See* ROI SOLEIL.

Sunna (Arab., custom). Term used to refer particularly to the deeds and practices of Mohammed which gradually came to denote Moslem orthodoxy as distinct from the heterodoxy of the SHI'ITES. The sunna of Mohammed affords a code of conduct which complements the injunctions of the KORAN. Its adherents are known as SUNNIS.

Sunnis. One of the two great Moslem sects (*see* SHI'ITES), the 'orthodox' believers who accept the SUNNA as well as the KORAN.

Supermac. Nickname of Harold Macmillan, British Prime Minister 1957–63. A cartoon by Vicky in the *Daily Express* on 6 November 1958 portrayed Macmillan as Supermac, a pun on Superman. Intended as an ironic commentary on his deft political touch, it became a central part of Macmillan's image, one which rebounded as his government drifted into crisis in 1962–63.

Super Tuesday. The key day when the most important PRIMARIES take place during the run-up to the American presidential election.

Supplicants. In England, those who signed the Supplication in 1637 opposing attempts to force a new prayer book on the Scottish Church. After 1638 they were known as COVENANTERS.

Supremacy, Acts of. (1) Act of 1534 establishing Henry VIII as head of the Church of England in place of the Pope and giving him control of church doctrine, ecclesiastical appointments and church income. It was repealed during the Catholic 'reaction' in the reign of Queen Mary (1553–58).

(2) Act of 1559 establishing Elizabeth I as supreme head of the Church of England. The British monarch is still head of the Church of England although in March 1982 a joint Anglican-Roman Catholic Commission suggested that eventually the Pope should become 'universal primate' of both churches.

supremo (Span.). Military overlord or commander-in-chief.

Sureté (Fr.). French criminal investigation department, equivalent to Britain's Scotland Yard.

suspending power. PREROGATIVE of the Crown to suspend a statute, used by Charles II and James II to relax the penal laws against Catholics and DISSENTERS in 1672, 1687 and 1688. It was abolished by the BILL OF RIGHTS.

suttee (Hind.). Ancient custom by which widows were burnt on the funeral pyres of their dead husbands. Lord William Bentinck's government made the practice illegal in India in 1826; during the 1850s it was put down by the Viceroy, Lord Dalhousie.

suzerainty. The control by one state of another which nevertheless retains an element of internal autonomy. Derives from 'suzerain', a feudal overlord.

swainmote (ME, attendant - *mote*. In early Norman England, the court of the forest freemen, modelled on the SHIRE MOOT or county court.

SWAPO. South West Africa People's Organization for Namibia, founded in 1960 by Sam Nujoma and Herman Toivo Ja Toivo. In 1920 the League of Nations gave Namibia (South West Africa), which had previously been a German colony, to South Africa as a MANDATE. From 1948 the South African government sought ways to integrate it into its other sovereign lands; in 1964 it was suggested that the territory be divided into BANTUSTANS and a 'White homeland' consisting of 70 per cent of the territory.

During the late 1950s nationalist sentiment had grown amongst the majority Ovambo tribe of Namibia and SWAPO was one of a number of organizations founded. It was immediately banned and its leaders driven into exile but since 1966 has mounted guerrilla actions against South African military units. In 1966 the UN general assembly passed a resolution revoking South Africa's mandate over Namibia and in 1971 the UN recognized SWAPO as 'the sole authentic representative of the people of Namibia'.

Elections for a Namibian National Assembly were boycotted by SWAPO in 1978 and South Africa remained in effective control of the country. By 1989, however, important progress towards an independent Namibia had been made.

Swaraj (Sansk., self-government). The Indian agitation movement under the British RAJ led by Gandhi.

Swarajya. Self-Government Party, founded in India in 1922 with the aim of reasserting the control of the CONGRESS PARTY over the Indian legislature following the failure of the movement of non-co-operation with the British authorities. Its leaders, C.R. Dois, Motilal Nehru and Vithalbhai Patel, hoped to force concessions from the colonial power by obstructing parliament. In the 1923 elections the Swarajists became the largest party in the central assembly and gained control of a number of the provincial assemblies, but only in Bengal and the Central Provinces did they have the power to obstruct business. In November 1924 Gandhi recognized them as the legislative wing of the Congress Party, but he found it difficult to approve of their tactics until they accepted his 'constructive programme'. Indeed, in 1926 a group centred on the Bombay and Central Provinces left the party in protest at its obstructionism, badly damaging the party. In 1929 its activities ceased, but it was revived, with Gandhi's blessing, to conduct the Congress Party campaign in the 1934 central assembly elections.

swastika (Sansk., well-being or luck). Ancient religious symbol, in the shape of a hooked cross, linked in European mythology with the revival of interest in Germanic legends at the end of the 19th century. It appeared on the helmets of the Erhardt Brigade, a body of FREIKORPS active in the Kapp PUTSCH of 1920. A number of extreme right-wing groups in interwar Germany adopted it and it was chosen by Hitler as the emblem of National Socialism. In September 1935, with Hitler in power, it became NAZI Germany's national emblem.

syndicalism. Form of SOCIALISM based on the theory of ownership and control of industry directly by the workers, rather than the more common doctrine of ownership and control by the state. Syndicalism would abolish the state, replacing it with a federation of units based on functional economic organization as opposed to geographical representation. Syndicalists have sought to further workers' interests by direct action in the form of strikes, industrial sabotage and working to rule, rather than through parliamentary procedures. Hence they have been linked with ANARCHISTS and are sometimes termed anarcho-syndicalists. Prior to 1914 the movement was strong in France, Italy, Spain, Mexico and Argentina, and exercised considerable influence on the British guild socialists. After World War I many syndicalists became communists or FASCISTS. Georges Sorel influenced syndicalism with his concept of the 'myth of the general strike', an emotive image and ideal goal aimed at stirring the passions rather than appealing to reason. Mussolini substituted the myth of the state for that of the general strike as a means to mobilize revolutionary forces.

In Britain, syndicalism in the trade unions was crushed in the 1920s by union leaders such as Ernest Bevin, who feared that if workers were directly involved in running their industries they would limit their powers in traditional union areas such as wage negotiations.

syndicat (Fr., trade union). The basic unit of syndicalist activity (see SYNDICALISM).

T

Taal. A form of Dutch spoken in Boer areas of South Africa, corrupted through intercourse with the native races and because of the high proportion of non-Dutch among early immigrants.

Tables, The. Group of four representative committees which virtually assumed control of Scotland in 1637 and organized the resistance to Charles I's religious innovations. They consisted of four members of each of the four classes of nobles, lesser barons, clergy and burgesses and were chosen by the SUPPLICANTS originally with the object of bringing about agreement between Archbishop Laud and the PRESBYTERIANS. *See also* COVENANTERS.

Taborites. Sect of militant HUSSITES, led by John of Zisca, whose name was taken from Tabor, their fortress and base south of Prague which was founded in 1420. They began as a religious movement with eschatological expectations, preaching the abolition of almost all the visible Church and practising a primitive communism. Drawing their strength from the rural areas and the lower orders, they later developed a political and military organization that proved essential for Hussite success.

Tackers. Extreme Tories who in 1704 tried unsuccessfully to secure the passage through parliament of the Occasional Conformity Bill by TACKING it on to the Land Tax Bill which the Lords could not reject without stopping supply.

tacking. Constitutional device used in the British parliament by which controversial matter is included in a vital money bill in order to get it accepted. *See* TACKERS.

tactical voting. A voting decision based on support for the candidate who appears to have the best prospect of defeating a least preferred candidate rather than party loyalty. Although such voting has taken place in British by-elections there is little evidence of it having been significant in general elections.

Tadpole and Taper. Two unscrupulous politicians, characters in Benjamin Disraeli's novel *Coningsby* (1844). Both unprincipled office-seekers and also party managers, one worshipped organization and the other a 'cry' or attractive policy in their search for votes. It is possible that they were based on two actual politicians Charles Ross and Alexander Pringle. As a leading opponent of repeal of the CORN

LAWS, Disraeli was seen to portray the Conservative Prime Minister Peel (1788–1850) and his followers as popularity-seeking traitors to TORY principles. When Disraeli later became Prime Minister (1868 and 1874–80) his prestige and his widespread political writing resulted in the phrase 'Tadpoles and Tapers' being widely used to denote timeserving and vote-seeking politicians.

Taff Vale. In July 1901 the House of Lords granted the Taff Vale Railway Company an injunction against the Amalgamated Society of Railway Servants for damages caused by picketing in an official strike, enabling the company to win £23,000 compensation. The result, seen as an attack on the right to strike, encouraged increased union support for the Labour Representation Committee, the forerunner to the Labour Party, and prompted a Liberal Government to give unions immunity from similar actions by the 1906 Trades Disputes Act.

Tag, der (Germ., the day). German expression for the start of World War I and hence of German military hegemony in Europe.

taille (Fr.). A tax in France which took two forms, personal and 'real'. Personal taille, a direct tax levied from the 15th century to 1789, was assessed on personal possessions at a rate determined by the tax collector. Because the First and Second Estates together with many of the Third Estate (*see* TIERS ÉTAT) were exempt, it bore heavily on the peasantry. 'Real' taille was levied over a similar period in the Midi and south-west of France and fell on common land. Less arbitrary than personal taille, it raised more revenue.

tallage. In medieval England, a tax paid by VILLEINS that was levied at the lord's will and based on special assessment. It was usually a means of financing military campaigns. Royal tallage was levied on the ancient DEMESNE, particularly the boroughs and towns. Parliament abolished tallage in 1340 but by then new taxes such as AIDS and SUBSIDIES had largely replaced it as a source of revenue.

tally. In medieval England, a wooden peg notched with cuts representing various monetary units that was used as an accounting device. When notches indicating the value of a transaction had been cut, the peg was split down the middle, and the two parts given to the creditor and debtor. When the debt was paid the parts were reunited to check that they tallied and were then kept by the debtor.

talukdar (Urdu). Hereditary revenue collector in the Indian state of Oudh, who received land taxes from a particular district and paid them to the government. In 1856 under the British RAJ, the government, represented by Lord Dalhousie, began collecting the taxes directly from the villages, thereby dispossessing many talukdars of a profitable living. Their system closely resembled that of the ZEMINDARS. *See* RYOTWARI.

Tammany. Headquarters of the Democratic Party in New York county and a political term used to signify 'machine' control of the political process and the corruption that goes with it. The Society of St. Tammany was founded as a club in 1789 but by the early 1800s had become a political organization. It came to exert a very powerful influence over New York politics, particularly after 1860 when William Marcy Tweed made it the city's dominant organization.

In the 19th century Tammany made itself responsible for the welfare of European immigrants and thus secured their votes, but usually, when the Democrats were in office, the leaders of the organization used their power to fill prominent positions with their own followers and to exact bribes for concessions and privileges. Tammany rule therefore became synonymous with large-scale corruption and most Tammany 'bosses' became very wealthy. Its control extended beyond the city to embrace New York state government and until 1932 it had an important and sometimes decisive role in Democratic politics.

Tamworth Manifesto. Name given to a speech made by Sir Robert Peel (1788–1850) in his constituency of Tamworth, Staffordshire in 1834. Peel's speech enunciated many of the new Conservative principles of reform, and signalled his party's shift from a position defending aristocratic and landowning interests to a stance more representative of the rising industrial middle classes.

Tánaiste (Ir., second in line). Deputy prime minister of Ireland appointed by the TAOISEACH, who acts in his place if he is absent, dead or permanently incapacitated. He must be a member of the DÁIL ÉIREANN and is a member of the Council of State.

tanist (deriv. Ir. *tanaiste*). In Celtic Ireland, the successor apparent to a local chieftain.

Tanker War. Bomb, rocket and mine attacks on oil tankers in the Gulf during the 1980–88 Iran–Iraq war. In 1984 Iraq attacked ships trading with Iran who retaliated by raiding tankers using the ports of Iraq's Arab backers. Iran's attacks on Kuwait-linked shipping provoked the United States into encouraging the reflagging of Kuwaiti tankers, allowing American naval protection and opening up the possibility of US–Iran confrontation.

Tanzimat (Turk 'reorganization'). Generally unsuccessful reforms undertaken between 1839 and 1876 to modernize the OTTOMAN Empire. Edicts in 1839, 1856 and 1876 promised equality, justice and a share in decision-making to all citizens and efforts were made to improve government administration and to professionalize the army.

Taoiseach (Ir.). Prime Minister of Ireland and head of government, appointed by the president 'on the nomination of DÁIL ÉIREANN' according to Article 13 of the constitution. He must be a member of the Dáil and is a member of the Council of State. He advises the president on domestic and international policy and nominates ministers for appointment.

Taoism (Chinese *tao*, way). One of the great religions of the east, surviving now only in a degenerate form. It is alleged to have been founded by Lao-tze, born in Honan, China, in 604 BC, who is said to have written the Taoist 'bible' *Tao-te-ching* ('The Way of Life'). But the poems of *Tao-te-ching*, apparently anonymous and written by numerous people, are probably the work of recluses in isolated valleys which were collected in the 3rd century BC and attributed to Lao-tze. It is in fact doubtful whether Lao-tze, whose name means 'old philosopher', ever existed.

Taoism was originally a mystical religion, a development of Brahmanism, which denied the existence of a personal God or of any deities such as men imagined; there were only emanations of the Tao which gave life to all. But later Lao-tze was worshipped as a divinity, one part of a trinity worshipped in the form of idols. Next came the worship of natural forces such as the tide, sun, moon, stars and hundreds of other deities including Confucius. In fact *Tao-te-ching* strongly disapproves of CONFUCIANISM. Taoism taught that 'the way' cannot be explained in words but is attained by virtue, humility, compassion and passivity. Weakness breeds true strength; violence defeats its own ends; words are useless but internal renunciation is of great value. Passive resistance alone can convince others of error.

Tariff Reform. Programme of the Tariff Reform League formed in July 1903 by Joseph Chamberlain (1836–1914, Colonial Secretary 1895–1903) advocating protection of British industry from foreign, predominantly German, competition and preference for Imperial goods. Chamberlain's policy divided the Conservative Party, ensuring its defeat in the 1906 General Election. *See also* EMPIRE CRUSADE.

Tartan Tories. Labour Party description of the Scottish National Party (SNP) as it made electoral progress in the 1970s, winning 30% of the Scottish vote and 11 seats at the October 1974 General Election. As the strongest party in Scotland, Labour felt it ultimately had most to fear from a Nationalist advance. The SNP soon afterwards began to decline, although a by-election victory in 1988 hinted at a resurgence.

taua. A Maori war party, not as large as an OPE.

Tausendjährig (Germ., a thousand years, a millenium). Term used by the German NAZI party to refer to Hitler's THIRD REICH.

tchinovniks (Russ.). Holders of official appointments in Tsarist Russia, generally drawn from the nobility and the clergy, with certain influential noble families supplying a great many. There were 14 classes or tchins of official, everyone entering the service in the lowest tchin and, nominally at least, being promoted by merit alone.

Teachta Dála (Ir.). Title of a member of parliament in the Republic of Ireland, abbreviated to TD.

Teapot Dome Scandal. Scandal displaying the links between American politics and the US oil industry which occurred during the administration of Pres. Harding (1865–1923). His term of office from 1920 to 1923 was marked by corruption amongst his friends, known as the 'OHIO GANG' because Harding came from Ohio. Harding transferred control of naval oil reserves held at Teapot Dome, Wyoming, from the Secretary of the Navy to his old friend Albert Fall, Secretary of the Interior. In 1922 Fall was responsible for leasing further reserves at Elk Hill, California, to a different oil developer. A Senate investigation resulted in Fall's imprisonment in 1929. The leases were cancelled and there was posthumous criticism of Harding's role in the affair.

Templar. A member of the order of the Knights Templars, founded in Palestine in 1118 (confirmed by Pope Honorius II in 1128) to protect Christian pilgrims travelling to the Holy Sepulchre; the order took its name from its headquarters on the site of Solomon's Temple in Jerusalem. It became very rich and powerful and spread widely over Europe, but was accused of heresy in the 13th century and proscribed by Pope Clement V and its property confiscated in 1312.

tenmannetale. In northern parts of medieval England, name given to the system of FRANK PLEDGE.

Tennessee Valley Authority (TVA). A controversial Federal agency established in May 1933 as part of Roosevelt's NEW DEAL, the TVA developed hydro-electric power in the Tennessee Valley watershed, providing cheap electricity, employment and improved social welfare across seven states.

Tennis Court Oath. Sworn by deputies of the French Third Estate on 20 June 1789 when their chamber at the Palace of Versailles was locked and they feared this was a threat of dissolution. Convening in the royal tennis court, they pledged to meet 'wherever circumstances may dictate, until the constitution of the realm is established and consolidated on firm foundations', a radical demand which opened the French Revolution.

Tenno. *See* MIKADO.

terrorism. Attempt to achieve political ends by creating a climate of fear through bombing, assassination, kidnapping and seizure of aircraft, undermining confidence in a state's ability to protect its citizens, or to gain publicity for a cause. Few non-communist countries have been free from terrorism since the 1960s.

Test Acts. Acts designed to exclude members of churches other than the Church of England from certain positions of authority. The 1673 Test Act excluded Catholics and NONCONFORMISTS from military and civil office by requiring office holders to repudiate the doctrine of TRANSUBSTANTIATION, receive Anglican communion and take an oath of allegiance to the monarch as head of state and of the Church of England. It was not repealed until 1829. An act of 1678, passed in the aftermath of the POPISH PLOT, prohibited Roman Catholics (except for the Duke of York, future King James II) from entering parliament. In Scotland an act of 1681 required all government office holders to subscribe to the Protestant faith.

Test-Ban Treaty. Treaty signed on 5 August 1963 whereby the USA, the USSR and Britain agreed not to test nuclear weapons under the ocean, in outer space or in the atmosphere. Underground testing was not prohibited. The treaty, the conclusion of five years' negotiation, formalized the voluntary restraint from nuclear testing exercised by the signatories between 1958 and 1961. Between 1963 and 1965 more than 90 other nations signed it though of course the majority of these were not at the time in positions to test military nuclear devices. France and China refused to sign and have continued nuclear tests.

Tet (Vietnamese). Period during which the lunar new year is celebrated in Vietnam. During the celebrations in early 1968 the VIET CONG and regular North Vietnamese troops commenced a major offensive against Saigon (now Ho Chi Minh City), Hué and 140 other towns and villages. Known as the 'Tet Offensive', it lasted from 29 January to 25 February 1968 and resulted in heavy casualties on both sides before the communists were forced to withdraw. Their material gains were insignificant.

Psychologically, however, the offensive undermined South Vietnamese belief in the ability of the USA and themselves to win the war with the North. In addition, the belief that many 'collaborators' with the Americans had been murdered during the offensive by the Viet Cong alienated South Vietnamese public opinion and diminished support for the war. In the USA it convinced public opinion that to 'win' the war would require a far greater commitment than many were prepared to give. It therefore eventually helped force the US administration to consider withdrawal from Vietnam.

Teutonic Knights. The Teutonic Knights of the Hospital of St. Mary of Jerusalem, a military fraternity established in 1198 that evolved from a hospital in the Holy Land established by German merchants in 1190 to care for German pilgrims at the siege of Acre. It was based on the orders of the HOSPITALLERS and TEMPLARS. Although it took part in major engagements in Palestine in the 13th century its main activities were against the pagan tribes of eastern Europe. Between 1211 and 1225 it was active in Hungary, and between 1230 and 1288 it conquered Prussia in a series of bloody campaigns and established a sovereign state, the Ordenstaat. The papacy and the German Emperor confirmed its right to the Baltic lands. The order's headquarters officially remained at Acre until the city fell to the Moslems in 1291; they were then transferred to Venice and finally, in 1308 to Marienberg in Prussia.

The order continued to exist until 1809 when Napoleon confiscated its properties but in 1840 it was revived as a semi-religious association in Austria. The exploits of the Teutonic Knights figured often in NAZI propaganda. Their habit was white with a black cross on the left shoulder and their banner a white field and plain black cross: the black cross remains part of Germany's national insignia today.

textura (Germ.). Late medieval form of handwriting.

Thatcherite. Supporter of Margaret Thatcher (b.1925), leader of the Conservative Party since 11 February 1975. Thatcherites give active support to Mrs Thatcher's extreme right-wing policies on the economy, defence and foreign affairs; they include the 'DRIES'. The term is increasingly applied to the radical Conservative Governments under Thatcher elected in 1979, 1983 and 1987.

Theatins. Religious order founded in 1524 by members of the Oratory of Divine Love, notably Gian Pietro Caraffa, Archbishop of Brindisi and later Pope Paul IV; their name comes from the Latin form of Chieti, one of Caraffa's bishoprics. Pastoral priests who lived and worked in society, they also took monastic vows and set an example to the regular clergy. They concentrated on preaching, and though few in number exerted a strong spiritual influence on the Roman Catholic Church in the mid-16th century.

thegn (OE, one who serves). In Anglo-Saxon England, a hereditary noble who held land in return for service; the title superseded GESITH in the 9th century. Their influence was closely related to that of their lord; the king's thegns, therefore, being important. They attended the court and the WITAN, performing administrative duties and, together with their own vassals, rendering military service. Their importance declined with the formation of the HOUSECARLES and had finally ceased by the time of the Norman conquest.

theows (OE). In Anglo-Saxon England, the slaves of feudal lords, reduced to a servile condition by debt or by being taken as prisoners in war.

Thermidor (Fr., month of heat). Eleventh month in the French revolutionary calendar, from 19 July to 17 August. The era of Jacobin dictatorship ended on 9 Thermidor (27 July) 1794 when the CONVENTION secured the proscription of Robespierre.

Thermidoriens (Fr.). Those who passed the decree of accusation against Robespierre and his followers on 9 Thermidor 1794. Until the DIRECTORY was established, the Thermidoriens ruled France through the CONVENTION and eradicated the machinery of the Terror and JACOBIN dictatorship. They achieved the ascendancy of the middle classes by breaking the power of the SANS-CULOTTES and the Paris Commune, but under the Directory proved to be in favour of maintaining the decrees against the clergy, the ÉMIGRÉS and the nobility.

thing (ON). Amongst the Norsemen, an assembly of freemen which could be convoked for a variety of purposes, varying in importance and bearing a different name for each one. The ALTHING was the general assembly of the nation and the Konungsthing a meeting specially convened by the king. On the lower end of the scale was the Husthing, originally a meeting summoned by a minor chief of his own men and later any of a variety of minor open air meetings. The term has come into English in its meaning of a meeting in connection with parliamentary elections. *See* HUSTING.

Thingamen. Alternative name for King Cnut's HOUSECARLES.

third estate. The common people. *See* STATES-GENERAL, TIERS ÉTAT.

third penny. Custom referred to in the DOMESDAY BOOK by which the EARL received one-third of any fines collected by the courts of the shire.

Third Reich. Phrase invented in the 1920s by the German nationalist writer Moeller van der Bruck in a book of that title; used by the NAZIS to describe their regime in Germany (1933–45). Hitler prophesied that it would last 1,000 years. The First Reich was the Holy Roman Empire; the Second Reich lasted from the unification of Germany in 1871 up to 1918.

Third Republic. The unstable French Republic which emerged out of defeat in the Franco–Prussian War on 4 September 1870, was divided by the DREYFUS AFFAIR, and came close to collapse in World War I. Permanently politically weak, the Republic had 108 governments in 70 years, 44 of these between 1918 and 1940. Though nominally in existence until 1946, the Republic effectively ended when the National Assembly voted by 569 to 40 to give full power to Marshal Pétain at VICHY in July 1940 following defeat by Germany.

Third Section (Russ., Tretye Otdeleniye, Third Section of His Imperial Majesty's Own Chancery in Russia). Secret police department created by Tsar Nicholas I on 15 July 1826, led until 1844 by Count Benckendorff. It was abolished in 1880 when responsibility for political security was transferred to the police under Interior Ministry control.

Third World. Poorer nations of the world which are far from full development in economic terms. Usually located in Latin America,

Asia and Africa, they are neither part of the CAPITALIST industrialized West nor of the communist EASTERN BLOC.

Thirteen Colonies. The American colonies which broke with Britain, fought the War of Independence and formed the United States: New Hampshire, Massachussets, Connecticut, New York, Rhode Island, New Jersey, Pennsylvania, Maryland, Virginia, North Carolina, South Carolina, Georgia, Delaware.

Thirty-eighth Parallel. Latitude 38° north which divides communist North Korea from South Korea, a demarcation line established at the Yalta conference of 1945 as a preliminary to the unification of Korea as a democracy. But the Korean War (1950–53), in which the north effectively invaded the south, ended any hopes of peaceful unity. *See also* DEMILITARIZED ZONE.

Thirty Years War. A political-religious conflict lasting from 23 May 1618 to 24 October 1648 which began in the Austrian Monarchy, spread into the German Holy Roman Empire and soon involved Denmark, France, Spain and Sweden. The resulting Treaty of Westphalia left Germany a patchwork of absolute monarchies in which Catholic counter-reformation had failed to eradicate Protestantism.

Thorough. Policy of Strafford and Laud in the reign of Charles I (1625–49) who were determined to carry through their schemes whatever obstacles were placed in their way.

'Thousand Days'. Days of office occupied by US Pres. John F. Kennedy (1917–63). He was inaugurated on 1 January 1961 and assassinated on 22 November 1963. During his term of office he initiated social and CIVIL RIGHTS legislation, proposed talks leading to a TEST-BAN TREATY and displayed firmness in the CUBAN MISSILE CRISIS. He also presided over the BAY OF PIGS fiasco and increased US involvement in Vietnam.

thralls. Amongst the Norsemen, slaves, usually captives taken in war.

three-day week. Result of an economic crisis in Britain which faced the 1970–74 Conservative government. The YOM KIPPUR war forced up the cost of oil imports and reduced supplies in late 1973. In November 1973 the National Union of Mineworkers voted to ban overtime in support of a pay claim. The fuel situation therefore deteriorated rapidly, and was further aggravated by industrial action by electricity and railway workers. It was thus not possible to supply adequate electricity in peak hours and on 13 November 1973 a state of emergency was declared. Restrictions were placed on domestic and commercial use of electricity.

The Government continued to refuse to allow the miners' pay claim and had to introduce stricter controls on the use of fuel. The most important, in force from 1 January 1974, was that electricity would only be supplied to industry on three specified days a week meaning that many people could only work a three-day week. On 2 February 1974 a general election was called to test support for the government's policy, but it produced no clear result. The Conservative Prime Minister, Edward Heath (b. 1916), resigned on 4 March and a Labour government took office. On 9 March 1974 the restrictions were lifted and Britain returned to a normal five-day working week.

Three Principles. Core of the philosophy of the Chinese nationalist revolutionary Sun Yat-sen (1867–1925), who believed in nationalism (the ending of foreign domination of China); democracy, and livelihood (the right of everyone to have the opportunity of earning a reasonable standard of living).

Thug (Hind., strangler). Member of a religious Indian sect, notorious for committing *thuggee*, murder by strangulation. It was suppressed by the British in the 1850s. The word now has a general connotation.

Thunderer, The. Sobriquet earned by *The Times* of London under the editorship of Thomas Barnes, a radical liberal, between 1810 and 1841 for the trenchancy and forthrightness of its political journalism and comment.

Tiempistas (Span.). Paraguayan liberals, who campaigned for constitutional government in 1944 in opposition to the dictatorship of Higinio Moríngo; their name came from their newspaper *El Tiempo*. Moríngo had many of them jailed and the movement was effectively suppressed.

tiers état (Fr., third estate). In pre-Revolutionary France, all the social classes other than the aristocracy, the higher clergy and the privileged magistracy. It is sometimes held that the third estate was first consulted by the Crown when Louis IX (1214–70) summoned 12 citizens from principal towns to advise him on the national coinage.

tithe (OE, tenth). Ecclesiastical tax, consisting of a tenth part of the annual produce of the laity, used to maintain the ministers of the Church. Known to the ancient Jews, tithes were first imposed by Christian authorities in the 4th century and were made compulsory in England after the 9th century. They were connected with the land and took three forms: praedial tithes such as corn, hops and wood; personal tithes, assessed on the profits of industry and labour; and mixed tithes, which combined the two. A tenth part of the gross amount had to be paid on praedial and mixed tithes, but only a tenth of clear profit on personal tithes, which were not always collected and which depended on local custom. The major praedial tithes were known as 'great tithes'; the others, together with mixed and personal tithes were called 'small tithes' but clear distinguishing lines were not drawn. Tithes belonged to the rector of a parish; if a deed of endowment or proof of ancient usage was shown, part of the tithe could sometimes be claimed by the vicar. A common arrangement was for all 'small tithes' to be vested in the vicar. Tithes were for centuries a source of controversy, especially during the 1640s and 1650s. They were gradually commuted into rent charges and these were abolished by the 1936 Tithe Act. The redemption annuity made payable on abolition will, in due course, terminate.

tithing (OE). In medieval England, a group of ten men whose members were mutually responsible for each other's behaviour. All freemen over 12 years of age belonged to tithings. They first appeared in the reign of Cnut (1017–35) and developed into the FRANK PLEDGE.

Togakuto. The Society of Oriental Learning, a Korean party which violently opposed Western influences in the late 19th century. It sought to exclude all foreigners from Korea and in 1893 some 200,000 of its members gathered in Seoul in an unsuccessful attempt to force their demands on the king.

tohunga. A Maori native priest.

toisée (Fr.). Order issued in 1644 by Louis XIV's finance minister, Emery, that owners of houses built in Parisian suburbs that contravened a century-old and partly forgotten edict would be liable to heavy fines. The order created such discontent that it had to be withdrawn.

Tokugawa. SHŌGUN dynasty which ruled in Japan from 1603 to 1867.

toll. Originally, the right to levy a duty; later, the duty itself. Tolls were a common form of taxation in medieval English boroughs and were imposed at markets and on sales, etc., for municipal purposes such as the maintenance of bridges. The king could grant freedom from a toll to individuals or boroughs and boroughs sought such exemptions as a means to freer trading. Today tolls survive on bridges and roads to pay directly for their upkeep.

Tolpuddle Martyrs. Six agricultural workers from Tolpuddle in Dorset who formed a union branch in 1834, were found guilty of taking a seditious oath and who were given the maximum sentence of transportation to Australia for seven years. A widespread public outcry led to their pardon in 1836.

Tonkin resolution. Resolution passed on 7 August 1964 by both Houses of the US Congress authorizing Pres. Johnson (1908–73) 'to take all necessary steps, including the use of armed forces' to help SEATO members defend their freedom. It followed North Vietnamese attacks on the destroyer USS *Maddox*, and other

vessels in the Gulf of Tonkin on 2 August 1964. Retaliatory raids on North Vietnamese naval depots and oil refineries were authorized but Johnson took the resolution as carte blanche for a general escalation of US involvement in Vietnam. In 1968 a number of senators, including the Democrat J. William Fulbright (b.1905) sought clarification or repeal of the resolution.

Torch. Code name for the Anglo-American landings in French North West Africa on 8 November 1942. The aim was to take Morocco, Algeria and Tunisia and support the British offensive started the previous month with the victory at El Alamein (23 October– 4 November). The VICHY forces in Tunis received AXIS support and delayed clearance of the Mediterranean sea routes, although the operation did achieve success in Algeria and Morocco. It took until May 1943 to drive the last Germans and Italians out of North Africa.

Tory (deriv. Ir. *tóraghe*, pursuer). Originally, one of the Irish bandits and plunderers active in the 17th century after the Irish rebellion; by extension, an insulting name for a Catholic. In 1680, the name was given by English Protestants to those who did not wish to exclude a Catholic heir from the succession to the throne of Charles II. It then remained the name of one of the two great political parties (*see* WHIGS) until 1832, when the Tory Party restyled itself the Conservative Party. The term now denotes a supporter or member of the Conservative Party.

total war. Term of 20th-century origin meaning a war in which all of a nation's resources (economic. human, ideological, etc.) are mobilized in the effort to win. Applicable.

for example, to the war efforts of Germany, the Soviet Union and Great Britain in World War II.

Totenkopfverbände (Germ., death's head units). Para-military sub-unit of the SS, who served from 1935 onwards as CONCENTRATION CAMP guards. In 1940 the youngest and fittest were formed into an élite fighting division, the Totenkopf Division, and integrated into the WAFFEN SS; by 1943 the majority serving in concentration camps were elderly or wounded.

Tractarian. *See* PUSEYITE.

Trades Union Congress. *See* TUC.

trail baston (OFr., a man with a club). Armed robber active in England in the periods of lawlessness during the wars of Edward I and Edward II in the late 13th and early 14th centuries.

Trail of Tears. Trek made by the Cherokee Indian nation in 1838 from their homeland in the east to territory in the west of the USA. By the terms of the 1830 Indian Removal Act all tribes east of the Mississippi River were obliged to cede their lands for exchange areas in the west. Suffering great hardships on their trail, 4,000 of the 13,000 Cherokees died en route.

train-bands. Trained bands of citizen soldiers which originated in 1573 when Elizabeth I ordered that a 'convenient number' of men in every county be grouped and trained for military service. They were not, in fact, well trained but Charles I used them against the Scots in 1639 and both sides tried to use them in the civil war, but with the exception of the London train-band they refused to serve outside their localties. *See* MILITIA.

transportation. Deportation of convicts to overseas penal colonies practised in England from the reign of Charles II (1630–85) until 1868. The American colonies were the main destination and deportation was an alternative to execution. After the American War of Independence (1775– 84) it was decided to transport convicts to Australia, often for minor offences. Transportation to New South Wales ended in 1840, to Tasmania in 1853 and to Western Australia in 1868.

Transport House. Headquarters of the Transport and General Workers' Union in Smith Square, London. For many years the Labour Party also used it as their headquarters but these have now been moved to Walworth Road in South London. The name signifies the power of the Labour Party nationally.

transubstantiation. Roman Catholic doctrine which holds that the sacrament of the eucharist transforms bread and wine into Christ's flesh and blood. The 39 Articles regulating the Church of England (issued in 1563) deny the doctrine, pointing instead to a position somewhere in between consubstantiation (co-existence of bread and wine and Christ's flesh and blood) and virtualism (that communicants receive the 'virtue' of Christ's body and blood). NONCONFORMISTS prefer to see the eucharist simply as a memorial service.

Treasury Bench. In the British HOUSE OF COMMONS, the front bench to the right of the Speaker which is occupied by members of the government.

Tricoleur. French national flag, made

up of red and blue colours of the city of Paris and the white Bourbon emblem. It was adopted on 17 July 1789 to signify the victory of the people of Paris three days earlier when they stormed the BASTILLE.

tricoteuses (Fr., knitters). The Tricoteuses de Robespierre ('Robespierre's knitters') were a group of women who during the Terror sat knitting at the meetings of the CONVENTION and the Tribunal and around the GUILLOTINE. They were also called 'Les furies de la Guillotine'.

Triers and Ejectors. The 'Triers' were an examining body drawn from the ranks of the INDEPENDENTS, BAPTISTS and PRESBYTERIANS which was appointed by Cromwell in March 1654 to inquire into the qualifications of clergy to be appointed to benefices by lay patrons. In August, local commissions of 'Ejectors' were also set up to eject all 'scandalous, ignorant and insufficient' clergy and schoolmasters from their livings. Immorality and the Prayer Book were condemned but generally both bodies were moderate and in practice almost anyone, other than a Catholic, whose creed was fundamentally orthodox was allowed to hold his post.

trinodas necessitas. In Anglo-Saxon England, an obligation on every freeman to bear his share in war service, the repair of bridges and roads and the upkeep of fortifications.

Triple Alliance. (1) Alliance formed between Germany, Austria-Hungary and Italy in 1882.
(2) A pledge of mutual aid in industrial disputes negotiated by the mining, railway and transport unions in 1914–15. Put to the test on 15 April 1921 (described as BLACK FRIDAY), the Alliance collapsed when the transport and rail unions refused to support miners striking against wage cuts.

Triple Entente. Agreement of Britain, France and Russia to pursue ways of resolving their outstanding colonial differences; it became a military alliance in 1914. *See also* ENTENTE CORDIALE.

Triumvirate (deriv. Lat., three men). (1) In England, Grenville's ministry of 1763, so-called because the secretaries of state, Egremont and Halifax, were held to be sharing the direction of public affairs with the prime minister.
(2) In Russia, the group of Czartoryski, Novossiltsof and Strogonof, principal advisers of Tsar Alexander I at his accession in 1801.

Trizonia. Term used in the 1940s and 1950s to denote the combined British, French and American zones of occupation in Germany.

troika (Russ.). Properly, a carriage drawn by three horses, hence used to refer to any organization run by three different persons or authorities.

Trotskyist. Communist who supports the views of Leon Trotsky, the assumed name of Lev Bronstein (1870–1940), who was ousted from power in the USSR by Stalin in 1924 and later assassinated by Russian agents in Mexico. Trotsky held that the excessive Russian nationalism developed under Stalin was incompatible with genuine international communism, and that Stalin's concentration on the economic development of the USSR could only result in a cumbersome bureaucracy and a purely nationalist outlook. After the Soviet invasion of Hungary in 1956 many members of western communist parties resigned their allegiance to Soviet communism and turned to Trotskyism.

Trucial States. Name given to the seven emirates of the lower Persian Gulf from the early 1820s until they became the United Arab Emirates in 1972: Abu Dhabi, Ajman, Dubai, Fujaira, Sharja, Ras al-Khaima and Umm al-Qaiwan. The name came from the 'truce' – an annual assurance from local leaders that they would not indulge in piracy – gained by the British resident agent at Sharja in 1823.

Tsar (*also* Czar; Russ., emperor). Title of the Russian rulers adopted by Ivan IV in 1547 and meant to express the highest form of dominion, equivalent to that of the Holy Roman Emperor in western Europe. It was used until the abdication in 1917 and execution in 1918 of Tsar Nicholas II. The Tsar's eldest son was known as the Tsarevitch, and his wife as the Tsarina.

Tsarevitch. *See* TSAR.

Tsarina. *See* TSAR.

Tsung-li-Yamen. Institution founded in China in 1861 on the recommendation of Prince Kung to handle foreign affairs. It was also active in promoting projects of modernization such as a postal service, railways, telegraphy and maritime defence. It had no power to make policy decisions but it was the most significant innovation of the T'ung-Chih restoration. Its recommendations to the Grand Council, the highest authority in the bureaucracy, were usually accepted since the personnel of the two institutions overlapped. But its power was limited by the pressure of work put on its members who all held at least one other office,

and by the fact that provincial officials continued to handle foreign affairs. The decline of Prince Kung and the creation of the Board of Admiralty in 1885 decreased its influence and in 1901 it was replaced by a Western-style foreign office as specified in the BOXER protocol.

TUC. Trades Union Congress, the federation of about 160 British trade unions founded in 1868 when the Manchester and Salford Trades Council took an independent lead in organizing a union congress. Its basic function is to co-ordinate union action by means of annual conferences of union representatives at which matters of common concern are discussed. The conference, or Congress, elects a general council which has executive functions and seeks to consult with government on matters affecting organized labour. Member unions retain their autonomy and the Congress cannot control their individual actions, although it can bring pressure to bear on particular unions by means of moral persuasion and the ability to influence the decisions of other unions in supporting strikes.

Tuchins (Fr.). French peasants of the Cévennes who rose in revolt in 1381 against all those who were not of the labouring classes.

Tudeh. Iranian left-wing group with communist sympathies founded in 1941. Although it had three Cabinet members in 1946 the party was suppressed in 1949, revived with a more radical programme between 1951–53 and again outlawed in 1954. Tudeh has again been suppressed by the Islamic Republic since 1979.

Tudor. The dynasty of Welsh origin which ruled England from 1485 to 1603 (Henry VII, Henry VIII, Edward VI, Mary, Elizabeth I), a period marked by religious controversy in which Henry VIII severed the English Church from Rome, and under Elizabeth I a growth in national self-confidence and rivalry with Catholic Spain.

Tugendbund. German secret society established in 1808 to rouse the spirit of nationalism against the domination of Napoleon.

tun (OE). In Anglo-Saxon England, originally an enclosure; later , a large isolated farm or a village.

tunnage or poundage. SUBSIDIES of separate origin but granted together by the English Crown from 1350 onwards. Tunnage, which dated from the 12th century as a levy on wine imported in tuns (casks), was a national subsidy from 1350. Poundage arose in the 13th century as a custom levied on all imports and exports at the rate of 3*d.* in the pound. From 1415 tunnage and poundage were granted by parliament to each new sovereign for life. They were the source of trouble in the reign of Charles I when he began collecting them without parliament's prior consent, which he regarded merely as an 'act of manners'. They were put on a statutory basis in 1641.

Tupamaros. Small but effective body of urban guerrillas in Uruguay, whose aim is to create the conditions for a Marxist revolution. Apart from bank robberies to secure funds, they have blown up official radio stations, raided government depots for arms and fomented and led strikes. Amongst the 1,000 or so members are many highly placed professional men. In 1972 the police and right-wing para-military groups carried out intensive actions against them and since then they have been relatively inactive and probably in decline. They took their name from the 18th-century Peruvian Indian Tupac Amaru who led a revolt against the Spanish.

Turnip Winter. The winter of 1944/45 in German-occupied Holland. Desperate by lack of food, the Dutch were driven to eat anything they could find. This last winter of the war was also known as the HUNGER WINTER.

Twenty-One Conditions. The terms left-wing parties seeking affiliation to the COMINTERN had to accept. They included organizing on the Russian party model and acknowledging ultimate Comintern authority; agitating for a DICTATORSHIP OF THE PROLETARIAT; creating an illegal organization for subversive work; rejecting SYNDICALISM and reformism; conducting revolutionary propaganda in the armed forces; and supporting colonial liberation.

Twenty-One Demands. List of demands issued by the Japanese government on 18 January 1915 in an attempt to turn China into a Japanese protectorate. Having seized the former German territory of Kiaochow on 7 November 1914 (with the approval of Britain, France and Russia) the Japanese threatened military action against China: if she did not settle 21 'outstanding questions'. Britain persuaded Japan not to pursue her demands to the full, but she did receive important concessions from China: a half-interest in China's most valuable iron and steel company; stronger control over Shantung and Manchuria; and promises that foreign powers would not be allowed to lease any further Chinese coastal areas. The other demands would have forced China to appoint Japanese political, financial and military advisers. The 21 demands caused alarm in the USA regarding Japan's territorial ambitions and caused lasting resentment in China.

Two Nations. From the subtitle of the novel *Sybil* published in 1845 by Benjamin Disraeli (1804–81) which suggested a society divided between rich and poor. In 20th-century Britain used to describe the division between the depressed North and the prosperous South in the 1930s and again in the 1980s.

Tycoon. *See* SHŌGUN.

Tynwald (deriv. ON *thing*, assembly + *vollr*, field). The parliament of the Isle of Man which comprises the governor and council (the upper house) and the House of Keys (the representative assembly). Acts passed by the Tynwald require simply the assent of the sovereign of the United Kingdom.

U

U-2 incident. The shooting down of a US Lockheed U-2 reconnaissance aeroplane over Sverdlovsk in the USSR on 1 May 1960. Its pilot, Gary Powers, was taken prisoner but returned to the USA in February 1962. Such flights had occurred since 1957 but the Russians used the incident for propaganda purposes, demanding an apology from the USA and breaking off the Paris summit conference (16–19 May 1960) when this was refused. Both the American intelligence service and American diplomacy were heavily criticized over the affair, after which U-2 flights ceased.

U-boats (Germ., *Untersee*, under the sea). Submarines. In both world wars the German U-boat squadrons posed a serious threat to British merchant ships transporting vital supplies across the Atlantic. Their attacks were countered by the use of CONVOY tactics, weapons such as depth charges and, in World War II, the use of radar.

udallers. Name given to holders of ALLODIAL LAND in the Orkneys.

UDI. Unilateral Declaration of Independence, such as that made by the Rhodesian Front government headed by Ian Smith, on 11 November 1965. The action was rejected by the British government and condemned by the United Nations who saw it as a rebellion caused by Rhodesia's refusal to introduce majority rule by extending the franchise to black Africans.

Uhlan (Fr.). Light cavalry soldier armed with lance, pistol and sabre, mainly employed as a skirmisher or scout in the Polish and later the German armies. The Prussian Uhlans won fame in the Franco-Prussian war of 1870.

uhuru (Swahili). Freedom, i.e. independence from colonial rule.

uitlander (S. Afr., foreigner). Name given by the BOERS to newcomers to the Transvaal in the late 19th century, mainly British subjects attracted by the discovery of gold in the Witwatersrand in 1886. The inferior position of the uitlanders under the Transvaal Constitution and their demands for equality with the Boers helped precipitate the South African War of 1899-1902 between Britain and the Boers.

ukase (Russ.). In Russia, originally a decree by the TSAR which, since he was an absolute monarch, had the force of a legal enactment. Today such decrees are issued by the PRAE-SIDIUM of the supreme SOVIET of the USSR and have a similar authority.

ulama (Arab., those with knowledge). Theologians and legal experts in ISLAM, who include the QADIS and MUFTIS.

Ultramontanism (deriv. Lat. *ultra*, beyond + *mons*, mountain). Belief in the ultimate authority of the papacy above that of loyalty to the state, particularly evident in 19th-century France, and encouraged by Pope Pius IX's decree of 1870. In Germany it contributed to the KULTURKAMPF. The long-term consequence of the ultramontanist movement was to free the papacy from dependence on civil powers and to give the Catholic Church freedom of action.

Umkhonto we Sizwe. 'Spear of the Nation', the guerrilla wing of the African National Congress which has mounted attacks on police stations, police officers, state witnesses as well as carrying out sabotage. *See* ANC.

UN. *See* UNITED NATIONS.

un-American activities. Activities of the exponents of anti-democratic movements, such as Nazism, fascism and communism. In 1938 Texan congressman Martin Dies founded a committee of the House of Representatives to investigate such activities; it was often referred to as the 'Dies Committee'. One of the first organizations it investigated and exposed was the Nazi Bund in the USA. There was a mixed reaction to the committee and Pres. Roosevelt was critical of its methods. Little was heard of it between 1944 and 1947 when it re-emerged to investigate the spread of communism, reaching the peak of its influence in the era of MCCARTHYISM. Again it was critic-

ized for its methods and accused of indulging in WITCH-HUNTS.

Unauthorized Programme. The programme of radical Liberal Joseph Chamberlain (1836–1914) put to the electorate at the 1885 General Election to attract the rural vote. It promised free education, compulsory land purchase to restore a peasantry with 'three acres and a cow' and a graduated property tax. 'Unauthorized' was intended to contrast Chamberlain's programme with that authorized by Gladstone, the Liberal leader.

Uncle Joe. Term of affection in Britain between 1941 and 1945 for the Soviet leader Joseph Stalin (1879–1953), signifying British recognition of the sacrifices forced on the USSR after BARBAROSSA and the endurance of the Russian people before the opening of a 'second front' by D-DAY.

Undertakers. (1) A group of English gentlemen who undertook the settlement of Ulster in 1569. They were to settle on forfeited lands, taking 240 acres per family, and allow no Irish as tenants. Neither condition was adhered to and little English settlement was achieved until the plantation of Ulster in 1606.

(2) Those members of the ADDLED PARLIAMENT of 1614 who undertook to control parliament in the interests of James I but failed to do so.

Unequal Treaties. Agreements reached at the 1921 Washington Conference by Belgium, Britain, China, France, Italy, Japan, the Netherlands, Portugal and the United States on an OPEN DOOR policy in China. Though soon objected to by China, civil war made the emergence of a stable government capable of renegotiating the treaties impossible. The term was used by the Chinese to refer to all agreements imposed on it by the imperialist powers.

UNESCO. United Nations Educational Scientific and Cultural Organization, established on 4 November 1946 to further peace and security by promoting collaboration on education, science and culture in order to increase 'universal respect for justice, for the rule of law and for the human rights and fundamental freedoms' enumerated in the UN charter. A specialized agency of the UN, it has a General Conference of one representative from each member state (meeting every two years), an Executive Board meeting twice a year and a Director-General and Secretariat based in Paris.

Uniformity, Acts of. Series of Acts designed to provide the legal and doctrinal bases on which the Church of England stands. The first two were passed in the reign of Edward VI. That of 1549 specified that the moderately Protestant Book of Common Prayer, written by Archbishop Cranmer, should be used in church services. Penalties on the clergy for non-compliance were, however, light. That of 1552 marked a move towards a more clearly Protestant position. A more Protestant prayer book was to be used and stricter penalties were enforced for failure to do so. Both Acts were repealed in the reign of Queen Mary I (1553–58). However, in 1559, a third Act was introduced following the accession of Queen Elizabeth I. This required the use of a modified version of the 1552 Prayer Book and imposed fines of a shilling a week on persons who failed to attend church services using the new book. In 1662 a fourth Act was passed (*see* CLARENDON CODE), which required

the use of yet another revised prayer book and a new liturgy. Over 2,000 members of the clergy who could not accept the provisions of the Act were obliged to resign their livings.

Unilateral Declaration of Independence. *See* UDI.

Unilateralists. Those who advocate implementing a policy in one country irrespective of whether – but often in the hope that – other countries follow suit. Used especially in reference to nuclear disarmament by one country undertaken for moral, economic, defence or political reasons but not based on reciprocal agreements with other nuclear powers. (*See* MULTI-LATERALISTS.)

Unionist. Supporter of the union of Ireland and Great Britain. The term became current in British politics following the introduction of the 1886 Irish HOME RULE bill. The Conservatives opposed the Bill and supported the Union, as did the LIBERAL UNIONISTS. The alliance of these two parties and their amalgamation in 1912 gave rise to the use of the term Unionist to denote both wings, first of the alliance and then of the party. Following the Irish Free State Act of 1922 the term lost most of its meaning in England but is still retained in the official title of the Conservative and Unionist Party. In Ulster unionism remains strong: the Unionist Party of Northern Ireland was the ruling political party from 1921 to 1972.

Union Sacrée (Fr. Sacred Union). Government formed in France at the outbreak of World War I which included, for the first time and as a symbol of national unity, two socialists among its members.

UNITA. National Union for the

Total Independence of Angola which fought alongside the MPLA and FNLA between 1961 and 1975 to achieve Angolan independence. Following independence on 10 November 1975, the MPLA and UNITA set up rival governments and civil war broke out. UNITA, in alliance with the FNLA, received aid from South Africa and her satellites but by February 1976 the MPLA, with Soviet assistance, had captured most of the country. However, a decade later, UNITA forces still control areas of southern Angola and continue to make raids into MPLA territory.

Unitarianism. Religious movement, whose members believe in the single person of God, which is generally thought to be heretical and anti-trinitarian. They first appeared in England after the REFORMATION and increased in numbers under the COMMONWEALTH and PROTEC-TORATE. They were excluded from the Toleration Act of 1689 and from the DISSENTERS' conference at Salter's Hall, London in 1719. From 1813 they were legally tolerated, but attempts were made to turn them out of their chapels on the grounds that their preachers did not hold the same views as the founders of the endowments. This conflict ended with the 1845 Dissenting Chapels Act. In 1825 the British and Foreign Unitarian Association was founded though it issued no authoritative confession of faith.

In the USA some New England PURITANS developed along Unitarian lines and the movement influenced the Harvard Divinity School. In 19th-century Boston many literary figures e.g. Longfellow and Lowell, were Unitarians. Ralph Waldo Emerson guided the movement towards humanitarianism and rationalism; in 1910 the American Unitarians joined the International Congress of Free Christians and other religious liberals. Today many deny a personal God and interpret their religion purely in moral terms, putting their faith in the value of love and brotherhood of man.

unitarios (Span.). In early 19th-century Argentina, advocates of strong central government as opposed to provincial autonomy and federalism. They were bitterly opposed to the dictatorship of Juan Manuel de Rosas and drew most of their support from the wealthy classes of Buenos Aires.

Unitas Fratrum. The Bohemian Brotherhood, a small, rigorous HUSSITE sect influenced by the pacifist ideas of Peter Chelčický which split from the UTRAQUIST Church in 1467. Its members were the forerunners of the MORAVIANS.

unite (deriv. Lat., join together). English gold coin worth 20s. Also called a broad, it was first minted by James I in 1604 and takes its Latin name from the union of England and Scotland. It was replaced by the GUINEA in 1663.

United Front. A Communist Party tactic which attempted to build temporary alliances with other socialist and working-class parties, ostensibly to face a common enemy, for example fascism. *See* POPULAR FRONT.

United Irishmen. Society formed by Wolfe Tone in 1791 to unite Irish Catholics and the republican northern Protestants in attempts to force reform on Grattan's parliament. It drew support from both northern PRESBYTERIANS and from Catholic peasants in the south and soon turned to revolutionary means to secure independence. Its leaders were arrested on the eve of an attempt to seize Dublin with French help in March 1798; after further sporadic outbursts of violence the movement was suppressed.

United Nations. Term first used by the Allied powers of themselves in a joint pledge of 1 January 1942 that none of their number would make a separate peace with the AXIS. A conference between China, Britain, the USA and the USSR in October 1943 recognized the need for an international organization, based on the principle of the sovereign equality of all peace-loving states, for the maintenance of international peace and security. At Dumbarton Oaks, near Washington, the same powers outlined its structure between August and October 1944; further details were refined at Yalta in February 1945 between Britain, the USA and the USSR. These were finalized by 50 nations at war with Germany at the San Francisco Conference between 15 April and 26 June 1945.

Membership is open to any 'peace-loving' state which the UN's general assembly considers able and desirous of fulfilling its obligations under the UN charter. Membership is by a two-thirds vote of the assembly. The main executive organ of the UN is the Security Council on which Britain, the USA, the USSR and China are permanently represented. 'Nationalist' China (Taiwan) sat from 1949 until 25 October 1971 when it was expelled in favour of the People's Republic of China. Until 1965 six other countries served two-year periods on the council; from 1965 their number was ten. The secretary-general is appointed for five years; past holders of the office have been Trygve Lie, Dag Hammarskjöld, U Thant and Kurt Waldheim. The present Secretary-General (since 1982) is the Peruvian, Sr. Perez de

Cuellar (b. 1920).

The permanent headquarters of the UN is in New York on land paid for by the city and by John D. Rockefeller. The General Assembly, which ultimately takes decisions and hears the Secretary-General's reports, has tended to become an 'arena for propaganda, but the UN has successfully mediated in numerous international disputes, for example Palestine (1947), Kashmir (1948), Indonesia (1962), Cyprus (1964), the Middle East ceasefires (1956, 1967 and 1973), and the Gulf War. It has not yet been able to enforce its will on South Africa.

The UN has proved more effective than the previous LEAGUE OF NATIONS because of the stronger powers of its Security Council and because member states have to provide armed forces for peacekeeping missions or to resist aggression. The UN's 15 specialized agencies have done much work to improve human conditions and further human rights. The UN's other main organs are the Economic and Social Council, the Trusteeship Council, the International Court of Justice and the Secretariat.

United Provinces. The seven Dutch-speaking provinces of Friesland, Gelderland, Gröningen-Drente, Holland, Utrecht, Zeeland, and Overijssel which – in alliance with ten other Spanish occupied provinces – fought a war of independence from 1568 until their independence as the Dutch Republic was recognized in 1648.

Untergang des Abendlandes, der (Germ.). *The Decline of the West*, title of a work by the philosopher Oswald Spengler, published 1918–22, which argued that civilizations naturally go through periods of growth and decay.

Untouchables. People considered unclean by 'caste Hindus' and given the title 'outcastes' because of the allegedly ritually unclean nature of their menial occupations. At the end of the 19th century the Untouchables began organizing against their status and in 1950 India abolished untouchability and made discrimination illegal.

urban guerrillas. Persons using terrorist tactics in cities in order to achieve political ends, for example the RED BRIGADES in Italy; the RED ARMY in Germany, and also the IRA in Ulster.

urbi et orbi (Lat., to the city and the world). Phrase used in formal declarations by the Pope.

Uštaše (Serbo-Croatian). Traditional name employed by Croatian nationalist rebels specifically adopted in 1929 by a secret terrorist organization led by the fervent nationalist Ante Pavelić. During the 1930s the Uštaše committed numerous acts of terrorism against Yugoslavia, including the assassination of King Alexander in 1934. They operated from Austria, Hungary and Italy. In 1941 they set up an independent Croatian state, collaborated with the Germans and Italians, and committed atrocities against non-Croats in Yugoslavia, against communists and members of the Serbian Orthodox Church. Pavelić fled to South America after 1945 where he died, but the Uštaše survived as a Croatian separatist and anti-communist organization responsible in the late 1960s and early 1970s for acts of terrorism including murders and bombings in West Germany, Sweden and Australia.

Utfangentheof. *See* INFANGENTHEOF.

uti possidetes (Lat., as you possess). Rule that property remains the possession of a conquering state at the end of hostilities, unless treaties are signed agreeing otherwise.

Utilitarianism. School of moral philosophy in the 19th century whose main proponents were James Mill, John Stuart Mill and Jeremy Bentham. Bentham's theory was based on the principles that the greatest happiness of the greatest number is the criterion of the highest good; and that good can be measured on a 'felicific' calculus, i.e. if people act on the basis of self-interest and pursue their own happiness, then what they do will automatically conduce to the general good. Mill (*Utilitarianism*, 1861) modified this theory of self-interest and suggested rather that the social consequences of an act be taken as the criterion of good and also that intellectual pleasures rank higher than sensory ones.

The utilitarians were a strong intellectual force for reform in the first half of the 19th century and their doctrines helped shape the Liberal Party. Theirs was one of the strands of thought represented in demands for 'LAISSEZ-FAIRE'.

Utraquists. Movement in Hungary, Bohemia and Poland in the 15th century which evolved from the moderate wing of the HUSSITES. Their main demand was for communion in both kinds (*sub utraque specie*) for the laity, from which they take their name. Such a form of communion was initiated in Prague in 1414 but condemned by the Council of Constance the following year. In 1485 the Utraquist church became the state church of Bohemia.

V

vali (deriv. Arab.). Title of a civil governor of a *vilayet*, a Turkish province.

Valor Ecclesiasticus (Lat.). Tax book in which all the ecclesiastical property in England was valued, with great speed and efficiency. by the commissioners appointed by Thomas Cromwell as a prelude to the dissolution of the monasteries in 1535.

Vandals. Germanic tribe from eastern Europe which settled in the Danube Valley, but under Hun pressure invaded Gaul in 406, moving on to Spain and into Africa. After conquering Carthage in 439 the Vandals used sea power to dominate the Mediterranean and in 455 captured and plundered Rome. Their power was destroyed by the Byzantium in a military defeat in 533.

Vasa. The ruling Swedish dynasty from the accession of Gustavus I in 1523 until 1818.

vassalage. Condition of feudal dependence on the LORD PARAMOUNT in the case of landed magnates and upon the vassals of the Lord Paramount in others.

Vatican 1. First ecumenical council of the Roman Catholic Church for 300 years, summoned by Pope Pius IX in 1869 to bolster confidence in the church at a time when the faith was under attack from new doctrines and the papacy was losing its temporal possessions in Italy. It produced the doctrine of PAPAL INFALLIBILITY.

Vatican 2. Second ecumenical council of the Roman Catholic Church in modern times, summoned by Pope John XXIII in January 1959. Its purpose was to consider increased collaboration with other churches and renewal of the faith. Over 8,000 bishops attended in Rome when the council opened on 11 October 1962, including many observers from other churches, especially the ANGLICAN and Orthodox faiths. The council lasted a year and published 16 decrees pointing towards a closer relationship with non-Catholic churches, the use of the vernacular rather than Latin in the liturgy and a greater humanism in Catholic doctrine. Many people expected that the tone of the council presaged a relaxation of the church's position on birth control, but the 1968 ENCYCLICAL, *Humanae Vitae*, condemned its use.

vavassor (ME). In feudal Europe, all the vassals of the great lords under the feudal system. In Normandy and later medieval England it had the more specific meaning of a freeman holding less land than a baron but still with some military obligations.

V-E Day. Victory in Europe Day. 8 May 1945, the date of the Allies' victory in Europe in World War II.

Vehmgerichte (Germ.). In medieval Germany, secret tribunals for trying people arraigned on capital charges and for executing sentences on conviction. The most famous was in Westphalia. Any free-born German was eligible to be an initiated member (*Freischöffe*) and many German princes sat on the tribunals. Their original function tended later to give way to their employment as vehicles of private vengeance, which led the emperor Maximilian greatly to curtail their activities. They gradually lost all influence and were abolished by Jerome Bonaparte in 1811.

veillée des armes (Fr., vigil of arms). In medieval times, the vigil held by a contender for knighthood alone in a chapel the night before his investiture.

Veishya (Hind.). Third or agricultural Hindu caste.

Velvet Chancellors. Term applied to the first Chancellors of the post-war Federal Republic of Germany (e.g. Konrad Adenauer).

Ventôse, Laws of. Although never implemented, the 1794 Laws of Ventôse were designed by some of the French JACOBINS, including St. Just, to secure the support of the SANS-CULOTTES for the government by introducing the free distribution of estates and property that had been confiscated during the revolution.

Verkramptes. *See* VERLIGTES.

Verligtes (Afrikaans, 'The enlightened ones'). Liberals among the Afrikaners who acknowledge the need for a modification of South Africa's APARTHEID policy. Whites who take a more rigid line are known as Verkramptes, 'the narrow minded ones'.

Vernichtungslager (Germ.). An extermination or CONCENTRATION CAMP.

Versailles, Treaty of. Treaty signed on 28 June 1919 by Germany and the victorious powers of World War I. It was the fruit of the Paris peace conference of 1919–20 and established the LEAGUE OF NATIONS. The treaty, forced on Germany by the BIG FOUR, was signed by her only under protest. It was criticized for its harshness in Germany and the USA (where CONGRESS refused to ratify it) and for its supposed leniency in France and Britain.

Its terms included the surrender of German colonies to the League of Nations as MANDATES; surrender of German-held territory to Belgium, Lithuania and Poland; surrender of Alsace-Lorraine to France and of Danzig to the League as a FREE CITY; French control of the Saar, occupation by the Allies of the Rhineland for 15 years; payment of REPARATIONS; prohibition of Austro-German union; limitation of the German army to 100,000 men; suspension of conscription; and limitation of the German navy to vessels under 10,000 tons. The army was to have no tanks, heavy artillery or poison gas and there was to be no German airforce or submarines. Germany had to accept a clause admitting her guilt for the war and another providing for the trial of the Kaiser and other military leaders. In practice, there were no trials of war leaders and ways were found of circumventing the clauses that restricted German military forces. The NAZIS, who derived great propaganda from the treaty and the NOVEMBER CRIMINALS, refused to continue paying reparations when they came to power in 1933.

Vestiarian Controversy. A dispute within the Anglican Church in 1566–67 over details of ecclesiastical dress which focussed Puritan dissatisfaction with the Elizabethan church settlement.

veto (Lat., I forbid). Power or right of forbidding or rejecting, for example the power of any of the five permanent members of the United Nations Security Council to prevent the council from making a decision on a non-procedural matter. In Britain the monarch has a power of veto over parliamentary legislation, though in practice it is never used.

viceroy. Chief Crown officer in a Spanish American colony who had the final responsibility for administration and military actions. Viceroys usually came from the nobility and by the 18th century military experience and prior service were generally required of candidates for the position. In theory they enjoyed wide powers, but these were limited in practice by the Crown's efforts to centralize decision-making in Madrid and by the need to consult the AUDIENCIA.

The office of viceroy was established in 1763 in Portuguese Brazil but had more limited powers than the Spanish model. The British employed viceroys on a similar basis in India during the RAJ.

Vichy. Provincial French spa town where the interim French government established its capital from July 1940 to July 1944. The Vichy régime

was autocratic and anti-republican; it collaborated with the Germans who occupied Vichy France in November 1942. After the liberation of France, Marshal Pétain, its prime minister, and the rest of the Vichy government established headquarters in Germany.

Victorian. The period of Queen Victoria's reign, 1837–1901. Sometimes seen as an era of complacent stability, with a literary and cultural style to match, it was one of rapid industrial, political and social change. 'Victorian values' of self-reliance, morality and the paternalistic family co-existed with exploitation, hypocrisy and imperialist arrogance. *See* WORKSHOP OF THE WORLD.

Viet Cong. A name meaning 'Vietnamese Communists' given to the supporters of the 'Front for the Liberation of South Vietnam' (founded in 1960) by the South Vietnamese government. The government were anxious to distinguish between the communists and the VIET MINH which had included non-communist nationalists in its ranks. The Viet Cong took an active part in the Vietnam War (1965-73) fighting the forces of the South Vietnamese government and the Americans. The Viet Cong were responsible for attacks on US bases at Pleiku and Qui Nhon in February 1965 which led to an escalation of American involvement and for the TET offensive of February 1968 which, although a military failure, badly undermined American morale.

Viet Minh. An abbreviated form of Viet-Nam Doc-Lap Dong-Minh, the Vietnam Independence League. It was founded in May 1941 to resist Japanese occupation of Indo-China after the VICHY French had agreed to co-operate with the Japanese.

Although the Viet Minh was made up of both communists and nationalists it was dominated by its leading communist members Ho Chi Minh, Pham Va Dong and Vo Nguyen Giap. The Viet Minh received the Japanese surrender in 1945 in Tonkin and Annam and declared a Democratic Republic of Vietnam. Negotiations with the French colonial authorities broke down in 1946 and in December of that year the Viet Minh attacked Hanoi. In 1951 it was transformed into the Lien Viet Front (also known as the Fatherland Front) and working closely with the Dang Lao Dong or Workers Party and the republic's efficient and politically-educated army, helped inflict a decisive defeat on the French at Dien Bien Phu in 1954.

Vikings. Norse or Scandinavian pirates who terrorized northern waters between the 8th and 10th centuries. Their raids reached south as far as the Mediterranean and east to the White Sea. Icelandic Vikings under Eric the Red discovered Greenland *c*980 and other Viking expeditions went to Newfoundland and Labrador. They excelled in ship-building and were fine sailors and craftsmen.

vilayet. *See* VALI.

villein (ME). In medieval England, an unfree peasant bound to his lord who, in return for land, gave his lord service and dues. These obligations could be commuted to rent but the villein could only free himself by escape, by entering the clergy or through MANUMISSION. Villeins were the chattels of the lord and could be sold or granted away with no protection from common law except in the ancient DEMESNE; they were judged in the manorial court according to manorial custom. Labour shortages

in the 14th century helped many villeins become COPYHOLDERS though they remained liable for some services. Villeinage had quite died out in England by the 17th century.

vingtième (Fr., twentieth). In France, a direct tax based on the earlier DIXIÈME introduced in 1710. The vingtième was levied by Machault in 1749 as a universal tax of 5% on incomes derived from rents, property, feudal rights, business and office holdings. The privileged classes attempted to restrict its operation and to evade it but it proved the most efficient and just form of taxation available. Further vingtièmes were levied in 1756 and 1760–63, both times of financial stringency.

virgate (deriv. Lat. *virga*, rod or yard). Feudal land measure of a quarter of a hide or carucate, equivalent to two BOVATES and measuring about 30 acres.

Visigoths. Western branch of the Germanic Goths who were ejected from southern Russia by the Huns in the 4th century. Settling south of the Danube under Roman control, the Visigoths rebelled, sacked Rome in 410 and moved to southern France where they were defeated in 507 by the Franks and forced into Spain. *See also* OSTROGOTHS.

visita (Span.). Investigation in the Spanish American colonies of any area from an entire viceroyalty to a single province, conducted by *visitadore*, who made recommendations for action to the Spanish Crown. Visitas usually occurred following charges of mismanagement or in times of serious emergency.

V-J Day. Victory over Japan Day. 15 August 1945, the date on which

Japan accepted the terms of surrender offered by the Allies, thereby bringing World War II to an end.

Voivodes. Name given to the princes of Moldavia and Wallachia up to 1789 when the principalities fell under Russian protection.

Völkisch (Germ.). Militant, aggressive nationalism, used particularly with reference to NAZI policies.

Volkskammer. The parliament of the post-war German Democratic Republic (East Germany) in East Berlin.

Volksraad (S. Afr.). Popular assembly of the BOER republic of the Orange Free State.

voortrekkers (S. Afr.). BOERS who took part in the GREAT TREK.

vox populi (Lat., voice of the people). Expression of the popular mood or opinion in a country.

vulgar Marxism. A rigid reading of Marx which overemphasizes the role of the economic factor to the exclusion of the complexities of human action and creativity and which rests too mechanically on a belief in historic inevitability.

Vulgate. Latin version of the scriptures, translated by St. Jerome in the late 4th century and sanctioned by the Council of Trent in 1545. They remain the authorized Bible of the Roman Catholic faith.

W

Wafd (deriv. Arab., delegation). The main nationalist party of inter-war Egypt, founded after a delegation in 1918 to the British government to request independence. Its leader Nahas Pasha headed several governments in the late 1920s and early 1930s. In April 1936, when the Wafd won a large majority in the general election, he became prime minister and regent during the minority of King Farouk. In 1938 Farouk dismissed the Wafd but the British, considering it to be less susceptible to Italian influence than Farouk's own choice of ministers, secured their reinstatement in February 1941. The Wafd's collaboration with the British discredited its claim to lead the nationalist movement and younger army officers such as Nasser and Sadat regarded it as corrupt and effete. When it won the 1950 election the 'Free Officers' encouraged rioting and civil disturbance. Following severe unrest in 1952 Farouk dismissed the Wafd ministers before being himself deposed in July 1952 by Neguib. In January 1953 the Wafd and all other parties were dissolved.

Waffen SS (Germ., armed guards detachment). Elitist military organization, a sub-unit of the SS, with intense loyalty to Hitler. Waffen troops were all ARYANS, but not necessarily German: they included volunteers from France, the Netherlands, Belgium, Norway, Denmark, Sweden, Hungary, Lithuania and Romania who joined primarily to fight against BOLSHEVIKS. There were 40 Waffen divisions in the field in World War II; it provided 1,500 men for the EINSATZGRUPPEN and helped put down the Warsaw rising in April 1943. *See also* TOTEN-KOPFVERBÄNDE.

Wahabis. Arabian sect of ISLAM originating in the teaching of Mohammed Ibn 'Abd-al-Wahab. Born in the late 17th century, he strongly opposed Turkish rule because of its tyranny and innovations to Islam which he sought to restore to its primitive form. Sheikh Mohammed Ibn Saud provided him with military support and his followers spread throughout Arabia and still dominate it today. They follow a literal acceptance of the teachings of Islam and refuse to accept any symbolic or mystical interpretations. The Turks again attempted to suppress them in the early 19th century but their beliefs remain an important element in the Moslem world.

Waldensians. Religious movement founded c1170 by Peter Waldo of Lyons which fell into heresy after being refused the right to preach and was subsequently condemned by Pope Lucius III in 1184. Split into two factions, the LYONISTS and the POOR LOMBARDS, they survived in France, Germany and parts of Italy and eastern Europe into modern times.

Wall Street. Site of the New York Stock Exchange; a synonym for US finance and banking.

Walloons. The French-speaking minority which inhabits industrial southern Belgium, comprising 45% of the population. Although the constitution guarantees the protection of cultural and political rights, a Mouvement Populaire Walloon agitates for autonomy within Belgium. *See* FLEMINGS.

Walworth Road. The South London thoroughfare housing the headquarters of the Labour Party since 1978.

Wanderers. COVENANTERS who left their homes in order to follow their dispossessed ministers in 1669.

Wandervögel (Germ.). Popular left-wing youth movement in Germany prior to 1914.

wapenshaw. In ancient Scotland, a gathering of the people to ascertain that each man was supplied with arms and was ready to fight if called upon to do so.

wapentake. In Anglo-Saxon England, territorial and administrative units in the northern shires corresponding to the HUNDREDS in the south.

waqf (Arab., pious foundation, pl. *awqaf*). A foundation for the purpose of pleasing Allah either by religious observance of the ISLAMIC faith or promoting the social welfare of the community. The establishment of a mosque or a hospital might constitute a waqf. It is administered by a nazir (superintendent) who may also be the founder and who is paid for his services. Awqaf within the legal jurisdiction of a QADI were subject to his management and grants of awqaf made the ULAMA financially independent. In the 19th and 20th centuries Moslem governments have tried to confiscate or control awqaf.

warband. The fighting men who accompanied Anglo-Saxon kings or chiefs at the time of their invasion of England. It could consist of hundreds, perhaps thousands, who were directed under the leader, by the comitatus or the chief's bodyguards. The comitatus remained an element in English armies up to the 10th century.

war communism. BOLSHEVIK policy in 1918 to meet the pressures of civil war and economic collapse, including nationalization of larger enterprises and a state monopoly of exchange; the partial militarization of labour, and the forced requisition of agricultural produce. War Communism's unpopularity and failure led to the NEW ECONOMIC POLICY in March 1921.

war criminal. A concept first enunciated in the 'Hang the Kaiser' campaign at the end of World War I. In the 1946 Nuremburg Trials 177 Nazis were indicted as war criminals for genocide and planning aggressive war, new and controversial concepts in international law. Ten were sentenced to death.

Wardrobe. Financial department of the royal household in the reign of Henry III (1216–72) which arose and came to dominate household finance, receiving cash and credit from the EXCHEQUER but without much Exchequer control of its accounts. Such lack of accountability alarmed the barons and in the late 13th century they demanded that all revenue should pass through the Exchequer, but for a time the Wardrobe continued to develop, organizing finance, victualling and transport for armies as well as the household. As it became more rigidified it was more susceptible to baronial opposition and declined in importance: under Edward II (1327–77) it was increasingly subject to Exchequer control. It survived for some centuries longer as the centre of household finance and repository for clothes, arms and armour in part of the Tower of London.

wardship. An incident of feudal tenure by which the lands of a minor heir to a tenant in chief were held by the king until the heir reached the age of majority. Wardships were often sold and the buyer could abuse his trust. Despite regulations laid down in MAGNA CARTA, wardships remained vigorously enforced, especially by the Tudor monarchs who used them to increase their personal revenue, investigating all lands held by tenants in chief to the crown. By measures such as the 1535 Statute of Uses they maintained the rights of the Crown over wards. Henry VIII appointed officers to supervise them and established court machinery in 1519–20 to deal with any disputes that arose. This court was given statutory powers and a seal in 1540 and, though unpopular, it was not abolished until 1646.

War Guilt Clause. Article 231 of the VERSAILLES TREATY, compelling Germany to accept responsibility for World War I and its ensuing damage. Intended to provide a legal basis for REPARATIONS claims made by the victors, it encouraged a bitterness which added to the difficulties of the WEIMAR Republic.

warlords. Provincial Chinese leaders, very powerful between 1916 and 1928, who maintained private armies to dominate their locality.

War of the Cities. Two phases in the Iran–Iraq war, 1980–88, causing heavy casualties. (1) March–July 1985, Iraq bombed Iranian civilian targets, Iran retaliating with missiles on Baghdad. (2) February 1988, missile attacks by both sides in which Iran's capital Tehran was hit for the first time.

Warsaw Pact. Eastern European Mutual Assistance Treaty, signed in Warsaw on 14 May 1955 by Albania, Bulgaria, Czechoslovakia, East Germany, Hungary, Poland, Romania and the USSR. A Soviet response to West Germany's joining NATO in October 1954, it reaffirmed the USSR's hold over eastern Europe following agreement to withdraw all occupying forces from Austria. The treaty established a unified command structure controlled from Moscow and obliged all signatories to give armed help to any cosignatory who was attacked. Albania formally withdrew in September 1968. Member countries engage in annual joint military manoeuvres but their only joint military action has been the occupation of Czechoslovakia in 1968.

Watergate. US political scandal of the early 1970s. On the night of 17 June 1972, five men were arrested while burgling the DEMOCRATS' campaign headquarters in the Watergate Hotel, Washington, DC. They were attempting to remove electronic bugging devices which had previously been placed there. Pres. Nixon's staff kept the affair out of the public eye until November 1972 but Bob Woodward, a reporter on the *Washington Post*, had attended the court when the five were arraigned and by the time they appeared before the Washington Federal District court on 8 January 1973 he and his fellow-reporter, Carl Bernstein, were accusing the WHITE HOUSE of a 'cover-up'.

On 7 February the Senate established a select committee to investigate the affair, but as late as 15 April Nixon met his adviser, John Dean, to discuss a further cover-up. At that meeting he revealed that all White House conversations were taped. On 30 April, Nixon's principal advisers – Haldeman, Ehrlichman and the attorney general, Kleindienst – were forced to resign.

In June, Dean testified against Nixon and in July the system of tapes was disclosed to the Senate Committee by a White House aide, Alexander Butterfield. Nixon persistently delayed surrender of the tapes to the Committee and only released them on 23 October under threat of impeachment and on the order of the Supreme Court. It was then found that some parts of the tapes had been erased and others were missing. On 27 July 1974 the House Judiciary Committee passed the first article of impeachment, charging Nixon with obstruction of justice. On 29 and 30 July the second and final articles were passed. On 8 August Nixon resigned; he received a pardon from his successor Gerald Ford.

Weathermen. Group on the far left of American politics whose aim was the total overthrow of the US political structure. They took their name from the lyrics of a song by the folk-rock singer Bob Dylan. They committed specific and carefully planned acts of violence including bombings and the murder of policemen. They drew their members from the well-educated strata of society but little is known of the movement's origins. It appeared to have ceased its activities in the early 1970s but bomb outrages in 1975 were committed in its name.

Wee Frees. 'Independent Liberals' who refused to support Lloyd George (1863–1945) as prime minister of a coalition government of Liberals and Unionists. Very much in the minority in the Liberal Party, most lost their seats in the House of Commons at the COUPON election of 1918. Asquith (1852–1928), their leader, lost his own seat in 1918 and the group was then led by Donald Maclean until he re-entered parliament in 1920. The independents were only truly reconciled to Lloyd George in 1926 when he replaced Asquith as official leader of the Liberal Party.

Wehrwirtschaft (Germ.). An economy made in wartime.

Weimar. Town where the German National Constituent Assembly met in February 1919, which gave its name to the constitution drawn up in July and hence to the German Republic of 1919–33. The economic problems of the Weimar Republic – hyper-inflation followed by mass unemployment – undermined its authority and facilitated the rise of Hitler and the NAZIS. In March 1933 Hitler suspended the Weimar constitution to make way for the THIRD REICH.

welfare capitalism. Post World War II West European mixed economies in which free enterprise capitalism co-existed with a state commitment to low unemployment, extensive social security and the provision of health and other social services.

Called into question by the ascendancy of right-wing Conservatism and the pressures of economic depression in the 1970s and 1980s.

Weltpolitik (Germ., world politics). New trend in German foreign policy which emerged at the end of the 19th century when Kaiser Wilhelm II determined to transform the country into a first-rank global power. Ultranationalistic fervour was combined with internal social and economic forces to promote a new interest in colonial expansion, German participation in the scramble for China and the foundation of a powerful navy. The term is sometimes applied with a more general meaning.

weregild (OE). In Anglo-Saxon England, the money paid by the family of a murderer or by the murderer himself to the relatives of his victim. The amount due in compensation varied according to the victim's social status. Weregild marked an advance on the primitive blood feud, but with the growth of the authority of the king it declined in importance; it characterized a stage of development when the Crown's interest was in securing justice for a victim's kin rather than in eradicating crime itself. After the Norman conquest it survived only in the small portion of the fine for the offence that was allotted to the relatives.

West Bank. Area on the west bank of the River Jordan occupied by Israel in the 'Six-Day War' (5–10 June 1967) between Israel and the Arab states. The Palestinians regard it as a homeland but the Israelis are intent on retaining possession of the area and of colonizing it.

Western Front. Battle-zone between Germany and her enemies France and Britain in World War I, extending from Nieuport on the coast of Belgium through Ypres, Arras, Soissons and Rheims to the area around Verdun. The battle-line remained static through most of the war, until the German spring offensive of 1918.

Westernizer (Russ., Zapadnik). 19th-century Russian intellectuals, particularly in the 1840s and 1850s, who saw Russia's progress as inevitably linked with the West. *See* SLAVOPHILES.

Wetbacks. Illegal immigrants into the USA from Mexico, so-called because for many years they were forced to swim the Rio Grande. Thousands of Mexicans still attempt to enter the USA illegally and many are deported after being caught on the border. Large landowners in California have to some extent encouraged them, since they supply a source of cheap and unorganized labour.

'wets'. Derisory term applied to members of the British Conservative Party who do not support the more radical policies of their leader and Prime Minister, Margaret Thatcher. They are generally perceived to be opposed to strict MONETARISM, concerned at the level of unemployment and cautious in foreign policy.

Whig (deriv. Sc. *whiggamaire*, drive a horse). Name originally given to rebels in the Scottish lowlands who continued their activities after the failure of the 1679 insurrection, opposing attempts to bring Scotland into ecclesiastical uniformity with England. In 1680 the term was derisively applied to politicians who sought to exclude Roman Catholics from succession to the throne, it thereafter became the name of the political party opposed to the TORY party. At first dominated by the nobility, it represented those forces which hoped to limit the power of the monarch and to increase the power of parliament. It became the governing party under Gladstone, Prime Minister from 1868.

Whimsicals. English TORIES who supported the House of Hanover on the accession of George I.

whips. Parliamentary party managers responsible for enforcing attendance at divisions and for the instructions they give MPs, the number of lines marked under an order denoting how crucial voting is.

Whiteboys. Irish agrarian bands, also known as Levellers, first founded in Limerick in 1761 and active until 1800. They were a product of rack renting, the poverty of rural life and opposition to the ENCLOSURE of common lands which they fought by levelling the fences put up around them. The name Whiteboys derives from the white shirts they wore over their other garments.

Whitecaps. Secret organization formed in Indiana, USA in the late 19th century, whose original purpose was to serve as a vigilance society but which later committed many outrages.

White Friars. *See* CARMELITES.

Whitehall. District of London where a number of government buildings are situated; the word is synonymous with the higher echelons of the British civil service.

White House. Official residence of the President of the USA in Washington, DC.

White Man's Burden. An expression of the Anglo-Saxon imperial mission

by Rudyard Kipling (1865–1936) in a poem of that title. 'Take up the White Man's burden –/ Send forth the best ye breed –/ Go bind your sons to exile/ To serve your captives' need'.

White Rajahs. Term applied to the Brooke dynasty who were the effective rulers of Sarawak during the colonial period.

Whites. Reactionary opponents to the 1789 French revolution and numerous subsequent revolutions. Most frequently used of the opponents of the Bolshevik Revolution of 1917 in Russia. The anti-Communists organized the White Armies. *See also* WHITE TERROR.

White Terror. Attempt by the KUOMINTANG to massacre their former allies the Chinese communists between 1927 and 1931. *See also* LONG MARCH.

Widow of Windsor. Queen Victoria (1819–1901, reigned 1837–1901), who went into permanent mourning on the death of Prince Albert in December 1861. Her decreasingly frequent public appearances encouraged complaints and a growth in the 1870s of republican sentiment. Her longevity, the rise of IMPERIALISM and the 1887 Jubilee restored Victoria's popularity and that of the monarchy.

wind of change. Phrase used by British Prime Minister Harold Macmillan (1894–1986) in a speech made to the South African parliament in 1960 to describe the strengthening of national consciousness amongst black Africans all over the continent, and to warn white South Africans that they should be aware of it.

winning hearts and minds (WHAM). Propagandist exercise carried out by US forces in Vietnam during the Vietnam war (1965–73), involving active attempts to convince the Vietnamese people of the value of western democracy and of the friendship of the USA and that communism was not to their benefit. Large-scale expenditure in the interests of the Vietnamese also played a part. WHAM was an implicit recognition of the success of VIET CONG propaganda; coercion – though not an official policy – played a part in it, and severe punishment was inflicted on communist sympathizers.

Winter of Discontent. A wave of strikes in the private and public sectors in 1979–80 against the Labour government's ultimately unsuccessful attempt to limit wage increases to 5%. Picket-line violence and the distress caused by local government manual workers' action played a significant part in the Tory victory at the May 1979 General Election.

Winter War. Invasion of Finland by the USSR RED ARMY. Intensive fighting in harsh conditions took place between 30 November 1939 and 12 March 1940.

Wirtschaftswunder (Germ., economic miracle). The rapid recovery of the West German economy after 1945.

Witan (OE, pl. of *wita*, one who knows). In medieval England, the king's council, a national assembly, which met at various times and in various places. Consisting of the higher clergy and the nobility, including the king's THEGNS, it gave the king advice and consent with regard to foreign policy, the raising of the FYRD, the levying of GELD and other legislation. It also elected new kings, though this was merely a formality.

The term witan also had a more general use and was applied to smaller formal assemblies such as the burhwitan, the town council.

Witch-hunt. Investigation and persecution of people without any real regard for their innocence or guilt, usually occurring for political purposes and accompanied by a certain element of hysteria. Witch-hunts of 'communists' were a common feature of MCCARTHYISM.

wite (OE, avenge). In Anglo-Saxon England, a fine in addition to compensation or WEREGILD, payable to the Crown or other public authorities, imposed for offences such as disturbing the king's peace.

Wobblies. *See* IWW.

Woolsack. Seat of the LORD CHANCELLOR when he attends the HOUSE OF LORDS. A large square sack of wool, it was first used in the reign of Edward III (1327–77) when wool was the largest staple commodity produced by England. Edward chose it to remind his judges that wool was the major source of the national wealth.

workers' control. Ambiguous concept which can mean management of industry in which all decisions are made by revocable delegates or mass meetings of the workforce; or workers being consulted and directing some aspects of production but with ultimate authority being retained by management. *See* AUTOGESTION.

workhouses. Locally funded institutions which grew rapidly in number in 18th-century Britain intended to house the poor and to fund themselves by utilizing the labour of their inmates. The 1723 Workhouse Test Act obliged those people receiving poor relief to enter a workhouse where conditions, though hardly luxurious, were usually not uncomfortable in practice. Indeed, many early workhouses were run by religious groups which sought to impose on the needy a regimented but also kindly régime run along more or less communistic lines.

The character of workhouses changed markedly in accordance with the 1834 Poor Law Amendment Act which enacted the concept of 'less eligibility' – i.e. that conditions inside workhouses should be worse than the inmates might expect to encounter outside. This attempt to deter 'indolence' made the poor unsurprisingly fearful of the workhouse but did nothing to reduce poverty.

The development of alternative forms of poor relief in the 20th century and the introduction of national insurance gradually led to the eradication of workhouses by World War II.

Workshop of the World. Description applied to Britain in the mid-19th century when industrial dominance made her the main international source of iron, steel, coal, shipping and machinery. The emergence of Germany and America as industrial rivals in the 1880s ended this monopoly position, opening a period of relative decline. *See* AILING GIANTS.

Wounded Knee. Scene of the massacre of at least 200 Hunkpapa SIOUX, mostly women and children, by a unit of the US Seventh Cavalry shortly after Christmas 1890. The events at Wounded Knee Creek, South Dakota, now symbolize the end of the Plains Indians' resistance to American expansion.

Wycliffite. Follower of John Wycliffe, or Wyclif (c1320-84). Master of Balliol College, Oxford, and rector of Lutterworth, he published *De dominio divino* and *De dominio civil* in 1376 in which he criticized the church for holding temporal possessions and intervening in state affairs. Later he denied the authority of the pope and the doctrine of TRANSUBSTANTIATION. His followers took up his attacks on ecclesiastical abuses and on transubstantiation. From about 1380 onwards they were known as LOLLARDS.

Y

yankee. Nickname first given to American colonists in New England, the derivation of which is obscure. In the USA, it is used specifically with reference to northerners (as in the War of Independence); in other countries it is used more generally to mean an American.

Yellow Book. *Britain's Industrial Future*, published in January 1928 by the Liberal Party under the leadership of Lloyd George (1863–1945), so called from its yellow cover. Two sections of the book were written by the economist John Maynard Keynes (1883–1946). The work contained far-seeing recommendations for curing unemployment and, amongst other things, advocated an extensive policy of state intervention in the economy to create semi-public corporations, and a public investment board to provide a large and general stimulus to domestic investment.

Yezhovshchina (Russ.). Word used to describe the Stalinist PURGE, derived from the name of the head of the Soviet secret police, N.I. Yezhov (1894–1939).

Yippie. Close contemporary of the HIPPY, but more actively involved in political action, particularly in protests against American involvement in Vietnam and the methods of the US police. The term was coined by one of the movement's leaders, former journalist Jerry Reuben, and is derived from the initials of Youth International Party and hippy. The Yippie movement faded in the early 1970s, possibly because of the cessation of US involvement in Vietnam.

Yishuv. The Jewish community in Palestine under the British mandate.

Yom Kippur (Heb., day of atonement). Jewish period of religious observance and fasting. On 6 October 1973, while the Israelis were observing Yom Kippur, Egyptian forces crossed the Suez Canal and moved 15 miles into Israel, while Syrian troops made a similar penetration into the Golan Heights. On 8 October, Israeli troops counter-attacked, moving to within 65 miles of Cairo and 35 miles of Damascus. On 24 October the 'Yom Kippur war' or 'October war' was nominally ended by a ceasefire arranged by the United Nations and later by a military disengagement along the Suez Canal between 18 January and 5 March 1974. A UN peace-keeping force of 1,200 men created a buffer zone between Syria and Israel on the Golan Heights in May 1974.

Yorkists. (1) The kings of the English House of York, comprising Edward IV (1461–83); Edward V (not crowned); Richard III (1483–85); and Edward, Earl of Warwick, executed by Henry VII in 1499.

(2) The supporters of Richard Duke of York and his sons Edward IV and Richard III in the Wars of the Roses against Henry VI and the LANCASTRIANS (1455–85).

Young England. A party of paternalistic Toryism formed in October 1842, led by Lord John Manners and George Smythe, with Benjamin Disraeli as a supporter. It opposed FREE TRADE and Conservatism's increasingly middle-class tone, which it felt threatened the traditional relationship between benevolent aristocratic landowners and the obedient poor. The party divided over the IRISH QUESTION and collapsed in 1845.

Young Pioneers. Communist youth organization.

Young Plan. Plan proposed by US businessman Owen D. Young (1874–1962) on 7 June 1929 as a means of settling German REPARATIONS. He suggested that the level of reparations should be reduced by 75 per cent and that remaining payments should be made in the form of annuities paid into an international bank until 1988. Germany accepted the plan in August 1929, but when Hitler became Chancellor in 1933 he refused to pay and thus ended the plan.

Young Turks. Movement by young army officers for liberal reform of the OTTOMAN empire between 1903 and 1909. A rebellion of army officers in Salonika in July 1908 led to the establishment of a 'Committee of Union and Progress' in Constantinople, headed by Enver Bey (1881–1922), Ahmed Djemel (1872–1922) and Mehmed Talaat (1874–1921). They persuaded Sultan Abdul Hamid to re-establish constitutional rule and to convene a parliament in December 1908. But splits arose between radicals who had been living in exile and the three leaders who adopted a purely nationalistic stance. The result was an increase in the prestige of the three Young Turks during the Balkan Wars of 1912 to 1913; they were also influential in establishing closer links between Germany and Turkey. Their influence lasted throughout World War I, with Enver and Talaat playing a leading role in Turkish politics until 1918.

Yuan. Dynasty established in China in 1206 by Mongol nomads under Genghis Khan (c1162–1227) and whose possessions reached through Asia to eastern Europe. Yuan power ended in 1238.

Z

zaibatsu (Jap., wealth + family). Large family-run business corporations which dominated the Japanese economy prior to World War II.

zambos. Spanish-American persons of mixed African and Indian blood.

ZANU. Zimbabwe African National Union, founded in August 1963 by former ZAPU members, including the Rev. Ndabaningi Sithole (b. 1920), to force the minority white government of Rhodesia to grant majority, i.e. black, rule. It was immediately banned from political activity and formed bases in Zambia where from 1967 onwards it launched armed incursions into Rhodesia. In 1976 Sithole and Robert Mugabe (b. 1925), as part of a Patriotic Front including both ZANU and ZAPU, represented ZANU at talks in Geneva on the future of Rhodesia.

The failure of those talks led to increased guerrilla activity up to 1979, when it was agreed that free and democratic elections would be held and the ban on ZANU's political activity lifted. Elections were held in 1980; the ZANU (PF) Party led by Mugabe won 57 seats and 63 per cent of the vote. Mugabe became Prime Minister in a coalition government which included ZAPU members.

On 17 April Zimbabwe became an independent republic; by May 1981 all former guerrilla troops had supposedly disarmed. But in February 1982 it was alleged that stockpiles of arms belonging to ZAPU members were found on farms owned by ZAPU leader Joshua Nkomo. Nkomo and three other ZAPU members left the government and, though a token ZAPU presence remained, the coalition was dead.

Throughout 1982 and early 1983 Mugabe accused ZAPU of planning a military takeover. Nkomo fled the country for Britain and Mugabe warned that ZAPU must disperse or be forcibly disbanded. The eventual outcome was the merger of ZANU with ZAPU in December 1987.

Zapadnick. *See* WESTERNIZER.

ZAPU. Zimbabwe African People's Union, founded in 1961 by Joshua Nkomo (b. 1917) with the aim of achieving majority rule in Rhodesia (now Zimbabwe). Banned from political activity, it commenced guerrilla warfare in alliance with ZANU. The two movements formed the Patriotic Front which helped to secure free and democratic elections and Zimbabwe's independence in 1980. In the elections ZAPU won only 20 seats and thereafter it became clear that the ZANU government intended to destroy ZAPU and make Zimbabwe a one-party state. The conflict was eventually resolved when ZAPU merged with ZANU in December 1987.

zek (Russ.). Prisoner in a penal labour camp in the USSR.

zemindar (Hind., land-holder). An officer charged with the collection of taxes over a certain district under the Moslem rulers of India. In 1793 Cornwallis converted such officers into landowners in their own districts; they alone paid land-tax to the government and recouped themselves by rents received from the peasants (*ryots*). This system of tax collection was known as the zemindari.

zemstvo (Russ.). Russian provincial or district councils first established by Tsar Alexander II in January 1864. They were active between 1865–66 and 1917 in the fields of public health, agricultural development, road building and primary education. Although dominated by the gentry they became a genuinely liberal force and succeeded in raising political awareness at local level.

Zentrum. The conservative Roman Catholic Centre Party in Germany from 1871 to 1933. Developed in response to Bismarck's anti-Catholic policies, it was influential in early 20th-century coalitions and again in the post-World War I WEIMAR Republic. Dissolved by the NAZIS in July 1933.

Zeppelin. Dirigible invented in 1900 by Count Ferdinand von Zeppelin (1838–1917), used by both the German army and navy in World War I. Antwerp, Warsaw, Liège and Paris were all bombed by Zeppelins but their largest bombing raids were on England. Between January 1915 and the end of the war, 53 raids were made on England, killing 566 civilians. After the war they were used for commercial service, making transatlantic passenger flights between 1928 and 6 May 1937 when *Hindenburg* burst into flames while landing at Lakehurst, New Jersey. In 1939 they were used to reconnoitre British air defences, but were scrapped soon afterwards.

Zionism. Belief in the need to establish an autonomous Jewish homeland in Palestine which in its modern form originated with Theodor Herzl (1860–1904), a Hungarian journalist living in Vienna. The DREYFUS AFFAIR and the POGROMS of eastern Europe convinced him that the Jews could have no real safety until they had a state of their own. They had always regarded Palestine as a spiritual homeland but had not up to then considered forming an actual state there. Herzl faced opposition from assimilated Jews who felt safe in the countries where they lived. Even after the 1917 Balfour Declaration supporting a Jewish homeland in Palestine, few Jews went to Palestine until the horrors of the NAZI régime and the HOLOCAUST had led them to reassess their position in Europe.

The Jewish state was proclaimed in 1948 and today most Jewish communities support Zionism, denounced by the USSR as 'western imperialism'. It is now an active international force concerned to extend the influence of Israel.

Zollverein (Germ.). The Customs Union, founded under Prussian auspices, which created a free trade area amongst the states of Germany. Custom duties on imports from German states were abolished in Prussia in 1818 and by the end of 1833 most of the small German states had been in effect forced into the Zollverein, thought by many to have been one of the influences which ultimately led to German political unity.

Zoroastrianism. At one time one of the great world religions, which flourished in Persia until conquest by Moslem Arabs in the 7th century forced it to give way to ISLAM. A number of its devotees fled to India to become PARSEES. Its basis was the age-long war between good and evil, Ahura Mazda heading the good spirits and Ahriman the evil ones. By doing right the believer supports Ahura Mazda; wrongdoers will be punished in the last days when Ahura Mazda achieves his inevitable victory. The religion has little influence today but its doctrines penetrated Judaism and, through Gnosticism, Christianity. The ALBIGENSIAN heresy was a medieval relic of the belief.

Zouave (Fr., deriv. *Zouatta*, name of Algerian tribe). Body of French light infantry, originally recruited amongst Algerians, who were dressed in quasi-oriental uniforms.